Judicial Soup

By Shannon Bohrer

At his best, man is the noblest of all animals; separated from law and justice he is the worst.

−Aristotle.

Copyright © 2024 by Shannon Bohrer

All rights reserved. No part of this book may be reproduced or transmitted in any form or by any means, electronic or mechanical, including photocopy, recording, or any information storage and retrieval system, without prior permission from the publisher (except by reviewers who may quote brief passages).

First Edition

Hardcover ISBN: 978-1-62720-519-1
Paperback ISBN: 978-1-62720-520-7

Internal design by Brian Barth
Cover by Apprentice House Press
Editorial development by Jack Stromberg
Promotional development by Riley Mitchell

Published by Apprentice House Press

Loyola University Maryland
4501 N. Charles Street, Baltimore, MD 21210
410.617.5265
www.ApprenticeHouse.com=
info@ApprenticeHouse.com

Contents

PROLOGUE   **VII**
Opening Remarks

PART I. The Incident, Arrest, Investigation & Grand Jury
Chapter 1: The Beginning   1
"This case is so weak it will never go to trial"
Walter Forbs: The Witness was Coerced

Chapter 2: How Did This Happen?   9
"Things that are obvious are not necessarily true, and many things that are true are not at all obvious." —Dr. Joseph LeDoux
Juan Rivera: DNA Exoneration after Three Trials

Chapter 3: Do We Find What We Seek?   25
If you ask the same question several different ways, it does not mean you will find the answer you seek.
Ronnie Long and Physical Evidence

Chapter 4: Sometimes the Facts Do Not Fit   47
There are at least two sides to every story and sometimes more.
David Camm: Inadmissible Evidence, Witness, and DNA

Chapter 5: Is This the Same Event? The ABRA Report and the Alcohol Beverage Control Board Hearing   55
Sometimes what we say depends on who we are talking to.
Kevin Green: Witness Misidentification by the Wife of the Accused

Chapter 6: Heath Patrick Thomas   64
"The last of human freedoms—the ability to choose one's attitude in a given set of circumstances." —Viktor Frankl
Thomas Haynesworth: False witness and DNA

PART II. The Trial

Chapter 7: Day 1: Opening Remarks and Confusion — 75
"Most of us regard good luck as our right, and bad luck as a betrayal of that right." —William Feather
James Owens: Exculpatory Evidence Withheld

Chapter 8: Day 2: The Heart of the Prosecution's Case — 89
"The serpent in the Garden of Eden, a prosecutor once told me, could produce both character witnesses and alibi witnesses." —J. Michael Hannon
Roger Logan and Police Corruption

Chapter 9: Day 3: Witnesses for Both Sides — 111
"Some minds are like concrete—thoroughly mixed up and permanently set." —Anonymous
Kirk Bloodsworth: The First DNA Exoneration

Chapter 10: What Time Did the Event Occur, and Why Does It Matter? — 140
"Anyone who doesn't take truth seriously in small matters cannot be trusted in large ones either." —Albert Einstein
Kristine Bunch: Fabricated Evidence

Chapter 11: Day 4: Apologizes, Hills and Witnesses — 147
"Facts are stubborn things; and whatever may be our wishes, our inclination, or the dictates of our passions, they cannot alter the state of facts and evidence." —John Adams
A Dangerous Situation

Chapter 12: Not Trusted Before You Testify — 167
Anthony Ray Hinton: Bad Science and a Gun

Chapter 13: Was Carole on Trial — 177
"To be persuasive we must be believable; to be believable we must be credible: to be credible we must be truthful." —Edward R. Murrow
Joyce Ann Brown: The Wrong Joyce Ann Brown

Chapter 14 Heath Testifies — 194
"When you have eliminated the impossible, whatever remains, however improbable, must be the truth." —Sherlock Holmes
Wilton Dedge: Questionable Identification by a Witness and a Dog

Chapter 15: Who Can Testify to What? 220
"Belief perseverance" – we look for what supports our positions and
  disregard information that challenges our positions.
William Dillion: Dog Identification, Witness and DNA

Chapter 16: Our Perceptions 241
"Our past influences our perception of the present."
  —Anthony Pinizzotto, Ph.D.
Henry McCollum and Leon Brown: False Confessions

Chapter 17: The Experts Testimony is Limited 253
"This is a Court of Law, young man, not a Court of Justice."
  —Oliver Wendell Holmes
Glen Ford: The Witness was the Girlfriend of Another Suspect

Chapter 18: Day 7, Continued: The End of the Line 277
"If the facts don't fit the theory, change the Theory." —Albert Einstein
Michael Morton: Concealing Exculpatory Evidence

PART III. The Verdict & Appeal
Chapter 19: Guilty, the Decision, an Appeal, and the Sentencing 298
"The last of human freedoms—the ability to choose one's attitude in
  a given set of circumstances." —Viktor E. Frankl
Cathy Woods: False Confession, and more

Chapter 20: The Appeal and the Aftermath 314
"The evidence of intent to injure or frighten was insufficient to
  support a conviction of assault with a dangerous weapon."[1]
Lukis Anderson: When DNA points in the Wrong Direction

Chapter 21: Final Thoughts 327

Epilogue 333
Acknowledgments 337
Appendix 339
References 385
Photographic/Materials Index 399

---

[1] Brief for Appellant, District of Columbia, 11-CFG-14222, Heath P Thomas v. United States of America, p 5

PROLOGUE
Opening Remarks

In August 2010, Heath Patrick Thomas, an off-duty agent with U.S. Immigration and Customs Enforcement (ICE), was arrested for assault with a deadly weapon. Over the next three years, he would be indicted, tried, and convicted of that crime, which, as this book will show, he did not commit. Today, Heath lives with that wrongful conviction on his record and has paid the consequences.

Before the incident, Heath was in federal law enforcement for 18 years; he held high-security clearances and was widely respected within his agency and allied agencies and by his co-workers. Heath was also familiar with the criminal justice system, having investigated and arrested numerous individuals and had been involved in a wide variety of prosecutions. Considering his background, one might believe that he would understand better than anyone the alleged charges against him and be capable of defending himself. Yet, he was found guilty of a crime he did not commit and lost his career.

If someone with the knowledge and expertise Heath possessed can be convicted of a crime they did not commit, what happens to ordinary citizens who lack knowledge of or practical experience with our judicial processes?

We hear about problematic cases where individuals are found guilty of serious crimes and spend years in jail before the convictions are overturned. This is not one of those cases. In this case, the penalty was a fine and probation. The alleged offense was serious, but minor compared to many of the serious crimes that occur. Nevertheless, the fallout of this wrongful conviction has been significant for the people involved. This one event permanently changed the trajectory of Health's life. If this can happen to Heath, it can happen to anyone.

The heavy impact of this relatively minor incident highlights another, more serious truth about the justice system. Over the years we have heard of numerous death penalty cases—people on death row—that have had their convictions overturned. Often, innocent people have spent decades incarcerated, and it shocks our belief and trust in the criminal justice system. If we find injustice, misconduct, and incompetence in death penalty cases which are examined and reviewed many times over, how many problems like Heath's exist in lesser cases?

How did this Happen?

I first met Heath weeks after the incident when his lawyer asked me to be an expert witness in the case. I had been in law enforcement for 42 years and testified in court hundreds of times. What I saw unfold, and what I have since learned through transcripts, interviews, and case notes, was unlike anything I had experienced before.

Beginning with my first contact with Heath and his lawyer, the book summarizes the grand jury process and questioning, the criminal trial transcripts, the motions, and some correspondence and contains numerous quotes. I had hoped to contact every person involved in the trial, interview them, and offer them an opportunity to contribute to the book. Not everyone involved with the case agreed to be interviewed, which was not unexpected. I have included my own opinions where they differ from others and give my reasons for them. I also explain some legal terms and processes, but there are a few instances where words and actions are not explainable. Sometimes, asking two lawyers the same question will result in different answers.

Early in the book, the eventual outcome is known that Heath was found guilty, and his appeal denied. However, as the chapters unfold, peripheral and subsequent issues, mistakes, conflicts, and false information become more apparent. These unexpected issues often seem to confuse and cloud the process of finding the truth. Additionally, the court often failed to recognize obvious problems and conflicts with some of the information presented. This story is not a who-done-it. Instead, it asks, how and why did this happen?

Important information that would question the prosecution's case was not entered into evidence or testified to during the trial. In some cases, information favorable to the defense was prohibited from being entered into evidence, often after objections by the prosecution but sometimes directly by the court. The limitations imposed by the judge even included what the defense's expert witness could testify to at the trial. In addition to the restrictions and constraints placed on the defense, the prosecution's presentation during the trial described an event that literally did not occur.

After the conviction, Mr. Thomas appealed, and the appeal was denied. The appellate court said that the defense expert testimony should not have been limited and restricted by the court. The appellate court asserted that if the expert had been allowed to testify, the testimony would not have changed the outcome, so "... *any error was harmless.*" The court even cited the fact that the expert was not a witness to the alleged crime. As the defense expert, I had never experienced anything like this case.

In this case, the person arrested was a police officer with extensive experience. Police are certainly not immune from criminal behavior. One study showed about 1,000 officers being arrested each year. We hear valid calls for police reform but reforming the

---

[1] Transcript of the memorandum opinion and judgment, District of Columbia, Court of Appels, Case No. 11-CF-1422, Heath Patrick Thomas, Appellant v. United States, Appellee decided February 27, 2013, p 8.

[2] A study funded by the National Institute of Justice, and conducted by Bowling Green State University, found that police officers are arrested about 1,000 times each year. The study found that 5,545 officers were arrested between 2005 and 2011.

police without examining the judicial system as a whole only addresses one part of the problem. This case demonstrates numerous issues and the lack of checks and balances within the criminal justice system.

Over the course of the investigation and trial, numerous factors came together to produce a negative but not unexpected outcome. Like ingredients melding together in a soup, these factors included a series of errors, omissions, and mistakes, some of which almost appear intentional. But no matter how minor or seemingly insignificant the mistakes appeared; they became significant when connected with other information associated with the case. The noteworthy effect of these mix-ups is that a court can be taken down a road believing it is traveling in the right direction, all the while going the wrong way.

Even with my four-decade-plus career in law enforcement and being Heath's expert witness, and knowing he was not guilty – I still was not sure of what could be done. Heath and I talked by telephone on many occasions to discuss the case and any options, thoughts, and ideas. We continued to talk and sometimes would repeat our conversations. These conversations became the foundation and impetus for the book. Documenting this case seemed obvious, if only for the purpose of shining a light in the right direction.

I have been questioned numerous times about who the book is written for and who I expect to read it. My general response is that I hope attorneys, judges, police, criminal justice employees, lawmakers, and anyone interested in examining the criminal justice system will read and learn from it. There are numerous parts of our criminal justice system that should be studied and analyzed with the intention of improvement. How these parts are interconnected and work together, or just as important, do not work together, is often overlooked when we talk about reform. In the concluding chapter, I offer a few suggestions for improvements in our system, and I also challenge others to be involved. It is time to take a full account of our criminal justice system and right the wrongs that have been done to too many innocent people.

Shannon Bohrer
Judicial Soup

PART I
The Incident, Arrest, Investigation & Grand Jury

1

The Beginning...
AUGUST 2010–JULY 2011
"This case is so weak it will never go to trial."

On March 3, 2013, I opened my email to find the following message:

> *Sorry for this message on a Sunday, but because of all the faith and support you all have shown, I felt you should know as soon as I did. I received a call early this afternoon from my attorney. She informed me that while the appellate court contradicts itself in the memo of ruling, they went ahead and up held [sic] my conviction. My recourse is limited, (the Supreme Court—unlikely) and in 4 years I can apply for a Presidential pardon.*[1]

It was signed by Heath Thomas.

In 2010, Heath had been charged with two counts of assault with a dangerous weapon. The alleged victims were Mr. Marshall Brackett, a bouncer at The Guards, and Cpl. Brandon Holubar, a bystander. For over two years, I worked with and for Heath as his expert witness. His appeal had just been denied.

The alleged crime occurred on August 28, 2010, in the District of Columbia. Heath's trial was in August 2011, and he was found guilty on August 30 of that year. While I believed—and still believe—that Heath was not guilty, the guilty verdict was not unexpected. It was not surprising because of the series of mistakes, misjudgments, and other events that had played out. From my perspective, no single factor was responsible, but the adverse events just kept piling up. In the middle of the trial, I told Heath, *"You may have to appeal this."* I could see even then that the mistakes and misinformation presented a false story to the Court, and the Court might believe it.

---

[1] Heath Thomas, Email message to the author, March 3, 2013

My involvement with Heath's case started on September 8, 2010, when I was contacted by Heath's attorney, Mr. Michael Hannon. He inquired about my criminal justice and police training expertise and then explained that he wanted to hire me. His client was Mr. Heath Patrick Thomas, employed by U.S. Immigration and Customs Enforcement (ICE). I agreed to examine the case.

My first meeting with Heath was about a month later, on October 7, 2010, in the Washington D.C. area. My first impression of Heath was positive. I found him reasonably pleasant, especially under the circumstances. I took him to be 5 foot 7 or 8 inches in height, about 40 years old, and in particularly decent shape. I thought him to be around 175 pounds and later found out that he was around 190 pounds. In an unconscious way, I think I was assessing his physical appearance, probably related to the struggle he encountered over control of his gun. I remember wondering, how big was the bouncer?

We met at an empty gym early in the evening, and everyone seemed relaxed. In addition to Heath and me, Mr. Garrett Olsen, a coworker of Heath's, and Ms. Emily Brant, an attorney in the Hannon Law Group, also attended the meeting. Mr. Hannon had told me, in general terms, what had occurred, but I wanted to hear Heath's version of the incident and then film a re-creation in the event a defense would be needed.

At the gym that evening, Heath explained that he and his girlfriend had been out with two other couples on the night of the incident. They had dinner, and after leaving the restaurant, they stopped for a nightcap at a bar called The Guards. They ordered two rounds of drinks, both of which had several problems, including drinks made with the wrong alcohol, spilled drinks, and more. Because of the poor service and the lateness of the hour, they decided to leave. When Heath went to the bar to pay the tab, however, he encountered some trouble. The bar staff seemed to ignore him. He began to get impatient, and he approached a person he believed to be the manager to get some help. The manager appeared to be Spanish, so Heath spoke to him in Spanish, attempting to keep the conversation private. He explained to the manager that his group had problems with their drinks, and now he was having trouble paying his bill. The manager seemed upset that he had been approached and replied with a threat to call the police. To this Heath replied, "I am the f—— police." Heath said he immediately calmed down and went back to the bar, wanting to pay his tab.

Unexpectedly, while facing the bar, Heath was picked up from the rear in a bear hug and carried out of the establishment. His arms were pinned at his sides, and his assailant's head was in Heath's back. The distance he was carried was estimated to be over 40 feet and included going down two short flights of stairs. Heath was carrying a concealed weapon, inside his waistband, at the time, and while being carried, he felt the weapon becoming dislodged from its holster.

When Heath and his escort were outside, the person carrying him (later identified as the bouncer) released him. Heath believed his weapon could be dislodged from his holster and fall to the ground, so he reached for it as soon as he was released, with the intent to reset the gun—that is, push the gun into the holster. The person carrying him never really left him, and the momentum of both men carried them forward. As Heath raised his shirt, which had been covering the gun, and grabbed the pistol grip with his strong hand, the bouncer reached for the gun with his left hand and grabbed Heath's waist with his right arm. Heath said the bouncer's right arm hit his right forearm just before the gun was dislodged. The bouncer's action probably helped to further dislodge the gun.

At that point, a struggle occurred between Heath and the bouncer for control of the gun. The struggle lasted several minutes, during which time some patrons from the bar, including Corporal Holubar, exited the building and watched the events before returning inside. At 11:58 p.m., the police were called; they arrived and arrested Heath.

To the police, the bouncer claimed that he took Heath outside, dropped him, and then backed up about three feet. He claimed Heath then turned with a gun in hand, so the bouncer reached out and prevented Heath from pointing the gun at him. That is when the struggle ensued.

From my perspective and experience, I found Heath's version of the event believable. Although I had not talked to or read any statements from the bouncer, the story related to me, attributed to the bouncer, was difficult to believe. I taught action vs. reaction training in weapon retention classes, and although what the bouncer described might happen in movies, this was not a movie.

Under the circumstances that Heath described, I would have expected his weapon, at a minimum, to be partially dislodged from his holster. I wanted to film the re-creation of the event to use if the case ever went to court. I saw this as the key to the case: Could Heath's gun have become dislodged? If yes, then Heath's claim that he was securing the weapon would be believed, and he would be found not guilty.

For the re-creation, Mr. Olsen would play the role of the bouncer, and Ms. Brant would film it. Heath, who wore similar clothing to what he was wearing when arrested—shorts and a polo-type shirt—would play himself. The script was for Mr. Olsen to bear hug Heath from behind, pick him up, and then carry him 20 to 30 feet. The actual distance Heath was carried was 40-plus feet, but we had limited space for the re-creation.

As we were preparing to film, I remember my thoughts at that time: *This is nice, and it is good to prepare, but this case is so weak it will never go to trial.* So much for my insight.

To best replicate the circumstances, we used a Crayola gun, a molded plastic replica of a Sig-Sauer 229. Heath normally carried an H & K P2000, a smaller gun, but that gun was being repaired. The Crayola gun would be a sufficient stand-in. Heath's belt and holster were the same ones he was wearing when the incident occurred. This style of holster is worn inside the waistband and is attached to the wearer's belt. The holster is worn on the person's strong side but more to the front of the body. This type of holster is popular with the law enforcement community, especially in warm weather, because it is very concealable. The holster's downside is that the weapon can move around, depending on the person's movements. When a weapon is holstered, most of the gun is concealed, with only the pistol grip visible above the waistband.

When Heath placed the Crayola gun in the holster, his shirt was not tucked in and the gun was concealed, just as it was on the night of the incident. To draw the weapon, he used his weak hand (his left hand) to raise his shirt, exposing the pistol grip, and his strong hand (his right hand) to grab the pistol grip. This procedure reflects formal police training used for this type of holster.

During the re-creation and filming, Mr. Olsen picked up Heath several times, replicating Heath's and the bouncer's positions when the incident occurred. When lifted, Heath's feet were about a foot in the air, and Mr. Olsen's head was in Heath's back. Mr. Olsen's arms were around Heath's waist, and his hands were clenched together in front of Heath. Mr. Olsen's arms were over the top of Heath's arms, pinning Heath's forearms to his body. In this position, Heath could not move his arms.

After Mr. Olsen set him down some 20 to 30 feet away, Heath raised his shirt, and we could see the gun had moved from his right side toward the center of his body and, at the same time, moved higher on his beltline, several inches in each direction. Heath readjusted the weapon by pushing the gun down into the holster and pushing it back to his right.

This part of the re-creation was reasonably accurate. However, during the actual event, the bouncer carried Heath down two short flights of stairs, and there were no steps in the gym for us to use. The two short flights of stairs would have resulted in significant downward pressure on Heath's body weight with each step. That much jostling would have further dislodged the weapon.

Now, to simulate the struggle for the gun, Mr. Olsen released Heath and then grabbed at the gun and tried to take control. The simulation demonstrated Heath's desire to keep possession of the weapon and, while doing so, to keep the gun pointed in a safe direction.

After the reenactment, I asked Heath why he had readjusted the firearm when Mr. Olsen set him down. He responded that he did it without thinking about it. Officers not in uniform, carrying a concealed weapon, often touch the clothing covering the weapon. The touching ensures the security of the weapon's location. Sometimes, when needed, the touching is for readjusting the gun in its holster. In police weapons training this behavior is called a "security check." It is often done unconsciously.

While at the gym, I questioned Heath if he could have gained full control of the weapon during the actual event. He said on the night of the incident; he was aware that he was getting tired. He knew he would have to do something to end the event before losing control of the weapon. He explained that one option was "shooting the bouncer off the gun." To perform this, the weapon is fired while someone is holding onto the barrel/slide area of the weapon. The barrel's muzzle end—where the bullet comes out—is not necessarily pointed at anyone. The person holding the barrel/slide area will naturally release their hold as the weapon fires.

Another option would have resulted in the gun being pointed at the bouncer. With this option, Heath would allow the bouncer to pull the gun toward him while Heath maintained control of the grip. Heath would move toward the bouncer as the bouncer backed up, pulling on the weapon. The bouncer would have ended up in front of the gun. Typically, when this tactic is employed, the person with the gun pointing at them releases the gun.

To document what Heath described, he demonstrated the defensive moves he had just described. His actions were videoed, and they demonstrate that he could have gained complete control of the gun, but only by using tactics that would have caused the weapon to fire or be pointed at the bouncer. Heath had strong concerns about this because he considered it dangerous to fire a gun or point a weapon at someone.

After we concluded the filming and before leaving the gym, there was a brief discussion of the value of the film. The intent of the video was to demonstrate what occurred from Heath's perspective if there was a trial. It was my opinion that the video accurately represented what happened and what actions Heath was reluctant to take. When we left the gym that night, I was reasonably confident the case would not go to trial.

I had several contacts with Mr. Hannon's office after the filming, but each was brief, either a short telephone conversation or an email. Then on May 26, 2011, seven months after the re-creation, I received an email from Mr. Hannon requesting that I call him. In the same email, he stated, "Heath was indicted. Trial date is August 15. Can you be available?"[2]

I responded, "Yes."

*   *   *

On July 6, six weeks after I agreed to be Heath's expert witness, I talked to Mr. Hannon by telephone, and we discussed the case. At that time, he felt the charges still might be dropped. His office had sent me additional file materials about the case, and I asked whether there was a complete list of witnesses to the event. The only names I had at that time were individuals who testified before the grand jury. There was no police report and nothing about any officers testifying in the grand jury. Since this incident occurred on a Saturday evening in Georgetown, Washington, D.C., there had to be other witnesses. Mr. Hannon assured me that there were other witnesses, but he did not have their information.

---

[2] Hannon Law Firm, Email to the author, May 26, 2011

Later that month, on July 27, I met Mr. Hannon at his office, and we took a trip to The Guards, the restaurant and bar where Heath and his party had gone for a nightcap. While there, I noticed that they had cameras inside and outside of the areas where the purported assault took place. I asked Mr. Hannon if there was any film of the incident, and he told me that the cameras were not operating at the time of the alleged assault. I wondered why. Were the cameras fake, broken, or just not turned on?

I later did a little research and found that The Guards was well known as a glamorous establishment in the center of Georgetown, an historic area in Washington D.C. The restaurant had been visited by celebrities, including the likes of Frank Sinatra, Sylvester Stallone, and John Travolta. The establishment had fallen on hard times, however, and today it is closed for business.

The same day we visited the Guards, Mr. Hannon held a meeting at his office with Heath, me, and a few other people. We were there to prepare for the trial. Mr. Hannon advised everyone that he had elected a trial by judge rather than a jury. He believed the judge would be more informed with the law, and sometimes juries can be anti-police. Since Mr. Hannon practiced law in the area and was familiar with the judicial system, I thought this to be the right decision. The trial would start in just over two weeks.

Before leaving Mr. Hannon's office I was given additional materials to review, such as case law on officers and assault cases. I remember expressing some concern about one defense Mr. Hannon planned to use: the claim that Mr. Thomas was assaulted. Mr. Hannon explained that he was trying to cover everything. That did make sense to me since, from the information we had, Heath was assaulted when he was picked up and carried out of the bar. But I also asked whether Mr. Hannon believed that the assault would warrant Heath's drawing his weapon. Mr. Hannon's response was not absolute, but it was my impression that he intended to include every possible defense. His strategy also included hiring a self-defense expert. Mr. Hannon's defense strategy sounded logical.

My impression of Mr. Hannon was positive. He appeared to be in his late fifties, of medium build and height. I knew he was a former federal prosecutor with many years of experience. Mr. Hannon was the movie or screen image of an attorney. Not Atticus Finch—he is not that tall—but the way he carried himself, his manner in asking questions, and he seemed confident, but not overconfident.

At that time my thoughts were that the trial would be brief, Heath would be found not guilty, and the incident would be over by the end of September. I never envisioned the complexities, the insinuations, and the volume of materials and witnesses the prosecution would use at the trial. I also know I could not have predicted the outcome.

1A

Walter Forbes: The Witness Was Coerced

In 1982, Mr. Walter Forbes was attending Michigan's Jackson Community College. While he was out one night, he witnessed a bar fight and intervened, thus breaking up the altercation. He had no idea that his actions that evening would contribute to his incarceration for more than 37 years.

The following day, Mr. Dennis Hall, a participant in the bar fight, sought out Mr. Forbes and shot him. Mr. Forbes was wounded but survived the shooting. However, his injuries took months to heal.

On July 12, 1982, about one month after Mr. Forbes was shot, Mr. Hall died in an apartment fire that was determined to be arson. The police considered Mr. Forbes a suspect in the arson because of the bar fight and the shooting. They found a witness, Ms. Annice Kennebrew, who said three men burned down the apartment home (an old house converted to apartments), and Mr. Forbes was one of them. (In 1982 Annice Kennebrew was Annice Gibson.)

In 1983, Mr. Forbes was tried and convicted of murder and arson and sentenced to life in prison on the basis of the evidence from Ms. Kennebrew. However, the account from the key witness had significant discrepancies. One of the three men she identified passed a polygraph test, and the charges against him were dropped. A second suspect was tried for the crime but was acquitted. That left Mr. Forbes as the only person convicted of the crime.

Mr. Forbes was released in 2020 after the "star witness admitted fabricating her story and evidence surfaced that the fire may have been part of an insurance fraud scheme orchestrated by the apartment building owner."[1] The new evidence led to a hearing, in which the Judge vacated the conviction, after which the prosecution dismissed the charges.

The apartment owner, Mr. David Jones, was a suspect in the apartment fire in 1982 but was not charged. In 1990 Jones was charged and convicted in another arson fire, part of an insurance scheme, in Livingston County, Michigan. He died in 2010.

When retracting her story, Ms. Kennebrew said that several local men had made threats against her and her family, instructing her to implicate Mr. Forbes. Giving false testimony is perjury (lying under oath); however, the statute of limitations for perjury

---

[1] Omar Abdel-Baqui, "Michigan man imprisoned for nearly 4 decades exonerated after witness admits lying," *USA Today*, December 14, 2020, https://www.usatoday.com/story/news/nation/2020/12/14/jackson-michigan-walter-forbes-exonerated-4-decades-prison/6537810002/.

in this jurisdiction is six years, so she faced no consequences for her actions. The men that threated Ms. Kennebrew, had both died before she came forward.

After being released, Mr. Forbes said, "Up until I was convicted, I thought the system would work, that it would correct itself. In hindsight, I was naïve."[2]

Mr. Forbes's conviction appears to have been based on one witness's testimony, and the witness's credibility was questionable. When the other two persons that Ms. Kennebrew implicated in the crime were excluded, one passing a polygraph test and the other found not guilty, should the authorities have questioned her story?

References

Omar Abdel-Baqui, "Michigan man imprisoned for nearly 4 decades exonerated after witness admits lying", Detroit Free Press, USA Today December 14, 2020.

https://www.usatoday.com/story/news/nation/2020/12/14/jackson-michigan-walter-forbes-exonerated-4-decades-prison/6537810002/.

Vimal Patel, "Convicted Using False Testimony, Michigan Man Is Free After 38 Years", New York Times December 17, 2020, https://www.nytimes.com/2020/12/17/us/walter-forbes-freed.htm.

---

[2] Omar Abdel-Baqui, "Michigan man imprisoned for nearly 4 decades exonerated after witness admits lying", Detroit Free Press, USA Today December 14, 2020, https://www.usatoday.com/story/news/nation/2020/12/14/jackson-michigan-walter-forbes-exonerated-4-decades-prison/6537810002/.

2

How Did This Happen?
AUGUST 29–OCTOBER 25, 2010

*"Things that are obvious are not necessarily true, and
many things that are true are not at all obvious."*
—Dr. Joseph LeDoux

After the altercation between Heath Thomas and Marshall Brackett, the bouncer at The Guards, Mr. Brackett, told the police that Heath had drawn his weapon and that Heath was turning with the purpose of pointing his gun at him. So, he grabbed Heath's arm. Heath's version was that the gun was being dislodged. He reached to secure it, and that's when Mr. Brackett grabbed his arm, which caused the weapon to further dislodge from the holster. The nanosecond during which the gun came out and how it came out is the whole case.[1]

Heath was arrested on Saturday, August 28, 2010, and a Statement of Charges was completed by Officer Steve Andelman, Metropolitan Police Department (MPD), on August 29, 2010. Heath was subsequently taken to a detention center, processed, and interviewed by Detective Keith Tabron. Heath was then taken to a holding cell where he would wait for his first court appearance; his arraignment was on Monday morning, August 30, 2010. On Monday, in the courthouse, the prosecuting attorneys were trying to locate Ms. Carole O'Connor, Heath's girlfriend at the time. The prosecutor's office had someone calling her name in the court hallways. Apparently, they wanted to subpoena her to the grand jury, but the police failed to obtain her name and address when the alleged crime occurred, or if they did have it, it might not have been given to the prosecutor's office. In the months following the incident, Carole had hired an attorney, Charles I. Cate, who provided her information to the prosecution.

On Wednesday, September 1, Heath's case was taken to a grand jury, just four days after his arrest. On the same day, Heath's attorney, Mr. Hannon, received a letter from the U.S. Attorney's Office offering a plea agreement. It was written as a "pre-indictment plea offer for your client, Heath Thomas."[2] The government's offer for a plea of guilty included "a fine not exceeding $5,000.00 or [] imprisonment for not more than 5 years,

---

[1] Mr. Brackett's written police statement on the night of the incident and his grand jury testimony, along with interviews with Mr. Thomas.

[2] Letter dated September 1, 2010, see Appendix A

or both."[3] Believing he would be found not guilty, Heath did not take the plea offer. Heath was in jail until September 2, 2010.

What follows is a summary of the grand jury process and the grand jury testimony of the first five witnesses.

The Grand Jury Begins

Three grand juries heard testimony for this case over a span of seven months. The first grand jury testimony was given on September 1, 2010, and the last grand jury was given on March 25, 2011.

Grand juries are generally limited to witnesses summoned by the prosecution. Persons testifying in the grand jury are entitled to have legal representation, but the legal representation (the lawyer) cannot enter the room. To consult with the lawyer, the witness leaves the room, talks to their attorney, and then reenters.

Prosecuting attorneys run grand juries. There are no lawyers for the defendants, and objections cannot be made. If a defendant is indicted, the defense is entitled to the transcripts. Defendants can offer to testify, but they are not required to testify.

Mr. Sean Lewis, an assistant United States attorney, represented the government in all the grand jury testimony related to Heath's case. In a grand jury, the prosecution asks questions. Normally, after the prosecutor finishes, he or she will allow questions from the jury members. Heath's grand jury followed this practice.

Mr. Marshall Brackett

Mr. Brackett, the bouncer at The Guards, testified at the grand jury on September 1, 2010, for twenty minutes. By his own testimony, Mr. Brackett did not identify himself to Heath during the incident, nor did he know why he was to remove Heath. Accordingly, he said, "I was asked by one of the waitresses to come and help escort a gentleman out of the bar."[4] He followed the waitress inside to where Heath was standing.

> Mr. Sean Lewis: *To your knowledge, had any of the other employees of the bar had any problems before the incident that you were going to—*
> Mr. Brackett: *I have no idea.*[5]

According to Mr. Brackett, he asked Heath to leave several times, and he touched his arm each time. When Heath did not comply, he picked him up from the rear in a bear hug and then walked out with him. He walked about twenty feet through one door, eight or ten feet more (with three steps down in the middle), through another door, and then down two more steps. When he reached the sidewalk, he set Heath down and then

---

[3] Ibid
[4] Testimony of Mr. Brackett from his grand jury transcript from September 1, 2010, p 6
[5] Ibid, 8

Top left: Inside of bar with view of the pillar. The table Heath's party sat at was behind the pillar. *Top Right*: Inside of bar looking at the first set of exit doors to the atrium area. *Bottom left*: View of the front entrance door from the street. *Bottom right*: View from the atrium with the front door closed.

took a step back, stepping up onto the bottom step. According to Mr. Brackett, when he set Heath down, Heath drew his gun and turned toward him. At that time, he said, there were several feet between the two of them. Mr. Brackett grabbed the gun and the struggle ensued. Mr. Brackett stated that during the struggle, Heath put his hand into his pocket to show him his badge, identifying himself as a police officer. However, Mr. Brackett said he was not letting go of the gun until the police arrived.

When questioned as to whether he noticed anything about Heath's demeanor and whether Heath said anything when he was carrying him out, Mr. Brackett responded, "No he just smiled and he was drunk."[6]

A question-and-answer exchange between Mr. Brackett and a juror followed. The juror asked where the barrel of the gun had been pointed.

> Mr. Brackett: *I didn't give him a chance to point it directly at me, but he was coming around like to point it at me. So—.*
> Juror: *But it was not pointed at you?*
> Mr. Brackett: *At the time, no. When I grabbed it, it wasn't.*[7]

If you believe Mr. Brackett's testimony, you could infer that Heath intended to point the gun at Mr. Brackett; however, because of Mr. Brackett's quick response, the gun was never really pointed at him. The most significant revelations that came from Mr. Brackett's testimony were his admission that he did not know why he was to remove Heath and did not identify himself to Heath, even while struggling with him.

Mr. Brandon Holubar

Three weeks later, on September 23, 2010, Brandon Holubar testified in the grand jury for twenty minutes. He would later be added to the case as a victim; at this point, however, he was only a witness. Mr. Holubar was a corporal in the U.S. Marine Corps, but he was not in uniform while out with friends when he witnessed the incident. He and his friends had been at the Georgetown waterfront earlier in the evening, and he was questioned as to whether he was drinking that night. Corporal Holubar stated he had a Long Island Iced Tea and one beer before the incident. According to his testimony, he consumed both drinks over the course of ten to twenty minutes.

After the drinks, he and his friends split up and headed to different bars. Corporal Holubar testified, "We headed to The Guards, where the incident took place."[8] He said that after entering the bar, they all "went downstairs."[9] Corporal Holubar stated that he stayed downstairs for only ten to fifteen minutes before going back upstairs, intending to leave.

---

[6] Testimony of Mr. Brackett from his grand jury transcript from September 1, 2010, p 10
[7] Ibid, 19
[8] Testimony of Corporal Holubar from his grand jury transcript from September 23, 2010, p 4 - 5
[9] Ibid, 5

Once upstairs, he witnessed an argument between a customer and the bartender. Corporal Holubar testified, "The individual [Mr. Heath Thomas] was trying to order a glass of champagne or wine of some sort; I'm not sure which kind. The bartender asked him for two names, I'm guessing for the tab of whoever he was with … he told the bartender, I just gave you two names. The bartender replied, Sir, you didn't tell me anything."[10] Corporal Holubar said that after some more exchanges, the bartender said, "sir, if you don't calm down we're going to ask you to leave and call the cops."[11] Corporal Holubar said that Heath replied, "I am a fucking cop, excuse my language."[12] Corporal Holubar continued, "He didn't say anything after that, but you could tell he was physically irked."[13] According to Corporal Holubar, he was about fifteen feet away from the exchange.

Corporal Holubar then testified that a bouncer appeared, approached Heath, and said, "sir, you can come with me?"[14] And according to Corporal Holubar, Heath answered, "I'm not leaving."[15] The bouncer then picked up Heath, from behind, in a bear hug and took him outside. Corporal Holubar followed them. He stated that he saw the bouncer move across the sidewalk into the street between two parked cars. From that location, he said the bouncer dropped Heath and took a step back. He then saw Heath turn with a black gun in his hand.

> Mr. Sean Lewis: *And then what did this individual do once you observed him with the black pistol in his hand?*
> Corporal Holubar: He [Heath] *had both hands* [on the gun] *turned around, he had the pistol chest high, he had his finger on the trigger, it wasn't straight or anything, it was on the trigger, trying to make his way towards the bouncer. The bouncer put his hand out, grabbed the top of the pistol, wrapped his arm around the individual, and tried to pull the pistol out of his hand, but he* [Heath] *had it in both hands, so it was very unlikely he was going to do that.*[16]

Corporal Holubar said he witnessed this while standing in the doorway to the bar. He said that he did not hear Heath say anything during the struggle, but he heard the bouncer say, "Let go of the gun."[17] He also believed that the bouncer said, "I'm not getting shot tonight."[18]

---

[10] Ibid, 6
[11] Ibid
[12] Ibid
[13] Ibid
[14] Ibid, 7
[15] Ibid
[16] Ibid, 9
[17] Ibid, 10
[18] Ibid

Corporal Holubar stated that the gun was pointed at the door and the front of the building during the struggle, and the gun was "flagging" (moving around like a flag). Since the gun was pointed at the front door, it was also pointed at him. He was questioned as to whether anybody else was there during this event. He answered, "There was a female [Carole O'Connor] to the right, just outside the door."[19]

Corporal Holubar said he had thought about helping the bouncer during the incident, but he deemed it dangerous with the gun pointing in his direction. He also said that he checked the door, blocking anyone else from coming out, for safety reasons.

He was asked if he heard the woman in front of him (Ms. O'Connor) say anything. He said, "I believe she said, 'he's a cop' to the bouncer, but I'm not sure if he [the bouncer] heard her."[20]

When questioned whether Heath was intoxicated, he said, "I couldn't tell. All I know is he was trying to purchase another bottle. I'm not sure if he was drinking before or at that moment."[21]

Questions by Jurors
When the prosecutor concluded his questions for Corporal Holubar, he yielded the floor to the jurors. One juror asked if Corporal Holubar saw anybody try to stop, run, or call the police. Corporal Holubar responded, "I was actually in a doorway, so my peripheral vision was partially blocked. So mostly the only thing I had in front of me was the individual and the bouncer."[22]

Another juror asked about the woman who was standing outside.

> Juror: *Did the young lady come outside when, when the man with the gun – I mean, the lady what was with him, did she come outside too?*
> Corporal Holubar: *Yes, she was outside as this happened.*
> Juror: *Oh, she was already out there.*[23]

Mr. Lewis, the prosecutor, asked Corporal Holubar whether he saw Ms. O'Connor leave the bar, and he said he had not.

A juror also asked Corporal Holubar if he witnessed the initial incident outside. Corporal Holubar said he did see the initial confrontation, and he did not see the individual pull the gun out. "At that time the bouncer was blocking my view of the individual."[24]

Corporal Holubar's testimony prompts another essential question. Mr. Brackett carried Heath out of the bar, and Corporal Holubar said he followed them. However, when

---

[19] Ibid, 11
[20] Ibid, 12
[21] Ibid, 16
[22] Ibid
[23] Ibid, 17
[24] Ibid, 19

asked about others outside, he said Carole O'Connor was already outside. So, did he follow her too? Unfortunately, this question was not asked.

Mr. Oscar Viricochea

Mr. Oscar Viricochea testified before the grand jury on Monday, September 27, 2010; his testimony lasted twenty-two minutes. Mr. Viricochea was the manager of The Guards when the incident occurred. Heath had approached him for help when he had trouble paying the tab.

Mr. Viricochea speaks broken English and there were several times when the transcriber of his grand jury transcript wrote "(unintelligible)" within the text. Within the transcripts there is no mention of a translator in attendance.

Mr. Lewis began with some ordinary questions.

> Mr. Sean Lewis: *Tell us what happened and where it started.*
> Mr. Viricochea: *It was around 10:30, and I was in the back. We had a function for about 50 people in the big room.*[25] *There was a guy there* [in the service area] *asking to close his credit card.*[26]

Mr. Viricochea said the person left the bar area and then returned. "When he came back, [he] was using bad words, he was very rude with my bartender."[27]

Mr. Lewis asked what Heath said to him, and Mr. Viricochea answered, "He said, 'son-of-a bitch bartender.'"[28] Mr. Viricochea said he then tried to calm Heath down, and when doing so, Heath asked, "Who are you?"[29] To which Mr. Viricochea responded, "I'm the manager here."[30] And, according to Mr. Viricochea, Heath then said, "fuck you."[31] That is when Mr. Viricochea called for a busboy to get the bouncer.

When questioned about Heath's behavior after this, he said, "He was trying to jump me. Trying to fighting [sic] with me, you know. I was really tried to cool down this guy because he was very hyper and I was – it was really busy at that time. There was a lot of people and I tried to take care of the waitress who serve the drinks."[32]

Regarding what happened after Mr. Brackett arrived, Mr. Viricochea said that Heath was rude and tried to fight with the bouncer. According to Mr. Viricochea, Mr. Brackett grabbed Heath from the rear and carried him out of the bar. Mr. Viricochea testified that the bouncer had some words with Heath, but the testimony is confusing. He testi-

---

[25] Ibid
[26] Ibid
[27] Ibid
[28] Ibid
[29] Ibid
[30] Ibid
[31] Ibid, 7
[32] Ibid, 7 - 8

fied, "The security came and then Marshall [Brackett] he told spoke to my security very rude and you need to get kicked out. You know. And he was trying to – how to you call this – fighting with him."[33]

Mr. Lewis asked if Heath had said anything about being a police officer, and Mr. Viricochea said, "I did not hear that."[34] After Mr. Brackett picked Heath up, Mr. Viricochea said, he walked behind him and opened the door for Mr. Brackett to go through.

Mr. Lewis asked, "What did Marshall [Mr. Brackett] do with the man?"[35] Mr. Viricochea responded, "Threw on the floor...After that I don't know. The guy went out. He just up and left."[36]

Mr. Lewis asked where the bouncer released Heath, saying, "At the time that Marshall is setting this man down, is he setting the man down outside of The Guards?"[37] Mr. Viricochea answered, "Yeah, outside of the Guards."[38]

Mr. Viricochea was questioned about what he saw outside. He said he could not see because he was still between the two doors, and other people were blocking his view.

> Mr. Sean Lewis: *When you first come outside, where is Marshall?*
> Mr. Viricochea: *He was between two cars outside on the sidewalk. There were two cars between the – and then forcing with the gun up and down. I don't know if he want [sic] to drop the gun, the guy or not because Marshall grabbed his arm.*[39]

Mr. Viricochea testified he heard Mr. Brackett say, "Call 911"; he did not remember if Heath said anything. "I call 911 and Marshall was freak out in a minute because that. "[40]

Mr. Lewis asked where the gun was pointed while the struggle was going on, and Mr. Viricochea said, "Right in front of me because I was looking out and there was a lot of people here waiting in the line."[41] He said that is when the police came. "The man [Heath] who had the gun dropped the gun."[42]

In his written statement on the night of the incident, Mr. Viricochea said that Heath had been drunk. During the grand jury, he was asked how he came to that conclusion. "Because – I wrote it on there because of his attitude. His attitude was really like when some people are drinking. He was very hyper and talking very loud and saying very rude things. That's when we see the guy maybe was really drunk. I'm not even can say

---

[33] Ibid, 8
[34] Ibid, 9
[35] Ibid
[36] Ibid
[37] Ibid, 10
[38] Ibid
[39] Ibid, 11
[40] Ibid
[41] Ibid, 13
[42] Ibid

– I can talk to him. He was very drunk or I don't know because I didn't have too much conversation with him."[43]

Mr. Lewis asked whether the restaurant's surveillance cameras were on during the incident. Mr. Viricochea answered, "No. It was not on because they usually – I put them on at 10:30 because we open the disco downstairs. We're no using it for the restaurant and what happened it's no on. This started at 8, I think and we start the program at 10:30 and I don't have time to go put on the cameras."[44]

At the start of his testimony, Mr. Viricochea said the incident began at 10:30. Here we are left to wonder, what started at 8?

Mr. Viricochea later added that when a representative from the Alcoholic Beverage Regulations Administration (ABRA) came that night, they went to the office and then turned on the cameras. He was also asked if there was a functioning camera inside the bar around the main level where the incident occurred, and he said, "No."[45]

Notably, when I visited the Guards with Mr. Hannon in 2011, I saw a camera over the bar. It may not have been on, or maybe it was broken, but a camera was there.

Back at the grand jury, there was an exchange between Mr. Viricochea and several jurors.

Juror: *What is your procedure for removing an unruly client from out of your restaurant?*
Mr. Viricochea: *Was no procedure.*
Another juror: *It appeared that no one talked to the gentleman beside you and your bouncer to come behind him and grab him and take him out. Is that normal procedure?*[46]

Mr. Viricochea restated some facts without addressing the question. His statement was a little confusing. A juror asked again: "When was the conversation to calm him down because—"[47] Mr. Viricochea again repeated or restated some testimony and added, "I tell him can you cool down please... not much I went to do for him because I was very, very busy."[48]

After that question, Mr. Lewis said that there was time for one more question. A juror asked how often something like this occurs, a customer with a gun. Mr. Viricochea said this was the only time.

What observations can we make about this testimony? Mr. Viricochea speaks English and Spanish, and even with the grand jury transcripts, it was sometimes difficult to follow his answers. There were several times that his answers did not seem

---
[43] Ibid, 14 - 15
[44] Ibid, 15
[45] Ibid, 16
[46] Ibid, 17 - 18
[47] Ibid, 18
[48] Ibid

to address the question(s), and as mentioned earlier, there were times when the transcriber wrote "(unintelligible)" within the text.

Mr. Viricochea testified that Heath was trying to fight with Mr. Brackett; however, Mr. Brackett did not testify that Heath was trying to fight with him.

Marina Yudina
Ms. Marina Yudina, a bartender at The Guards when the incident occurred, testified at the Grand Jury on October 8, 2010. Her testimony lasted eighteen minutes. She said her shift started at 10 p.m. She remembered Heath coming to the bar with the waitress, Graciela Perez, wanting to pay his tab. There was a discussion between her and Heath about the names on the bar tabs. During this conversation, another bartender, Mr. Mark Fleming, got involved. According to Ms. Yudina, Heath asked Mr. Fleming who he was while using curse words.

Ms. Yudina went to the front of the bar to close one of the tabs while Mr. Fleming talked to Heath.

> Mr. Sean Lewis: *Could you hear what this man was saying to Mark?*
> Ms. Yudina: *Not at that point, for a few minutes, a good few minutes, because I was – we were busy so I was really busy period that time.*[49]
> She was asked if she heard any of the conversations when she returned.
> Ms. Yudina: *Yeah, I came back with the closed tab and I saw my manager standing there and Mark was still there. It was all happening in the service area. And the guy was up in my manager's face and very angry and cursing. There were a lot of curse words flying around.*[50]

Ms. Yudina said the manager asked Heath to leave, and then one of the bouncers (Mr. Brackett) asked him to leave, "And he wouldn't so he took him outside."[51]

Mr. Lewis asked about the noise level inside. Ms. Yudina stated, "It was very noisy. It was very busy. We had music on, it was very noisy."[52] She was also shown a copy of a check and was asked if that had been the check she had closed. She said that the name "O'Connor" was on the check she had closed.

Graciela Perez
The next witness for the prosecution at the grand jury was Ms. Graciela Perez, a waitress at The Guards. She testified on Monday, October 25, 2010, and her testimony lasted twenty-one minutes. Ms. Perez testified that she thought the group of people (four to

---
[49] Testimony of Ms. Yudina from her grand jury transcript from October 8, 2010, p 8
[50] Ibid
[51] Ibid
[52] Ibid, 9

six) were seated at a table "Between 10:00 and 11:00."[53] When asked if she noticed anything about the group, she said, "They were drunk already."[54]

> Mr. Sean Lewis: *And what was it about this party that made you conclude that they were drunk?*
> Ms. Perez: *They were complaining of their drinks, they were a little loud, that's basically about it.*
> Mr. Lewis: *And after you had seated this party, did there come a time when there was a problem of some kind?*
> Ms. Perez: *Yeah, they complain about their drinks two times.*[55]

She remembered that one drink was returned for not being what was asked for, another drink had a bug in it, and she also spilled part of one drink.

When asked about the person complaining, she described him as the "*Spanish guy.*"[56] She may have confused Heath with Dennis Jones[57] (another member of Heath's party), because it was Dennis who complained about the drinks, and either man could be viewed as appearing Spanish.

Ms. Perez was asked about the party's reaction when they had complaints and returned drinks. She said, "I don't remember exactly what he said, but he took it back."[58]

> Mr. Lewis: *Did he appear to be upset at all when he took it back?*
> Ms. Perez: *Kind of. I cannot tell. Like I say, "they were drunk."*[59]
> Mr. Lewis: *Now, at some point that night, while you were waiting on the table did you, yourself, spill a drink?*
> Ms. Perez: *By accident, a little bit.*[60]

She said when she was putting the drinks down, she spilled one a little. She apologized and offered to bring another, but she said the party said, "no that's fine."[61]

Ms. Perez said she was asked for the tab and was told the party would pay at the bar. She knew she would not receive a tip since they were paying at the bar.

---

[53] Testimony of Ms. Perez from her grand jury transcript from October 25, 2010, p 7
[54] Ibid
[55] Ibid
[56] Ibid
[57] Dennis Jones and Jane Jones, his wife, are not their real names. They were contacted about the book, and during that contact, they requested that I not use their names. I honored their request. All official records contain their real identification.
[58] Ibid, Testimony of Ms. Perez from her grand jury transcript from October 25, 2010, p 8
[59] Ibid
[60] Ibid, 9
[61] Ibid

Ms. Perez: *He [Heath] went to the bar and pay; he was trying to pay.*

Mr. Lewis: *Could you see what he was doing? The Spanish man?*

Ms. Perez: *He was trying to pay his tab, trying to talk to the bartender.*[62]

Ms. Perez was asked if Heath talked to anyone else, and she said, "Yes, he talked to the manager."[63] Ms. Perez added that Heath appeared "*Mean and upset … because he wanted to pay and the bartender was not getting – he wasn't getting the attention of the bartender.*"[64]

Mr. Sean Lewis: *Did you see the first interaction between the manager and the Spanish gentleman?*

Ms. Perez: *Yes, I heard the guy told the manager if want him to speak in Spanish or in English because he's Spanish.*

Mr. Lewis: *And is he saying this in English or Spanish?*

Ms. Perez: *Spanish.*[65]

Mr. Lewis questioned her about what "*the Spanish man was saying to Oscar.*"[66]

Ms. Perez: *Basically that sentence, you know, like, whether you want to speak English or Spanish because, you know, like, trying to say I'm Spanish like you, something like that.*

Mr. Lewis: *When the Spanish man was speaking to the manager, can you describe how his voice was? Did he sound happy, or upset or something else?*

Ms. Perez: *Upset and loud.*[67]

Ms. Perez described the noise level at The Guards: "it was getting loud."[68]

She said that she never saw Heath touch the manager, and she never saw the manager touch Heath. She said she later saw the security guard (Mr. Brackett) carry Heath out, and at the same time, she heard clapping.

Mr. Lewis: *Did you actually see the moment when Marshall [Brackett] —*

Ms. Perez: *No.*

Mr. Lewis: *— Grabbed the man?*

Ms. Perez: *No.*

Mr. Lewis: *And do you know about what happened because somebody later told you about what had happened?*

Ms. Perez: *Well, yeah, I heard.*[69]

Ms. Perez did not see Mr. Brackett pick up Heath, but she did see him next to the bar carrying Heath. She did not see them exit the building. The last place she saw Heath was outside the

---

[62] Ibid, 11
[63] Ibid, 12
[64] Ibid
[65] Ibid, 12 - 13
[66] Ibid, 13
[67] Ibid
[68] Ibid, 14
[69] Ibid, 15

window with the police. She did not see what happened outside, but she saw the police. While Ms. Perez said she believed the whole party was drunk, she never said anything about foul language being used, even when describing how Heath spoke in Spanish to Mr. Viricochea.

*   *   *

After reviewing the grand jury testimony, I remember thinking, "This will never go to trial." The only person to have alleged that the gun had been pointed at him, Corporal Holubar, gave suspect testimony. It was suspect because he said that he followed the bouncer out of the building, and yet Carole O'Connor was already outside when he arrived. This also conflicts with the manager's testimony, when he said he followed the bouncer so that he could open a door.

Further, Corporal Holubar said that Heath's finger was on the trigger, as he testified, "...he had his finger on the trigger, it wasn't straight or anything, it was on the trigger."[70] Heath is right-handed, so his trigger finger would be along the right side of the weapon's frame. Corporal Holubar said he only saw the left side of the gun. Because Heath had two hands on the gun and Mr. Brackett had one hand on the gun and Cpl. Holubar was viewing the incident in low light from a distance of ten feet; seeing a trigger finger on the trigger would be exceedingly difficult.

The credibility of the description that Mr. Brackett gave of the incident is also suspect for several reasons. Mr. Brackett may have believed his perception of the event was accurate, but his description is not corroborated by other witnesses or science. Mr. Brackett said he set Heath down on the sidewalk and then stepped back up on a step. At least two witnesses who followed the men outside, Mr. Viricochea and Corporal Holubar, observed Mr. Brackett and Heath on the curb's edge or in the street between two parked cars, which is about eight to ten feet from the steps.

Additionally, Mr. Brackett's description of Heath turning with the gun in hand and himself grabbing the gun before it was pointed at him is not believable. Why? Because his actions would not be physically possible. If someone is turning with a gun in hand to point it at someone behind them, the person behind them—just a few feet away—would not be able to grab the gun before it was pointed at them.

Physical laws of human performance tell us that a stimulus is followed by a response selection and then a response. In motor-skill learning terminology, the space between the stimulus and the response is called the reaction time—meaning a reaction to a stimulus is not instantaneous. Stimulus—space—response (action-reaction models) is well documented in kinesiology and motor-skill learning and refutes Mr. Brackett's description of events.[71]

---

[70] Ibid, 9

[71] Motor Learning & Performance, by Richard A. Schmidt, copyright 1991, Chapter 2, Processing Information and Making Decisions, p 15 to 25

An essential element of the stimulus-response model is that the reaction time depends on the action's compatibility and has a linear relationship to the stimulus and response. If the stimulus is expected, as a jab when two boxers are sparring, the response is much quicker since the person blocking the punch expects a punch to be thrown. Conversely, if someone sucker punches someone (the person being hit is not expecting to be hit), the person being punched will have a much longer reaction time. In Heath's case, Mr. Brackett's stimulus would have been seeing the gun, and it would have been much like a sucker punch in that he would not have been expecting it.

I acknowledge that I have summarized the testimony given in the grand jury and that the prosecution might have a different perspective of the events. But I do believe that there were enough inconsistencies to question what really happened that evening. The next two chapters cover the witnesses who were with Heath on the evening of the incident.

2A

Juan Rivera
DNA Exoneration After Three Trials

In 2012, Mr. Juan Rivera was released from prison after serving 20 years of a life sentence. He had been convicted in the 1992 rape and murder of an 11-year-old girl in Waukegan, Illinois. He was released because DNA evidence exonerated him. In Mr. Rivera's case, the prosecution tried him three times, the last in 2009, long after the DNA results were known. In fact, the prosecutors had known the DNA results when they retried Mr. Rivera the second time, in 2005. The appeals judge who reversed his conviction finally prohibited the prosecution from trying him again.

Mr. Rivera was 19 years old when the crime occurred. He was a former special education student. When arrested, he was interrogated for four days before confessing, signing the confession the police had typed. According to media reports, "The document, a narrative account of what the investigators claimed Mr. Rivera told them, was so riddled with incorrect and implausible information, that Lake County State's Attorney Michael Waller instructed investigators to resume the interrogation in an effort to clear up the inconsistencies. The interrogation resumed, resulting in a second signed confession, which contained a plausible account of the crime."[1]

The problems with the police and the prosecutors in this case were so numerous that one might think it was a poorly written novel. The police and prosecution worked hard to convict an innocent person.

After Mr. Rivera was freed, his attorneys filed a civil suit against multiple entities and parties that participated in the case. A settlement was reached in 2015, where Mr. Rivera was to receive $20 million. The settlement cost was to come from the towns, as well as Lake County, which had police officers working with the Lake County Major Crime Task Force.

The City of Waukegan was responsible for $7.5 million, the largest share. The mayor of Waukegan said the city's insurance would cover only part of the settlement, so the taxpayers would have to pay the rest. Lake County was responsible for $3.5 million, and the attorney for Lake County said the county had no insurance, so again the citizens would pay the bill. The civil cases against the police officers involved in this case were dismissed, so they were absolved of any financial responsibility.

---

[1] Article in the Chicago Tribune, March 20, 2015

Mr. Steve Art, one of Mr. Rivera's attorneys, said, "The settlement should send a message that wrongful convictions come at a steep price." He also said, "It demonstrates that there was serious alleged misconduct and that this case was very winnable for Mr. Rivera at trial," adding, "It also shows taxpayers in Lake County that there's a serious price to pay when police and other actors in the criminal justice system violate individual rights."[2] He did not elaborate on the misconduct or the violation of rights.

Four other Lake County murder or rape prosecutions were reversed in the five years from 2010 to 2015, all with DNA evidence. The five men who were wrongfully convicted and later exonerated were incarcerated for a combined total of 80 years.

Cases like this bring up important questions. For example, if Mr. Rivera did not rape and murder this little girl, who did? Victims' families deserve answers, and justice is never served when the wrong person is imprisoned.

Should there be an investigation of what evidence was presented at all these trials? With so many cases called into question, could there be other convictions that should be reexamined?

References

Mary Wisniewski, "Illinois man freed after 20 years in prison gets $20 million", Chicago Tribune (Reuters) dated March 20, 2015.

Rob Warden, Juan Rivera, National Registry of Exonerations, Posting Date: Before June 2012

Last Updated: 11/21/2019 https://www.law.umich.edu/special/exoneration/.

---

[2] Ibid

3

Do We Find What We Seek?
OCTOBER 2010

If you ask the same question several different ways, it does not mean you will find the answer you seek.

During the grand jury testimony, the federal prosecutor called a total of ten people to testify. Chapter 2 reviewed the testimony of the two alleged victims—the bouncer, Mr. Brackett, and a bar patron, Corporal Holubar—along with the bar manager and two other bar employees. The next two chapters will review the testimony of four individuals who were with Heath on the evening of the event, along with Heath's direct supervisor, John Eisert.

While Heath was with five people at the time of the incident, he did not know four of them before that evening. Two of the four were friends or associates of his date, Carole O'Connor. Carole had previously worked with Jane Jones and Terry Spradlin.[1] On the evening of the event, Ms. Jones was with her husband, Dennis, and Mr. Spradlin was with his wife, Vickie. Vickie Spradlin was the only member of the party that evening who did not testify at the grand jury.

Ms. Carole O'Connor

The first member of Heath's party to testify in the grand jury was Carole O'Connor. She testified on October 1, 2010, and her testimony lasted for one hour and twenty-five minutes. She was Heath's companion on the evening in question and was represented by an attorney, Mr. Edward Sussman. Although Mr. Sussman was not allowed in the grand jury room, which is normal grand jury procedure, he was seated just outside. Carole was told that if she had a question and wished to consult with her attorney, she could ask the foreperson to excuse her. She could then step outside, consult with her attorney, and reenter the grand jury room.

Mr. Sussman was not Carole's first attorney. Her first attorney was Charles I. Cate[2]; however, the U.S. Attorney's Office objected to her counsel, citing a conflict of interest.

---

[1] Jane Jones and Dennis Jones are not their real names. They were contacted about the book, and during that contact, they requested that I do not use their names. I honored their request. All official records contain their real identification.

[2] Letter from Charles Cate to Mr. Lewis, dated September 16, 2010, and a letter from the U.S. Attorney's office dated September 30, 2010.

In a telephone interview, Mr. Cate told me that the prosecutor objected to his representation, but it was fair. Mr. Cate said that the only thing he knew about the case was what he was told by Carole and Mr. Hannon, Heath's attorney.[3] Carole then hired another attorney, Edward Sussman, and he represented her when she testified at the grand jury.

Carole told the grand jury she was with Heath, Jane, Dennis, Terry, and Vickie when the incident occurred. She said they arrived at The Guards around 11:10 or 11:15 p.m. They seated themselves at a table, which she described as eight to ten feet from the bar.

Carole said they were not at the bar that long—maybe a half hour—before they decided to leave. She said, "Heath went to go ask the bar for the tab… a couple of minutes went by, not all that long. And then I saw - I saw the bouncer had him [Heath] grabbed from behind, like in a big bear hug, and he had him off, lifted up like off the ground and he was carrying him out."[4]

When questioned what she saw and heard during the time after Heath left the table until he was carried out, Carole answered, "There was nothing unusual at all about anything. It was just- it seemed like a perfectly normal, non-eventful evening. That's what struck me. I was like, 'What's going on?' when I saw that."[5] The only thing she heard was the normal chatter of people at a bar.

When questioned about her position at the table—where she was sitting—she responded that she was standing when the bouncer went past, carrying Heath. She had stood up because she believed they were leaving. As she described it, she was about seven to eight feet from the bouncer, who had Heath in a bear hug, when she saw them, and they were moving in her direction toward the front door.

Mr. Lewis asked if she heard the bouncer saying anything when she first observed them, and she answered, "They were both - I don't remember hearing them say anything. I remember that Heath was very still. He wasn't like flailing or moving. He was just very still, and that's one of the things that struck me, like he just almost looked like a doll like just being picked up."[6]

She testified that as they moved past her, she followed them and saw that they turned into the first door, which opened into a vestibule area. At that time, she was only about five or six feet behind them. After exiting the building, Carole said she stopped and stood on the bottom step. (There were two steps in front of The Guards, so this would be one step down from the entrance door.)

> Carole: …*they* [the bouncer and Heath] *were at the curb by the time I came through, completely through the vestibule* [through both doors]. … *The first thing I saw was the bouncer trying to take his gun.* …

---

[3] Telephone interview with Mr. Cate on October 28, 2014
[4] Testimony of Ms. Carole O'Connor from her grand jury transcript from October 1, 2010, p 9
[5] Ibid, 10
[6] Ibid, 14

> Mr. Lewis: ...*When you first see the bouncer and Mr. Thomas down by the curb, how is the bouncer positioned with respect to you?* ...
> Carole: ... *Both of them are face to face. The bouncer is on my right. Heath Thomas is on my left and there's a black SUV right there and the bouncer is kind of pushing Heath up into it as he's trying to take his gun.*[7]

According to Carole, she said, "Stop. What are you doing? He's a federal police officer."[8] And the bouncer answered, "He has a gun, you know, nobody waves a gun at me. I'm trying to get it. I'm going to take it away."[9] She later added that after she had told the bouncer that Heath was a federal police officer, the bouncer said, "I don't care."[10]

She described the gun as being in Heath's hand, and the bouncer also had a hand on the gun. The two were close, and the gun appeared to be on the bouncer's hip. She did not see how the gun came out, and she observed the gun always pointing down. She was unsure if Heath said anything but thought he might have said, "I'm a federal police officer."[11] However, she was unsure when he said that—if it was before or after she had identified him as a federal police officer.

Carole said that the manager was standing next to her; she told him that Heath was a federal police officer. According to her, the manager never answered her, possibly because he was dialing a phone. She believed he was calling the police. The manager then walked away from her, toward the curb, but away from the struggle.

> Mr. Lewis: *Did anything else happen in the course of that struggle besides what you've told us about?*
> Carole: *No, ... While they were, you know, still struggling, someone came out of the bar behind me and said, hey look out. He has a gun. And I'm like he's a federal police officer. You know, I told everybody. Anybody I could tell, I said he's a federal police officer... I'm his girlfriend, you know, he's fine, you know, just go back inside.*
> Mr. Lewis: *And the man who came up behind you, white, black, Hispanic, some other race?*
> Carole: *White, youngish, you know, twenties I think, light brown hair.*[12]
> Carole also said that she had to turn completely around to see him. He was standing directly behind her.
> Mr. Lewis: *Now, during the ... struggle ... does Mr. Thomas's gun ever point at you?*
> Carole: *It never pointed at anybody... it's always aimed toward the ground.*[13]

---

[7] Ibid, 17-18
[8] Ibid, 18
[9] Ibid
[10] Ibid, 21
[11] Ibid
[12] Ibid, 24-25
[13] Ibid, 25

When asked about the manager, when he came outside, Carole said that the manager followed the bouncer and Heath, and she was right behind him. She was also asked if anybody was warning people on the street about the gun, to which she said, "No."[14]

When the struggle seemed like a stalemate, and after the white youngish male subject (Corporal Holubar) came up behind her, Carole ran back in to tell her friends what was happening. Once inside, she grabbed her purse before going back outside. When she returned, the police were there. Several police cars had arrived, and the police were talking to people, but she could not hear what was being said.

She said, "they seemed to be interested in talking to everyone but me."[15] She waited a while and then approached an officer. The officer asked her if she saw how the gun came out, and she responded that she did not. She only talked to the officer for about a minute because he turned and left.

> Mr. Lewis: *...do you remember whether you told people in the area that what happened was none of their business?*
> Carole: *I did.*[16]

She explained that while the police were there, people were gathering on the street, and the police did not seem to be controlling the scene. People were asking, "what happened?"[17] She said she "intentionally didn't tell them because it really wasn't their business."[18] When questioned further, she said, "They were just walking by. And that was all I said to them. I had no discussion. I just said it's none of your business. It's a police matter."[19] She was asked if she said that to the young man behind her, and she replied, "I never said that to him. I never told him it was none of his business."[20]

Mr. Lewis then asked who had what to drink and other details about the bar tab. Carole said she had the Maker's Mark for the 7&7 that she was drinking. Dennis Jones ordered a Bombay Sapphire, and Heath had one with him.

> Carole: *... But when the waitress brought them to the table, she spilled one on Dennis and then the other one spilled all over the table in front of Heath...*
> Mr. Lewis: *Did getting spilled on make Mr. Thomas upset, that you could tell?*
> Carole: *Not at all. He laughed.*[21]

---

[14] Ibid, 26
[15] Ibid, 31
[16] Ibid, 32
[17] Ibid
[18] Ibid
[19] Ibid, 33
[20] Ibid
[21] Ibid, 38

When asked about the drinks the group had earlier at dinner, she related that the group had ordered four rounds, but the last round did not arrive until they were paying the bill. Some people may have taken a sip or two of the last drinks, but they left right after paying their bill. She could not remember what everyone was drinking at the restaurant. She testified they arrived at the restaurant for dinner at "seven o'clock and… we left right around eleven."[22]

This topic, of who had what to drink and when, would be revisited several times in the grand jury and again in the trial.

At this point Mr. Lewis began asking about any conversations Carole had with Heath about the incident. She said they had not talked about the incident because of advice from her lawyer. She was questioned extensively about what she was testifying to—whether she was coached or instructed about what to say—and she repeatedly said no.

After Mr. Lewis finished his questions, some jurors questioned her for a lengthy period about the incident, about the gun, about the holster, and about the bouncer and Heath.

> Juror: *What was his [Heath's] demeanor? He's like a soft-spoken gentleman or a hot-head or a —*
> Carole: *He's always very calm, very even keeled …. He's been trained to … think before you act. … I've never seen him as a hot head or anything else.*[23]

When Carole finished her testimony, she had a conversation with her attorney, Mr. Sussman, in the hallway in the prosecutor's presence. During that conversation, she asked her attorney about what information she could talk about and with whom. She was told she could talk to anybody she wished—that it was her testimony.[24]

Mr. Terry Spradlin

The next member in Heath's party that evening to testify was Terry Spradlin. Mr. Spradlin testified on October 21, 2010, for forty-seven minutes. He had previously worked with Carole O'Connor at the Transportation Security Administration (TSA) for about two years. He met Heath on the evening of the incident.

Mr. Spradlin was questioned about the dinner at the restaurant, Old Glory, specifically whether the party members had anything to drink. He could not remember who had what drinks, but he did remember that he was drinking beer.

---

[22] Ibid, 39
[23] Ibid, 53
[24] Telephone interview with Ms. O'Connor on October 13, 2014, I telephoned Mr. Susman's office and left a message for him to contact me on 10/28/2014, and on 01/30/2015 and on 03/10/2015 but the calls were never returned.

Mr. Lewis: *Do you know how much Mr. Thomas had to drink while he was at Old Glory?*

Mr. Spradlin: *No... He drank some portion of what's on that receipt. But I really don't know what... I don't even know what my wife drank...*

Mr. Lewis: *Do you recall if he was drinking beer or wine?*

Mr. Spradlin: *I think he drank beer...*[25]

After leaving Old Glory, Mr. Spradlin said, the group stopped at another establishment—The Guards—where someone in the party bought him "a shooter" (a shot of alcohol) for his birthday. He was not sure what the shooter was; he said it tasted fruity.

Mr. Lewis: *While you were sitting at the table did anything out of the ordinary happen?*

Mr. Spradlin: *I don't know that it was out of the ordinary. Whatever they ordered didn't have an olive in it.*[26]

Mr. Spradlin explained that he was referring to the mixed drinks that Dennis Jones and Heath ordered. Another round of drinks was made with the wrong liquor. Heath and the waitress discussed the incorrect drinks, and, from Terry's perspective, the waitress seemed upset.

Mr. Lewis: *And the conversation that Heath is having with the waitress, does he appear to be upset?*

Mr. Spradlin: *No, I think the waitress was a little agitated. ... They weren't yelling at one another. They didn't disrupt the restaurant. So anyway, they had a debate over that was the proper drink or not.*

Mr. Lewis: *So you are not sure—if you already answered this I apologize. Did it appear to you that Mr. Thomas was upset by the problem he was having?*

Mr. Spradlin: *No, I mean, it really didn't.*[27]

Mr. Spradlin remembered that Jane Jones said something about Heath being outside with the police. Mr. Spradlin was questioned about Heath's whereabouts from the time of the conversation with the waitress to the point when Heath was in police custody. Mr. Spradlin answered, "I have no idea."[28] The prosecutor then asked whether the waitress had spilled any drinks.

---

[25] Testimony of Mr. Spradlin from his grand jury transcript from October 21, 2010, p 13
[26] Ibid, 16
[27] Ibid 17-18
[28] Ibid, 19

Mr. Lewis: *While you were there at the Guards, did a waitress ever spill a drink on anyone?*
Mr. Spradlin: *I should know that. I don't know. She didn't spill it on me. I'm certain on that.*

When questioned further, he said, "I don't recall a drink being spilled."[29]

He was asked again about the time between Heath's conversations with the waitress and when Heath was outside—specifically, did he "see any kind of altercation, or along those lines happening inside the bar?"[30] He answered, "No." When asked how Jane Jones knew that Heath was outside, Mr. Spradlin said, "I don't know how she knew that."[31]

Mr. Lewis: *Did anyone, to your knowledge, dash outdoors—Ms. O'Connor, Jane, Dennis—*
Mr. Spradlin: *I don't know that… I don't know if she ran out.*[32]

Mr. Spradlin eventually did go outside, and he saw Heath in police custody. He believed Heath was handcuffed because his hands were behind his back. He also saw a gun on the ground with a police officer standing over it. After a short time, Mr. Spradlin and his wife left the scene and went back to their hotel. When they left, Heath was still in police custody. According to Mr. Spradlin, when they left the bar that evening, he did not know what had happened. It was after midnight, and they had an early flight the next morning.

Mr. Lewis: *About how long were you all at the bar before Jane told you that the police had Mr. Thomas outside?*
Mr. Spradlin: *I think I had two drinks, maybe an hour or so…*[33]

Mr. Lewis returned to the bar tab and questioned Mr. Spradlin about who had what drinks. He said he had the martini, and his wife may have had the wine. He remembered that Heath and Dennis had the Bombay Sapphires. He did not know who had the sodas, the Maker's Mark, or the premium beer.

Mr. Lewis: *Now, can you tell us, while you were there with Mr. Thomas at the bar, did he appear to you to be intoxicated?*
Mr. Spradlin: *No.*[34]

---

[29] Ibid, 20
[30] Ibid
[31] Ibid
[32] Ibid, 21-22
[33] Ibid, 25
[34] Ibid, 29

Mr. Lewis questioned Mr. Spradlin about what he had discovered since the incident and if he knew Heath was carrying a gun that evening. He said he had not talked to Heath, but he said that he did talk to Carole. She had called him, but the discussion was limited. He said, "I mean we've talked about it but not about the case necessarily."[35] Mr. Lewis pressed on.

> Mr. Lewis: *My question is what did Ms. O'Connor tell you about what had happened that led to Mr. Thomas being arrested?*
>
> Mr. Spradlin: *She really didn't talk about it. I mean we knew it had something to do with a gun because it was laying in the street…*
>
> Mr. Lewis: *So let me make sure I understand this. When you asked Ms. O'Connor she said it was something about a gun and that was it, and you just left it at that?*
>
> Mr. Spradlin: *You know I don't recall the whole conversation.*
>
> Mr. Lewis: *What was the gist of it?*
>
> Mr. Spradlin: *The gist of it was Heath had his gun in the bar. Now I don't know how they ended up outside. I don't know how the gun ended up on the street. I really don't know how he ended up in handcuffs. I didn't see it. I thought he had gone to the men's room.*[36]
>
> Mr. Lewis: *The question is what were you told by Ms. O'Connor…*
>
> Mr. Spradlin: *… I don't really recall the real details of the conversations. We hadn't talked about what he was charged with. I had no idea of what he was charged with.*
>
> Mr. Lewis: *So is it your testimony that Ms. O'Connor didn't tell you about what the allegations were as to why he got arrested?*
>
> Mr. Spradlin: *No, she didn't.*[37]
>
> Mr. Lewis: *Did she [Ms. O'Connor] tell you what you should say when I contacted you or when the U.S. Attorney's contacted you?*
>
> Mr. Spradlin: *Did she—*
>
> Mr. Lewis: *Did she tell you what you should say when we contacted you?*
>
> Mr. Spradlin: *No.*
>
> Mr. Lewis: *Did she tell you about the questions that you would be asked.*
>
> Mr. Spradlin: *She told me what you asked her.*
>
> Mr. Lewis: *Did she tell you about the answers that she had given?*
>
> Mr. Spradlin: *I don't recall everything that she told me. She just said that— she said I would be contacted by Heath's lawyer and she said I would probably be contacted by you.*
>
> Mr. Lewis: *And the question was, whether or not she told you about the answers she had given when she had come down here.*

---

[35] Ibid
[36] Ibid, 32
[37] Ibid

Mr. Spradlin: *No, not really.*

Mr. Lewis: *You say not really. What does that mean?*

Mr. Spradlin: *I mean she told me what you had asked her. Well, I mean – She talked about the environment in the bar and the things you would be looking for.*

Mr. Lewis: *And again, you didn't answer the question. Did she tell you about the answers that she had given in some way, shape or form?*

Mr. Spradlin: *We talked about your conversation with her; yes.*

Mr. Lewis: *Yes, that includes the answers she gave. Is that correct?*

Mr. Spradlin: *I don't remember specifically. I don't think she said okay he asked this question and here's your answer. I mean it was more of a conversation. But she did tell me that she had to testify before the Grand Jury and that you asked about the environment in the bar; was it loud, was it dark, was it light.*

Mr. Lewis: *Let me ask you this, after you got done with that conversation with Ms. O'Connor, did you have a pretty good idea of what she had testified to when she came down here?*

Mr. Spradlin: *Yeah.*

Mr. Lewis: *And that was based on what she told you?*

Mr. Spradlin: *Yes.*[38]

The questions continued regarding whom Mr. Spradlin had talked to about the incident, who knew he was testifying at the grand jury, whether he knew of any other witnesses, and whether he knew if the incident had been filmed (he did not know if it had been filmed).

Mr. Lewis: *Were you intoxicated that night by the time that you left the bar?*

Mr. Spradlin: *No.*

Mr. Lewis: *Was anybody from your party intoxicated?*

Mr. Spradlin: *No. I don't think so. No.*[39]

Mr. Lewis concluded his examination, and the jurors were then allowed to ask a few questions.

Juror: *When you guys were outside, how was Jane acting? Was she outside with you?*

Mr. Spradlin: *Yes.*[40]

Later, a juror asked Mr. Spradlin if he could remember what Heath was wearing. Mr. Spradlin said he could not. When questioned further about Heath's appearance that evening, he said, "I'm not even sure if I would recognize him if he walked in here. I met him that one night."[41]

---

[38] Ibid, 33-34
[39] Ibid, 36-37
[40] Ibid, 37
[41] Ibid, 38

Mr. Spradlin's testimony sheds some light on what the prosecution was trying to establish. Mr. Lewis questioned Mr. Spradlin as if Carole were being investigated. Mr. Spradlin's testimony is typical and expected in that, to him, nothing of significance occurred before he was informed of Heath's being outside with the police.

I interviewed Mr. Spradlin by telephone. He said that if there had been a disturbance at the bar, he would have heard it. He added that he would not have witnessed it since his view of the bar area was blocked by a pillar and his back was to the bar. I asked him if he used the men's room at The Guards, and he remembered that he did. He said that he had to go down a flight of steps to a lower level to do so. When asked if anyone else was downstairs, he did not remember, saying, "I don't recall."[42]

Mr. Dennis Jones

The next member of Heath's party to testify was Mr. Dennis Jones. Mr. Jones testified on October 22, 2010, one day after Mr. Spradlin, for about fifty minutes. He had just met Heath and Carole that evening; Carole had previously worked with Mr. Jones's wife, Jane.

Mr. Jones believed that his group arrived at The Guards at seven or eight o'clock. When they first arrived, they were at the bar, but moved to a table that was behind them. While seated at the table, he was facing a wall. He ordered a dirty martini and he had to send it back. It did not have olives in it, and it was not made properly. He said other drinks in his party also had to be sent back. He said the waitstaff seemed to have an attitude, and he believed it might have been because the party sent the drinks back.

Mr. Jones remembered Heath going to the bar to pay the tab, and then he "heard someone say – They're throwing him out of the bar."[43]

> Mr. Jones: *I got up and I walked outside to see....*
> Mr. Lewis: *And at the time that you stepped outside of the bar, what did you see?*
> Mr. Jones: *I saw Heath and the bouncer wrestling— well not –wrestling is the wrong term. Both of them were trying to control a gun that was already out.*[44]
> Mr. Jones heard someone say, "Call 911."[45]
> Mr. Lewis: *Could you see what – the bouncer had his hands on Mr. Thomas at the moment that you're standing outside and the gun is pointing at you.*
> Mr. Jones: *Yes, he was bent over and the bouncer was definitely a taller guy was almost on top of him. ... the bouncer was behind him.*[46]

---

[42] Telephone interview with Mr. Spradlin on October 21, 2014
[43] Testimony of Mr. Jones from his grand jury transcript from October 22, 2010, p 14
[44] Ibid, 16
[45] Ibid, 18
[46] Ibid, 19-20

Mr. Jones said that at some point the gun was pointed at the doorway—which was where he was standing—so he reentered the bar. When he peeked outside after reentering the bar, "the positions of both individuals didn't really change much."[47]

After the police arrived and he went back outside, he said, "Heath was handcuffed and he was standing in front of a police vehicle, and there were – obviously there was a lot of people surrounding that scene just because Saturday in Georgetown, they wanted to see what was going on."[48]

Mr. Jones said the noise level in the bar was a five or six out of ten, but it was not hard to hear conversations at their table. He could not hear conversations at the bar (which was about fifteen feet away).

When questioned about bar tabs from Old Glory, the restaurant where they had dinner, he could not remember who had what drinks. He believed he had, "Probably five or six beers."[49]

> Mr. Lewis: *Sir, do you remember how much Mr. Thomas had to drink while you were at Old Glory?*
> Mr. Jones: *I do not.*
> Mr. Lewis: *So he was drinking about the same as you or different? Do you remember that?*
> Mr. Jones: *I would think the same as me.*[50]
> Mr. Lewis: *At the time, Sir, you left Old Glory, how would you say that the beers that you had affected you? Were you buzzed? Were you drunk? Not affected at all?*
> Mr. Jones: *Between not affected and buzzed.*[51]

At The Guards, Mr. Jones had a beer when they first arrived, and he then ordered a martini, to which he added, "I may have had two dirty martinis."[52] He could generally not remember who had what drinks, from a receipt in his name. He did remember that Heath had one of the martinis. The prosecutor asked Mr. Jones how the alcohol had affected him at that point, to which he answered, "I was definitely very buzzed at that point."[53]

Mr. Lewis continued his questioning about the bar tabs from that evening and who paid for what. Mr. Jones could not remember the details.

---

[47] Ibid, 21
[48] Ibid, 22
[49] Ibid, 30
[50] Ibid
[51] Ibid, 32
[52] Ibid
[53] Ibid, 36

Mr. Lewis: *Do you know whether or not Mr. Thomas was under the influence of any drugs or alcohol that night?*

Mr. Jones: *I do not know.*[54]

When Mr. Lewis was finished, the jurors were invited to ask Mr. Jones questions.

Juror: *Do you remember when Mr. Thomas got up to ask about the tab, do you remember what his statement was like or what he said or—*

Mr. Jones: *I don't know what he said.*

Mr. Lewis: *Actually, if I can follow up on that. The last time you saw Mr. Thomas before he had – he was outside with a gun, did he appear to you to be drunk or intoxicated?*

Mr. Jones: *I don't know. I know I had a few drinks... and I was pretty buzzed. So I would imagine everyone else in the table were too.*

Mr. Lewis: *And was Mr. Thomas pretty much keeping up with you while you were drinking over the night?*

Mr. Jones: *I think so. I don't recall.*[55]

Juror: *When Mr. Thomas got up from the table to – do you know what he was getting up from the table ... I thought I heard you say he was going to pay the tab.*

Mr. Jones: *... I think he was going to go and try to get the drink that we sent back taken off his tab.*[56]

Mr. Jones's testimony is like Mr. Spradlin's in that, to him, nothing of significance, other than the drink problems, occurred before he was informed of Heath's being outside with the police. He did say that he arrived at the Guards around 7 or 8 p.m., so he may have been thinking about the restaurant where they had dinner.

Mr. Jones is also the only witness from Heath's party who implies that Heath, not unlike himself, could be "buzzed." At dinner, he said he had five or six beers, but other testimony and evidence show the party only had four rounds. Mr. Spradlin is also small in weight, which means he would be more affected with his consumption, which would also affect his memory. Over a three-hour period, four beers would have more of an effect on him than it would on Heath, for example. A general estimate is that a person weighing 150 pounds will eliminate ¾ of one beer, or 3/4 ounces of alcohol, in one hour. Heath was 190 pounds and would be less affected.

Ms. Jane Jones

Ms. Jane Jones, Dennis Jones's wife, was the next individual to testify in front of the Grand Jury. She testified on Friday, October 22, 2010, the same day as her husband, for fifty-four minutes. Like her husband, Ms. Jones did not know Heath before the night of the incident.

---

[54] Ibid, 37
[55] Ibid, 39-40
[56] Ibid, 41

When asked to recount the events of that night, Ms. Jones said that she and her husband drove to Georgetown on the night in question to meet the other two couples for dinner. The group, except for herself, consumed alcohol with dinner. When questioned if she consumed any alcohol, she said, "No."[57] They arrived at the restaurant around 7:00 and left, "Between 10:00 and 11:00."[58]

When the group was seated at The Guards, the bar area was behind her and to her right.

> Mr. Lewis: *… did there come a time when something out of the ordinary happened?*
> Ms. Jones: *Yeah. We were having problems with the drinks.*[59]

Ms. Jones explained several problems with the drinks. First, they were supposed to have olives but did not. To correct that issue, the waitress brought a cup of olives to the table. Second, the next drink order was made with the wrong liquor; they had ordered gin martinis, but they were made with vodka. The waitress disagreed with their assertion that the drinks were made with the wrong alcohol and went to the bar to talk to the bartender. Third, when the waitress returned to the table, she tried to take the drink from Dennis's hand, and it spilled in his lap.

> Mr. Lewis: *When your husband had the drink spilled in his lap, did that make him upset?*
> Ms. Jones: *Well, he was – he wasn't angered by it, but he was like, you know, 'Come on. You brought us the wrong drink first. And now it spilled.' It just wasn't a good experience, but he wasn't irate. He wasn't rude to the waitress or anything like that.*
> Mr. Lewis: *How about Mr. Thomas? Did these series of interactions or problems seem to make him upset?*
> Ms. Jones: *No. Again, I wouldn't say that he was visibly angry.*
> Mr. Lewis: *You say he wasn't visibly angry. Did he seem to be angry in some other way?*
> Ms. Jones: *No. He just – I looked at him and he did not appear angry.*[60]

Ms. Jones said she believed it was maybe five minutes after the spilled drink incident that Heath got up from the table, but she did not see where he went.

Mr. Lewis then questioned Ms. Jones about the lighting and noise in the bar. She said, "It was moderately lit where we were sitting. We had no trouble seeing each other. No trouble seeing the bar."[61] As to the noise, using a one-to-ten scale, she said it was a five.

---

[57] Ibid
[58] Ibid, 9
[59] Ibid, 11
[60] Ibid, 13-14
[61] Ibid, 15

Mr. Lewis: *... After Heath got up and you're not sure where he went, did there come a time when he again came to your attention?*

Ms. Jones: *Well, Carole ran outside of the bar. And that's when it again came to my attention.*

Mr. Lewis: *Tell us about Carole running outside of the bar. Did she say anything before she got up and ran outside of the bar?*

Ms. Jones: *No. She just got up and left.*

Mr. Lewis: *Did she walk out or did she run out?*

Ms. Jones: *She moved quickly.*[62]

Ms. Jones did not know why Carole left, and after a few moments she followed her. When questioned why she followed Carole she responded, "Because she just got up and left without saying anything."[63]

Mr. Lewis: *Did you know why she was getting up.*

Ms. Jones: *No. She just got up. She didn't say anything.*

Mr. Lewis: *Then what happened?*

Ms. Jones: *I followed her outside. I take that back. I didn't follow her outside. I followed her out and I was standing in the portico. The Guards has like a covered doorway before you actually enter the street. I was standing in that covered doorway and I had a direct line of sight to the cars parked out in front of the bar. And I saw Heath laid out face down on the hood of a car and somebody on top of him and a gun in his hand.*[64]

Mr. Lewis: *And when you were in that foyer looking out, where was Carole?*

Ms. Jones: *She was — if I'm looking out the door, she was kind of standing to the left, on the left side of the doorway on the sidewalk.*[65]

Mr. Lewis: *... Do you have any idea based on your personal knowledge ... how it was that Mr. Thomas came to be outside?*

Ms. Jones: *No, I didn't see anything.*

Mr. Lewis: *Did you hear anything?*

Ms. Jones: *No.*[66]

Ms. Jones was questioned as to whether she heard any argument or scuffle or anything before the incident, and she said, "No."[67]

---

[62] Ibid
[63] Ibid, 16
[64] Ibid
[65] Ibid, 17-18
[66] Ibid, 18
[67] Ibid

When she was outside, she saw the bouncer, Heath, Carole, and a man who was standing to the right of Carole and with whom Carole was having a conversation. The man was an older gentleman with light skin. (She was referring to Mr. Viricochea.) She said it was dark outside, and the conversation seemed urgent. She did not notice anyone else outside.

When she first observed Heath, he was on the hood of a car with the bouncer over or on top of him. When questioned for more details, Ms. Jones answered, "I can't recall if it was one arm on top of Heath's back or two arms on top of Heath's back, but the individual was over Heath."[68]

> Mr. Lewis: *Were Heath's feet still on the ground or was he completely laying on the hood?*
> Ms. Jones: *I couldn't say for sure.*[69]

She was then asked about the gun she mentioned earlier and where she saw it. She said, "In Heath's hand. I believe it was in his right hand."[70]

Ms. Jones was questioned at some length about the position of the gun; she reiterated that she believed the gun was in Heath's right hand. She could not say where the gun was pointing.

> Mr. Lewis: *If the gun had shot at that moment, where would the bullet have gone? Would it have hit anything?*
> Ms. Jones: *I couldn't tell you for sure. I don't know.*[71]

When questioned further about the gun and the direction it was pointed, she said, "I really couldn't tell you. I couldn't see. I was too far away to see the details of how the gun was positioned in his hand."[72]

When outside she did not hear Heath or the bouncer say anything, but she heard Carole saying something to the older gentleman. "*She* [Carole] *was – at the time frame that I saw all of this, she was interacting directly with this other individual, this older gentleman.*"[73]

Ms. Jones said she was only in the portico for five to ten seconds, and she then reentered the bar. She remembered it was her husband who, when she was in the portico, had pulled her "back inside and said, 'Let's go.'"[74]

---

[68] Ibid, 20
[69] Ibid
[70] Ibid, 21
[71] Ibid, 22
[72] Ibid, 23
[73] Ibid
[74] Ibid

She returned to their table and told the others, "There is a situation outside. We need to get our bill."[75] The Spradlins were the only people at the table; Heath and Carole were outside, and Mr. Jones had followed his wife to the entrance.

Ms. Jones was questioned again about the gun and where it was pointed.

> Mr. Lewis: *Did the gun ever point in your direction?*
> Ms. Jones: *I couldn't tell you. I wasn't there long enough to see it. I couldn't see what direction the gun was facing.*
> Mr. Lewis: *Is it possible it was pointing in your direction?*
> Ms. Jones: *I couldn't say. I don't know. I didn't see it.*[76]

After returning to her table and taking care of the check, she went back outside. The police had arrived. Heath was in handcuffs and Carole was standing on the sidewalk.

She was then questioned about her time in the foyer when she first went out—whether anybody warned her of any danger. She answered, "I can't recall."[77]

Mr. Lewis asked about her interactions with Carole when she went back outside.

> Ms. Jones: *She [Carole] didn't know what was going on. She was flustered.*
> Mr. Lewis: *Did she appear – was she crying?*
> Ms. Jones: *At that point, no, she was not crying. She was upset.*
> Mr. Lewis: *Angry upset? Scared upset?*
> Ms. Jones: *Scared upset.*[78]

Ms. Jones said she was at the scene for some time before she left. She was asked if, before she left that night, Carole gave her any more information about the incident. She answered, "She [Carole] said she didn't know what happened."[79]

Ms. Jones could not remember if they left before or after Heath was taken away. She said, "All I know is that it was very late by the time we left. It was between 1:00 and 2:00… But probably closer to 2:00 by the time we left the scene."[80] When they left, they took Carole home, and at that time, Carole still did not know what had happened. Carole wanted to contact Heath's supervisors, but she did not have any contact information.

At that point the questions turned to the bar tabs and who drank what. When asked whether she had any drinks with alcohol, Ms. Jones said no, but later she corrected

---

[75] Ibid, 24
[76] Ibid, 25
[77] Ibid
[78] Ibid, 28
[79] Ibid, 29
[80] Ibid

herself and said she had a glass of wine with dinner.[81] She was generally unable to say who had what drinks, but she did remember a few. When questioned about the tabs from The Guards, she remembered that it was her husband and Heath who ordered the Bombay Sapphires.

Mr. Lewis then pursued a line of questioning about Heath's sobriety, beginning with when Heath got up from the table.

> Mr. Lewis: *Now can you tell us at the time that Mr. Thomas is getting up, how would you describe his level of intoxication or impairment from all the alcohol we just talked about?*
> Ms. Jones: *That was the first time I was meeting him. I had nothing to compare it to. So I really couldn't tell you if he was intoxicated or not.*
> Mr. Lewis: *Did he appear to you to be intoxicated?*
> Ms. Jones: *I really couldn't tell you. I don't know if he was intoxicated.*
> Mr. Lewis: *But the question is, did it appear to you, in your opinion, based on your life experience, that he was intoxicated?*
> Ms. Jones: *No.*
> Mr. Lewis: *Did it appear to you, based on your life experience, that the alcohol he had consumed had had some effect on him?*
> Ms. Jones: *No. He was not drunk.*
> Mr. Lewis: *So you're – let me just make sure I understand this. Your testimony is that from all that he had been drinking, he didn't appear to you to – strike that. It didn't appear to you that the alcohol had had any effect on him whatsoever?*
> Ms. Jones: *No. He did not appear to be drunk.*
> Mr. Lewis: *My question is, all the alcohol that was consumed, did it appear to you to have affected him at all?*
> Ms. Jones: *Well, we had been drinking since dinner. You know, there had been drinks throughout the night. So I really had nothing to compare it to because the whole time I saw him, you know, everyone had alcohol. I don't know.*[82]

Mr. Lewis's seventh, but not his last follow-up question was, "So your answer is you don't know whether or not it appeared to you that alcohol had affected him. I just want to make sure I understand what you're saying."[83] Ms. Jones answered, "Yeah. I don't know."[84]

Mr. Lewis continued asking questions about the whole party.

---

[81] Ibid, 33
[82] Ibid, 38-39
[83] Ibid, 39
[84] Ibid

Mr. Lewis: *How about anybody else you were with? Did it appear that all this alcohol had affected them at all?*

Ms. Jones: *We were having a good time. Again, I haven't drank with Terry and Vickie before. I haven't drank with Heath before. I don't know what they're like when they're drunk. We were just having a good time.*

Mr. Lewis: *Sure. You that night were sober because you only had one glass of wine—*

Ms. Jones: *Right.*

Mr. Lewis: *So is it your testimony that, stone cold sober, you were unable to tell whether or not all the alcohol we just went through had any impact on any of the people you were with?*

Ms. Jones: *Yes. I could not tell you that if that caused an impact – had any impact on folks. I had not drank with them before.*[85]

Mr. Lewis then asked Ms. Jones about her husband.

Mr. Lewis: *Did the alcohol he had appear to have influenced or impacted him in any way?*

Ms. Jones: *He was having a good time.*

Mr. Lewis: *How would you describe the effect? Was he stone cold sober or was he buzzed, was he completely drunk?*

Ms. Jones: *He was buzzed.*

Mr. Lewis: *Could you tell whether or not the other people were buzzed?*

Ms. Jones: *Again, we were having a good time, but I really couldn't say for sure whether or not the other people were buzzed?*[86]

Mr. Lewis changed the topic and asked her about conversations with Heath and Carole. Mrs. Jones testified that she had met with Heath once since the incident, but the incident was not discussed.

Mr. Lewis: *Have you had any conversations with Ms. O'Connor about what happened that night?*

Ms. Jones: *We discussed her Grand Jury testimony because her lawyer said it was okay.*[87]

She explained that Carole told her about what questions she could expect from the grand jury; generally, Carole had told her about her own experience with the grand jury. The conversation occurred the evening before Ms. Jones testified.

---

[85] Ibid, 39-40
[86] Ibid, 40
[87] Ibid, 41

> Mr. Lewis: *But she gave you a pretty good idea of what she has said in the Grand Jury; is that right?*
> Jones: *Yeah. She shared some of her answers with me, but again it was, you know, I said this and it wasn't — she didn't tell me her whole – she didn't go in verbatim to what she said.*[88]

Ms. Jones conveyed her belief that Carole shared the information with her because she, Ms. Jones, had never been to a grand jury. She asked Carole about what to expect. A few questions later, Mr. Lewis rephrased his questions about her conversation with Carole.

> Mr. Lewis: *Did you get the impression that she wanted your testimony to line up or be consistent with the testimony that she had given while she was down here?*
> Ms. Jones: *No. That's not something we discussed.*
> Mr. Lewis: *Was that implicit at all in your conversation?*
> Ms. Jones: *No.*
> Mr. Lewis: *Now before your conversation with Ms. O'Connor last night, between August 28 and then, had you had any conversations with her about what had taken place the night Mr. Thomas was arrested?*
> Ms. Jones: *No. She wasn't allowed to talk about the details of the case.*
> Mr. Lewis: *So, between August 28 and last night, she didn't tell you anything at all about what had happened or what led to Mr. Thomas's arrest.*
> Ms. Jones: *No. Again, she wasn't allowed to talk about the details of the case.*
> Mr. Lewis: *Did you ask her about it?*
> Ms. Jones: *No. She just – well, I asked her how everything is going. She said, 'I really can't say.' She said, 'I'm going for the Grand Jury.' And that's the only indication I had.*[89]

Ms. Jones said she had talked to her husband and Terry Spradlin about the incident. The conversations were just general.

> Mr. Lewis: *… Is there anything else that happened that night that the Grand Jury who is investigating this incident should know about?*
> Ms. Jones: *I found it interesting that while we were waiting on the street, the cops didn't interact with any of us. I don't know if they knew we were part of the group, but they didn't approach us for statements. I found that odd.*

---

[88] Ibid, 42
[89] Ibid, 42-43

Mr. Lewis: *Did you approach the police and let them know that you —.*
Ms. Jones: *We were told to stay back. We were told to stay away. They told everyone to stay away.*[90]

That concluded Ms. Jones's time on the stand. Ms. Jones's testimony and memory of the event corroborate the testimony from others in her party. It also seems to put in doubt when Corporal Holubar came to the doorway. If he did arrive before her, he was not there long. She testified that she did not see Corporal Holubar standing in the same location, in the same doorway, where she would have been standing.

Still to testify was Agent John Eisert, Heath's supervisor.

---

[90] Ibid, 46

3A

Ronnie Long: Physical Evidence?

On April 25, 1976, a 54-year-old woman in Concord, North Carolina, reported being assaulted and raped in her home. Several weeks later, at the request of the police, the victim was asked to observe people in the courtroom to see if any defendants in other cases resembled her assailant. According to media reports, "She ended up identifying Mr. Long, who was there on a trespassing charge"[1]—a charge that was later dismissed. Subsequently, the police gave the victim a photo lineup that included Mr. Long. From the photo lineup, the victim identified Mr. Long as her assailant.

After being identified by the victim, Mr. Long was charged, tried, and found guilty of rape and burglary and was sentenced to life in prison. On August 27, 2020, he was released from prison. Additionally, he later received a pardon of innocence. He was 64 years old when released and had spent 44 years of his life incarcerated for crimes he did not commit.

Mr. Long had been incarcerated for almost 30 years when, in 2005, a motion was filed by the North Carolina Innocence Inquiry Commission, a neutral state agency whose stated mission is "to investigate and evaluate post-conviction claims of factual innocence." The motion required the district attorney and the police department to turn over all the evidence related to Mr. Long's case. The motion was granted, and the authorities revealed that forty-three fingerprints and a hair sample existed from the crime scene. There had also been evidence from a rape examination, but it could not be located. The authorities admitted that the hair found in the evidence did not match Mr. Long. Although the evidence had been collected at the crime scene and from the hospital, it was not shared or even known to Mr. Long or his attorneys.

The Innocence Inquiry Commission ceased further investigation because there was no DNA evidence for testing, either overlooking or disregarding the forty-three fingerprints.

After numerous appeals, in 2012, Mr. Long's attorneys requested information on any and all evidence that was found in the Innocence Inquiry Commission's motion from 2005. Evidence from the rape examination—the DNA—was still missing, but they did find the forty-three fingerprints collected at the crime scene. Mr. Long's attorneys had the fingerprints in evidence compared to Mr. Long's prints. Mr. Long's prints did not match any of them and he was excluded from the evidence.

---

[1] CNN "A Black man is freed from prison 44 years after he was wrongly convicted of rape", August 28, 2020.

During one of Mr. Long's final appeals for a new trial Judge Stephanie Thacker wrote, "*A man has been incarcerated for 44 years because, quite simply, the judicial system has failed him.*"[2] Judge Thacker also said, *"a trickle of post-trial disclosures has unearthed a troubling and striking pattern of deliberate police suppression of material evidence."*[3]

The U.S. District Court granted Long's petition for a writ of habeas corpus on August 27, 2020, and he was released from prison that day. *"The Cabarrus County District Attorney's Office dismissed the charges on August 28."*[4]

Jamie Lau, a law professor and faculty adviser for the Duke Law Innocence Project, told CNN, *"Because of the deceit that occurred at trial, Ronnie and his counsel at the time didn't have the benefit of that evidence to present to the jury."* He added, *"So he's been wrongly incarcerated for 44 years."*[5]

Police and prosecutors are required by law to notify defendants if exculpatory evidence exists. "Exculpatory evidence is evidence that is favorable to the defendant in criminal trial that exonerates or tends to exonerate the defendant of guilt."[6] Will there be, or should there be, any consequences for the authorities that withheld the evidence? Who was the actual offender?

References

Harmeet Kaur and Amanda Watts, "A Black man is freed from prison 44 years after he was wrongly convicted of rape", CNN, August 28, 2020. (https://www.cnn.com)

Ken Otterbourg, Ronnie Long, National Registry of Exonerations (umich.edu), www.innocenceporject.org, Posting Date: 9/14/2020, Last Updated: 5/4/2021

---

[2] Ronnie Long, National Registry of Exonerations (umich.edu), www.innocenceporject.org
[3] CNN "A Black man is freed from prison 44 years after he was wrongly convicted of rape", August 28, 2020.
[4] Ronnie Long, National Registry of Exonerations (umich.edu), www.innocenceporject.org
[5] CNN "A Black man is freed from prison 44 years after he was wrongly convicted of rape", August 28, 2020.
[6] Wikipedia

4

Sometimes the Facts Do Not Fit
MARCH 11, 2011

There are at least two sides to every story and sometimes more.

The grand jury concluded with a final witness on March 11, 2011, more than six months after Heath was arrested. As with all previous witnesses, US Attorney Sean Lewis conducted the examination of Special Agent John Eisert, which lasted fifty-five minutes.

Special Agent John Eisert
Special Agent Eisert worked for U.S. Immigration and Customs Enforcement (ICE) and was Heath's supervisor. He visited Heath at the police station after he was arrested. While on the stand, Agent Eisert was questioned about the ICE policies for firearms and holsters. He read and described the holster policy, stating that the policy for holsters is guidance. He explained that the regulations for holsters are not specific to make and model; the holsters must be approved and should offer security—meaning the gun stays in the holster. One bullet point of the policy reads, "Holsters must have at least one retention device that requires some deliberate action by the wearer to release such as a thumb break."[1]

The prosecutor, Mr. Lewis, asked about an agent's responsibility when displaying a weapon in public. Should the officer identify himself? Agent Eisert agreed that if an agent displays a weapon, the agent should yell, "Police," to identify himself.[2]

Mr. Lewis asked, "Does ICE have a policy about what an agent is supposed to do if he's simply trying to maintain control or keep his weapon from falling to the ground?"[3] Agent Eisert said the agents have training about weapon retention. The prosecutor narrowed his question, asking how the officer could prevent the weapon from falling to the ground. Agent Eisert said, "I would be hard pressed to take an opportunity where I'm walking down the street and a gun would just fall out."[4] The specific situation that occurred in Heath's case was not posed.

---

[1] U.S. Immigration and Customs Enforcement; <u>Guidance for Primary Firearm Holsters</u>, December 2004
[2] Testimony of Agent Eisert from his grand jury testimony from March 11, 2011, p 10
[3] Ibid, 11
[4] Ibid

The question most closely related to Heath's experience was about what ICE officers are taught if their weapon is in danger of being taken. Mr. Lewis asked, "If an agent is trying to maintain control, maybe keep a weapon from getting to somebody else's hand, what training do they receive, what steps are agents supposed to take?"[5] Agent Eisert said that an officer should keep the weapon in the holster at all costs. The officer should ensure the holster is well made and will not let the weapon fall out.

Agent Eisert was also questioned about his meetings with Heath after the arrest. He reported that he drove to the police station just hours after Heath's arrest. He was not on official business; he volunteered to go as a coworker and supervisor. He said their first meeting occurred while Heath was in a holding cell. Agent Eisert stood just outside of the cell while Heath was seated in the cell. Heath sat on a bench against the wall, next to the cell bars. Heath's left side was next to the bars where Agent Eisert was standing. So, Agent Eisert was looking at Heath's profile, the left side of his face.

According to Agent Eisert, he told Heath he was not there on official business but as a friend to see if Heath needed anything. A separate office—the Office of Professional Responsibility (OPR)—would be investigating the incident in the federal system. He did offer Heath some personal advice, saying, "Heath, if you were drinking … throw yourself on the sword. You're not the first one to drink with your firearm and you're not going to be the last one to drink with your firearm, and you're not going to get fired for drinking with your firearm. You're going to get in trouble, but you take that on the chin. It's these criminal charges you need to worry about."[6] He told Heath that lying would get him fired.

Mr. Lewis asked if they had any conversations about the incident. Agent Eisert said any conversation about the incident was brief and vague, as he did not want to hear what happened. He repeated that another organization would be investigating the incident, and, in Agent Eisert's words, it could create "a conflict of interest."[7]

> Agent Eisert: *And the conversation was in the sense that there was a weapon retention issue and that he was trying to retain his weapon.*
>
> Mr. Lewis: *Can you remember, as best as you can, the words of the way he phrased that?*
>
> Agent Eisert: *It was just, you know, it was vague as I'm holding onto my gun, I'm not letting someone touch my gun. But those are not his words, though. It was just the substance of the conversation.*[8]
>
> Mr. Lewis: *Did Mr. Thomas say anything to you about what he thought was going to happen as a result of this incident?*

---

[5] Ibid, 12
[6] Ibid, 18-19
[7] Ibid, 19
[8] Ibid, 19-20

> Agent Eisert: *He did. It was one of those things that I clearly remember. I remember his sitting back. He had a very straight look, and he was acting* [acting supervisor] *at the same time looking for a promotion, and he said, I see my career going poof, and he made an explosion sign with his fingers, as he said, poof, I see my career going poof.*[9]
>
> Mr. Lewis: *And during this time you're having this conversation with Mr. Thomas, can you describe his demeanor?*
>
> Agent Eisert: *Very straight, very calculated, very — his wheels were turning in his head at that time. There were probably 1,000 thoughts going on in his head at the time.*[10]

Mr. Lewis asked Agent Eisert if Heath was looking at him during his visit. He answered that Heath was sitting perpendicular to him, so he was looking at Heath's profile. Mr. Lewis asked, "So… could you smell…anything on his breath?"[11] Agent Eisert said, "No. I could not."[12]

Agent Eisert had two meetings with Heath that evening; the first was about twenty minutes long. After the first meeting, he was told that Heath had not been interviewed yet by a detective. After a detective interviewed Heath, Agent Eisert had a second meeting with him.

> Mr. Lewis: *During that second meeting did you say anything to Mr. Thomas to indicate that he's required to speak to you?*
>
> Agent Eisert: *No.*[13]

Mr. Lewis would come back to this topic later. However, the reason for this question is unclear. The prosecutor was aware that Agent Eisert was visiting Heath as a friend, coworker, and supervisor. He also knew the OPR would be investigating the incident. So why ask that question? He seemed to be laying the groundwork for future questions.

When asked, Agent Eisert said the second meeting was very brief. He asked Heath if he needed anything, something to eat or drink, to make a telephone call, and so on. Heath asked to make a phone call, so Agent Eisert loaned him his cell phone. Before handing over his phone, Agent Eisert asked the detectives if this was allowed, permission was granted, and officers were present when the cell phone was used. Agent Eisert knew that Heath was calling his girlfriend, but he could not hear the exact conversation. He said, "I don't remember anything offhand other than I'll be all right, and things along those lines. There wasn't a conversation of what happened that night or anything like that."[14]

---

[9] Ibid, 20
[10] Ibid, 20-21
[11] Ibid, 21
[12] Ibid
[13] Ibid, 23
[14] Ibid, 25

Mr. Lewis asked additional questions about Heath's demeanor during his meeting.

Mr. Lewis: *And you indicated today that he was very straight, or something along those lines …*
Agent Eisert: *Yes, like rigid, just stiff, looking straight ahead.*[15]

Agent Eisert said that this was not Heath's normal demeanor.

The questioning continued about any conversations Agent Eisert had with the watch commander. The watch commander, who went unnamed during the grand jury, is usually the highest-ranking officer on duty and is responsible for the work during that shift. Mr. Lewis wanted to know whether the commander said anything about Heath's being intoxicated, and if anyone offered or asked if Agent Eisert wanted Heath to take a breath test.

Again, the reasoning behind this line of questioning is unclear if we assume the prosecutor is attempting to elicit new information. Agent Eisert was clear that he was not investigating the incident, so why would the watch commander ask him if he wanted Heath to take a breathalyzer?

Asked about who else he had spoken with, Agent Eisert said he had conversations with Carole O'Connor that same evening via telephone and email. He said, "She gave me bits and pieces of a story, but once again, I was there for one thing only. I thought I was going to be driving Mr. Thomas home that night and things along those lines. As to the story, like I said, that's another agency's purview that I just can't get involved in." He added, "she did give me bits and pieces of her perception of what happened."[16]

Mr. Lewis asked what he remembered about the conversation. Agent Eisert said Carole told him that the group was seated at a table when Heath got up to talk to the manager. Then Carole saw Heath being carried out, and she followed. A gun was unholstered, and there was a scuffle over it. Agent Eisert also said Carole told him that she identified Heath as a police officer during the scuffle.

Next, Mr. Lewis questioned Agent Eisert about what he knew that evening and who he talked to about the incident.

Agent Eisert: *Well, obviously I know from the complaint what the police officers' view is, the complaint written for the presentment on Monday morning… I did speak with the Watch Commander, the arresting officer, the Desk Sergeant, and we didn't get into any specifics of what happened… I got the understanding that Mr. Thomas was involved in an incident in a bar involving his gun, and that's why I showed up… that was my understanding throughout the whole night.*[17]

---

[15] Ibid
[16] Ibid, 29-30
[17] Ibid, 31

That ended Agent Eisert's testimony. Taken all together, Agent Eisert's comments seemed beneficial to Heath, in that Heath conveyed to him that the incident had been a weapon retention issue. This information, if testified to during the trial, would help Heath's case.

Upon reviewing the materials, I thought it peculiar that Agent Eisert was summoned to testify while the MPD police officers involved in the investigation were not. It remained to be seen whether any of these people would be called to testify at the trial.

The Grand Jury Concludes

Agent Eisert was the last witness to testify at the grand jury. The entire process had spanned three grand jury seatings over a period of nearly seven months.[18] In reviewing the materials that Mr. Hannon and Heath provided me, I found several aspects of this case to be abnormal. First, the U.S. Attorney's Office took the case to a grand jury on September 1, 2010. This was peculiar because of the brief time span—it was just four days after the arrest. Under normal circumstances, from my experience, a police investigation is conducted, and then everything is given to the prosecuting attorney. However, under federal law, all criminal charges that are felonies and have possible incarceration of one year must be presented to a grand jury. That requirement does not preclude a police investigation, but in this case, it appears that the grand jury was the only investigation.

Second, it seemed unusual for the U.S. Attorney's Office to offer a plea agreement with only an initial idea of what appeared to be an incomplete investigation. I say "incomplete" because the police files included only three written statements from the alleged crime scene. The statements were from the bouncer, the manager, and the one independent witness, Cpl. Brandon Scott Holubar. One would think that the police would have a long list of witnesses that would include bar patrons, bar employees, and, at the very least, the five people with Heath at the time of the incident.

Third, as mentioned earlier, the case had been taken to the grand jury on nine different dates over a period of six months. Ten individuals testified from September 1, 2010, through March 11, 2011. While investigations by grand juries are not uncommon, the use of three different grand juries to conduct one investigation—from my perspective—is not common.

Regarding the grand jury testimony, my opinion is that it was mixed. While one-person, Corporal Holubar, said a gun had been pointed at him, there was no testimony that went to intent. The intent seemed implied with Heath's descriptive pre-incident behaviors, which suggested he was intoxicated and out of control. That appeared to be the prosecution's perspective. But this view was countered by the people who were with

---

[18] Grand Juries in Washington D.C. are empaneled for 25 working days and two extra days if needed. The testimony of nine witness was taken from September 1, thru Oct. 25. The last witness testimony was taken on March 11, 2011.

him that evening, testifying that he was not drunk. Also, several prosecution witnesses did not think Heath was intoxicated, and Carole testified that he was not out of control.

Additionally, reading the grand jury testimony, I discovered numerous contradictory statements. Some disagreement should be expected at any hearing. We do see things differently. But sometimes the difference is more significant than it should be. The bouncer's story regarding where he set Heath down was contradicted by other witnesses. Corporal Holubar's testimony that he followed the bouncer and Heath out of the building was contradicted by his own testimony—in that he said Carole was outside when he arrived.

The story that Mr. Brackett told of Heath turning with a gun in hand is difficult to believe. Mr. Brackett may have intended to set Heath down and then step back. It is possible and more probable, however, that Mr. Brackett was still in contact with Heath as they were moving forward after releasing Heath. From this position, looking over Heath's left shoulder, Mr. Brackett could have observed Heath's hand on his gun and may have thought Heath was going to turn to face him. So, he just grabbed for the gun.

The testimony of the first five witnesses—the prosecution witnesses—lasted one hour and forty-one minutes, or around twenty minutes per person. The next five witnesses' testimony, the individuals with Heath that evening plus Agent Eisert, was four hours and fifty-one minutes, almost an hour for each witness. The time of the testimony, taken as it was by several grand juries, is important. To obtain an indictment, the prosecutors would first have had to read all the testimony to the final sitting grand jury. The total time in the grand jury, as recorded, was six hours and thirty-one minutes.

Also of concern is that the witnesses for the prosecution were sometimes questioned as if they were victims. By contrast, the witnesses with Heath that evening were often questioned as if they were not being completely honest—as if they had something to hide. The prosecution witnesses, again from my perspective, were believed, while the witnesses that were in Heath's party were questioned - what they believed.

Although out of necessity I have summarized the testimony, what I have written from the transcripts is, from my perspective, a fair account. Evaluating the material as a whole, I have come to believe the grand jury was not used as an investigative tool but was used to justify what the government believed occurred.

4A

David Camm: Inadmissible Evidence, Witnesses, and DNA

In 2002, David Camm, a former Indiana State Trooper, was found guilty of killing his wife and two children. The crime occurred in 2000 in the garage at his residence. All of the victims had been shot.

Physical evidence and testimony from the prosecution's expert at the trial included blood spatter on Mr. Camm's shirt. The prosecution said the "tiny droplets of his [Camm's] wife's blood on his shirt, … could only be spatter from a gunshot."[1] The prosecution also implied marital infidelity and implied that he molested his daughter. One theory was that he killed his family to hide the child molestation. The theory was raised in Court with no evidence.

Mr. Camm's defense was that the blood on his clothing was transferred from his son. His son's body was in a vehicle, and he moved his son from the vehicle. He also had an alibi, with eleven witnesses who testified that he was playing basketball when the crime occurred.

In 2005, Mr. Camm appealed his conviction, and the initial convictions were overturned because of the inadmissible evidence about his alleged affairs and the accusation of child molestation. He was then retried and reconvicted in 2006.

During the appeal, the defense requested that the DNA discovered at the crime scene be retested. A sweatshirt, which was found at the crime scene, had been tested for DNA, and the prosecution said two different samples were found, but there were no matches, including Mr. Camm's, at that time. When retested, a match was found to a Charles Boney. Mr. Boney was located and questioned about the sweatshirt. He said he had donated that sweatshirt to charity and proffered someone else acquired it from there. He also agreed to take a polygraph test, which he did take, and his responses were deemed deceptive. Yet, Mr. Boney was then released and not considered a suspect.

Several weeks after Mr. Boney was released, the physical evidence was reexamined and a palm print that had been found on the vehicle at the crime scene was matched to him. He was arrested. The prosecution then put forth a theory that both men, Camm and Boney, conspired to commit the crime. They charged Boney as an accomplice to the crime. Boney eventually confessed to being at the crime scene, saying he witnessed Mr. Camm shoot his wife and children.

---

[1] David Camm was found not guilty after two convictions for killing wife, two kids." ABC News, October 25, 2013.

On Mr. Camm's next appeal, the prosecution used Boney to testify against Mr. Camm. However, the defense presented evidence at the trial that indicated that Boney was the assailant. The retesting of evidence showed that Boney's DNA was on the victim's clothing and fingernails.

During this appeal, the defense called on their own blood spatter expert. The expert testified that the bloodstains found on Mr. Camm's shirt were consistent with his story, that he lifted his son out of the vehicle. The defense's expert also testified that the analysis presented at the first trial—by the prosecution expert—was faulty. The prosecution's expert was recalled and admitted through his testimony that he previously lied about his credentials and perjured himself.

Mr. David Camm was found not guilty after spending 13 years in jail. An anonymous juror said, "She felt that the prosecutors and investigators… had fallen victim to a phenomenon called 'confirmation bias,' which simply means you see what you want to see."

"We all felt that he [the state police crime scene investigator] was definitely looking for evidence to support the conclusion he'd already come to and that's not the way you should investigate a case."[2]

Mr. Boney was convicted of the crime and is serving 225 years. Mr. Boney had a criminal record for burglary before this crime occurred.

Examining this case, one could understand the defense's claim that the DNA evidence was not tested before the first trial. Boney's DNA was on file when it was alleged that the evidence was tested, so there should have been a match before the first trial.

It appears that the only evidence used to convict Mr. Camm was the false testimony from the prosecution's bogus blood expert. Should it be incumbent for the prosecutor to verify an expert's credentials? When a person is incarcerated and later found to be innocent, should there be a mandatory review to determine how or why the event and the investigation came to a false conclusion?

References

Richard Schlesinger, "Walking Free - 48 Hours - investigates the David Camm case", on ET/PT on CBS, Associated Press aired August 3, 2014 (This story first **aired** on November 30, 2013).

Linsey Davis, "Former Indiana Trooper David Camm Found Not Guilty After 3rd Trial in Family's Slaying.

David Camm found not guilty after two convictions for killing wife, two kids." ABC News, October 25, 2013. https://abcnews.go.com/US/indiana-trooper-david.

David Camm - National Registry of Exonerations, no reporter listed https://www.law.umich.edu/special/exoneration/.

Posting Date: 10/25/2013, Last Updated: 5/26/2021

---

[2] CBS video of anonymous Juror, interviewed by Richard Schlesinger and aired on the 48 hours, on August 3, 2014

5

Is This the Same Event? The ABRA Report and the Alcohol Beverage Control Board Hearing

NOVEMBER 2, 2010, AND JANUARY 19, 2011

Sometimes what we say depends on the person to whom we are talking.

In Washington, DC, the regulations for businesses that sell and serve alcoholic beverages fall under the Alcoholic Beverage Regulations Administration (ABRA). ABRA investigates complaints and submits reports to the Alcohol Beverage Control Board, the governing body for ABRA. The Alcohol Beverage Control Board also holds hearings and takes testimony on reported incidents. After the incident at The Guards, when Heath was arrested, ABRA investigators responded to the scene and conducted an investigation.

The police were also called and responded to The Guards for a reported crime. The role of the police was to stop any criminal behavior, investigate any alleged crimes, arrest perpetrators, gather evidence, interview witnesses, and complete a report on the investigation. The role of the ABRA investigation of the same incident was to determine compliance with alcohol regulations. ABRA completed a report and, subsequently, the Alcohol Beverage Control Board held a hearing to determine whether The Guards was complying with regulations.

This chapter presents ABRA's investigation of the incident, as well as the hearing held by the board. It also examines a request by The Guards to eliminate a security detail. The security detail consisted of off-duty Metropolitan Police officers, paid to work as security at The Guards during certain business hours. A portion of the cost of the security detail is reimbursable through the board.

ABRA Response

On the night of Heath's arrest, investigator Donnell S. Butler from ABRA responded to The Guards to investigate a reported incident.[1] The subsequent report Mr. Butler submitted contains a summary, the investigative details, an investigative history (previous complaints), a security plan, and statements from two employees of The Guards.

---

[1] The Guards restaurant held ABRA license number ABRA 916 and the ABRA investigation case number for this incident was 10-251-00188

The summary of the investigation states:

Alcoholic Beverage Regulation Administration (ABRA), investigator Donnell Butler was able to determine that on Saturday, August 28, 2010 at approximately 12:20 am., a Felony Assault occurred outside The Guard's located at 2915 M Street, N.W., Washington D.C. Specifically, a patron who was escorted out of the establishment by security personnel, pulled a handgun from his waist, and security personnel struggled with the patron until MPD arrived. The patron was arrested by Metropolitan Police Department (MPD) for Assault with a Deadly Weapon ADW Gun. It was also determined that The Guards failed to follow its documented security plan.[2]

The report was submitted on November 2, just over two months from the date of the incident. No one from Heath's party—including Heath and his attorney—was ever contacted or interviewed as part of the ABRA investigation.

The Case Report

The written investigative report states that another investigator, Vincent Wills, assisted Mr. Butler at the scene. It was Mr. Wills who interviewed the bouncer. He referred to him as "Brackett Marshall Cornell." Mr. Brackett's middle initial is C, so possibly he reversed the order of the names. According to the investigator, Mr. Cornell (meaning Brackett) requested the subject (Heath) to leave, and when he did not, he made a second request and then carried him out. The report also says that when the gun was pulled, he (Mr. Brackett) "grabbed the gun and the patron's waist and a struggle ensued."[3]

Mr. Butler interviewed the manager, Mr. Oscar Viricochea. Mr. Viricochea said that after the bouncer carried the patron out, "he went back to catering other patrons when he heard Mr. Cornell [Brackett] yelling for someone to call the police," and the police were called.[4] Mr. Viricochea said that "the complainant and his companion had entered the establishment before 5:00 pm, and therefore has not been patted down."[5] Additionally, Mr. Viricochea said that there were eight cameras located throughout The Guards, but they were not operating at the time of the incident because he had forgotten to turn them on.

If Mr. Butler correctly recorded the information that he received from Mr. Viricochea, in which he stated that Heath and Carole arrived before 5 pm, that would conflict not only with the testimony of other witnesses, but also Mr. Viricochea's own testimony at the grand jury and evidence from the restaurant where Heath had dinner. This dis-

---

[2] ABRA investigative report on The Guard's incident, case number 10-251-00188, occurred August 28, 2010, Defense Exhibit 11, p 1
[3] Ibid, 2
[4] Ibid
[5] Ibid

crepancy could become a key point in the trial and may point to differing agendas among the witnesses.

Mr. Butler said The Guards security plan was not being followed; the cameras were not on, and there were no police officers posted outside, as they were supposed to be. Attached to the investigative report was a copy of The Guards Security Plan, dated 2008. Part of the security plan states:

Our restaurant operation encourages an atmosphere of minimal incidents; however, in an effort to maintain such an environment we have developed this security plan, the majority of which is for the days and time we offer entertainment. During such times we will have a minimum of three hosts working from 10:00 pm until close, in addition to 2 police officers hired to start at 11 on Friday and Saturday nights through ABRA reimbursement program.[6]

Hosts are security personnel. On page 6 of the security plan, the two police officer requirement is repeated for Friday and Saturday nights, from 11 p.m. until the restaurant closes. This incident occurred on a Saturday night, around 11:58 p.m., but there were no police officers present at the time.

On page 7, the security plan says, ". . . eight cameras monitoring and videotaping all entrances and inside. These cameras will be employed during the hours we have entertainment."[7] It also says, "When a guest is asked to leave or is escorted to the front door the Hosts are instructed to handily [sic] it as gently as possible."[8] Two lines later: "If there is resistance the next and final action is to call for police assistance."[9] Under the heading "Rules of the Floor" the third rule reads, "Never act aggressive or use physical force with guest."[10] The security plan is well written and goes into more detail than what is related in this brief description. (At the grand jury, Mr. Viricochea testified that there was no procedure for removing patrons.)

The last section of Mr. Butler's report included statements on the incident, written by two employees at The Guards. The first was from Mr. Mark Fleming, a bartender who had contact with Heath the evening of the incident. Mr. Fleming described Heath as swearing, and he thought Heath was going to start a fight. He did write that Heath identified himself as a police officer. Shortly after that, he noted that Heath "was calmly and firmly escorted to the door."[11]

The second statement was from Mr. Cesar Siles, who was a waiter that evening. Mr. Siles described Heath as argumentative and cursing. He said Heath was arguing with Mr. Fleming, and the manager asked him to move from the service area. He said Heath

---

[6] The Guards Security Plan, Defense Exhibit 10, p 3
[7] Ibid, 7
[8] Ibid, 8
[9] Ibid
[10] Ibid, 9
[11] Mr. Fleming's written statement, p 1, contained within the ABRA investigative report Defense Exhibit 11

identified himself as a police officer, but then, "this person got extremely irritated and started screaming and yelling that he was a cop."[12] He concluded, "The security guy grabbed him from the waist lifted him up and took him outside."[13]

Employees made the two witness statements, but neither employee testified at the grand jury. Neither witness reported the bouncer saying anything or asking Heath to leave. And both wrote that Heath did identify himself as a police officer before being removed from the restaurant. Conspicuously, neither witness reported anything about Heath trying to pay his bill or Heath talking to the manager in Spanish. Both would become sticking points in the trial.

The last attachment to the initial report was the Investigative History of The Guards, dated January 20, 2011. The summary report outlined eleven incidents at The Guards that were investigated by ABRA from December 2005 through August 2010. When asked by a juror during the grand jury about previous incidents, Mr. Viricochea maintained there were none. Mr. Viricochea may have misunderstood the question, he may have been unaware of the eleven incidents, or he may have been not telling the truth.

The Alcohol Beverage Control Board Hearing

On January 19, 2011, the Alcohol Beverage Control Board held a hearing on this incident. The acting chairperson, Nick Alberti, started by saying, "This is a fact-finding hearing in a case involving a disturbance where I believe a patron was being escorted out and pulled a gun on the security personnel."[14] He continued, "Fact findings are non-contested cases. As such, there won't be any cross-examination. We're just here to kind of get the facts, review the facts, hear everybody's version of what transpired that evening."[15]

Persons at the hearing included six members of the Alcohol Beverage Control Board; investigator Donnell Butler from ABRA; Mr. Michael Fonseca, counsel representing Hossein Shirvani, the Guards owner; Hossein Shirvani; Mark Fleming; and Oscar Viricochea.[16]

Mr. Donnell S. Butler

Investigator Butler was first to give his testimony, which included his interview with the police, as well as his interviews with the manager and the bartender. Accordingly, the police told him they had someone in custody for felony assault. Mr. Viricochea told him he had forgotten to turn the cameras on around 10:00. Specifically, Mr. Butler reported,

---

[12] Mr. Siles' written statement, p 1-2, contained within the ABRA investigative report Defense Exhibit 11
[13] Ibid, 2
[14] Alcohol Beverage Control Board Fact-Finding Hearing, case number 10-251-00188, January 19, 2010, Defense Exhibit 2 p 4
[15] Ibid, 4
[16] Mr. Viricochea is the manager of The Guards. In the ABRA investigative report, his name is spelled "Viricohea," while in the grand jury testimony, it is spelled "Viricochea."

"I didn't get into a lot of the other details regarding the cameras situation because the cameras wasn't [sic] turned on. So I didn't get a copy of the incident as it occurred."[17]

According to the security plan, The Guards was supposed to have a security detail outside, but Mr. Butler said he did not see one. He said the only security working at the time of the incident was Mr. Brackett.

Mr. Brooks, a board member, asked, "And it appears from your report that I guess the assailant was bear hugged, but this occurred before they called the police?"[18] Mr. Butler answered, "Yes," and Mr. Brooks continued. "Okay. So the police was [sic] not notified until they actually put hands on him—"[19]

A discussion followed regarding the security plan and how someone could have entered the establishment with a gun. Investigator Butler said that the cameras and security checks at the door both typically started around 10:00 p.m. He then repeated Mr. Viricochea's statement that the individual with the gun came in before or around 5:00 pm, before people were being checked at the door.[20] Sometimes what we say depends on who we are talking to.

Mr. Michael Fonseca, Counsel for The Guards

Mr. Fonseca presented The Guards' position. He outlined the restaurant's security procedures and how they related to entertainment. In summary, he testified that if there was no entertainment, the security procedures were not required. Mr. Fonseca also said that when there was entertainment, it was usually in the basement.

Responding to questions from Mr. Fonseca, Mr. Butler stated that he did not go into the basement on the night of the incident, and he did not remember hearing any music. Mr. Fonseca then questioned Mr. Butler as to whether the security plan said anything about pat-downs or security devices to check for weapons. Mr. Butler said he thought the security plan did include pat-downs; it does not. The Guards security plan provides information about checking IDs and checking bags, but not pat-downs.

Mr. Hossein Shirvani

Mr. Hossein Shirvani, the owner of The Guards, told the board that Heath came in after 10:00 p.m., saying, "I have it on a check in here around 10:17."[21] Mr. Shirvani added that Heath and his girlfriend came in first, and later, four other people joined them. The wide discrepancy in time for when Heath's party arrived was not noticed, or at least not mentioned.

---

[17] Alcohol Beverage Control Board Fact-Finding Hearing, case number 10-251-00188, January 19, 2010, Defense Exhibit 2 p 7
[18] Ibid, 12
[19] Ibid
[20] Ibid, 13-14
[21] Ibid, 23

At that point, Acting Chairman Alberti interjected with questions about the entertainment at The Guards that evening. He stated that the board's concern was, if there was entertainment that night, what procedures were followed and what was The Guards required to do? He ended with, "I personally am not so concerned with how you handled that particular incident."[22] His and the board's focus was on the security plan and whether it was followed, not Heath's case. He added, "I don't see, but I'm hearing that there are questions that you mishandled the patron and reacted to the situation appropriately. That's my assessment."[23]

The meaning of this last statement is unclear. Can one mishandle a patron—and then react to the situation appropriately? Did Mr. Alberti misspeak? No clarifying statements were included in the transcript.

Next, the chairperson opened the hearing to questions from board members, which Mr. Shirvani answered. The first question was how many security personnel were working that night. Mr. Shirvani said there were three security personnel, one at the door and two downstairs. He added that they did not have entertainment that night, so they were not required to have the police officers outside.

Mr. Fonseca, counsel for the Guards, commented that the security plan does not require the cameras to be on unless there is entertainment. The chairperson asked why the cameras were not on that night, and Mr. Shirvani responded, "Well, we put it on around 10:30 when we have entertainment."[24]

A rather lengthy discussion followed regarding the cameras—why they were not on, how they were always off in the daytime, and so on. It was also discussed that if the cameras had been on, the hearing might not be necessary, and the process could have been much shorter. In that same discussion, a board member, Mr. Jones, noted that if the staff forgot to turn the cameras on, and at the same time the security plan did not require it, it would appear they never intended to turn on the cameras. Later, Mr. Shirvani told the board that in the future, the restaurant would always turn the cameras on after 10:00 p.m.

During the hearing, Mr. Fonseca requested that the security plan be changed to eliminate the police security for outside. He told the board, "The Guards do not have the crowds it used to have and it is very expensive—about $2,500 per month."[25]

The Board's Decision

The board told Mr. Shirvani no action would be taken at that time. However, the board wanted the security plan updated and recommended that the cameras be

---

[22] Ibid, 26
[23] Ibid, 27
[24] Ibid, 35
[25] Ibid, 43

on whenever the restaurant was serving alcohol. The board asked that the plan be updated within 30 days.

The Follow-Up
In the end, the Alcohol Beverage Control Board took no action and only required The Guards to update the security plan within 30 days. On January 28, 2011, nine days after the hearing, The Guards submitted a formal letter to the board requesting approval to eliminate The Guards' use of the Metropolitan Police Departments' reimbursable detail. The Guards said it was a financial hardship and had not had any actionable incidents in two years.

The board responded three weeks later: "The Board relies on the investigative history of the establishment and the absence of any actionable incident to underscore the success of the Reimbursable Detail's present at this establishment. Thus, the Board denies this request."[26]

As Mr. Alberti indicated, this hearing was not about Heath and whether or not he pulled a gun on the bouncer. It was about the way the establishment managed the disturbance and whether it followed its own security plan. However, the testimony revealed some concerning discrepancies when compared to the grand jury. In some instances, these discrepancies may reflect an agenda different from the facts.

---

[26] Alcoholic Beverage Control Board's official response to The Guard's request to eliminate the reimbursable detail, p 1 dated February 16, 2011

5A

Kevin Green: Witness misidentification by the wife of the accused.

Late in the evening on September 30, 1979, Mr. Kevin Green and his pregnant wife argued. After the argument he left his residence, in Orange County, California, and went to a hamburger stand where he purchased a hamburger. When he returned home with his hamburger, he found his wife had been assaulted. Because of the extensive wounds, he first believed she had been shot in the head. He called the police.

Ms. Green was transported to a hospital, where it was determined that she had not been shot but was severely beaten. She was pregnant and several hours later it was determined that the unborn child was deceased. Surgery was performed to end the pregnancy and Ms. Green went into a coma. When she emerged from the coma, she had no memory of the event.

When the crime was reported, Mr. Green explained to the police that he had left his residence and purchased a hamburger. An employee from the hamburger stand told the police that Mr. Green had indeed been there and made a purchase and the police noticed the hamburger he purchased was still warm. While he had an alibi that he was at the hamburger stand, he was nevertheless charged with the crime.

In 1980, Kevin Green was convicted of second-degree murder of an unborn fetus and attempted murder of his wife, Dianna Green. He was sentenced to 15 years to life. The principal witness that testified against him was his wife, who had suffered head trauma during her attack. There was also physical evidence that she had been sexually molested.

Prior to Ms. Green's testimony a psychiatrist, Dr. Brenner, testified that Ms. Green was a reliable witness for the prosecution. The defense had requested to have their expert examine her, but the request was denied. Ms. Green had suffered brain damage from the attack, and while testifying, she had difficulty spelling her name.

At trial, testimony revealed that the Greens had previous domestic issues, and the police had been to their apartment before this incident. It was stated that the argument on the night of the crime was because Ms. Green refused to have sex with her husband.

In 1996, Kevin Green was exonerated after being incarcerated for 16 years. The State of California had created a DNA database, and evidence from the sexual assault excluded Mr. Green as the offender. The DNA testing found a match to a Mr. Gerald Parker. Mr. Parker was called the "Bedroom Basher" because he broke into bedrooms, where he raped and killed women. Parker confessed to the crime, along with five other murders.

Without DNA and a confession from the real killer, the conviction stood with the testimony of a mistaken witness, who was the wife of the accused. If the prosecution's psychiatrist had been allowed to examine the victim, would there still have been a guilty verdict? Due to the victim's diagnosis of brain damage, is it possible that she was coached before testifying?

References
The National Registry of Exonerations, associated with the University of Michigan Law School and https://www.law.umich.edu/special/exoneration/Kenvin Lee Green, no reporter listed.

Posting Date: Before June 2012, Last Updated: 6/20/2020

6

Heath Patrick Thomas

"The last of human freedoms—the ability to choose one's attitude in a given set of circumstances."

—Viktor Frankl

Heath Patrick Thomas is the principal individual in this book, but the book is not about him. It is about the bigger picture—the problems and issues within the criminal justice system that led to Heath's wrongful conviction. It is about police investigations, prosecution lawyers, our grand jury system, defense attorneys, and our court systems. It is about how all these parts work together and—sometimes—do not work together.

Although this book is about more than Heath and his particular case, he is at the center of these issues because of his arrest and conviction. His experience is the lens through which we view these larger problems. Further, his background in law enforcement makes the fact of his wrongful conviction all the more perplexing. He was in many ways the last person one might expect to end up in these circumstances.

I have had the privilege of knowing Heath for more than a decade. I can tell you, Heath Patrick Thomas is not your average person, although he would disagree with that. He is a man who has dedicated his adult life to service to his country, to the criminal justice system, and to the safety and well-being of the country and its citizens. In his attitude toward the case, he reminds me of the bull rider who did not make the eight seconds. When asked what went wrong, the rider says, "I fell off." And when the rider is asked what he should do the next time, he says, "Stay on." Heath is understated, he does not make excuses, and he has not, nor would he, let this incident define him.

In some of our discussions, Heath has sometimes expressed anger and frustration, usually when reviewing parts of the book that contributed to his being found guilty. Even then, his perspective is often directed inward—what he could have done differently. From my perspective, he has a right to be annoyed, irate even, especially when examining the story that changed his life and ended his career. How should someone who dedicated his life to a justice system feel when that same justice system found him guilty of a crime he did not commit? In the law enforcement community, the department for which one works, and the justice system as a whole, are often viewed as a second family. How are you supposed to feel when your family turns on you?

The Thomas Family

Heath's mother, Ms. Alda Perez Salazar, was from San Antonio, Texas, and was the youngest of seven siblings and three half-siblings. Alda's mother, Ms. Guadalupe Perez, had immigrated to the United States from the Mexican state of San Luis Potosi, fleeing the 1913 revolution when she was only 13 years old. Heath's immediate and extended family was rather large and primarily resided in the San Antonio area.

Heath's father, Robert M. Thomas, was from New Jersey; his family was from West Virginia, and his ancestors were originally from Ireland. Robert was in the U.S. Army when he met Alda at a USO dance while stationed at Fort Sam Houston in San Antonio. They became engaged in San Antonio. Heath learned from his mother and a few other family members that when she became engaged, her family was not happy. Since she was the youngest, she was expected to take care of her mother, Heath's grandmother. His father's family also was not happy about the marriage; Heath's mother told him that some members of Robert's family viewed the marriage as interracial, which was not to their liking.

Heath was told that his father was a good soldier, but he liked to gamble, drank a lot, and was unfaithful to his wife. When his father was deployed to Korea, his mother stayed in New Jersey with Robert's family. It was not a pleasant stay. Alda was pregnant when she arrived in New Jersey, and Heath was born there on May 7, 1968. Heath later learned his mother was somewhat ostracized or shunned by her own family. It is believed that the marriage already had problems, and a few family members thought she was not being a "good military wife."

When his father was deployed to Germany, Heath and his mother joined him there. Heath's only sibling, Nathan, was born in Germany. His father continued drinking and cheating on his wife, and he also started physically abusing her. After a particularly bad incident, Alda called the base chaplain.

The chaplain's involvement was significant for two reasons: First, the chaplain had Robert Thomas arrested by the military police. He was in jail for a few days before being released. Second, following the arrest, the military offered to have Alda and her two sons flown back to the U.S. The family did return to the U.S.—without Robert. They landed in New York and spent their first night in a shelter. Heath's mother contacted his grandmother for help, and the grandmother provided transportation from New York to San Antonio, where they moved in with her. Heath later learned that this caused additional friction with a few of his mother's siblings. It was years later that the relatives found out that the grandmother brought them to Texas from New York. The family believed that the grandmother brought them home from Germany. The difference was never explained to Heath.

For several years Heath, Nathan, and Alda lived with his grandmother in San Antonio. When he would ask about his father, he was always told he was at work. It was not until much later that he was told his father had deserted the army. Robert knew where they lived but never made any contact with the family.

Heath's mother went to work, so for a few years, he and his brother were raised by their grandmother. To speak to his grandmother, Heath had to speak Spanish, since she did not speak English. He does not remember learning to speak English or Spanish, but he remembers being told to use the language that was spoken. When he attended school, he used English, and when home, he used Spanish. He understood at an early age that much of their family thought poorly of his mother. The family members would visit and converse in Spanish, not realizing he spoke Spanish. They seemed to blame his mother for problems with her marriage, and they even questioned his and his brother's legitimacy. Even today, he has relatives who speak Spanish in front of him, forgetting that he also speaks Spanish.

The grandmother lived in one of the prominent Hispanic neighborhoods in San Antonio. When it was time to go to school, looking Hispanic but having a *gringo* name was problematic for Heath. Like his mother's family, the children at school taunted him because of his name. He thought this strange since many of the Mexican-looking children with Hispanic names could not speak Spanish. He remembers asking his mother to change their last name. His mother, of course, refused.

The family stress increased when Nathan developed medical issues and other children teased him. Heath was protective of his younger brother, resulting in some physical altercations.

When Heath told his mother that school was boring, she introduced him to the public library. The library opened his mind, as he said, "These books had stories that formed my thoughts about what was possible, what was right and what was wrong, even explained some of the conflicts that were happening to me. These books helped me understand the things that the adults wouldn't tell, like what my father's desertion meant."[1]

When they eventually moved from his grandmother's house, his brother Nathan's medical issues seemed to increase, and he began having seizures. Heath believed that his grandmother blamed him for some of his brother's medical problems. He recalls his grandmother feeling that he should be there if his brother had a seizure. In instances when he was not present, he was often punished. Being held responsible for something he had no control over was confusing for him.

Around this same time, his mother started dating another service member, a Marine, whom she eventually married. The family moved to Camp Lejeune, North Carolina. Heath believed that his mother felt it important that he and his brother had a father.

The move to Camp Lejeune had an unintended impact on Heath. He felt accepted as Hispanic, but at the same time he felt discriminated against for being Catholic. It was as if the discrimination he experienced in San Antonio because of his English name

---

[1] Information from Heath's written accounts of his early childhood, along with interviews.

was now reversed. Even with these new circumstances, he did well in school, and he believed his mixed heritage was a good thing. He feels he was well adjusted and remembers being optimistic.

Unfortunately, Alda's second marriage turned in the same direction as her first. Her Marine husband cheated on her and became abusive. He was medically discharged from the service, and Heath remembers the family's long drive back to San Antonio. At only 12 years of age, he recalls intervening in a domestic dispute between his mother and stepfather. His mother eventually had a nervous breakdown and was hospitalized. While she was in the hospital, Heath and his brother stayed with other family members. By that time his grandmother had passed.

After being released from the hospital, Heath's mother went back to work. She also got her second divorce. Things were going well until Nathan began to have more frequent medical problems. This time it was not just the seizures. Nathan had already undergone several operations, and the doctors wanted to perform more surgery on him. His mother refused the surgery, primarily because of the risk. She was told Nathan would function at a 12-year-old level for the rest of his life. Heath remembers his mother taking his brother to different facilities that were supposed to help him. But his brother had a challenging time adjusting, and the help she sought never materialized.

Heath had started high school about that time. His grades were good, but he knew he could not go to college since he had no money. Throughout high school, his mother prohibited him from playing sports because they had no medical insurance. Instead of sports, he enrolled in the Junior Reserve Officer Training Corps (JROTC), influenced by an uncle he admired. The uncle was in the Special Forces, and when he visited the family, Heath would shadow him. To Heath, his uncle was a good role model. Heath graduated in the top 10 percent of his class and did very well on the armed forces exam.

After high school, he enlisted in the navy. His mother wanted him to leave; it was her belief that if he stayed, he would be responsible for his brother and his future would be limited because of family obligations.

A Career in Service
Heath entered the navy in 1986, graduated from boot camp, and was sent to an officer preparation school. The program, run by the Marines, was for minorities, which Heath believed was a break for him. After nine months, however, he failed officer training when he did not pass calculus. After that, he returned full-time to the navy and went to basic electricity and electronics school. Later, he became a gunner's mate and did two tours in the Persian Gulf. After his tours, he tested for entry into Basic Underwater Demolition/SEAL School (BUD/S), and he passed.

After being accepted into BUD/S, he reported to the Navy Special Warfare Center, Navy Amphibious Base, Coronado, California. He was incredibly happy that he passed

Heath in his Navy uniform...

In his diving gear...

At Graduation with his mother...

With his mother at a sporting event...

In front of his patrol vechile...

In Bosnia...

Receiving an award.

his first physical and swim class, which some did not. Heath credits a lot of his character to this training, even though he was eventually dropped. He says, "I was performance dropped, I blame no one but me."[2] After being dropped, he was assigned to the school's armory, which meant he might have another chance at completing the program. Altogether, he was at Coronado for almost 19 months and was promoted to 2nd class petty officer. He had classed up three times, meaning he had repeated the training process three times but could not pass the final benchmarks. He says of his time there, "While I didn't finish, that school really impacted me; it is really a place where you learn so much about yourself and what you can achieve. In fact, after being there so long, I think I had to relearn how to be around people who constantly give reasons for not doing something or who regularly blame others for their actions."[3]

Heath was nearing the end of his obligated navy enlistment and intended to transfer to the army. He had been preselected and was informed that he would have a Special Forces assessment and selection. However, there was a reduction in force order (RIF) by President George H.W. Bush the week of his discharge, and that opportunity was now closed.

Before being discharged, he had also made applications to several law enforcement agencies. He returned home to San Antonio in July 1992, staying with his mother. He took a job as a lifeguard at the local community college and then received a call from the U.S. Border Patrol; he was selected. After reporting to his California sector, he was sent to the academy at the Federal Law Enforcement Training Center in Georgia.

Heath did very well at the academy, graduating third in his class. To his surprise, his mother and an uncle attended his graduation. At first, he thought something was wrong since no one had attended any of his other graduations. But to his delight, they just came to see him graduate and congratulate him.

His first assignment was San Diego. He was there for five years and had a variety of law enforcement experiences. He patrolled the border, was assigned to a task force, led multiple interdictions, and participated in numerous felony arrests. He also applied to and was accepted to a Regional Emergency Action Team (REACT), looking for violent offenders and developing criminal intelligence.

In 1997, Heath transferred to the Immigration and Naturalization Service (INS) as a criminal investigator. At that time, the U.S. Border Patrol and INS were both under the Department of Justice. Later, in 2003, his part of INS became U.S. Immigration and Customs Enforcement (ICE). ICE is part of the Department of Homeland Security. Heath worked with multiple agencies targeting violent gang offenders and investigating organized crime. He also worked undercover investigating alien smuggling and later the identification of Russian organized crime members. His work involved inter-

---

[2] Information from Heath's written accounts of his service time
[3] Ibid

national investigations, including money laundering, document fraud, immigration fraud, and extortion.

In May of 2001, Heath went to Bosnia-Herzegovina to represent the Department of Justice and INS at the embassy. His position included working with multiple agencies and the International Criminal Investigative Training Assistance Program (ICITAP). The Bosnia-Herzegovina assignment was supposed to be temporary but was extended after the terrorist attacks on 9/11. He was there for more than five years. Bosnia was skeptical of its neighbors due to terrorism and threats. Heath said that many of its neighbors were dealing with similar problems.

After 9/11, Heath's skills in boarder security became more valuable and kept him busy. He often coordinated with the host country and U.S. law enforcement agencies. He assisted with border security related to immigration and customs laws, identity and travel document fraud, smuggling, and counterterrorism. He engaged in multiple task force issues and was used as a subject matter expert for legislative issues and new laws encompassing international standards and U.S. government interests.

While in Bosnia, Heath's free time and social life were limited, as one might expect. He prided himself on staying fit and was an avid runner. He joined a running group called the Hash House Harriers and spent what time he had on his physical fitness. He did date a few times but dating in Bosnia was complicated. At that time there was a requirement to report any romantic relationships with non–U.S. citizens.

Returning to the United States in September 2006, Heath was assigned as a desk officer for Mexico in the Office of International Affairs. He was responsible for the support and coordination of five ICE offices in Mexico. From September 2007 until March 2009, he was the lead liaison to the Central Intelligence Agency. He developed a targeting protocol utilizing information from the Department of State's Security Advisory Opinion (SAO) Program. The idea was to identify potential threats in conjunction with other agencies. In March 2009, Heath was assigned to the National Security Investigations Division, National Security Integration Center, as the acting section chief. The position included outreach to joint interagency partners.

After Heath's arrest in August 2010, he was placed on administrative duties, which meant he was given a desk job and could not carry a firearm. This was difficult for him, but at the same time, he expected to be found not guilty and would then go back to full service. At age 42, he still had many years of service to give.

6A

Thomas Haynesworth: False witness and DNA

Within four weeks in early 1984, five women were victims of sexual assault or attempted sexual assault in one neighborhood in Richmond, Virginia. Because all the assaults occurred in one geographic area, the police believed they were all committed by one person.

One of the victims observed Mr. Thomas Haynesworth walking down a street. He was going to a store to buy groceries. The victim called the police to report him as suspicious because he looked like the person who attacked her.

The police responded and questioned Mr. Haynesworth, asking him to let a woman (the woman who called the police) observe him. He agreed, and the woman identified him as the person who attacked her. Mr. Haynesworth, an 18-year-old Black male, was later arrested and charged with rape.

Subsequently, Mr. Haynesworth was identified in a lineup by four of the five known victims. He was tried for four different offenses and found guilty in three cases. In the three cases he was sentenced to 10 years, 36 years, and 28 years, each to be served consecutively, meaning the sentences were added together for a total of 74 years. (More than a few documents found with this case report that he was sentenced to 84 years.)

While the authorities believed they had caught a serial offender, after Mr. Haynesworth was in custody the crimes continued. In less than one year ten additional offenses occurred until Mr. Leon Davis was arrested. After Mr. Davis was arrested on December 19, 1984, the crimes stopped. He was convicted and sentenced to several life terms. According to documents, Mr. Davis and Mr. Thomas Haynesworth resembled each other.

A state law that allowed for DNA testing was enacted in Virginia in 2009. When Thomas Haynesworth's DNA was tested, he was excluded from the evidence collected from the first attack.

The local prosecutor took the case to the Virginia Attorney General's Office, and subsequently, all of the cases against Mr. Haynesworth were vacated. He was released (on parole) in March 2011 and was exonerated in December 2011. Arrested when he was eighteen, he had been incarcerated for twenty-seven years for crimes he did not commit.

In this case, several victims of the crimes identified Mr. Thomas Haynesworth as the perpetrator of the crimes. Charging someone under those circumstances should be expected. However, since the police believed that one perpetrator committed all the offenses, they should have expected the offenses to stop. Since ten additional offenses occurred after his arrest, all in 1984, that should have been a clue that Mr. Haynesworth was not the perpetrator. Because the crimes continued, and because of the reported resemblance between Mr. Haynesworth and Mr. Davis, you could expect at a minimum that the police would investigate further.

When the local prosecutor went to the Virginia Attorney General's Office with the test results, he did the right thing. Too many times when exculpatory evidence is discovered and that evidence questions the prosecution's case, the burden still rest with the defense to prove their innocence.

"The DNA exoneration cases where the false conviction is established with near certainty show that eyewitness evidence has been largely responsible for false conviction in more than 70% of cases."[1]

References

Steve Broader, "The case of Thomas Haynesworth," The Washington Post, February 14, 2011

John Schwartz, "Virginia Man Jailed for 27 Years is Exonerated", The New York Times, December 6, 2011

---

[1] www.Innocenceproj.org.

PART II
The Trial

7

Day 1: Opening Remarks and Confusion
AUGUST 15, 2011

*"Most of us regard good luck as our right, and
bad luck as a betrayal of that right."*

—William Feather

It was just under one year from the time Mr. Hannon first contacted me, and five months since the conclusion of the grand jury, to the trial start date of August 15, 2011. In that time, I had met with Heath and his team and created the film simulating the incident, reviewed the grand jury transcripts, and participated in several phone calls and two meetings with Mr. Hannon. Heath was present at the last meeting. He seemed relaxed, but also reserved, probably believing the trial would be brief and he would be exonerated.

I had learned through experience that when a case goes to trial, the testimony and evidence can be so contradictory that people often wonder if both sides are even talking about the same event. Even with that understanding, I believed that Heath would be found not guilty.

Before the trial started, I told Heath that he was in his current situation because of a series of events that could only be referred to as bad luck. There was poor service at The Guards, and he was frustrated that he could not pay the tab. Of course, if he had left without paying, he could have been arrested. Then he was thrown out, actually carried out, of the bar, and his gun was dislodged. Subsequently, when he tried to reposition his gun, the bouncer fought for control of it. The police responded, and any investigation appeared to be limited to taking statements that supported Heath's guilt. The prosecutor's office investigated the incident through the grand jury with questions that also appeared to reflect a predetermined assessment of guilt.

It was time for the bad luck to change. Heath did not need good luck. He just needed to be heard and to have the truth told. All he had to do was to relate the facts and testify as to what happened.

At 11:57 a.m. on the morning of August 15, the court was called to order to hear *United States of America v. Heath Patrick Thomas,* Defendant, Criminal Action Number

2010-CF3-16079, Washington D.C. The Honorable Herbert Dixon, Associate Judge, Trial Judge. Representing the government were Assistant U.S. Attorneys Stephen Rickard and Katherine Sawyer. Representing the defendant, Mr. Michael Hannon, Esquire, and Emily Brant.[1]

Courtroom 215, where the trial took place, was small to medium in size, allowing everyone to hear and see the proceedings. The presiding judge, Herbert Dixon, was in his sixties, of good height with a little extra weight, and I was told he had a solid reputation in the legal profession. He presented the physical appearance of what you might expect a judge should look like. In 2011 he had been a circuit judge for 26 years, first appointed in 1985 by President Ronald Reagan. Both prosecutors appeared young, in their late twenties, and had limited courtroom and trial experience.

Then there was Michael Hannon, Heath's defense attorney, with many years of experience and an air of decorum. While no one really knew how the trial would end, my first impressions were favorable for the defense.

Pretrial Time and the Missing Witness

In any trial, certain matters are discussed before the trial starts. One issue in this trial was the estimated time for both sides to present their case. The prosecution's estimate was two days, and the defense's estimate was one and a half days. Unknown to anyone at that time, the trial would take eight days to complete. I did not think much of the estimates at that time. But I later wondered if some things, as the trial dragged on beyond the estimated time, were shortened or abbreviated for the sake of saving time.

Another pretrial matter was the location of a witness, Yuliga Vetlugeena. The defense submitted a motion to compel, as they could not find Ms. Vetlugeena. According to the motion, "There is a witness who the government is not calling who apparently has a statement or made a statement that contradicts a portion of the government's theory in this case that the defense has characterized as Brady evidence."[2] Brady evidence is exculpatory evidence, which is evidence that is or can be favorable to the defense in a criminal trial. The government provided the defense the contact information for the witness, but Mr. Hannon and his team could not locate her. The defense requested that the government turn over any information they had, "including all statements so that the defense can determine if there is, perhaps, some other substitute that they might offer in the absence of the witness to be able to present the testimony that they feel the witness would give."[3]

The government opposed the motion. Judge Dixon heard from Mr. Hannon, who argued that the information the witness had was not known. Mr. Hannon said, "Well,

---

[1] Information from the trial transcript, Criminal Action Number 2010-CF3-16079, dated August 15, 2011
[2] Ibid, 7
[3] Ibid, 8

I simply don't know if there's any other information that was provided by this witness that I would want to use in cross-examination of the other employees … of The Guards. So to the extent, if it is indeed Brady information … there's no harm to the government, we would like it now."[4]

The judge declined the motion at that time, saying he would wait until he had heard the government's case. The judge added that the witness might still be found.

The Brady Rule
The Brady Rule is from a Maryland case in which a defendant in a murder trial was found guilty and sentenced to prison. In *Brady v. Maryland*, a co-defendant in the case, at a separate trial, had confessed to the actual murder, and this information was withheld at the defendant's trial. The defendant argued that his sentence would have been less if the co-defendant's confession had been entered at his trial, since he did not physically commit the murder. The case went to the Supreme Court, and the defense's argument was upheld.

The Brady Rule requires the prosecution to disclose material exculpatory evidence to the defense. Material exculpatory evidence is evidence that would create a reasonable probability that a conviction or sentence would be different. Of course, the material exculpatory evidence must be introduced, and for it to be introduced, it must be known. Material exculpatory evidence can include witness statements and physical evidence that challenge the prosecution's witnesses and their physical evidence.

The Witness
Ms. Yuliga Vetlugeena was summoned to be a witness for the defense, but she could not be located and served. On the summons, it stated that she was employed at The Guards. Before the trial, Mr. Hannon had requested, through discovery, a list of the employees at The Guards who were employed on August 28, 2010.[5] Ms. Vetlugeena's name was not on the employee list. In researching the book, I found a current address for her and sent letters to her regarding this case and the book, but she never responded.

The Trial Begins
After the preliminaries were dealt with, as with every trial, each side made opening statements. An opening statement is a brief summary of what each side intends to show and prove to the court. For the prosecution, Mr. Rickard put forth the idea that Heath was drunk, insulting the restaurant employees, and being a nuisance. Mr. Rickard said, "He [Heath] didn't feel that he was getting enough attention and he began yelling about his tab."[6] The

---
[4] Ibid, 10
[5] One-page document titled List of Employees working August 28, 2010, at the Guards, see Appendix B
[6] Information from the trial transcript, Criminal Action Number 2010-CF3-16079, dated August 15, 2011, p 18

prosecutor argued this was why Heath was evicted from the bar, and then, to save face, he drew his weapon with the intent to scare the bouncer. Mr. Rickard continued, "Mr. Thomas made a decision and took an action. And the next thing Mr. Brackett saw was Mr. Thomas as coming around with his weapon drawn, his arm extended coming around towards him."[7]

Mr. Rickard did not just summarize what he believed the trial would show; he added intent and meaning to Heath's alleged actions. Mr. Rickard argued that Heath drew his weapon intentionally to frighten the bouncer.

In Mr. Hannon's opening remarks, he talked extensively about witnesses who would be called, including character witnesses. He did give credit to the police department, saying, "The Metropolitan Police Department investigation is worth highlighting just a bit. And the evidence we expect will show that the uniformed officers on the scene diffused [sic] the situation. And had it not been for events that I think the court will hear about, I don't believe we would be here today."[8]

Mr. Hannon then reviewed some of the prosecution points without refuting them. At one point, he talked about elements of the alleged crime saying, "But the government is going to have to show that it was Agent Thomas who engaged in the Act that they're going to ask the court to find him guilty of and that it was a threaten [sic] act. And he didn't do it voluntarily, on purpose, and not by mistake of accident. That means he did it on purpose. He did it to threaten. He did it to threaten another person with a dangerous weapon and that was in his mind when he engaged in that activity. And if Agent Thomas was acting for some other purpose, then he can't be convicted."[9]

He continued, "And then we are asserting that Agent Thomas had the privilege to act in self-defense. And your Honor knows, the government has the burden of proving that he did not act in self-defense beyond a reasonable doubt."[10]

The Prosecution Begins

The prosecution called two witnesses, Marina Yudina and Graciela Perez, to open the trial. The two women, both employees at the Guards, described what they observed on the night of the incident.

Marina Yudina

The first witness, Marina Yudina, was a bartender at The Guards who was working on the night of Heath's arrest. Mr. Rickard, a youthful-looking attorney, of average height and weight with just under two years of experience with the U.S. Attorney's office, conducted the direct examination.

---

[7] Ibid, 19
[8] Ibid, 29
[9] Ibid, 32
[10] Ibid

Ms. Yudina stated that Graciela, a waitress, came up to the bar with Heath and said that he wanted to pay his tab. To close the tab on the computer, she needed Heath's last name. He gave his name to her, and she started to close the tab. Heath then stated that he wanted to close the tabs for the rest of his party as well. Ms. Yudina asked for their names, and he responded that he did not know the names. According to Ms. Yudina, Heath was angry and aggravated and started using profanity. Heath was getting louder, she said, and the bar was packed and becoming busy. At that time, Mark, another bartender, stepped in to manage the customer.

Ms. Yudina went to the other end of the bar, processing Heath's tab. Mr. Rickard asked, "While you were at the front computer [at the end of the bar] could you see what was going on in the service area?"[11] She answered, "No."

She said upon returning to the service area, the conversation was louder, and Heath seemed "angry."[12] The bouncer was there, and "He [Mr. Brackett] was just trying to get his attention and then he tried to tell him that he has to step outside."[13]

After this, the bouncer picked up Heath in a bear hug, "and he carried him outside."[14] Mr. Rickard asked, "Did you see where on this man's body the bouncer grabbed him with the hugging motion?"[15] Ms. Yudina answered, "I would say kind of the shoulder, like upper arm area."[16]

Ms. Yudina's description aligned with testimony from the grand jury. However, picking up someone using a bear hug around the shoulders is extremely difficult and most often impossible.

She was asked but did not remember Heath saying anything as he was being carried outside.

Mr. Rickard asked about Heath's tab, and Ms. Yudina said she "closed it. And later on, a woman came up and she signed it."[17] Mr. Rickard introduced Government's Exhibits 15 and 16. Exhibit 15 was a check from The Guards with the name "O'CONNOR/CAROLE" on it, for $13.15. On the bottom, it stated, "Check Closed" with the date, "Aug 28'10," and time, "11:57 p.m." The Government's Exhibit 16 was a credit card copy (the Merchant's copy) for Exhibit 15, and it was closed at 11:47 p.m. Both were for $13.15, and both were marked "213 Xan X."[18] Since the check was closed at 11:57 p.m., and the credit card slip was closed at 11:47 p.m., that would indicate that Ms. Yudina was at the front, closing the check, for at least 10 minutes.

---

[11] Ibid, 40
[12] Ibid, 41
[13] Ibid
[14] Ibid
[15] Ibid, 42
[16] Ibid
[17] Ibid, 44
[18] U.S. v. Heath Thomas, U.S. Government's Exhibits 15 & 16, Case No. 2010 CF3 016079

```
          The Guards
        2915 M St. NW
      Washington, DC ·20007

213 Xan X
-------------------------------------
Chk 2146    O'CONNOR/CAROLE    Gst 0
            Aug28'10 10:17PM
-------------------------------------
1 PREMIUM BEER              5.45
1 Call                      6.50
XXXXXXXXXXX4007 03/12
   Amex                    13.15

   Subtotal                11.95
   Sales Tax                1.20
   Payment                 13.15
--------213 Check Closed-----------
----------Aug28'10 11:57PM---------
```

```
                         The Guards Restaurant
Date:           Aug28'10 11:47PM
Card Type:      Amex
Acct #:         XXXXXXXXXXX4007
Exp Date:       03/12
Auth Code:      545599
Check:          2146
Check ID:       O'CONNOR/CAROLE
Server:         213 Xan X

Subtotal:             13.15

Tip:_____

Total:_____

Signature_____
I agree to pay above total
according to my card issuer
agreement.

* * * * Merchant Copy * * * *
```

Bar tab from the guards, Government Exhbiit 15.

Bar tab from the guards, merchant copy, Government Exhibit 16.

Mr. Rickard asked about the "relationship between Exhibit 15 and Exhibit 16."[19] She answered, "It is the same tab. This – the previous one [Exhibit 15] was just a tab with how much money customer owes and this one [Exhibit 16] is already a closed tab because it already has a signature. So it's ready to be processed, like, closed, just to – go into the system."[20]

That concluded the prosecution's questions.

During the cross-examination, Mr. Hannon asked Ms. Yudina if the employees had talked a lot about this incident. She answered, "There was talk about it that same night because everyone was just shocked and it was a lot of police everywhere. So, of course, everyone was talking; not only employees, customers as well."[21]

Mr. Hannon also asked her whether the employees talked about the grand jury.

Ms. Yudina: *Yes, I did. Because – we all did because some of us had to take a day off...*
Mr. Hannon: *And have you talked to other employees about coming down for this trial?*
Ms. Yudina: *Yes. Some of them are here—*[22]

Mr. Hannon turned to the bar tab and the credit card slip. Ms. Yudina said that she printed both slips so the customer could see what they were paying for when they signed

---

[19] Information from the trial transcript, Criminal Action Number 2010-CF3-16079, dated August 15, 2011, p 45
[20] Ibid, 45-46
[21] Ibid, 53-54
[22] Ibid, 54-55

the credit card slip. She gave both slips to the customer before the incident occurred. Mr. Hannon continued, "And this was before Mr. Brackett picked up the man?"[23] Ms. Yudina answered, "Yes."

She testified she knew the lady; Ms. O'Connor signed the credit card receipt. She believed she left the slips on the bar, "So she [Ms. O'Connor] came and she closed it."[24]

Mr. Hannon next asked Ms. Yudina about Heath going into the service area to close out his check. A wedding party had come into the bar at some point, causing the noise level to rise. Mr. Hannon asked whether Heath tried to pay before or after the wedding party arrived. She said, "That was before the bachelor party.[25] . . . They [the bachelor party] just walked in so they were mainly at the front – mainly at the main bar area."[26]

Mr. Hannon: *And when the bachelor party came in, were they ordering drinks at the bar?*
Ms. Yudina: *Yes, they were ordering drinks at the bar.*
Mr. Hannon: *And did that mean you were busy?*
Ms. Yudina: *I – on the way back while the tab was running,* [she had been at the front bar closing Heath's check] *I might have made a drink or two.*
Mr. Hannon: *Just a drink or two?*
Ms. Yudina: *Yes.*[27]

After another question about how busy the bar was, she talked about returning to Heath. She said, "I was trying to get back with the tab to the gentleman because he was waiting."[28]

After the defense finished, Judge Dixon asked some questions about what she did with the bar check and credit card receipt. As one would expect, her memory was not that specific, but she believed she just left them on the bar next to Heath. Judge Dixon asked whether she witnessed Ms. O'Connor sign the receipt. She said, "Yes, I remember the lady signing the tab."[29] He then asked if she noticed that she did not receive a tip. She did not remember.

To me sitting in the gallery, the question about a tip seemed a little unusual. Many people leave a cash tip, which is not on the credit card receipt. Also, at that point, Carole's friend, Heath, had just been carried out of the bar. I would believe that most people in Carole's position would just sign the check and hurry back outside. Under the circumstances, concern for leaving a tip might not be foremost in the customer's mind.

---

[23] Ibid, 59
[24] Ibid, 60
[25] Ibid, 61
[26] Ibid
[27] Ibid, 61-62
[28] Ibid, 62
[29] Ibid, 68

Ms. Graciela Perez

The government's next witness was Ms. Graciela Perez, the waitress who served Heath's group. Mr. Rickard questioned her for the prosecution. She said that Heath's table had tried to return a drink because it was made with the wrong alcohol, but the bartender told her it was made correctly. So, she took it back to the table. Mr. Rickard asked, "How did the customer respond?"[30] Ms. Perez answered, "He looked upset. He wasn't, like, too happy."[31]

Ms. Perez said the guy she was dealing with looked drunk, and when asked who she was talking about, she replied, "The guy because he was the one who was talking to me."[32] When another drink was ordered, it was also returned, this time because it had a bug in it.

She also said that when she was delivering drinks to the table, she spilled one.

> Ms. Perez: ... *I was putting the drink from the tray to the table. I spilled one a little bit and I apologized.*
> Mr. Rickard: *What happened after the drink spilled?*
> Ms. Perez: *He — he kept the drink and then they ordered me the tab. They wanted to check their tab.*[33]

Ms. Perez said the same guy who requested the check told her that he was taking it to the bar to pay. She was asked how she felt about this, and she said, "bad." When asked why, she said, "Because that mean he will not tip me."[34]

After she took Heath to the bar, she heard him "talking to the bartender trying to pay his tab."[35] She described the conversation as "kind of arguing."[36] Mr. Rickard asked, "Did you hear what they were arguing about?"[37] Ms. Perez answered, "he wanted to pay his tab and the bartender said to hold on a second because he was busy and he will take care of him."[38]

Ms. Perez said that while this was occurring, she was tending to other tables. The tables were in the rear of the restaurant.

> Mr. Rickard: *...Did you ever notice anything else going on in the service area while you were attending your other tables?*

---

[30] Ibid, 73
[31] Ibid
[32] Ibid, 74
[33] Ibid, 76-77
[34] Ibid, 77
[35] Ibid, 79
[36] Ibid
[37] Ibid
[38] Ibid

Ms. Perez: *...he [Heath] was talking to the manager at that time because, apparently, the guy was upset that he couldn't pay ...*

Mr. Rickard: *Did you hear any part of their conversation?*

Ms. Perez: *...this guy was telling Oscar [Viracocha], like, he was really upset, mad... he was saying, like, do you want me to speak in Spanish or English ...*

Mr. Rickard: *You heard the customer say, "Do you want me to speak in English or Spanish."*[39]

Ms. Perez said, "yes,"[40] she heard those words, and Heath was speaking in Spanish.

Mr. Rickard asked what occurred in the service area, and she said, "I saw the bouncer ... like, grab him [Heath] from his back, but I did not see the beginning. I just saw them walking out."[41] Mr. Rickard asked if she actually saw the bouncer grab Heath, and she said she did not.

Mr. Rickard: *Did you notice anything going on when the bouncer was taking the customer out?*

Ms. Perez: *I just saw the police officers' cars outside from the window.*[42]

Mr. Rickard: *In the instant when the bouncer was actually taking the customer out of the bar, did any of the other customers in the bar react in any way?*

Ms. Perez: *Yeah. They were, like, clapping and saying...*[43]

Before she finished, the judge asked, "They were like what?"[44] Ms. Perez continued, "Like, they were, like, yeah and clapping like they were happy that the bouncer was taking this guy out."[45]

Whether the clapping was related to Heath being removed is debatable. During both her trial and grand jury testimony, when asked if she noticed anything when Heath was being carried out, Ms. Perez said she saw the police cars outside. That could mean that Heath was already outside when she heard the clapping.

Mr. Rickard asked Ms. Perez if the check for the table had been paid, and she said, "No."[46] She testified that she believed that at some point she asked Carole to pay the check, but the bartender told her that the check had already been paid. Mr. Rickard concluded his questioning.

---

[39] Ibid, 81-82
[40] Ibid, 82
[41] Ibid
[42] Ibid, 83
[43] Ibid
[44] Ibid
[45] Ibid
[46] Ibid, 85

Mr. Hannon, standing at the defense table, started his cross-examination by asking Heath to stand and then asking Ms. Perez, "Have you ever seen him before?"[47] She said, "No."[48] Mr. Hannon then asked if the man who ordered the Bombay Sapphire was the one who wanted to pay, and she answered, "Yes."[49]

Mr. Hannon continued, "Is that the man on whom you spilled the drink?," and Ms. Perez answered that it had been.[50] In the same line of questioning, Mr. Hannon asked her if this was the same man who received the drink with the bug in it, and she said, "Yes."[51]

Mr. Hannon asked several questions about where Heath stood while at the bar, specifically whether he was inside or outside of a roped-off service area for staff. At one point, she talked about the roped-off area being moved, as if someone moved the rope barrier. Ms. Perez said, "I think by that point, they moved this already because the guy was, like, trying to fight. So they – I don't know who but they were in – in this area."[52] When she was testifying to where the roped-off area was, she was given a photograph of the bar that was entered into evidence.

Mr. Hannon asked if Ms. Yudina was working the night of the incident; Ms. Perez said, "Who is Yudina?"[53] When questioned further, Ms. Perez said three bartenders were working that evening, one male and two females, one of whose names she could not remember.

> Mr. Hannon: *Now, did you have any words with the man over the confusion regarding the drink?*
>
> Ms. Perez: *No.*
>
> Mr. Hannon: *The two of you didn't argue?*
>
> Ms. Perez: *Not that I remember.*
>
> Mr. Hannon: *Did anyone else at the table where this man was sitting argue with you?*
>
> Ms. Perez: *Not that I — no.*
>
> Mr. Hannon: *Did anyone else at the table where this man was sitting say anything offensive to you at all?*
>
> Ms. Perez: *Not offensive.*[54]

Mr. Hannon revisited the clapping that Ms. Perez described earlier.

---

[47] Ibid, 88
[48] Ibid
[49] Ibid
[50] Ibid, 88
[51] Ibid, 89
[52] Ibid, 93
[53] Ibid, 94
[54] Ibid, 97

Mr. Hannon: *... And where the people were who were clapping? ...*
Ms. Perez: *I heard. I was so busy in the back I heard people clapping. I didn't see exactly who was clapping.*

Judge Dixon then questioned her.

Judge Dixon: *... When the man went to the bar, you said you heard him say in Spanish, "Do you want me to explain in English or Spanish?" You heard him say that in Spanish; is that right?*
Ms. Perez: *Yes.*
Judge Dixon: *Now, had you heard the man speak Spanish earlier that evening?*
Ms. Perez: *No.*
Judge Dixon: *Did you hear anything leading up to "Do you want me to explain in English or Spanish?" Anything he said to the bartender or the bartender said to him –*
Ms. Perez: *Well, he was – he was not happy because Mark was not paying attention to him. So he was, like, I want to pay my tab ...*
Judge Dixon: *And it was to Mark that the person said, 'Do you want me to explain in English or Spanish?'*
Ms. Perez: *No. That's to Oscar, the manager. And the manager is Spanish.* [55]

Although the judge and others seemed to take Heath's offer to speak Spanish as condescending or inappropriate, Heath would later explain that he was trying to keep the conversation private.

Judge Dixon: *When you saw the bouncer holding the man from behind, was he just holding him or was he lifting him up or could you tell?*
Ms. Perez: *I saw that he hold [sic] him, like he was walking.*
Judge Dixon: *... So they both appeared to be walking?*
Ms. Perez: *Yes.* [56]

That concluded Ms. Perez's testimony and, after some procedural matters, the first day of the trial.

One point of interest on this first day of the trial was the motion to compel under the Brady Rule regarding the witness Ms. Yuliga Vetlugeena. In the materials I had from the case, I found a document that mentioned Ms. Vetlugeena. On August 15, 2011, the same day as the motion to compel, the government responded with "GOVERNMENT'S

---

[55] Ibid, 104-105
[56] Ibid, 105-106

OPPOSITION TO DEFENDANT'S SECOND MOTION TO COMPEL DISCOVERY."[57] In the opening paragraph, the government wrote, "Because the defendant is not entitled to such information under Rule 16, and because the defendant has not and cannot demonstrate a need for such information, the motion should be denied."[58]

In the same document, the government provided some information on Ms. Vetlugeena. It said that she was a waitress on the night of the incident and witnessed part of Heath's interaction at the bar. However, according to the government, "the only inconsistency with other witnesses to those events leading up to the offense, as disclosed, was that Ms. Vetlugeena described the defendant as 'probably' black."[59]

The defendant and his attorney were aware that a witness was identified and saw or said something. They knew someone talked to her. They wanted to subpoena her, and the government opposed it, saying they "cannot demonstrate a need for such information."[60] That sounds like the chicken-and-egg dilemma: to demonstrate a need for the information, one needs to know what information she could provide. And if the witness could not help the defense, why would the government oppose the motion?

Throughout the trial, there seemed to be a level of competitiveness between the prosecution and defense. Although that is normal in trials, in this case at least, it appeared to be detrimental to finding the truth.

And last, the prosecution seemed to find it unusual that a customer in a bar consumed alcohol and used profanity, as though that would be an infrequent event. Even more bewildering is the customer that becomes annoyed because they cannot pay the tab. Using such banal circumstances to explain assault with a dangerous weapon? Sometimes the more benevolent explanation, that he was trying to re-holster his gun, is the right one.

Day one was now in the books. Day two, it turned out, would present the heart of the prosecution's case.

---

[57] The government's response for Opposition to Defendants Second Motion to Compel Discovery, Case No. 2010-CF3-016079, dated August 15, 2011
[58] Ibid, 1
[59] Ibid, 4
[60] Ibid, 1

7A

James Owens: Exculpatory Evidence Withheld

In 1987 in Baltimore, Maryland, a young female college student was murdered. She had been beaten, stabbed, and sexually assaulted in her home. There was some property missing, and the following day the police offered a $1,000 reward for information about the case.

Mr. James Thompson came forward with evidence he said he found, a knife. Mr. Thompson said the knife was from his neighbor, Mr. James Owens. With the information and presumed evidence from Mr. Thompson, Mr. Owens was arrested and charged with burglary, rape, and murder.

When Mr. Thompson presented the knife, he was wearing what appeared to be blood-stained jeans. He later admitted that he was trying to collect reward money by offering information about the crime, information he did not have.

At Mr. Owens' trial, a jailhouse informant testified that Mr. Owens confessed to him while they were locked up. Mr. Thompson testified twice during the trial. After his first testimony, the prosecution believed that Thompson may have been involved with the crime, so he was recalled to testify a second time. When testifying the second time, Mr. Thompson changed his story again, this time placing himself at the crime scene and saying he and Mr. Owens broke into the home. He claimed to have witnessed the crime. The blood-stained jeans that Mr. Thompson was wearing when he first came forward were entered into evidence. The blood on the jeans was presumed to be the victims. Almost immediately Mr. Thompson recanted his testimony; however, he was charged with the crime.

In 1988, Owens and Thompson were found guilty and given life without parole. In 2004, defense attorneys for Owens filed a postconviction petition, seeking DNA examinations with the rape evidence. In 2005 the petition was granted, and in 2006 a DNA test eliminated both men from the evidence, proving that neither of them committed the crime. The bloody jeans that were in evidence were tested and it was found to be male blood. Because of the findings, they were both granted new trials.

Instead of having a new trial, however, the prosecutors first offered Alford Pleas to both Mr. Owens and Mr. Thompson. An Alford Plea is a guilty plea in a criminal court, where the defendant does not admit guilt. However, *"in entering an Alford Plea, the defendant admits that the evidence presented by the prosecution would be likely to persuade a judge or jury to find the defendant guilty beyond a reasonable doubt."*[1] An Alford Plea is not an exoneration.

When Mr. Thompson was offered the Alford Plea, he accepted it and walked out of prison after being incarcerated for nineteen years.

Mr. Owens, who was also offered an Alford Plea, refused the deal. He said he wanted to clear his name. He waited another 16 months for a new trial. However, the day the trial was to begin, the state declined to prosecute, as they had no evidence. In 2008 James Owens was finally released. He was incarcerated for twenty-one years for a crime he did not commit. Because he was exonerated, he could sue the state for wrongful imprisonment, which he did.

James Owens won his suit against the police and prosecutors, with a record award of $9 million. Part of the suit alleged that evidence of his innocence was withheld, evidence that was exculpatory in nature. The evidence included the fact that Mr. Owens's boss had said he was at work when the crime occurred, and this information was never given to the defense. The prosecution knew that the jailhouse snitch was lying. The snitch had submitted eleven letters to the prosecution, trying to improve his position. They also knew that Mr. Thompson was lying and there was no physical evidence connecting Mr. Owens to the crime.

Apparently, the prosecution's case depended upon the lies told by Mr. Thompson and the snitch, with no physical evidence.

If this case went forward with information known to be false or fabricated, how many other cases like it exist?

References

Christopher Zoukis, "$9 Million Settlement in Baltimore Wrongful Conviction Case", The Criminal Legal News, October 2018, Filed under Settlements, wrongful Conviction, Maryland location, online at https//www.criminallegalnews.org

Maurice Possley, Mr. James L Owens, The National Registry of Exonerations, before June 2012, last updated: 5/6/2019, https://www.law.umich.edu/special/exoneration/

---

[1] Wikipedia

8

Day 2: The Heart of the Prosecution's Case
AUGUST 16, 2011

"The serpent in the Garden of Eden, a prosecutor once told me, could produce both character witnesses and alibi witnesses."
—J. Michael Hannon[1]

During the second day of the trial, the prosecution put forth three witnesses. First to testify was the bar manager, Mr. Oscar Viricochea, who had spoken with Heath at the bar and witnessed the struggle between Heath and the bouncer. The bouncer, Mr. Marshall Brackett, was second to testify. It was Brackett who carried Heath outside and struggled with him over the gun. The third witness was Cpl. Brandon Holubar, who witnessed the argument at the bar and the struggle between Mr. Brackett and Heath. Corporal Holubar, who at the grand jury claimed Heath pointed the gun at him, had been added to the case as a second victim. Assistant U.S. Attorney Katherine Sawyer presented the case for the prosecution.

Mr. Oscar Viricochea
Ms. Sawyer began her examination of Mr. Viricochea by asking where he worked and what shift he was working on the date of the incident. The questions then went to the specifics of the incident. Immediately there was a discrepancy. Ms. Sawyer asked, "And at some point in time in the evening of August 28, 2010, around 10:30 p.m., did a verbal altercation commence at The Guards Restaurant?"[2] Mr. Viricochea answered, "Yes." Although Ms. Sawyer gave the time of the incident as 10:30 p.m., and Mr. Viricochea confirmed it, the police report and the statement of charges listed the incident time at 23:58 hours, or 11:58 p.m.[3]

Ms. Sawyer then asked the bar manager to describe the event. Mr. Viricochea said he went to the bar and witnessed Heath and the bartender, and "he [Heath] was very rude

---

[1] Quote from Mr. Hannon during the trial during closing arguments on August 25, 2011. Mr. Hannon attributed the quote to a prosecutor (not named) while talking about character issues. Trial transcript from August 25, 2011, p 344

[2] Information from the trial transcript, Criminal Action Number 2010-CF3-16079, dated August 16, 2011, p 117-118

[3] Superior Court for the District of Columbia, Criminal Division, United States vs. Thomas, Heath Patrick, Statement of Charges, completed by Officer Andelman, MPD, August 29, 2010

with the bartender and using bad words."[4] When Ms. Sawyer told him he could repeat the bad word, Mr. Viricochea said, "Where's the son of a bitch fucking bartender?"[5] Mr. Viricochea said the bartender told Heath, "Give me the names I'm going to close it," and Heath responded by saying, "Fuck." After that, "[Heath] go—he just disappear [sic]."[6]

Ms. Sawyer asked, "And when he came back from the table and returned to the bar, what is it that you heard him say to the bartender?"[7] Mr. Viricochea answered, "That's what I just told you few minutes ago."[8] When asked to repeat it, Mr. Viricochea said, "Where's the son of a bitch, the mother fucking bartender?"[9]

Mr. Viricochea said when the incident occurred, a party was coming in. "Oh, it was very busy at that time."[10] He added, "I was close to him… And I told him – I said, 'Sir – sir, let me – I can help you but give me one minute. I just move it a little bite [sic] because I have to pick up my drinks."[11] Mr. Viricochea said Heath asked, "Who are you?"[12] Mr. Viricochea responded that he was the manager, to which Heath said, "Fuck You." [13]

Mr. Viricochea said he told the busboy in Spanish, "Call security because he getting too much –a little hyper."[14] Heath interjected, "I can speak Spanish, too."[15]

Ms. Sawyer: *Well, did you feel that you could reason with him?*
Mr. Viricochea: *Really, I can't talk to him too much because he was really jumping and everything, it was fuck, fuck, fuck everything.*
Ms. Sawyer: *… Why did you feel the need to at that point to call security?*
Mr. Viricochea: *… Because I want to involve different kind of people or getting too much disturbing in the restaurant because it was really, really busy at that time.*[16]

Mr. Viricochea said when he called for security, Heath heard him and said, "You can call three or four securities."[17] Ms. Sawyer asked, "So at that point, based on your conversations with the gentleman, was it your understanding that he knew that security was being called?"[18] Mr. Viricochea answered, "Yes."[19]

---

[4] Information from the trial transcript, Criminal Action Number 2010-CF3-16079, dated August 16, 2011, p 121
[5] Ibid, 122- 123
[6] Ibid, 123
[7] Ibid, 124
[8] Ibid
[9] Ibid
[10] Ibid, 125
[11] Ibid,
[12] Ibid,
[13] Ibid,
[14] Ibid, 126
[15] Ibid, 127
[16] Ibid, 128
[17] Ibid, 131
[18] Ibid
[19] Ibid

Mr. Viricochea said Marshall Brackett responded, and Ms. Sawyer asked, "And what, if anything, did Marshall… say when he approached the gentleman?"[20] Mr. Viricochea answered, "Really, I don't hear nothing because I was moving to, like, a — from here to over there."[21]

Mr. Viricochea said he left the service area, and when he returned, he saw "Marshall pick him [Heath] up, and the guy - and keeping [sic] outside."[22] When asked if Mr. Brackett picked up Heath around his chest or his waist, he said his "chest."[23]

Ms. Sawyer then asked Mr. Viricochea if he heard the

View of the street, from the atrium with the front doors open.

man say anything while being carried out, and he said, "No."[24] She also asked if he heard Heath mention anything about being a police officer and he said, "No."[25] Responding to questions, Mr. Viricochea testified that Mr. Brackett carried Heath out of the restaurant through two doors and down some steps, and he followed them.

Ms. Sawyer: … *what did you do when you followed Marshall and the man out?*

Mr. Viricochea: … *I opened the door with my hand like this because Marshall was taking out the guy. And after that, I was holding and he went outside. I didn't even see what happened, you know, outside when he go [sic] out.*

Ms. Sawyer: *Why didn't you see what happened when they went out?*

Mr. Viricochea: *Because I was here between this door and — this mat here, when open this door, they were moving and I can't close it again. I was facing the other way with my - that's why I take time.*[26]

---

[20] Ibid, 132
[21] Ibid,
[22] Ibid, 135
[23] Ibid, 136
[24] Ibid
[25] Ibid
[26] Ibid, 138

Mr. Viricochea said he went outside after fixing the doormat and saw Mr. Brackett and Heath. He described what he saw, saying, "They was forcing ... Marshall and Mr. — he was like forcing like this up and down."[27] He described "forcing" as Heath and the bouncer both trying to control the gun. When Mr. Viricochea first saw the struggle, he said he was on the steps, and Mr. Brackett and Heath were in the street, between two parked vehicles. He stated that when the police came, they said, "drop the gun," and Heath "dropped the gun."[28]

Ms. Sawyer asked about surveillance cameras at The Guards, and Mr. Viricochea said, "No. We have cameras. But that time, it was off."[29] He explained that the cameras were usually turned on at 10:30 p.m., but, on the evening of the incident, he had been too busy to turn them on.

Mr. Hannon would offer his cross-examination next. Mr. Hannon was a career attorney, a former federal prosecutor with over thirty years of experience. Mr. Hannon questioned Mr. Viricochea as to whether the police were still there when the investigator from the Alcohol Beverage Control Board (ABC) arrived. Mr. Viricochea said the police were there.

> Mr. Hannon: *If there's a fight at The Guards, does someone from ABC come to investigate?*
> Mr. Viricochea: *Yes, Sir.*
> Mr. Hannon: *And that's what the ABC guy was there for that night, right?*
> Mr. Viricochea: *Yes.*
> Mr. Hannon: *Did they [ABC investigators] check the cameras?*
> Mr. Viricochea: *Yes.*
> Mr. Hannon: *And did you show them that the cameras weren't on?*
> Mr. Viricochea: *Yeah. They was [sic] off...*

That's what I explained to him, to ABC. I said I turn off because this is working manually. I have to go to my office to push the record on the – the button on the recording, and that's the time to start to [sic] recording everything.[30]

He explained that the cameras typically were not turned on until 10:30, which, according to him, is about the time this crime occurred. He also said the police detective wanted to see the tapes, but he told him the cameras were not on.

Mr. Hannon questioned Mr. Viricochea about the ABC investigation, The Guards' security plan, and a possible security plan violation. His questions implied that The

---

[27] Ibid, 139
[28] Ibid, 141
[29] Ibid, 142
[30] Ibid, 147-149

Guards and its employees had a motive to say Heath assaulted the bouncer. The security plan required the manager to call the police before having someone escorted out of the building.

Ms. Sawyer objected to the line of questioning, and the judge held a bench conference. Judge Dixon told Mr. Hannon to make his case regarding his line of questioning. Mr. Hannon, at the bench, referred to Mr. Rickard's opening remarks about the crime and said:

> [T]he government apparently takes the position that somebody is disruptive in a bar, they can assault him, pick him up and carry him out to the sidewalk…that's not the standard that ABC permits. ABC does not permit a bouncer to touch a patron. And there was actually a hearing on this incident. And certain information was withheld from the ABC and was withheld from the investigator by Mr. Viricochea at the time that he was interviewed. This witness and everybody else that works at The Guards has an incentive to try to exaggerate the conduct of Agent Thomas to comport with Mr. Rickard's view of things, that somehow or another, if you are swearing and loud, the bar can resort to self-help and commit what is clearly an assault. And they also have a policy that they file with the ABC that they're obligated to follow. And in that policy, they state that – that they will not touch a patron unless there is – I will paraphrase it – unless there is – there are circumstances which will permit a civilian person to engage in self-defense and that they train all of their bouncers not to do that. And I proffer that Marshall Brackett will say that he's never been trained and this is what they do all the time.[31]

Mr. Hannon was correct about what the security plan allows, but a violation of the security plan is not a criminal offense.[32]

The discussion continued at the bench about witnesses' testimony and impeachment of a witness—that is, showing that a witness contradicted himself or herself. During the discussion, Mr. Hannon said, "But I do have the ABC guy under subpoena," meaning the court would hear what he was alleging from the source, which is one of the criteria for getting the evidence admitted.[33] This was followed by a discourse among Judge Dixon, Mr. Rickard, Ms. Sawyer, and Mr. Hannon that centered on the questioning of Mr. Viricochea.

---

[31] Ibid, 156-157

[32] U.S. v. Heath Thomas Defense Exhibit 10, The Guards Security Plan, p 8: "*When a guest is asked to leave or is escorted to the front door the Host are instructed to handily it as gently as possible.*" Two lines later:" *If there is resistance the next and final action is to call for police assistance.*" P 9 of security plan: under the "Rules of the Floor:" number 3 says: "*Never act aggressive or use physical force with guest.*"

[33] Information from the trial transcript, Criminal Action Number 2010-CF3-16079, dated August 16, 2011, p 159

> Judge Dixon, addressing Mr. Hannon: *... I imagine this is to demonstrate some sort of bias that in a defense theory, that – that this witness knew that his employee had done something wrong by touching the person and deliberately withheld that information from the ABC Board. I suppose that's the bias that Mr. Hannon is attempting to show me ...*
>
> Mr. Hannon: *No.*
>
> Judge Dixon: *All right.*
>
> Mr. Hannon: *Just the manner in which he reported it that evening.*[34]
>
> Mr. Rickard: *Your Honor, if there is an ABC report that's provided the foundation for this line of questioning, then I would request a copy of it now. We're now in trial and counsel is using this line of questioning —*
>
> Judge Dixon: *There is nothing for me to order Mr. Hannon to give you at this point.*[35]

Judge Dixon ended the bench conference, and the objection was overruled.

The documents that Mr. Hannon was referring to were defense exhibits of the ABRA hearing where Mr. Shirvani, owner of the Guards, testified and Mr. Viricochea attended.[36] The prosecution should have had copies of those documents, as they were entered as exhibits in the trial. It appears the judge was not aware of that, however, and neither were the attorneys.

Mr. Hannon resumed his questioning of Mr. Viricochea regarding the ABRA fact-finding hearing and what was said and proffered there.

> Mr. Hannon: *... Were you with Mr. Hossein [Shirvani] when he was at the board telling them what happened?*
>
> Mr. Viricochea: *Yes.*
>
> Mr. Hannon: *Now, did you tell the ABC guy that Agent Thomas came into the Guards at 5:00?*
>
> Mr. Viricochea: *Another member is –.*
>
> Mr. Hannon: *Pardon?*
>
> Mr. Viricochea: *Another member, I think.*[37]

This part of the testimony was confusing, but I believe he was saying that someone else spoke at the hearing, which was correct. But the heart of the question was, did he tell the ABC investigator that Heath and his party arrived at 5 p.m.? At the hearing, Mr. Butler, the ABRA investigator, testified that Mr. Viricochea told him, "The complainant

---

[34] Ibid, 160

[35] Ibid, 160-161

[36] U.S. v. Heath Thomas Defense Exhibit 2, Alcoholic Beverage Control Board Fact-Finding Hearing, Criminal Case No. 2010 CF3 016079

[37] Information from the trial transcript, Criminal Action Number 2010-CF3-16079, dated August 16, 2011, p 161-162

and his companion had entered the establishment before 5:00 p.m., and therefore has not been patted down."[38]

Mr. Hannon continued asking Mr. Viricochea what Mr. Shirvani said to the board at the hearing, but Ms. Sawyer objected. Mr. Hannon stated, "— he was present?"[39] Judge Dixon responded, "That doesn't make it admissible. ... The objection's sustained."[40] Testifying about what someone else said is generally considered hearsay and not admitted in court.

Moving on, Mr. Hannon asked, "How many security people did you have working that night?"[41] Ms. Sawyer objected, but it was overruled.

Mr. Viricochea: *... They will usually have four securities._*
Mr. Hannon: *... besides Mr. Brackett, who else was the security working that night.*
Mr. Viricochea: *That night, there was Mark, — I mean, I'm sorry - Marshall, Shane – what's the name of this guy — Freddy, and there's another one. I don't remember the other one.*
Mr. Hannon: *Did you ever see them that night?*
Mr. Viricochea: *No. Marshall was the first one. Marshall usually come in - one security at 10:00, and the other guys come in at 11:00 because downstairs, we open at 11:00.*
Mr. Hannon: *What time did this incident happen?*
Mr. Viricochea: *At 10:30.*
Mr. Hannon: *And was the downstairs open?*
Mr. Viricochea: *No, not yet.*
Mr. Hannon: *So at 10:30, you only had one security person there?*
Mr. Viricochea: *Yes.*
Mr. Hannon: *And so nothing was going on downstairs?*
Mr. Viricochea: *Nothing was going on at that time.*
Mr. Hannon: *So, there's no reason for anybody to be downstairs?*
Mr. Viricochea: *No. Nothing. There was nothing. There was only upstairs.*[42]

Again, Mr. Viricochea's testimony seems to be either inaccurate or incomplete. Mr. Shirvani testified at the ABRA hearing there were three security personnel, one at the door and two downstairs, when the incident occurred.[43] A former employee from The Guards, Mr. Freddy Biloatoomez, told me in a telephone interview that he was

---

[38] U.S. v. Heath Thomas Exhibit 11, The ABRA case report on The Guard's incident, case number 10-251-00188, August 28, 2010, p 2 attributed to Mr. Viricochea

[39] Information from the trial transcript, Criminal Action Number 2010-CF3-16079, dated August 16, 2011, p 162

[40] Ibid

[41] Ibid

[42] Ibid, 162-163

[43] U.S. v. Heath Thomas Defense Exhibit 2, The Alcoholic Beverage Control Board Fact-Finding Hearing report on The Guard's incident, case number was 10-251-00188, January 19, 2011, p 48

employed as a security person on August 28, 2010. He was working in the downstairs area when the incident occurred. He also said that when he became aware of the incident, he went upstairs.[44] The information he related to me was never introduced at trial.

Mr. Viricochea continued his testimony, describing how busy the bar was with the wedding party and guests coming in. Mr. Hannon asked, "Before the wedding party came, The Guard's wasn't very busy, was it?"[45] He answered, "It was busy."[46]

Here again, the veracity of Mr. Viricochea's answers is in question. In a telephone interview, Ms. Alexandra Calomaris, who was tending bar upstairs the night of the incident, said she was on break when the incident occurred.[47] If the Guards was as busy as the bar manager said, why would an employee be on break?

Mr. Hannon returned to the topic of the security plan, asking if the plan was in effect on August 28, 2010. Mr. Viricochea replied, "No. They don't give you any – anything to the police officers guys, you know, not – I mean, you talking (sic) about August 28?"[48]

Mr. Hannon then referred to the part of the security plan that prohibits employees from touching patrons. To that, Mr. Viricochea said, "We touch? I mean, we're not punching something, just grabbing when something happen [sic]."[49]

Mr. Hannon asked Mr. Viricochea about his grand jury testimony and Ms. Sawyer said she was going to object. The judge asked, "Is this for impeachment?"[50] Mr. Hannon replied that it was. That began multiple conversations about the grand jury materials, with Mr. Hannon wanting to use Defendant's Exhibit 8 (Grand Jury transcript) to facilitate his questioning. After some discussion, Judge Dixon allowed Mr. Hannon to use the exhibit, now referring to the transcript as Exhibit 8A.

> Mr. Hannon: *Mr. Viricochea, did you tell us today that you didn't hear any of the conversation between Marshall and Agent Thomas when Marshall came up to him?*
> Mr. Viricochea: *No.*
> Mr. Hannon: *You didn't?*
> Mr. Viricochea: *No.*[51]

Earlier, under direct examination, Ms. Sawyer asked, "And what, if anything, did Marshall…say when he approached the gentleman?"[52] Mr. Viricochea answered at that time, "Really, I don't hear nothing because I was moving to, like, a — from here to over there."[53]

---

[44] Telephone interview with Mr. Freddy Biloatoomez on September 30, 2014
[45] Information from the trial transcript, Criminal Action Number 2010-CF3-16079, dated August 16, 2011, p 169
[46] Ibid
[47] Telephone interview with Ms. Alexandra Calomaris on October 22, 2014
[48] Information from the trial transcript, Criminal Action Number 2010-CF3-16079, dated August 16, 2011, p 173
[49] Ibid, 175
[50] Ibid, 180
[51] Ibid, 182
[52] Ibid, 132
[53] Ibid,

Mr. Hannon displayed Exhibit 8A. He reminded Mr. Viricochea that he was under oath when he gave his grand jury testimony and that testimony's date. He went to page 8 of the exhibit and, starting with line 15, read a question posed in the transcript: "What happened after you asked Felix to go to get the security?"[54] Mr. Hannon then read, "Answer: The security came. And then Marshall, he told – he spoke to my security very rude and you need to get kicked out, you know. And he was trying to, how do you call this, fighting with him."[55]

Mr. Hannon: *Do you remember that question and answer?*
Mr. Viricochea: *I remember it but...*
Mr. Hannon: *Do you remember saying that?*
Judge Dixon: *Mr. Hannon, I don't want to be impatient. But the question that led us to the grand jury testimony was whether he overheard anything between the person and Marshall. That doesn't refer to that.*
Mr. Hannon: *Very well, Your Honor.*[56]

Judge Dixon had asked if this line of questioning was for impeachment. Mr. Hannon said it was, and in fact there were discrepancies. As Mr. Hannon pointed out, Mr. Viricochea, in his grand jury testimony, said that Heath had been rude to Mr. Brackett and was trying to fight with him. In his trial testimony, he said he did not hear anything between Mr. Brackett and Heath as he moved away from the area to help other customers. While the discrepancy exists, the judge, for an unknown reason, wanted to move on. He seemed oblivious of the discrepancies.

Mr. Hannon moved on. "When Agent Thomas was next to you, did he tell you that he could speak to you in Spanish if you wanted?"[57] Mr. Viricochea answered, "Yes."[58]

Answering several questions about the struggle for the gun, Mr. Viricochea said that Mr. Brackett and Heath were between two cars. Mr. Brackett was behind Heath, and he believed Mr. Brackett was holding Heath's arm with only one hand. He thought Heath had two hands on the gun. He said that when the police came, Heath dropped the gun; he did not know if Mr. Brackett put his hands up.

Mr. Hannon yielded the questioning to Ms. Sawyer for redirect.

Ms. Sawyer's first question for Mr. Viricochea was about The Guards' camera system and how it was turned on. There was a pause for the interpreter, and Mr. Viricochea answered that the cameras start and stop when buttons are pushed. Ms. Sawyer then reminded Mr. Viricochea that he was questioned about The Guard's Security Plan by

---

[54] Ibid, 183-184 and information from grand jury transcript of Mr. Viricochea on September 27, 2010, p 8
[55] Ibid, 184 and information from grand jury transcript of Mr. Viricochea on September 27, 2010, p 8
[56] Information from the trial transcript, Criminal Action Number 2010-CF3-16079, dated August 16, 2011, p 184
[57] Ibid, 184
[58] Ibid

Mr. Hannon. She asked, "And the plan does not require that the cameras be turned on unless there is entertainment; is that correct?"[59] Mr. Viricochea answered, "Right."[60]

Ms. Sawyer continued, "Mr. Viricochea, going back to the moment when you got outside of the — of The Guards and saw Marshall and the defendant struggling... do you have any idea how Marshall got behind the defendant? Did you see that?"[61] Mr. Viricochea said he observed the struggle but did not see how they came to their positions.

When Ms. Sawyer concluded, Judge Dixon had a few questions for the witness, repeating and clarifying some previous points. Mr. Viricochea repeated that he saw Mr. Brackett carrying Heath, but this time he added, "I was behind the bar...when he picked up."[62] He remembered that Mr. Brackett told him to call 911, but he did not hear Heath say anything and did not hear Mr. Brackett say anything to Heath. He said it took the police four or five minutes to arrive, and there were numerous witnesses outside.

Mr. Viricochea was told he could step down.

Mr. Marshall Brackett

The next witness called was Mr. Marshall Brackett, the head bouncer at The Guards and alleged victim in the case. Mr. Rickard conducted the examination.

Responding to questions, Mr. Brackett stated that he was the head bouncer and was responsible for hiring the other bouncers. He said that his role was to "Escort people out."[63] Mr. Rickard asked, "Do you ever carry them out?"[64] He answered, "Every once in a while."[65]

Mr. Rickard asked how he escorted people out. He said, "It depends how rowdy the person is. Most of the time, I would say 80 percent of the time, they want to walk on their own. Then you've got someone who wants to - have to be carried all the way out to the front and then let go."[66]

Mr. Rickard asked Mr. Brackett what he was wearing on the evening of August 28, and Mr. Brackett said a red guard shirt. The shirt was then shown to the defense and entered into evidence as Government's Exhibit 11. It was noted that the shirt might not have been the exact shirt he was wearing on the evening the incident occurred.[67]

Describing the events of the night, Mr. Brackett said someone told him, "there's a guy in there that needs to be escorted out, walked out, he wasn't leaving on his own."[68]

---

[59] Ibid, 194
[60] Ibid, 195
[61] Ibid, 199
[62] Ibid, 202
[63] Ibid, 207
[64] Ibid
[65] Ibid, 208
[66] Ibid,
[67] Ibid, 209
[68] Information from the trial transcript, Criminal Action Number 2010-CF3-16079, dated August 16, 2011, p 211

When Mr. Brackett found the person, "he [Heath] was arguing with somebody. I want to say it was Oscar. They were arguing something in Spanish."[69] Mr. Brackett said he touched Heath on his shoulder and said, "it's time to go,"[70] and Heath ignored him. Mr. Brackett said he then touched Heath on the arm twice, and each time Heath pulled away, so he picked him up in a bear hug and carried him out.[71]

> Mr. Rickard: *Did you see what he [Heath] was doing?*
> Mr. Brackett: *... waiving [sic] his hand saying stuff. I mean, I don't understand what he was saying, but he was talking.*
> Mr. Rickard: *How was he waiving his hand?*
> Mr. Brackett: *I mean, you know —- you know – I don't know. He was just trying to explain – I don't know whether he was trying to explain.*[72]

Mr. Brackett continued, "I thought he [Heath] was talking to Oscar about something, you know, arguing about something. Then Oscar walked away. And he [Mr. Viricochea] was, like – you know, it's time for him to go."[73]

Responding to questions, Mr. Brackett described picking up Heath. When asked where he grabbed him, he said, "Right here I guess around his biceps and shoulder right here."[74] (Mr. Viricochea and Ms. Yudina were asked similar questions; both said that Mr. Brackett picked up Heath around his shoulders. I noticed the consistency.)

> Mr. Rickard: *Did he say anything when you picked him up like that?*
> Mr. Brackett: *No.*
> Mr. Rickard: *Did you feel any weapon on his person while you had him in this position?*
> Mr. Brackett: *No.*
> Mr. Rickard: *What happened when you got outside?*
> Mr. Brackett: *I put him down. And I, you know, backed up. And he's like simultaneously, as soon as I let go and put him down, he turned towards me and the gun was in his hand when he turned toward me.*[75]

When asked the specifics of where he put Heath down, he said on the bricks, about an arm's length from the steps. He said Heath turned toward him with the gun in hand. There was a long discussion in the courtroom about the gun's position, midlevel and

---

[69] Ibid, 211
[70] Ibid
[71] Ibid
[72] Ibid, 213-214
[73] Ibid, 214
[74] Ibid, 215
[75] Ibid, 215-216

arm extended or the elbow bent. The settled description was midsection, the waist area with his elbow bent, meaning the gun would have been close to Heath's body. Mr. Brackett said Heath was only three feet away, and "It was — when he turned around, it was all, like really, really fast. When he spun around, the gun was in his hand and I just automatically just grabbed it when I saw it."[76]

Mr. Rickard asked, "Did… this man show you, while he was pinned on the Suburban, that he was a police officer?"[77]

> Mr. Brackett: *I think he used his other – the offhand. I had both hands on the gun. He had one hand on the gun. So he used his – I guess his left hand to get his wallet out and try to show me his credentials.*
> Mr. Rickard: *And what did you do when you saw his credentials?*
> Mr. Brackett: *I still held him until the cops came.*[78]
> Mr. Rickard: *What happened when the police arrived?*
> Mr. Brackett: *He [Heath] let go of the gun. I had the gun in my hand. They told me to put it on the ground and I put it on the ground.*
> Mr. Rickard: *How is it that the gun came to be in your hands?*
> Mr. Brackett: *I had both hands on it. He released it.*[79]

Mr. Rickard questioned Mr. Brackett, again, whether he felt the gun when he first picked up Heath, and Mr. Brackett said no. He asked him if he felt the gun while carrying Heath out, and he said no. Mr. Rickard continued, "When you were holding him, did your arms ever go near his waistband area?"[80] Mr. Brackett answered, "No."[81]

Under cross-examination, Mr. Brackett identified Heath, seated at the defense table, as the individual with whom he had the encounter. Mr. Hannon then guessed that Mr. Brackett was about six feet tall, and Mr. Brackett agreed. When questioned about his weight, Mr. Brackett said he weighed 230 pounds.

With permission from the court, Mr. Hannon asked Mr. Brackett to step down from the witness stand and demonstrate how he picked up Heath on the night of the incident. Mr. Hannon played the role of Heath. When Mr. Brackett picked up Mr. Hannon, his arms were not around Mr. Hannon's biceps or shoulders, but around Mr. Hannon's waist, pinning Mr. Hannon's arms against his body. Mr. Hannon commented, "He's got me from behind the back, … over my arms. His fists are clenched together above my

---

[76] Ibid, 220
[77] Ibid, 225
[78] Ibid
[79] Ibid, 226
[80] Ibid, 227
[81] Ibid

navel and my feet are a foot off the ground."[82] Neither the prosecution nor the court responded or said anything about where Mr. Brackett's arms were in relation to Mr. Hannon's body.

Following the demonstration, Mr. Hannon asked Mr. Brackett when he first saw the gun. Mr. Brackett answered, "Soon as he turned – soon as he turned around, he turned around and faced me, and that's when I saw the gun."[83] With that answer, Mr. Hannon conducted another demonstration, this one intended to identify the moment when Mr. Brackett saw the gun. Standing about three feet away with his back to Mr. Brackett, Mr. Hannon turned toward the witness in small increments. He held a plastic gun, referred to as a training gun, at his waist. When Mr. Brackett finally said he saw the gun, Mr. Hannon was almost facing him.

Mr. Hannon asked, "Oh, so you didn't see it until it was actually pointed at you?"[84] Mr. Brackett answered, "Yes."

Mr. Hannon repeated the demonstration without moving incrementally. Mr. Brackett grabbed the defense attorney's right wrist with both hands, with the replica gun pointed at Mr. Brackett.[85] The demonstration confirmed that the incident did not occur as Mr. Brackett described it. He could not have prevented the gun from being pointed at himself. The court appeared to not take any notice of the significance of the demonstration, however.

It is possible for Mr. Brackett to have seen the gun before it was pointed at him. If, for example, Mr. Brackett had been right behind Heath—not three feet away as he testified—and Heath turned, moving his right side forward or away from Mr. Brackett, then Mr. Brackett could have observed the gun over Heath's left shoulder and reached for it with his left hand. In that scenario, Mr. Brackett could have grabbed Heath's arm before any turning took place. That is how Heath described the event. When Heath turned slightly to keep the gun side away, Mr. Brackett may have thought Heath intended to turn toward him.

Mr. Hannon's next line of questioning was about what happened after the police arrived. Most notable was the police treatment of Heath compared with Mr. Brackett. Asked if he put his hands up when the police arrived, Mr. Brackett answered, "No … When the police came, I had the gun. They asked me to put it on the ground and I put it on the ground. Then I didn't have to put my hands up. They didn't ask me to put my hands up."[86]

Mr. Hannon asked, "Do you remember telling Ms. Brandt [Emily Brant, an attorney in Mr. Hannon's office] that it [the gun] was always pointing down even though you

---

[82] Ibid, 232
[83] Ibid, 236
[84] Ibid, 238
[85] Ibid, 239
[86] Ibid, 247

moved in different directions?"[87] Mr. Brackett answered, "Yeah. It was pointing kind of down. But, you know, still, if it would have gone off, he probably could have shot somebody. Yeah."[88]

> Mr. Hannon: *…You had control of the gun when you had both arms on it, didn't you?*
> Mr. Brackett: *Mostly. I would say, yeah.*
> Mr. Hannon: *So no one's going to point that gun anywhere because you're not going to let them, right?*
> Mr. Brackett: *Right.*[89]

Mr. Hannon next questioned Mr. Brackett about his opinion that Heath was drunk that evening. Previously, in response to a prosecution question, Mr. Brackett had said he believed Heath to be drunk and that Heath smelled like alcohol. He said that in addition to the odor of alcohol, Heath's behavior—specifically, his refusal to leave when requested—made Mr. Brackett think Heath was drunk.[90]

> Mr. Hannon: *…But didn't you tell Ms. Brant when she came to talk to you at the Guards that you had no reason to believe he was intoxicated except what people told you?*
> Mr. Brackett: *No. I don't recall saying that to her.*
> Mr. Hannon: *Do you recall telling her that other than smelling the alcohol on him, you had no reason, yourself, personally, to believe he was drunk?*
> Mr. Brackett: *I mean, I didn't see him consume any alcohol, no.*[91]

Mr. Hannon revisited Mr. Brackett's version of how he had set Heath down, which way Heath had been facing, and how he had turned. Mr. Hannon referenced Mr. Brackett's grand jury testimony on page 10, reading the question, "At the moment that you put him down and let him go, was his back still towards you?"[92] Mr. Hannon then read Mr. Brackett's response, "Yeah. Kind of his back, his side – left side."[93]

Answering a follow-up question, Mr. Brackett said that when he set Heath down, "His left side is facing me."[94] Mr. Brackett also physically demonstrated how Heath turned; he turned to his left.

---

[87] Ibid, 248
[88] Ibid, 248
[89] Ibid, 250
[90] Ibid, 258-259
[91] Ibid, 259
[92] Ibid, 260
[93] Ibid
[94] Ibid, 260

Mr. Hannon continued, "Now, do you and I finally agree that the gun was never pointed at you?"[95] Mr. Brackett disagreed. After a few clarifying questions and answers, Mr. Brackett said, "At some point, when I saw it, it had to be – it was pointing right at my hip area."[96]

Mr. Hannon read from Mr. Brackett's grand jury testimony, saying, "'I didn't give him a chance to point it directly at me, but he was coming around like about to point it at me.'"[97]

Answering another question, Mr. Brackett said, "He didn't point it at my chest or face, no. That's what I was trying to tell the jury that day. They never got it – I never let him get that close enough to be pointed in my chest or my face. But he was standing right in front of me. I didn't give him a chance to raise it all the way up. No I did not."[98]

Mr. Hannon questioned Mr. Brackett about where he was that evening before the incident, whether he had been downstairs at The Guards, and whether other security personnel were working that night. He answered that he had not been downstairs, at least from his memory. He said other security personnel were working that night and that they were downstairs.[99] The importance of this exchange, seemingly missed by Judge Dixon, is that a prosecution witness—Mr. Brackett himself—said the downstairs was open when the manager said it was not. This also goes to the question of when the crime occurred.

Mr. Hannon revisited the matter of Mr. Brackett carrying Heath from the bar. He asked about Heath not saying anything from when he was picked up inside until after the gun was out. Mr. Brackett said that was true.[100] The significance of this fact seemed to change depending on perspective. The prosecution used Heath's silence as an indication that he was intoxicated. Conversely, an argument could be made that a drunk person would have been greatly annoyed, verbal, and irate while being carried out, while a sober person would stay calm.

Mr. Hannon asked, "How long ago did you learn that there was going to be a trial this week?"[101] Mr. Brackett answered, "I got a subpoena in the mail. Actually, one of the detectives brought it to me at work, so maybe a couple of weeks ago. Yeah."[102]

This concluded the initial cross-examination by the defense. Mr. Rickard then conducted a redirect examination, covering topics already discussed. After he finished, the court had some questions for the witness.

---

[95] Ibid, 262
[96] Ibid, 263
[97] Ibid and information from grand jury testimony of Mr. Brackett on September 1, 2010, p 19
[98] Information from the trial transcript, Criminal Action Number 2010-CF3-16079, dated August 16, 2011, p 264
[99] Ibid, 265
[100] Ibid, 267
[101] Ibid,
[102] Ibid,

Judge Dixon asked, "When the gun was released by the man, was it released into your hands or was it released onto the hood of the car?"[103] Mr. Brackett answered, "Into my hands."[104]

The judge also inquired about whether the bouncer was given any specialized training related to dealing with armed people, and he said no.

After Judge Dixon finished, Mr. Hannon asked, "May I make an application to the Court to either follow up on your questions or to reopen my cross on a couple issues?"[105] The court agreed, and Mr. Hannon inquired about any training Mr. Brackett had received from The Guards. He answered that the only training he received was from the Alcohol Beverage Control Board. Mr. Hannon pressed further about the security procedures, asking, "But at the Guards, you never saw any security plan or anything written about what you're supposed to do, right?"[106] The prosecution objected, and the objection was sustained. The judge explained that it was not a topic he had brought up.

Cpl. Brandon Holubar

Cpl. Brandon Holubar was the next person to testify. Before he was called to the stand, however, Mr. Hannon requested a bench conference.

Mr. Hannon told the judge a subpoena had been sent to the Navy looking for any reports by Corporal Holubar regarding this matter. He said that the Navy's Judge Advocate General (JAG) Officer faxed him a letter indicating that "they have no record of any communication from Corporal Holubar regarding this matter."[107] From the response, it appeared that Corporal Holubar did not inform the Navy of his involvement with this case as he was required to do. The point called his credibility into question. Judge Dixon accepted the subpoena, for the record, then continued with the proceedings.

Corporal Holubar was called to the stand and Ms. Sawyer began her questioning. The initial line of inquiry was about his occupation. He said he was in the U.S. Marine Corps, with the rank of Corporal Infantry 0311, and his duty assignment was in Hawaii.

> Ms. Sawyer: ... *what were you doing before you got stationed in Hawaii?*
> Corporal Holubar: *Guard Duty, Presidential Guard, D.C.*
> Ms. Sawyer: ... *where are you at that time?*
> Corporal Holubar: *Bolling Air Force Base.*
> Ms. Sawyer: *And Presidential Guard, can you give us some basic information about what that means?*

---

[103] Ibid, 272
[104] Ibid,
[105] Ibid,
[106] Ibid, 273
[107] Ibid, 274, Letter to Mr. Hannon from the Navy's Judge Advocate General, dated August 15, 2011, Appendix C

Corporal Holubar: *We're based out of Bolling Air Force Base. It's a White House communications agency. We're a small group of marines – marine security forces in charge of security over that complex. And we also travel with the President on some trips overseas and country, work with and around Secret Service, and security for all the communications equipment and vehicles that he uses.*[108]

Ms. Sawyer: *And is that in some respects a protective detail?*

Corporal Holubar: *Yes.*

Ms. Sawyer: *… did you carry a weapon back then?*

Corporal Holubar: *Yes.*

Ms. Sawyer: *And what kind of weapon did you carry then?*

Corporal Holubar: *It depends on where we were. If we were on a trip, it was just a sign-on 9 mm Beretta. If we were back at the complex, an assortment of weapons; MP-5, M4, shotgun, side Armageddon.*[109]

Ms. Sawyer next asked about the required skills for the position.

Corporal Holubar: *Security force training involved training from SWAT schools, pistol marksmanship, detainee handling training, including room clearing, vehicle checks, personnel searches and things of that nature.*

Ms. Sawyer: *And… did that assignment often require you to use focus [sic] in sort of high-stress intent situations?*

Corporal Holubar: *Yes.*[110]

On the night of the incident, Corporal Holubar and some friends were at the Waterfront in Georgetown. He described the Waterfront as a small bar. They were there for "maybe 30 or 45 minutes."[111] While there, he had a Bud Light and a Long Island Iced Tea, consuming both in 15 to 20 minutes. After leaving they went to The Guards, about a five- or ten-minute walk. The group then divided, some going to The Guards, the others going to McFadden's, another bar in the area.

Corporal Holubar said that at The Guards, "We went downstairs. Three of us went to the bar. It was really crowded. There was some kind of party or something going on."[112] Corporal Holubar said he texted his other friends, and he decided to leave. He went upstairs by himself, which is when he noticed "An argument at the bar."[113] He believed the argument was over a bottle between the bartender and a customer. He described it: "There was a bartender holding some type of bottle. I'm not sure exactly what. The

---

[108] Information from the trial transcript, Criminal Action Number 2010-CF3-16079, dated August 16, 2011, p 276-277
[109] Ibid, 277
[110] Ibid, 277-278
[111] Ibid, 278
[112] Ibid, 280
[113] Ibid, 281

gentleman on his side with his back to me, I guess, was trying to purchase or get the bottle for the party ... The bartender was disagreeing saying he needed two names or a name for a tab of some sort, and it just went from there. I guess he wouldn't give it up or give it to the individual."[114] When asked to explain "it," he said "it" was the bottle.[115]

Ms. Sawyer asked about Heath's interaction and demeanor. Corporal Holubar said the customer was "getting a little irritated, that he could not receive — the bottle."[116] He said the bartender was not getting the names, so he was not giving up the bottle. Later, when questioned about the meaning of "irritated" Corporal Holubar said, "He was raising his voice, going back and forth. His posture, he was starting to tense up a little."[117] He later said, "He was trying to lean in forward, just turning more authoritative, I guess."[118] At that time, the only thing he heard the bartender say was that he needed two names.

> Ms. Sawyer: *Did you hear the bartender say anything about the police?*
> Corporal Holubar: *Yeah. After he said, calm down, sir. I ask you to leave. And then we'll call the police and — where the individual then stated, I am the F'g police.*
> Ms. Sawyer: *...Was the individual also using profanity?*
> Corporal Holubar: *Yes.*[119]

Corporal Holubar testified that after the interaction with the bartender, the bouncer came in, approached the individual, and said, "Sir, can you come with me."[120] Ms. Sawyer asked, "And what was the man's demeanor like when he's having this exchange with the bouncer?"[121] Corporal Holubar answered, "Still in the irritated state. He didn't really calm down or get more aggressive."[122]

Corporal Holubar said the man refused to leave. The bouncer tried to escort him out, putting his hand beside him, and when he did not respond, the bouncer picked him up. Describing how the bouncer picked Heath up, he said, "The bouncer grabbed him from behind in a bear hug right under the arms across the chest and went to pick him up. The individual dropped his body weight, kind of spread out. And he picked him up again, turned, and walked towards the door."[123]

Corporal Holubar said he followed the bouncer and Heath out of the building, and when they got outside, "the bouncer dropped him right after the sidewalk in between

---

[114] Ibid, 282
[115] Ibid
[116] Ibid,
[117] Ibid, 283
[118] Ibid,
[119] Ibid, 284
[120] Ibid, 285
[121] Ibid, 286
[122] Ibid,
[123] Ibid, 287

two parked vehicles."[124] He said the bouncer took a step back, and when he did so, he was not touching Heath.

> Ms. Sawyer: *And what's the next thing you saw?*
> Corporal Holubar: *The individual spun around. He has some – hands kind of chest level, and the bouncer put his hand out and grabbed. I did notice there was a weapon in his hand.*
> Ms. Sawyer: *…what, if anything was in his hand?*
> Corporal Holubar: *It took a moment to notice it was a pistol.*[125]

Ms. Sawyer asked if he saw where the man got the pistol from, and he said he did not. She asked if Heath was "holding it [the gun] in one hand or two hands?"[126] Corporal Holubar said, "One."[127]

When describing how Heath turned, Corporal Holubar moved and turned slightly on the stand, which could be described as an unplanned demonstration. The unplanned demo position was identical to what you see in police magazines—weapon held high with both hands, muzzle pointed forward and down, and elbows in tight.

> Ms. Sawyer: *Now, what, if anything, did you notice about where his finger was positioned?*
> Corporal Holubar: *On the trigger.*
> Ms. Sawyer: *… And how is it that you noticed that?*
> Corporal Holubar: *Something I know to look for. It's just one thing I caught.*
> Ms. Sawyer: *And is that of any special significance to you in contrast, for example, having his finger straight as opposed to on the trigger?*
> Corporal Holubar: *Yes.*
> Ms. Sawyer: *… And what did that mean to you?*
> Corporal Holubar: *That he planned on using it, I mean to – to fire. If you put your finger on the trigger, you're going to fire the weapon. I mean, that's your – your intent.*
> Ms. Sawyer: *And based on those observations, how did you feel when you saw the man turning with the gun?*
> Corporal Holubar: *Threatened.*[128]

At that point, the judge asked a few questions for clarification.

> Judge Dixon: *The first time you noticed it was a gun, was it before or after the bouncer grabbed the arm?*

---
[124] Ibid, 288
[125] Ibid, 289-290
[126] Ibid, 290
[127] Ibid
[128] Ibid, 291

Corporal Holubar: *He – the bouncer grabbed the top of the gun.*
Judge Dixon: *… Was it after the bouncer grabbed the top of the gun that you then noticed it was a gun?*
Corporal Holubar: *It – about the same time, sir.*[129]

Using a photograph, Ms. Sawyer had Corporal Holubar identify where he was standing when he witnessed the event. Corporal Holubar said he had been standing in the doorway to the building; he was in the atrium.

Ms. Sawyer asked, "Did you ever make an attempt to go to try and help the bouncer?"[130] Corporal Holubar said he started to, but then stopped. "It was five, six feet to – or maybe a little bit more to get to the situation, and the gun was pointed at me with the finger on the trigger. I didn't feel comfortable enough trying to make transition or that movement to assist and have somebody feel that I was a target and pull the trigger – or a threat."[131]

Ms. Sawyer went back to the struggle for the gun.

Ms. Sawyer: *And what did you see?*
Corporal Holubar: *Bouncer grabbed the weapon and grabbed the individual at the same time and started struggling. Soon after that, … since I wasn't going to move forward, I kind of shifted my focus to the people that were behind me trying to push him back away from — the struggle outside.*
Ms. Sawyer: *And why did you take that action?*
Corporal Holubar: *In case the firearm went off, give everybody a little bit more of a chance not to get hit being away from the window further back into the restaurant or bar.*
Ms. Sawyer: *… And at the point where the bouncer grabs onto the man, does he ever identify himself as a police officer at that point?*
Corporal Holubar: *Not that I heard.*
Ms. Sawyer: *… did you ever hear the man identify himself as a police officer?*
Corporal Holubar: *Only when arguing at the bar. Other than that, I didn't, myself, hear him say it.*[132]

Ms. Sawyer asked where on his body the gun was pointing during the struggle, and he answered, "*Chest. To be – not exactly one point in particular. … It was flagging the front of the building, the doorway.*"[133] *Flagging* means to wave side to side.

That was the last question for the day, and Corporal Holubar was told he would resume his testimony the following morning.

---

[129] Ibid, 292
[130] Ibid
[131] Ibid, 293
[132] Ibid 293-294
[133] Ibid 294

8A

Roger Logan and Police Corruption

Mr. Roger Logan, 53, was released from prison in New York in 2014. He had been incarcerated for 17 years after being found guilty of a 1997 murder. The District Attorney, Kenneth Thompson, asked the judge to release Mr. Logan based on new evidence. The judge agreed and dismissed the case. Mr. Logan had always maintained his innocence.

When the murder occurred in 1997, New York City Police Detective Louis Scarcella questioned Mr. Logan about the crime. It had been reported that Mr. Logan was in the vicinity of the crime when it occurred. During the interview, Detective Scarcella asked Mr. Logan to frame another person for the crime. Mr. Logan refused.

Later Detective Scarcella produced a witness that said Mr. Logan was playing dice in the vicinity of where the crime occurred, implicating him in the crime. Mr. Logan was charged with murder. The witness testified at the trial, and Mr. Logan was found guilty and sentenced to 25 years to life.

While incarcerated, Mr. Logan heard of the David Ranta case, wherein Mr. Ranta was falsely accused, found guilty, imprisoned, and later exonerated and released. Mr. Logan contacted the prosecutor's office because Detective Scarcella was also the charging officer in Mr. Ranta's case. The Ranta case was instrumental in questioning Detective Scarcella's tactics and integrity in other cases.

Reviewing Mr. Logan's case, the prosecutor's office discovered that the only witness that testified against Mr. Logan was herself incarcerated when the crime occurred, so she could not have witnessed the crime. Mark Hale, an assistant district attorney, told the judge that *"the witness could not have made these observations because she was incarcerated."*[1]

It was believed that the witness had been coached by Detective Scarcella, who is now retired.

When District Attorney Thompson was elected, he created a unit to review wrongful convictions in old homicide cases. Mr. Logan was the seventh defendant released that year. District Attorney Thompson was quoted in the *New York Daily News* as say-

---
[1] New York Daily News, June 3, 2014

ing, "*Most of them stem from concerns about the investigative tactics of one now-retired police detective....*"[2]

By July 2018 fourteen people had been released and their convictions reversed in cases re-examined involving Retired New York City Police Detective Louis Scarcella.

If all of these convictions were overturned, not on technicalities but because they were innocent, who actually committed the crimes? Did the real offenders continue to commit additional crimes? Arresting the wrong/innocent person leaves the guilty party on the street.

Currently, and with good reason, all of Detective Scarcella's cases are being reexamined.

While Detective Scarcella is retired, are there, or should there be, any consequences for him?

References

Jennifer Dhanaraj, "After serving 17 years, New York man freed from prison," *New York Daily News*, June 3, 2014

Josh Soul, "Wrongful, 17-year conviction ends for 'framed' Brooklyn man," *New York Post*, June 3, 2014.

---

[2] New York Daily News, June 3, 2014

9

Day 3: Witnesses for Both Sides
WEDNESDAY, AUGUST 17, 2011

*"Some minds are like concrete—thoroughly mixed
up and permanently set."*

—Anonymous

Day three of the trial began, and the prosecution resumed questioning Corporal Holubar. Additional prosecution witnesses scheduled for the day were Mr. Dennis Jones, a member of Heath's party, and Officers Jeffery Cadle and Robert A. Anderson, members of the Metropolitan Police Department. This would conclude the prosecution's case.

The defense planned to call Mr. Terry Spradlin, who like Mr. Jones was a member of Heath's party, and Ms. Angela Parrott, an assistant federal defender who would serve as a character witness.

The majority of the testimony on day three did not put Heath in a good light. However, some testimony from prosecution witnesses seemed favorable to Heath.

The Prosecution Witnesses
Cpl. Brandon Holubar
Ms. Sawyer resumed her examination of Corporal Holubar with questions about where the gun was pointed when Heath turned around and Mr. Brackett grabbed it. Corporal Holubar said the gun was pointed at the bar.[1] She followed with, "Now at what part of your body was the weapon aimed?"[2] He replied, "Chest, generally."[3]

When asked to describe how the gun was moving, he said, "A few inches, not very much. The bouncer had the hand on top of the weapon, and it was kind of, I guess, pushing down; it was coming back up."[4] From Corporal Holubar's perspective, the bouncer was pushing down and Heath was trying to pull up.

Ms. Sawyer asked if anyone else had been outside during the incident. Corporal Holubar answered, "There were people outside, but none that interfered with the struggle between

---
[1] Information from the trial transcript, Criminal Action Number 2010-CF3-16079, dated August 17, 20112011, p 5
[2] Ibid, 6
[3] Ibid,
[4] Ibid

Left: View of the street, from the front door, (exhibit 93). *Middle and right*: Photographs taken at another location simulating the view from the doorway at the Guards. The photographs simulate the lighting conditions and distance to the street, showing a person facing right, with a gun in his right hand, then facing left, with the gun in both hands. Photo credit: Adam Enatsky.

the two."[5] When asked if he noticed anyone, he answered, "There was a female [Ms. O'Connor] to my right, right outside the door. Other than that, not anyone I could tell."[6]

He identified photographs of where he was standing and where the woman was standing, indicating that he had been in the doorway to The Guards, while the woman had been on the first step down. He then identified a photograph showing where the struggle took place—directly in front of the door and in the street between two parked cars.

> Ms. Sawyer: ... *What if anything during the course of the struggle, did you hear the bouncer say?*
> Corporal Holubar: ... *I can recall him actually saying ... I'm not getting shot tonight.*
> Ms. Sawyer: *Now, the woman you described who was to your right... did you hear her say anything?*
> Corporal Holubar: *The only thing I really remember her saying was, "you're not part of this." Whenever I'd noticed her to my right, it's like, "get back," I mean – I believe that's all I said was, "get back."*[7]

---

[5] Ibid, 8
[6] Ibid
[7] Ibid, 12

He could not remember if the woman in front of him said anything about Heath's being a police officer. However, after reviewing his grand jury transcript, he said, "She mentioned to the bouncer that he was a cop,"[8] but said he did not know if the bouncer heard her. While outside, he never heard the individual (Heath) identify himself as a police officer.

Corporal Holubar said it was dark outside, but he could see what was happening with the light of the streetlamps. When the witness first arrived in the doorway, the bouncer was blocking part of his view of Heath. At first, Corporal Holubar could only see Heath on Mr. Brackett's left side. As the incident unfolded, he could see more.

Mr. Hannon took over for his cross-examination, beginning with a question about Corporal Holubar's work assignment when the incident occurred. He asked if he guarded the communications equipment and Corporal Holubar responded, "Yes Sir." Mr. Hannon continued, "And are you telling the court that there is a designation of that assignment as presidential guard?" Corporal Holubar answered, "Yes Sir."[9]

Mr. Hannon then asked about any regulations concerning a marine's contact with police.

Mr. Hannon: *Corporal, are you required to report to your command any contact with civilian police?*
Corporal Holubar: *Yes.*
Mr. Hannon: *And you didn't do that, did you?*
Corporal Holubar: *Yes, I did.*
Mr. Hannon: *To which command?*
Corporal Holubar: *Beth Walker. I passed – I had White House communications, Izzy* [possibly referring to Ms. Elizabeth Walker].[10]

Mr. Hannon moved on to the night of the incident. Corporal Holubar said he was there to help celebrate the birthday of a fellow marine. Mr. Hannon reminded him of his testimony the previous day when he said he drank a Long Island Iced Tea and a beer just before arriving at The Guards. Mr. Hannon asked him if he knew that a Long Island Iced Tea was made from "five different kinds of alcohol."[11] Corporal Holubar said he did know that.

Revisiting previous testimony, Corporal Holubar said that after having drinks at the Waterfront—the Long Island Iced Tea and a beer—the group left the bar and split up. He went with the group to The Guards. They were met at the door by Mr. Brackett, who checked their IDs. After entering, the group went downstairs; they were there for ten to fifteen minutes. He described the downstairs: "there was a large crowd, and it was pretty

---

[8] Information from the trial transcript, Criminal Action Number 2010-CF3-16079, dated August 17, 2011, p 14
[9] Ibid, 18
[10] Ibid, 29-30
[11] Ibid, 20

packed down there…"[12] He began texting the other group and found out that they had gone to McFadden's, so he decided to go to McFadden's.

Corporal Holubar said there was music downstairs, and he did not tell the others in his party he was leaving. He could not describe the music. Nor could he estimate the number of people, but he said it was crowded.

Mr. Hannon turned next to what the Corporal saw when he was at the bar on the first floor.

> Mr. Hannon: *And there came a point in time when you heard someone say, "I'm going to call the police," right?*
> Corporal Holubar: *Yes, sir.*
> Mr. Hannon: *And then you heard the individual who was carried out say, I am the F'ing police?*
> Corporal Holubar: *Yes, sir.*[13]

Corporal Holubar said the bartender and Heath were at the bar, and it was the bartender who said he was going to call the police. When asked if he knew the manager, Corporal Holubar said he did not know who the manager was. He said that the only individuals he knew to be involved with the incident were the bartender and Heath. He described the bartender as "an older gentleman,"[14] and added that he might have had a mustache. He also said he might have seen him outside after the incident and when the police were there.

Corporal Holubar's description of the bartender more accurately describes the manager, Mr. Viricochea, who was outside after the incident. The bartender was said to be in his mid-thirties with blondish hair.

Mr. Hannon questioned Corporal Holubar about his observations when the bouncer arrived, picked up Heath, and carried him outside.

> Mr. Hannon: *Now, did you decide to follow the bouncer out because you wanted to see what was going on, or did you just use that as a moment to leave and go to McFadden's?*
> Corporal Holubar: *He [The bouncer] was clearing the way, so I might as well just follow him.*
> Mr. Hannon: *And how close behind the bouncer were you when you followed him?*
> Corporal Holubar: *Five feet, six feet.*[15]

---

[12] Ibid, 24
[13] Ibid, 40
[14] Ibid, 41
[15] Ibid, 43

Corporal Holubar's answer—that he was only five or six feet behind the bouncer—is the same distance that Carole O'Connor said she was behind the manager.

Mr. Hannon asked, "Did you ever see anyone at the Guards wearing a red shirt that said 'Staff' on it?"[16] Corporal Holubar answered, "Not that I can remember."[17] Answering another question, Corporal Holubar said that he told the prosecution that the bouncer's shirt was black or dark in color.

Mr. Hannon then showed Corporal Holubar some photographs from inside The Guards, looking out from the front door. He asked if this was the perspective he had on the evening of the incident. Corporal Holubar answered, "It looks about right, sir."[18]

> Mr. Hannon: *You even considered for a moment using your body to protect the woman who was standing to your ... right?*
> Corporal Holubar: *Not necessarily to protect the woman, but to assist with the de-handling of the disarming of the individual.*
> Mr. Hannon: *Well, you didn't do that, did you?*
> Corporal Holubar: *No, sir.*
> Mr. Hannon: *And you're trained in how to disarm someone with a weapon, aren't you?*
> Corporal Holubar: *Yes, sir.*[19]

Mr. Hannon introduced a training weapon and had Corporal Holubar assist with a demonstration. While Mr. Hannon stood in Corporal Holubar's position, the Corporal was to demonstrate to the court how Heath turned with a gun in hand. According to Corporal Holubar, the bouncer placed Heath in the street and then stepped back, but he was not certain if the bouncer stepped back up to the sidewalk or stayed in the street.[20] When he demonstrated, he turned to his left with the weapon in his right hand. He was not sure if Heath's left hand was on the gun, but he said that it had been close to the gun.[21]

Responding to a question, Corporal Holubar testified that Mr. Brackett saw the gun as it came around and he put his left hand on it. Mr. Brackett then grabbed the individual by putting his other arm (his right arm) around him. He said the gun was pointed at him after the bouncer grabbed it, not before.[22]

The questioning then moved to Corporal Holubar's view that Heath had his finger on the trigger.

---

[16] Ibid, 44
[17] Ibid
[18] Ibid, 48, photo, Exhibit 93
[19] Information from the trial transcript, Criminal Action Number 2010-CF3-16079, dated August 17, 2011, p 52
[20] Ibid, 54
[21] Ibid, 55
[22] Ibid, 57

Mr. Hannon: *And when was it that you concluded that the man with the gun had his finger in the … trigger guard?*

Corporal Holubar: *Whenever I saw the pistol. Whenever I recognized this pistol, I got a better look or focused more on it, and noticed his finger was in the trigger lock.*

Mr. Hannon: *Was that before the bouncer grabbed it?*

Corporal Holubar: *It was about the same time, sir.*

Mr. Hannon: *… - when you concluded that the man with the gun had his finger in the trigger, did the bouncer have his hands on the weapon?*

Corporal Holubar: *When he was going for it.*

Mr. Hannon: *So the answer is no?*

Corporal Holubar: *No to which part, sir?*

Mr. Hannon: *That when you noticed his finger was on the trigger, the bouncer's hand was not on the weapon; is that what you're saying?*

Corporal Holubar: *Not at that time, sir.*

Mr. Hannon: *And would you agree with me that the time during which you would have had to recognize his hand on the trigger was probably a portion of a second?*

Corporal Holubar: *Yes, sir.*

Mr. Hannon: *And after the bouncer got his hand on the weapon, could you see that he had his finger on the trigger, Corporal?*

Corporal Holubar: *Not directly, sir.*

Mr. Hannon: *What do you mean "not directly"? Did you see it or not?*

Corporal Holubar: *If I saw his finger on the trigger before he grabbed?*

Mr. Hannon: *… My question was: After the bouncer put his hand over the slide of the weapon, did you see the individual's finger on the trigger?*

Corporal Holubar: *No sir, I could not see his finger on the trigger.*[23]

He described the struggle and said, "After that, I wasn't going over there, and I told the lady, the female to my right to, like, move. After that, [I] kind of hit the window, trying to get people back away from the glass and the front."[24]

Mr. Hannon: *Did you see the man with the weapon get pushed up onto a vehicle or against a vehicle?*

Corporal Holubar: *No, sir.*[25]

He said that when the police arrived, the gun was still in Heath's hand or hands, and it was at waist level. The bouncer still had his left hand on the weapon and his right arm over Heath's shoulder, and they were both still in the street, between two parked cars.

---

[23] Ibid, 58-59
[24] Ibid, 60
[25] Ibid, 61

Mr. Hannon revisited previous testimony claiming Heath was trying to move the gun up, and the bouncer was trying to push it down. Corporal Holubar said that he believed this because it appeared that "he [Heath] was trying to keep the weapon close."[26] He said he recognized that keeping the weapon close was a defensive tactic.

Going over previous testimony of when the gun was pointed at himself, Corporal Holubar said that Heath only had one hand on the gun at that time, "One that I could tell, sir."[27] With that answer, Mr. Hannon referred to Corporal Holubar's grand jury testimony, and Corporal Holubar was given a copy of it. Mr. Hannon said, "I want to ask you if you were asked this question and gave this answer, Question: 'And then what did this individual do once you observed him with the black pistol in his hand?'"[28] Mr. Hannon then read Corporal Holubar's answer: "'He had both hands turned around. He had the pistol chest high. He had his finger on the trigger; it wasn't straight or anything; it was on the trigger, trying to make his way toward the bouncer. The bouncer put his hand out, grabbed the top of the pistol.'"[29]

Here Ms. Sawyer objected but was overruled. Mr. Hannon continued reading Corporal Holubar's answer. "'The bouncer put his hand out, grabbed the top of the pistol, wrapped his arm around the individual, tried to pull the pistol out of his hand, but he [Heath] had it in both hands, so it was very unlikely he was going to do that.'"[30] Mr. Hannon asked, "Were you asked that question and did you give that answer in the grand jury?"[31] Corporal Holubar answered, "Yes, sir."[32]

Mr. Hannon questioned him about his location in the doorway as he witnessed the struggle for the gun and his previous testimony that he was about five feet behind the bouncer as he left the bar area.

> Mr. Hannon: *And you were right behind him as he went through the first door, correct?*
> Corporal Holubar: *Yes, sir.*
> Mr. Hannon: *And you were right behind him as he carried him down several steps, correct?*
> Corporal Holubar: *Yes, sir.*
> Mr. Hannon: *And how did the bouncer get through the outside door? Was it –?*
> Corporal Holubar: *I can't recall, sir.*
> Mr. Hannon: *You don't remember if he had to push it open or if it was already open?*
> Corporal Holubar: *I don't remember, sir.*
> Mr. Hannon: *Do you know if there was another bouncer checking I.D.s at the door?*

---

[26] Ibid, 64
[27] Ibid, 65
[28] Ibid, 66, and information from grand jury transcript of Corporal Holubar on September 23, 2010, p 9
[29] Ibid, 67, and information from grand jury transcript of Corporal Holubar on September 23, 2010, p 9
[30] Ibid, 68, and information from grand jury transcript of Corporal Holubar on September 23, 2010, p 9
[31] Information from the trial transcript, Criminal Action Number 2010-CF3-16079, dated August 17, 2011, p 68
[32] Ibid, 69

> Corporal Holubar: *Not that I can remember.*
> Mr. Hannon: *So you were the second person out the door –*
> Corporal Holubar: *Yes, sir.*
> Mr. Hannon: *Behind the bouncer, correct?*
> Corporal Holubar: *Yes, sir.*
> Mr. Hannon: *And he [the bouncer] went directly from the stoop, all the way across the sidewalk with the man suspended off the ground, in his arms, correct?*
> Corporal Holubar: *Yes, sir.*
> Mr. Hannon: *And he put him down in the street?*
> Corporal Holubar: *Yes, sir.*
> Mr. Hannon: *And did you see who came out behind you?*
> Corporal Holubar: *No, I didn't.*
> Mr. Hannon: *Was the woman that you saw to your right already out there?*
> Corporal Holubar: *I'm not sure, sir.*
> Mr. Hannon: *Did she go out in front of you?*
> Corporal Holubar: *Not that I am aware of.*
> Mr. Hannon: *While you were watching this and waiting for the police, did anyone else come out the door behind you?*
> Corporal Holubar: *Not that I can remember. There was — nobody – whenever I took the next step back, there was nobody behind me. Unless they went back inside, I'm not sure.*
> Mr. Hannon: *And you stayed in what I call the alcove of the doorway until the police came, correct?*
> Corporal Holubar: *I went back inside after the second squad car came.*[33]
> Although Corporal Holubar did not recall it, the outside doors were propped open on the night of the incident.

Mr. Hannon continued, "Now, between the time you arrived on the stoop and the time that the first squad car arrived, did you hear anyone near you calling the police?" Corporal Holubar answered, "No, sir."[34]

Answering a series of questions, Corporal Holubar said he did hear a woman (Ms. O'Connor) saying something about Heath being police. He never heard Heath say anything about being a police officer while outside, but he was more than ten feet away. He also said he never saw Heath produce any credentials; he never saw anything lying on top of the vehicle and did not hear the bouncer say anything.[35]

Mr. Hannon returned to the activity inside The Guards, at the top of the steps, at the bar when "the bartender"—Mr. Viricochea—threatened to call the police.

---

[33] Ibid, 69-70
[34] Ibid
[35] Ibid, 73-74

Mr. Hannon: *And you heard Agent Thomas say, I am the F'ing police, did you have difficulty hearing that conversation?*

Corporal Holubar: *At the bar or?*

Mr. Hannon: *That occurred at the bar, when you heard Agent Thomas say, I am the F'ing police?*

Corporal Holubar: *No, sir.*

Mr. Hannon: *You were about 15 feet away, correct?*

Corporal Holubar: *Give or take, yes, sir.*[36]

Mr. Hannon revisited the struggle then, asking, "Is it true that when you were watching the struggle, it appeared to you as if the bouncer wanted to take the gun?"[37] Corporal Holubar answered, "Yes, sir."[38]

Mr. Hannon also inquired about any concerns he might have had since he believed that Heath was a police officer.

Corporal Holubar: *Other than what I've heard someone say, 'he's a cop,' other than that, I had no assumption that he was, or no reason to believe that he was.*

Mr. Hannon: *And you heard that in the bar?*

Corporal Holubar: *Yes.*

Mr. Hannon: *And did it occur to you that perhaps you might go to the assistance of a law enforcement officer – who was having his weapon taken?*[39]

Ms. Sawyer objected, and her objection was overruled.

Corporal Holubar: *No, sir.*

Mr. Hannon: *And is that because you didn't — you were concerned about your own safety?*

Corporal Holubar: *Partly, and the fact that the individual who draw [sic] the weapon, had possibly been drinking that night, and that was on my mind.*

Mr. Hannon: *A possibility?*

Corporal Holubar: *Yes, sir.*

Mr. Hannon: *But you didn't know whether Agent Thomas had been drinking, number one, or was intoxicated, number two?*

Corporal Holubar: *No, sir.*

Mr. Hannon: *… were you intoxicated, Corporal?*

---

[36] Ibid, 75
[37] Ibid, 79
[38] Ibid
[39] Ibid, 80

Corporal Holubar: *No, sir.*[40]

On redirect, Ms. Sawyer revisited the struggle, asking, if the trigger were pulled at that time, where would a shot have gone? Corporal Holubar answered, "Possibly to the side of the bouncer, to the left rib cage area, or past him into the bar."[41]

Answering a question about the distance between him and the bouncer and the danger, he said it was too dangerous for him to help. So, he said, "The female to my right. I verbally told her to get back or move. I'm not sure exactly what I said. It was as to that nature."[42] He then focused on the people sitting in the front of the bar, "trying to get their attention to move back."[43]

Ms. Sawyer reminded Corporal Holubar that in responding to Mr. Hannon's questions, he had said that he did not hear the bouncer say anything, but earlier, he (Corporal Holubar) had testified that he heard the bouncer say, 'I'm not getting shot tonight.'"[44] Ms. Sawyer asked, "And you were able to recall that? And you were able, in fact to hear that?"[45] Corporal Holubar answered, "Yes, that, but anything else he might have said, which I wasn't able to hear. I backed further into the doorway, so I wasn't able to hear anything else after that."[46]

Ms. Sawyer returned to the struggle between the bouncer and Heath.

Ms. Sawyer: *Did you feel that you were pulling for one side or the other in this case.*
Corporal Holubar: *Not necessarily.*
Ms. Sawyer: *And when you thought about going and getting involved, who did it cross your mind to assist at that moment?*
Corporal Holubar: *The bouncer.*[47]

After the prosecution finished its examination, Judge Dixon had questions. He repeated the question, already asked, and answered, about the conversation between Heath and the bartender. The judge also asked about Corporal Holubar's observations when he followed the bouncer carrying Heath. Specifically, he asked what he observed after the bouncer took a step back—did Heath go to the ground, did he bend down, did he say anything, and did he do anything before he turned around? The judge seemed to be probing for various reasons the gun may have come loose. Corporal Holubar said no to each question. Judge Dixon asked, "Is your impression or your memory that he was

---

[40] Ibid, 80-81
[41] Ibid, 83
[42] Ibid, 84
[43] Ibid
[44] Ibid
[45] Ibid
[46] Ibid
[47] Ibid, 86-87

standing up the full time before he turned around, or you just don't know?"[48] Corporal Holubar answered, "Standing up."[49]

The judge asked about the lady who had said, "You're not part of this."[50] Was she speaking to Corporal Holubar at the time?

> Corporal Holubar: *I wasn't really sure, sir. I was guessing through my best judgment that she was with him, and some sort of friend or something.*
> Judge Dixon: *What made you think that?*
> Corporal Holubar: *She was defending him, "You're not part of this," saying that she was and I wasn't. I wasn't really sure, sir.*
> Judge Dixon: *Was she behind you inside the bar or was she outside?*
> Corporal Holubar: *She was outside, to my right.*[51]

Taken as a whole, Corporal Holubar's testimony seemed genuine because, for the most part, he seemed very sure of his answers. Nevertheless, he did leave some room for doubt. Although he admitted he had consumed a beer and a Long Island Iced Tea before arriving at The Guards, he testified he was not impaired. According to an online blood alcohol calculator (BAC), a person weighing 155pounds (estimate of his weight) who drinks a beer, and a Long Island Iced Tea (5 oz. of liquor and one beer) would have an estimated BAC of .120, which is intoxicated.[52] This is only an estimate. The legal standard for intoxication in most states is .08 BAC.

In a telephone interview, Corporal Holubar told me that the downstairs at The Guards had been crowded and noisy on the night of the incident, but it was not crowded upstairs. The only conversation he witnessed at the bar was between the bartender and Heath. He saw no other conversations between Heath and anyone else, and he did not hear Heath speaking Spanish to anyone.[53]

Mr. Dennis Jones

The next witness to take the stand was Mr. Dennis Jones. He was the husband of Jane Jones, a former co-worker of Carole O'Connor, Heath's companion. Mr. Jones was called as a witness for the government.

To start, Mr. Jones stated whom he was with, which included Heath, and said that the group went to Old Glory for dinner. He was drinking at dinner and con-

---

[48] Ibid, 89
[49] Ibid
[50] Ibid
[51] Ibid, 90
[52] Web site www.thealcoholcalculator.com used to calculate an estimated Blood Alcohol Content. http://www.thealcoholcalculator.com/blood_alcohol_content_calculator.php
[53] Telephone interview of Mr. Holubar on November 16, 2014

suming beer. When asked how many drinks he had with dinner, he said, "I can't recall. Like, maybe four, three or four."[54] Mr. Jones was asked if Heath had any drinks with dinner, and he said, "He may have. I can't recollect."[55] Mr. Rickard then reminded him of his grand jury testimony, and he read from the grand jury testimony: "'So was he [Heath] drinking the same as you or different; do you remember that?' And you answered: 'I would think the same as me.'"[56] Mr. Jones said, "Yes," answering that he remembered.[57]

Mr. Hannon asked the court, "Under the rules of completeness, may I ask Mr. Rickard to read the question and answer at 18, line 18?"[58]

From the grand jury transcript, Mr. Rickard read the passage, "Do you remember how much Mr. Thomas had to drink while you were at Glory? The answer was, 'I do not.'"[59] Reading the next question, "'So was he drinking about the same as you or different; do you remember...?'" Reading the answer: "'I would think the same as me.'"[60] Mr. Jones remembered those questions and his answers.

Mr. Jones said that after dinner, they left Old Glory and stopped at The Guards for a drink. He identified his dinner tab from Old Glory.[61] He said that when they first arrived at The Guards, they ordered drinks from the bar. When they noticed that a table was open behind them, they went to the table. At the table, he was drinking martinis; he believed they were made with gin, but he was not sure.

> Mr. Rickard: *Did Mr. Thomas have a martini with you?*
> Mr. Jones: *I think so, yes.*
> Mr. Rickard: *I'm going to again ask you about a question and answer in the grand jury. From the Grand Jury, page 35, line 4. 'Question ... Do you recall who was drinking the four Bombay Sapphires? Answer: I recall having two. I know I had one martini with gin. I don't know who else had –. Question: Was Mr. Thomas also drinking? Answer: He definitely had one with me, yes.'*
> *Did you give that question and make that answer?*
> Mr. Jones: *Yes.*[62]

Mr. Rickard asked Mr. Jones to identify where everyone was sitting. He answered that he had been facing a wall.

---

[54] Information from the trial transcript, Criminal Action Number 2010-CF3-16079, dated August 17, 2011, p 93
[55] Ibid
[56] Ibid, 93-94, and information from grand jury transcript of Mr. Dennis Jones on October 22, 2010, p 30
[57] Information from the trial transcript, Criminal Action Number 2010-CF3-16079, dated August 17, 2011, p 94
[58] Ibid
[59] Ibid, 94, and information from grand jury transcript of Mr. Dennis Jones on October 22, 2010, p 30
[60] Ibid, 95
[61] U.S. v. Heath Thomas, Governments Exhibit 14 Case No. 2010 CF3 016079, Old Glory Restaurant Tab
[62] Ibid, 96 - 97 and information from grand jury transcript of Mr. Dennis Jones on October 22, 2010, p 35

Mr. Rickard said, "There were a number of problems – I'm sorry. Were there any problems with the drinks that you ordered from the table?"[63] Mr. Jones answered, "I had ordered a dirty martini and the martini came out that was not dirty and did not have olives in it, so, we sent it back. So that was the first problem. Then I believe the service was slow. But that's the problem that I recollect."[64]

Mr. Jones was asked if there had been other drink problems, but he said he did not remember. Mr. Rickard again referred to Mr. Jones's grand jury testimony. In the grand jury transcript, when asked about other drink problems, he answered, "I remember there were a couple of other drinks that were sent back."[65] Mr. Jones recalled saying that.

Mr. Rickard established that Heath had gone to the bar near the end of the night, then asked, "What is the next thing you noticed with respect to what was going on with Mr. Thomas?"[66] Mr. Jones answered, "After Mr. Thomas went up to the bar, I believe maybe a few minutes later I heard someone say that they're throwing Keath [Heath] out of the bar. I turned around to see what was going on and I saw two bodies, over my left shoulder, move very, very quickly toward the exit. I got up, went outside to see what was happening. I saw Mr. Thomas and the bouncer from the bar with a weapon, and then at that point I went back inside."[67]

Mr. Rickard continued, "Before you got up, had anyone beside Mr. Thomas left your table?" Mr. Jones answered, "I don't remember."[68]

Mr. Jones said that while he was outside, the gun was pointed at him, and he had been outside for only a few seconds. He did not know who was holding the gun, saying, "And if I remember correctly, both of them were near either – I forget if the car was in the front or the back, but they were in front of a car."[69] Once back inside, he went to the window area in the front of the building. He was trying to see what was happening, but his view was not good.[70] Mr. Rickard yielded for cross examination.

Mr. Hannon began his cross-examination with a question about Heath going to the bar to pay the tab. Mr. Jones said he only knew that Heath had left; "I just assumed he went to the bar."[71]

Mr. Hannon then reviewed the drink orders.

---

[63] Information from the trial transcript, Criminal Action Number 2010-CF3-16079, dated August 17, 2011, p 98
[64] Ibid, 98-99
[65] Ibid, 99, and information from grand jury transcript of Mr. Dennis Jones on October 22, 2010, p 13
[66] Ibid, 100
[67] Ibid, 100-101
[68] Ibid, 101
[69] Ibid, 102
[70] Ibid
[71] Ibid, 105

> Mr. Hannon: *And you're sure you had two martinis when you were at the Guards …?*
> Mr. Jones: *Right.*
> Mr. Hannon: *And the problems with the drinks, you felt that it was the problem with your waitress, right?*
> Mr. Jones: *Correct.*[72]

Mr. Jones said he did not remember what the waitress looked like. He did not remember her hair color or how she was dressed, but he thought she had an attitude.[73]

Changing the line of questioning, Mr. Hannon asked, "And at the time that the gun pointed in your direction, your impression was that Mr. Thomas and the bouncer were struggling over control of the gun; is that right?"[74] Mr. Jones answered, "That is correct."[75] Mr. Hannon read part of Mr. Jones's grand jury testimony: "the bouncer was trying to take it away from him, … and he was trying to control – he was trying to maintain control of it?"[76] Mr. Jones remembered that he had said that.

Mr. Rickard asked the judge, in the interest of completeness, that the next question be read.

Mr. Hannon continued, "So did it appear that the gun was in Mr. Thomas's hand and the bouncer was trying to take it away from him?"[77] Mr. Jones answered, "I have no idea whose hand the gun was. It just seemed like both of them were trying to take hold onto it."[78] Mr. Rickard corrected Mr. Hannon, saying, "were trying to hold onto it. There's no 'take.'"[79] Mr. Hannon then read it correctly.

Again, changing the line of questioning, Mr. Hannon asked, "Are you able to say, from your own observation, how much Agent Thomas drank when you were at The Guards with him?"[80] Mr. Jones replied, "No,"[81] then confirmed he did not recall seeing Heath drinking the martini.

Mr. Hannon asked, "And do you recall the waitress spilling any of the drinks?" Mr. Jones answered, "I don't recall that either."[82] That was the last question from Mr. Hannon.

On the prosecution's redirect, Mr. Jones said he was not aware, on the day of the incident, that Heath was in law enforcement, that he could carry a gun, or that he was carrying a gun that evening. That concluded his time on the stand.

---

[72] Ibid, 106-107
[73] Ibid, 108
[74] Ibid, 108
[75] Ibid
[76] Ibid, 109 and information from grand jury transcript of Mr. Dennis Jones on October 22, 2010, p 19
[77] Ibid, 109 -110 and information from grand jury transcript of Mr. Dennis Jones on October 22, 2010, p 19
[78] Ibid, 110 and information from grand jury transcript of Mr. Dennis Jones on October 22, 2010, p 19
[79] Ibid, 110 and information from grand jury transcript of Mr. Dennis Jones on October 22, 2010, p 19
[80] Information from the trial transcript, Criminal Action Number 2010-CF3-16079, dated August 17, 2011, p 110
[81] Ibid
[82] Ibid, 111

In hindsight, one question is conspicuously missing from Mr. Jones's testimony. After the bouncer removed Heath from the bar, Mr. Jones went outside; he was in the doorway and witnessed the struggle for the gun. Although he was only there for a moment, he was never asked if he saw Corporal Holubar.

Officer Jeffery Cadle
Officer Jeffery Cadle of the Metropolitan Police Department was the next witness called to testify for the government's case. He had been an officer for 19 years at the time of the trial and was working on August 28, 2010.

Officer Cadle said he responded to a call for a man with a gun. The description of the person with the gun was a subject with a black shirt. He said, "Once I arrived on scene, I did observe a gentleman wearing a black top who was involved in a struggle with a gentleman that I knew as a bouncer for 2915 M Street."[83] He knew the bouncer by face, not by name, and the bouncer was wearing a red shirt. He said the employees for The Guards wore red shirts, and "I saw the subject in a black top struggling with the – another gentleman wearing the red top, with their hands above their head, struggling with an unknown object. I did not see exactly what it was."[84] As he exited his vehicle, he heard Officer Andelman (another MPD officer) say, "Drop the weapon, drop the weapon."[85] He observed a weapon on the ground and handcuffed the man in the black shirt.

> Mr. Rickard: *Did you see how the gun got to the ground?*
> Officer Cadle: *I did not see it drop to the ground, I just noticed that it was on the ground.*
> Officer Cadle identified Heath Thomas as the person he handcuffed.
> Mr. Rickard: *What happened – what did Mr. Thomas do when you secured him?*
> Officer Cadle: *As I handcuffed him, he told me something to the effect, either by stating, I'm a cop, or I'm a police officer.*[86]
> Mr. Rickard: *… before you secured the defendant in the struggle. Did you ever see any part of the struggle taking place near or with respect to a vehicle?*
> Officer Cadle: *I did. Mr. Thomas and the gentleman in the red shirt, Mr. Brackett, were in between two parked cars, and that's when they were struggling… in the street area of the two parked cars.*
> Mr. Rickard: *Did you see any action take place on the hood of the car or up against the car?*

---

[83] Ibid, 114
[84] Ibid, 114
[85] Ibid, 115
[86] Ibid, 115 - 116

> Officer Cadle: *I did. I do recall that, for example, the hands were...were against the car.... And that's when Officer Andelman yelled, "Drop the weapon." The weapon dropped – the weapon was on the ground directly below where I saw their hands.*
>
> Mr. Rickard: *Did you see how the two struggling got from hands above their head to hands on the car?*
>
> Officer Cadle: *I did not.*
>
> Mr. Rickard: *After you handcuffed the defendant, without saying what you talked about, did you have any interactions with them?*[87]

Officer Cadle said he did; Heath had provided him with his phone and a code to get into the phone, with the intent to contact a supervisor.

Describing his observations of the defendant, Officer Cadle said, "Mr. Thomas... smelled of alcohol, to me. When he spoke, he said something to me, he would – I could tell he had slurred speech, and his eyes appeared to be glassy, to me."[88] Mr. Rickard asked, "If you had observed Mr. Thomas in the situation that you just described, after a traffic stop, what would you have done?"[89] Officer Cadle answered, "I would have requested that an officer who was certified in a field sobriety test to respond to my scene."[90]

Mr. Rickard finished the direct examination, and Mr. Hannon asked to approach the bench. At the bench Mr. Hannon explained that he had just received some materials from the prosecution that included Heath's statements to Officer Cadle on the night of the incident. Mr. Hannon described the materials: "In the upper right-hand corner it says 'AUSA notes March 4 of 2011.' And it contains a whole list of statements that were made to Officer Cadle by Agent Thomas. Quote, He grabbed me from behind."[91] Mr. Rickard objected, saying, "Those statements were all disclosed," adding, "I don't think they need to be read into the record."[92] Judge Dixon said, "Do I need to know the contents of this?"[93]

Mr. Hannon wanted time to go over the materials since he had just received them, and he wanted to do his cross-examination the following day. The prosecutor said the defense had the same materials earlier, that they were not new. Mr. Hannon answered, "My view is that he asked him, 'Did Agent Thomas say anything to you?' ... he said, 'Yeah, I'm a cop.' And therefore, I can speak to him about all these other statements that

---

[87] Ibid, 116-117
[88] Ibid, 118
[89] Ibid, 119
[90] Ibid, 119
[91] Ibid, 119-120, and Letter to Hannon Law Group ref., Heath Thomas case, 2010-CF3-106079, by the U.S. Attorney's Office, "In the upper right-hand corner it says 'AUSA notes March 4 of 2011.'"
[92] Ibid, 120
[93] Ibid

he made to him. Plus, he brought up the fact that he arrested him – excuse me, that he put handcuffs on him."[94]

Judge Dixon: "I don't think I agree, Mr. Hannon, that because he elicited this statement about, 'I'm a cop,' that that opens up everything else that Mr. Thomas may have said."[95] Mr. Hannon answered, "The officer didn't answer the question."[96] Mr. Rickard followed, "I didn't ask if he made any statements. I asked, 'Without telling me what the statements were, did you talk to him?'"[97]

Judge Dixon: "Whatever the question was, it's not going to entitle you to go into any other statement that Mr. Thomas may have made to this officer. If there is something that relates to that, you know, perhaps. But if it's something about what happened during the incident, no. If it's a protestation of innocence, no."[98]

Mr. Hannon continued, saying, "It's a statement to him of Agent Thomas's version of the facts," and Judge Dixon responded, "Then that definitely will not be admissible through this witness."[99] (Testifying to what another person said is considered hearsay and is inadmissible.)

Mr. Hannon argued that the actions of the officer, handcuffing someone and placing them in a patrol car, suggest guilt. The judge replied that the questions were related to Heath's sobriety and "so there was a reason for that inquiry."[100] Judge Dixon added, "The fact that you heard an open-ended question that wasn't answered does not entitle you to bring out everything that was said."[101]

The AUSA notes dated March 4, 2011, that Mr. Hannon cited—AUSA referring to the assistant U.S. attorney—were not in the materials that he and Heath turned over to me.[102] However, I did find a notice of filing for the Heath Thomas case, 2010-CF3-016079, by the U.S. Attorney's Office, dated July 5, 2011, which appears to be a later version of the same document. The document includes oral statements Heath made to Officer Cadle, a Sergeant Benton, and a Lieutenant Charland. The document states, "I'll disclose these statements without regard to whether they were spontaneous or in response to questions, and without regard to whether the government intends to elicit them at trial."[103] The document includes responses from three separate letters sent by Mr. Hannon's team to the U.S. Attorney's Office, the third being the oral statements.

---

[94] Ibid, 121
[95] Ibid
[96] Ibid, 122
[97] Ibid
[98] Ibid
[99] Ibid, 122
[100] Ibid, 123
[101] Ibid
[102] Ibid,
[103] Letter to Hannon Law Group ref., Heath Thomas case, 2010-CF3-106079, by the U.S. Attorney's Office, responding to three inquiries', dated July 5, 2011, Appendix D

According to the document, Heath made the following oral statements to the officers at the scene:

"Your client told Ofc. Cadle that he was a police officer and that he was not drunk. Your client stated that the bouncer grabbed him from behind and carried him out of the bar. Your client stated, in substance, that the bouncer must have felt the gun, and that your client was trying to keep the bouncer from getting it. Your client stated that he was out with a female witness, and further stated that he had 18 years on."

"Sgt. Benton asked your client if he was a cop, and your client responded affirmatively. Sgt. Benton asked if there was an official that your client wanted him to notify, and your client said he did not have the number for the official."

"Lt. Charland later asked your client if there was an official he should notify, and your client provided contact information."[104]

In my review, I thought the reported oral statements made to Officer Cadle, while not allowed in court, seemed important. Under certain conditions, when an officer arrests someone and the person being arrested blurts out a statement of guilt, the officer can testify to that at a trial. Should not the same apply to statements of innocence? The rules of evidence notwithstanding, not allowing these statements to be read in the courtroom was not helpful to Heath or to the finding of facts. Officer Cadle returned to the stand following the bench conference, and Mr. Hannon started his cross-examination.

> Mr. Hannon: *You went to the man in the black shirt and put your handcuffs on him because of the lookout.*
> Officer Cadle: *That's correct.*
> Mr. Hannon: *And did Agent Thomas, besides saying that he was a cop, tell you that he wanted Brackett charged —.*
> Mr. Rickard: *Objection.*
> Mr. Hannon: *— and locked up?*
> Judge Dixon: *The objection is sustained.*
> Mr. Hannon: *Did you consider whether the other individual who was struggling with Agent Thomas over a weapon ought to be locked up?*[105]

Mr. Rickard objected again. This time the judge overruled the objection and said to the officer, "You can explain why you went to this person rather than the other person."[106] Officer Cadle responded, "Well, the lookout was for the gentleman in the black top. ... And, again, I knew the security, Mr. Brackett, by face and by shirt, that he was a bouncer at the location."[107]

---

[104] Ibid

[105] Information from the trial transcript, Criminal Action Number 2010-CF3-16079, dated August 17, 2011, p 124

[106] Ibid, 124

[107] Ibid

I was sitting in the courtroom taking notes when I heard the judge's instructions and Officer Cadle's response—and I stopped writing. The first surprise was the wording of the judge's instructions. Saying "this person rather than the other person" would indicate the officer had a choice, as though he could only handcuff one person. I would expect any officer to handcuff both parties in this situation, at least while conducting an initial investigation. The next surprise was Officer Cadle's answer, saying that he did not cuff the bouncer because he knew him. I waited for someone to ask Officer Cadle, "If you knew both parties, would neither one be cuffed, or if you did not know either party, would they both be cuffed?" The questions were never asked.

Mr. Hannon hesitated after Officer Cadle's answer, then continued, "Well, as a police officer, if you gather information that suggests to you there's probable cause to believe that someone committed an offense, you have to do something about it, right?"[108] Mr. Rickard objected, and the judge sustained the objection.

Mr. Hannon asked Officer Cadle if he ever worked a "detail" at The Guards while off duty to provide security. Officer Cadle answered, "No, sir."[109] Mr. Hannon followed with, "Have any of the other 2-D officers [i.e., secondary officers] worked a detail at the Guards?"[110] Mr. Rickard objected, and it was sustained.

Continuing, Mr. Hannon asked about a holster.

Officer Cadle: *I believe there was a question about if Mr. Thomas had a holster on him.*
Mr. Hannon: *Did you observe a holster?*
Officer Cadle: *I did.*
Mr. Hannon: *And did you recover that holster?*
Officer Cadle: *I did not.*
Mr. Hannon: *Did anyone recover that holster?*
Officer Cadle: *I don't know who did. I believe it was recovered. I don't know who recovered it.*[111]

After Mr. Hannon finished, Judge Dixon asked, "Sir, where was the holster that you observed?"[112] Officer Cadle responded, "I believe it was on his right hip area."[113]

Officer Robert A. Anderson Jr.

The next witness to testify was Officer Robert A. Anderson Jr. Officer Anderson was with the Metropolitan Police Department, assigned to the Forensic Science Services Division. On the evening in question, he was assigned to the Crime Scene Search Unit. Replying to

---
[108] Ibid, 124-125
[109] Ibid, 125
[110] Ibid
[111] Ibid, 126
[112] Ibid, 127
[113] Ibid

Ms. Sawyer's questions, he said that he responded to the scene, where he took photographs and recovered a handgun from the street. During his direct examination, he identified the gun and photographs he had taken at the scene. Ms. Sawyer yielded for cross examination.

> Mr. Hannon: *Do you know whether Agent Thomas had a holster?*
> Officer Anderson: *Not – I didn't know on the scene.*
> Judge Dixon: *Did you see that anyone recovered a holster at the scene?*
> Officer Anderson: *No, I did not.*[114]

Answering further questions, Officer Anderson said he did not know if Heath had a holster, he saw no holster, and he did not hear anyone talk about a holster.

In fact, no one at the scene found a holster on Heath's person. On the night of the incident, while being booked at the police station, Heath took the holster off and turned it in as part of his property. Later the holster was given to Mr. Hannon, and at the trial, it was the defense that entered it into evidence as Defense Exhibit 102.

After Officer Anderson's cross-examination, the prosecution's case was completed. They would still question defense witnesses, but they had no further prosecution witnesses to call.

The prosecution helped their case when Officer Cadle described Heath as under the influence of alcohol. However, Officer Cadle's answer as to why he only arrested Heath seemed to call his judgment into question, at least from my perspective. Following that with his testimony that a holster was recovered at the scene, later shown to be false, questions an officer's memory.

Witnesses for the Defense

In a somewhat unusual move, the defense presented its first two witnesses, Mr. Spradlin and Ms. Parrott, before offering the motion for judgment of acquittal. At the end of any prosecution, the defense can request a judgement of acquittal if they believe the prosecution has not proven its case. Judge Dixon allowed the delay, saying it was "for purposes of time and efficiency."[115]

Mr. Terry Spradlin

As its first witness the defense called Terry Spradlin, a former co-worker of Ms. Carole O'Connor. He and his wife were in the group with Heath at the Guards.

After a few introductory questions, Mr. Hannon asked, "During the course of the evening, can you say today, with any firm recollection, how much alcohol you saw Agent Thomas drink?"[116] Mr. Spradlin answered, "Not exactly. I know while we ate

---
[114] Ibid, 134-35
[115] Ibid, 171
[116] Ibid, 138

dinner, I had two beers at the barbecue place. And then I know that I had two of those martinis over at the second place that we went to. And I really didn't pay attention to what everybody was drinking, but if somebody had really been tossing back drinks, I would — you know, I would have taken notice to that."[117]

Mr. Hannon asked about the incident at The Guards. "Did there come a point in time when you went out onto the street and you saw Agent Thomas in handcuffs?"[118] Mr. Spradlin answered, "Yes."[119] He did not remember when Heath left the table, and he had his back to the room, so he did not see anything. He said, "I think it was Jane [Jones], came to the table and said that 'Heath is outside in handcuffs.'"[120]

When questioned about the atmosphere and the noise level in The Guards, he said, "Yeah it wasn't loud. I mean, we were having conversation at the table. And I remember a group came in; it must have been a wedding party because they were all – it was a fairly casual place and they were all really dressed up. And I just remember… suddenly the place had twice as many people and it still wasn't crowded, but it wasn't loud. … it was just a casual atmosphere."[121]

> Mr. Hannon: *Mr. Spradlin, did you have enough opportunity to interact with Agent Thomas during the course of that evening to be able to form an opinion as to whether he was intoxicated when you were at the Guards before he left your table?*
> Mr. Spradlin: *Sure. I mean, we – there was [sic] three couples at the table, and we conversed all night.*
> Mr. Hannon: *And what's your opinion as to whether that night Agent Thomas was intoxicated?*
> Mr. Spradlin: *No, he was not.*[122]

When questioned about Heath's mood, he said, "It was fairly upbeat. I mean, we talked a lot about a workout that he and Carol had been doing, … just personal things. I mean, he didn't ask about my children and stuff like that because we had just met. But it was a fairly upbeat evening."[123]

Continuing, Mr. Hannon asked, "Was there anything about Agent Thomas's conduct at all that evening in terms of his behavior that concerned you?"[124] Mr. Spradlin said, "No."[125]

---

[117] Ibid, 138-139
[118] Ibid, 139
[119] Ibid
[120] Ibid
[121] Ibid, 139-140
[122] Ibid, 140-141
[123] Ibid, 141
[124] Ibid
[125] Ibid

Mr. Rickard stood to begin his cross-examination. "Do you recall that Mr. Thomas was drinking beer out of a plastic cup at Old Glory?"[126] he asked. Mr. Spradlin answered, "I – he may have been."[127] Mr. Spradlin was given a copy of his grand jury testimony, Government's Exhibit 32, and after reviewing it he stated he remembered "He [Heath] had a plastic cup of beer."[128]

Moving on to the drink issues at The Guards, Mr. Rickard asked Mr. Spradlin if Mr. Jones and Heath had ordered drinks that, when served, had the wrong type of liquor in them.

Mr. Spradlin: *According to them, yes.*
Mr. Rickard: *And the drink that they were ordering together was Bombay Sapphire, right?*
Mr. Spradlin: *I don't know.*[129]

Mr. Rickard showed Mr. Spradlin Government's Exhibit 17, part of the drink order at the Guards, and asked him to review part of his grand jury transcript. Mr. Spradlin, reading, "It says four Bombay Sapphire, three soda, one Maker's Mark and one Gray Goose. I had the Gray Goose. I think so. I know that at the grand jury testimony they showed me the receipts from Old Glory. I'm not sure – I don't know if I saw that or not."[130] Mr. Rickard then read a question and answer from the grand jury transcript: "'Do you have any recollection as to who it was that was drinking the four Bombay Sapphires?'[131] … 'That was Heath and Dennis.'"[132] Mr. Spradlin confirmed that he had given that answer at the grand jury.[133] Responding to other questions, Mr. Spradlin agreed that they were at the bar for an hour and a half or so, and everyone had two drinks while there.

Mr. Rickard turned his attention to Carole, asking if Mr. Spradlin had received a call from her before he testified at the grand jury, and he said yes.

Mr. Rickard: *And she told you about the questions and answers she had given to the grand jury, didn't she?*
Mr. Spradlin: She *talked about the questions and answers, yes.*
Mr. Rickard: *She told you about the things we would be looking for, the U.S. Attorney's office would be looking for when you testified in the grand jury, right?*

---

[126] Ibid, 144
[127] Ibid, 145
[128] Ibid, 146 and information from grand jury transcript of Mr. Terry Spradlin on October 21, 2010, p 13
[129] Ibid, 149-150
[130] Ibid, 150 and information from grand jury transcript of Mr. Terry Spradlin on October 21, 2010, p 27
[131] Ibid, 150-151 and information from grand jury transcript of Mr. Terry Spradlin on October 21, 2010, p 27
[132] Ibid, 151 and information from grand jury transcript of Mr. Terry Spradlin on October 21, 2010, p 27
[133] Ibid

Mr. Spradlin: *I don't know that she told me specifically, but she said that they really just asked her about the environment stuff; you know, was it loud, was it dark, was it bright. I mean, she really didn't dwell on it a lot...*

Mr. Rickard: *After you talked to her, you had a pretty good idea of what she told the grand jury, right?*

Mr. Spradlin: *Yeah. I mean, I had a good idea of what the grand jury asked her. I don't really recall what she told the grand jury.*[134]

Mr. Rickard went back to Mr. Spradlin's grand jury testimony, reading, "Question: Let me ask you this, after you got done with that conversation with Ms. O'Connor, did you have a pretty good idea of what she had testified to when she came down here?"[135] Mr. Hannon objected, but it was overruled. Mr. Rickard continued, "And that was based on what she told you?"[136] Mr. Rickard, reading Mr. Spradlin's answer: "Yeah." Mr. Rickard then asked Mr. Spradlin if he had been asked those questions in the grand jury and if he answered yes, and Mr. Spradlin said, "Yes."[137]

There were no further questions from the prosecution and no redirect from Mr. Hannon. Judge Dixon then asked a few questions. First, he asked Mr. Spradlin whether he had encountered any problems with the drinks that night, and he said he had not. The judge then asked, "The atmosphere, with respect to whether or not the service was bad or good, as expressed at your table, do you remember there being any concern about the service, or it was just a matter of fact it's not quite what I ordered, please replace it?"[138] Mr. Spradlin answered, "That was pretty much it. I don't think the waitress, or the bartender agreed with them. But they weren't yelling at one another. I mean, it was just a conversation about the drink."[139]

Ms. Angela Parrott

Mr. Spradlin stepped down and the defense called Ms. Angela Parrott, who was an assistant federal defender in Charlotte, North Carolina. At the time of her testimony, she had been an attorney for 17 years and a federal public defender for 15 years. She would serve as a character witness for Heath.

Asked how she knew Heath she said, "We met, I think it was 1999, 2000. We met professionally. He was the agent on a case, an alien smuggling case, and it was a seven-defendant case. And in Los Angeles, the federal public defenders would take material witnesses, and so I represented several material witnesses in the case. And it was a particularly terrible alien smuggling case; in that two of the women – two of my clients

---

[134] Ibid, 152-153
[135] Ibid, 153 and information from grand jury transcript of Mr. Terry Spradlin on October 21, 2010, p 34
[136] Ibid, 153-154 and information from grand jury transcript of Mr. Terry Spradlin on October 21, 2010, p 34
[137] Ibid, 154
[138] Ibid
[139] Ibid, 155

had been gang raped by the men over a period of several days. And one of my clients had part of his ear torn off with pliers by…"[140] Ms. Sawyer objected, and Ms. Parrott continued saying, "—the smugglers." Ms. Sawyer repeated her objection, and the court sustained it.[141]

Ms. Parrott told the court that she had a personal relationship with Heath, and they had dated for several years. She had not seen him since 2002 or 2003, but they did keep in touch.

> Mr. Hannon: *And what is Agent Thomas's reputation in his professional community for truthfulness?*
> Ms. Parrott: *He has a reputation for being truthful.*
> Mr. Hannon: *And do you have a personal opinion as to his truthfulness?*
> Ms. Parrott: *I believe he is very truthful.*
> Mr. Hannon: *What about the characteristic of sobriety?*[142]

Ms. Sawyer objected, and Judge Dixon overruled the objection. Ms. Sawyer asked to be heard, and she approached the bench. She said, "I would just object on the grounds that it's not an appropriate trait for her to be opining on."[143] The judge said, "Considering what the case is about, it's a trait that I'm going to allow the reputation testimony about."[144]

Mr. Hannon again asked Ms. Parrott about Heath's sobriety and she answered, "My opinion is that he, in terms of sobriety, he remains sober. He is sober when we went out, he was sober at work-related functions and in our personal life."[145]

Mr. Hannon asked, "Do you have an opinion as to his reputation for law abidedness [sic]." Ms. Parrott answered, "That he is law-abiding." When asked about whether Heath had any propensity for violent behavior, she replied, "Absolutely not."[146]

Taking the floor to begin the cross-examination, Ms. Sawyer went over questions about Ms. Parrott's relationship with Heath, including the fact that they remained friendly and that she served as an employment reference for him. Ms. Sawyer asked if she had ever gone out with him while they were both drinking, and she said yes. Ms. Sawyer asked if Heath was ever out without her. Ms. Parrott said that when they were dating, she was always with him, except if he was overseas. She said, "When he was in Bosnia, he went out with people, I'm sure. And I don't know what happened there."[147]

---

[140] Ibid, 156-157
[141] Ibid, 157
[142] Ibid, 159
[143] Ibid, 160
[144] Ibid
[145] Ibid
[146] Ibid, 161
[147] Ibid, 163-164

Ms. Sawyer: *And it's your testimony that you've never seen him intoxicated?*
Ms. Parrott: *I have never seen him intoxicated.*
Ms. Sawyer: *And have you ever seen him carry a weapon while off duty?*
Ms. Parrott: *Yes.*
Ms. Sawyer: *You ever see him consume alcoholic beverages with that weapon on him?*
Ms. Parrott: *Twice, yes.*[148]

Ms. Sawyer asked Ms. Parrott if she had a personal interest in the case, and she said she did not.

Ms. Sawyer: *Well, you didn't want this case to even go forward at the beginning, did you?*
Ms. Parrott: *No, I did not. I didn't think it was appropriate.*
Ms. Sawyer: *And you took efforts, you took it upon yourself to take efforts to do your part to see that it wouldn't, didn't you?*
Ms. Parrott: *Yes, I wrote a letter to you.*
Ms. Sawyer: *Well, to me. You wrote a letter directed to Ron Machen, the United States Attorney in the District of Columbia, right?*
Ms. Parrott: *Correct.*[149]

At Mr. Hannon's request, Judge Dixon convened a bench conference. Mr. Hannon explained that Ms. Parrott sent the letter to him at his request, and he never sent the letter to the U.S. Attorney's Office. Mr. Hannon was unsure if she even knew that he did not present the letter. There was a back-and-forth discussion, and Judge Dixon said, "I don't think it really matters whether or not it got to Mr. Machen. It's her addressing the letter to Mr. Machen."[150]

Ms. Sawyer continued her cross-examination. "Ma'am, you directed your letter to Ronald Machen, the United States Attorney in the District of Columbia, correct?"[151] Ms. Parrott answered, "Yes."[152] Ms. Sawyer stated that the letter contained information about Ms. Parrott's relationship with Heath, including her recollections of incidents where she was with him. She added that Ms. Parrott wanted her information to aid the decision process as to whether to charge or not charge Heath. Ms. Parrott said it was all true.

Ms. Sawyer asked, "You also stated that if Mr. Thomas had taken that weapon out of his holster and brandished it, he would have shot the person?" Ms. Parrott answered, "It's my belief."[153]

---

[148] Ibid, 164
[149] Ibid, 165, the letter from Ms. Parrott is Appendix E; it was Government's Exhibit 60.
[150] Ibid, 167
[151] Ibid, 167
[152] Ibid and the letter was written by Ms. Parrott, Appendix E
[153] Ibid, 168

Ms. Sawyer questioned Ms. Parrott whether she used her official letterhead, and she responded that she was not sure. The prosecutor then produced a copy of the letter, which was not on official letterhead, but Ms. Parrott had used her title and work address. Ms. Sawyer asked, "So you took steps to include your professional status in this letter to the United States Attorney, correct?"[154] She replied, "Yes."[155]

On redirect Mr. Hannon asked, "Who requested you to draft this letter?" Ms. Parrott answered, "You did."[156] Answering additional questions, Ms. Parrott said she sent the letter to Mr. Hannon, but she did not know if it was forwarded to the U.S. Attorney.

After Ms. Parrott's testimony, the government rested its case. Judge Dixon then stated that the trial would continue the next day, and they would start with the motion for judgment of acquittal.

It was at that point that Ms. Sawyer raised the issue of the defense experts whom the defense could call. I was in the courtroom at the time, and I was requested to step outside. The discussion covered possible defense experts and what they would be testifying about. Since I did not hear the conversation, the following information is from the transcripts.

Ms. Sawyer said, "Mr. Hannon has expressly declined to give us any information about the field in which he intends to qualify some of these experts, some of which can be gleaned from resumes; obviously, specific details of the contour of that testimony cannot be. And we have no information beyond that."[157] She was arguing that, without any knowledge of what an expert would say, she could not prepare a cross-examination and might request more time to prepare a cross-examination.

Judge Dixon asked Mr. Hannon for an explanation, and he answered that he knew that two of the experts would be called, and he provided their curricula vitae (CVs). He said, "Ms. Sawyer asked me only the subject matter of one of the four experts and I expressly declined to indicate to her the subject area that we might propose that expert in."[158] Mr. Hannon argued that he was not required to provide the information requested "under the rules of reciprocal discovery because we have not asked for discovery of the Government."[159]

What the defense was required to give, what the prosecution wanted, and what the court expected was discussed for some time. The prosecution argued, "There is … case law reports of excluded defense experts based on defense counsel's refusal to provide the materials and the bases for their opinions, under rule 705."[160]

---

[154] Ibid, 169
[155] Ibid,
[156] Ibid, 170
[157] Ibid, 174
[158] Ibid, 175-176
[159] Ibid, 176
[160] Ibid, 176-177

Based on the transcripts, each side seemed to be making good arguments about rules and procedures that fit their positions. What was missing was the need for the facts and evidence that would determine guilt or innocence.

Toward the end of the conversation, Judge Dixon advised Mr. Hannon that if the government requested time to prepare for cross-examination, he would grant it. Mr. Hannon responded, "The Government has set the field of battle for this, not current counsel, but – and that's partly the reason for our taking advantage of our rights under the rules not to have to provide this before. During the trial and accommodating the court's discretion to manage its calendar and the process of the case is a different issue."[161] The court was adjourned for the day and was to resume the following day at 11 A.M.

Later that evening, I received a message from Mr. Hannon asking me if I could be at the courthouse earlier than expected the following morning to meet with the prosecutors. I agreed to do so. I viewed it as an opportunity to explain how the incident could not have occurred as they believed it did and how it could have happened. At that point I still believed Heath would be acquitted if only the truth were allowed to come out. Whether the prosecutors would be open to hearing my expert opinion of the case, I did not know.

---

[161] Ibid, 178-179

9A

Kirk Bloodsworth: The First DNA Exoneration

Mr. Kirk Bloodsworth was the first person in the United States sentenced to death and later freed because of DNA evidence.

In 1984, Bloodsworth was charged with raping and killing a nine-year-old girl in Baltimore County, Maryland. In 1985 he was tried, found guilty, and sentenced to death. Five witnesses testified that Bloodsworth was in the vicinity or with the victim before the crime occurred. Additionally, there was physical evidence connecting a pair of his shoes to marks on the victim's body. He maintained that he was not with the victim, and he was not guilty.

Mr. Bloodsworth appealed the verdict because the state withheld exculpatory evidence. Part of the exculpatory evidence included the existence of a person of interest.

When the authorities were searching for the victim, before the crime was discovered, an individual interviewed in the vicinity of the crime was considered suspicious. The individual was carrying a police officer's nightstick (billy club) and wearing camouflage fatigues. He appeared dirty, except for his very clean hands. It was reported that this individual knew the location of the victims' underwear, which was reported to be hanging in a tree. Additionally, with a consensual search of his vehicle, a pair of child's underwear was found. With the discovery of the underwear the individual appeared nervous and vomited. He said he found the underwear in the woods, days before, and intended to take them home – to his wife or daughter.

Before the victim's body was found, before anyone knew the crime existed, the suspicious person said he hoped they caught the person responsible. A background check on this individual revealed a criminal history of indecent exposure and burglary. The subject underwent a polygraph test related to the crime, and he failed. The police eventually eliminated the individual as a suspect, but the information was never disclosed to the defense.

Because possible exculpatory evidence was not given to the defense, the conviction was overturned. Bloodsworth was retried and convicted again. This time the sentence was reduced to two life terms.

While incarcerated, Bloodsworth read about the new science of DNA, and he believed the science could exonerate him. His legal defense team requested the testing, and in 1992 the test was conducted. The testing excluded him from the crime but did not identify the offender. Bloodsworth was released in 1993 and pardoned by the Governor (a pardon is not an exoneration). He was incarcerated for nine years, which included two years on death row.

In 2003, almost ten years after his release, a DNA match was found. The suspicious person who had found the underwear was not the offender. The perpetrator of the crime was identified as Kimberly Ruffner, who was incarcerated at that time on other charges. He was charged with rape and murder in 2003 and pleaded guilty in 2004, twenty years after the crime. Only after his conviction was Bloodsworth fully exonerated.

When the DNA testing was initially requested, the physical evidence could not be located, and it was thought that evidence was either lost or destroyed. When the evidence was located, it was found in the courthouse, in the judge's chambers. If the evidence had not been found, would Bloodsworth still be incarcerated?

Should the evidence chain of custody procedures, at least in this case, be re-examined? How many other cases are there where the evidence has been lost, misplaced, or destroyed?

References

Rob Warden, Mr. Kirk Bloodsworth, The National Registry of Exonerations, before June 2012, last updated: 10/6/2021 https://www.law.umich.edu/special/exoneration/

Raju Chebium, "Kirk Bloodsworth, twice convicted of rape and murder, exonerated by DNA evidence", subtitled, "After spending two years on death row, Kirk Bloodsworth was cleared by DNA evidence that was nearly destroyed", CNN, June 20, 2000.

Full title: KIRK NOBLE BLOODSWORTH v. STATE OF MARYLAND, Court: Court of Appeals of Maryland, Date published: Sep 3, 1986, Citations Copy Citations, 307 Md. 164 (Md. 1986) 512 A.2d 1056 Bloodsworth v. State, 307 Md. 164 Case text Search + Citator*https://casetext.com/case/bloodsworth-v-state-1*

10

What Time Did the Event Occur, And Why Does It Matter?

"Anyone who doesn't take truth seriously in small matters cannot be trusted in large ones either."

—Albert Einstein

There are occasions when the time of an incident is unknown—usually when there are no witnesses and what occurred could have happened during an extended period. In Heath's case, which includes multiple witnesses and substantial documentary evidence, we should know the time.

What seems uncommon in Heath's trial is the wide range of times given for not only when Heath's party arrived but also when the altercation took place. The multiple times—reported in the grand jury testimony, the ABRA investigative report, the ABRA hearings, and courtroom testimony—span 110 minutes. In Mr. Brackett's written police statement, he said the crime occurred at 12:20 a.m. on August 29, 2010. In the ABRA investigator's report, Mr. Viricochea said the incident happened at 10:30 p.m. However, the official statement of charges gives the time at 23:58 hours, or 11:58 p.m.[1] Could the statement of charges have the wrong time?

When Mr. Viricochea was questioned in the grand jury about the incident occurring on August 28, 2010, just before midnight, he answered, "Yes. It was about 10:30. It was around 10:30 and I was in the back."[2] During the trial, the prosecutor, Ms. Sawyer, asked, "And at some point in time in the evening of August 28, 2010, around 10:30 p.m. did a verbal altercation take place at The Guards Restaurant?"[3] Since the prosecutor gave the time of the incident as being around 10:30, one would think that would be accurate. However, the evidence suggests otherwise.

We know that Heath and his party had dinner at Old Glory restaurant before going to The Guards. The dinner check (Exhibit 13) from Old Glory, in the amount of $270,

---

[1] Superior Court for the District of Columbia, Criminal Division, United States vs. Thomas, Heath Patrick, Statement of Charges, completed by Officer Andelman, MPD, August 29, 2010

[2] Testimony of Mr. Viricochea from his grand jury transcript on September 27, 2010, p 5

[3] Information from the trial transcript, Criminal Action Number 2010-CF3-16079, dated August 16, 2011, p 117-118

What time did the Event Occur, And Why Does It Matter? | 141

Left: Resturant tab from Old Glory, government Exhibit 13,. Above: Three resturant tabs from Old glory (merchant copies) Government Exhibit 14.

Bar Tab from the Guards, Government Exhibit 15.

Bar tab from the Guards, merchant copy, Government exhibit 16.

was closed at 11:02 p.m.[4] From the time on this check, one might conclude that the party was at Old Glory until at least 11:02 p.m., and therefore the crime could not have occurred at 10:30 p.m. This would also indicate that the party did not arrive at The Guards until after 11:00 p.m.

However, that time conflicts with Heath's tab at The Guards, which was opened at 10:17 (Exhibit 15), meaning at least a portion of the group arrived before 10:30. That fact, however, does not support the claim the crime itself took place at 10:30.

The differences can be explained with Exhibit 14, which is three separate checks from Old Glory. When the total check was presented to the group at the restaurant, the check was divided for each couple to pay their portion. The three separate checks

---

[4] Governments Exhibit 13, Case No. 2010 CF3 016079, Old Glory Credit card receipt.

reflected three separate bills that were paid.⁵ The times they were closed were 10:06 p.m., 10:08 p.m., and 10:05 p.m. Since each couple paid their portion of the bill, and given that the last of the three credit card receipts was stamped at 10:08 p.m., the party could have arrived at The Guards, a five-minute walk from the restaurant, at 10:17 p.m., as indicated on Heath's tab.⁶

While exhibit 14 indicates that Heath and his party could have been at The Guards before 10:30 p.m., Heath and Carole believed they arrived at the Guards after 11:00, relying on the Old Glory tab (Exhibit 13) being closed at 11:02 p.m.

But despite all of that confusion, there is one piece of evidence that can most closely confirm the time of the altercation between Heath and Mr. Brackett. The credit card receipt laid on the bar in front of Heath just before he was removed from the establishment was printed at 11:57 p.m., so we know the incident occurred either close to or shortly after 11:57 p.m.

Beyond the paper trail, there are also audio recordings that confirm the time of the incident. When the crime occurred, the Guards manager, Mr. Viricochea, reported it by telephone. He called 911 using a cell phone, and he was on the street in front of the establishment when he made the call. A recording of the call is on a CD labeled "United States v. Heath Thomas, 2010 – CF3 – 16079, Radio Run, Tac Radio run and 911 Call." On the CD, there are four tracks: the dispatching of the call to police units, tactical radio calls, the 911 call, and a short recording explaining that the CD was recorded on September 17, from the records created on August 28, 2010. I believe the CD was intended to be a government exhibit, but I do not have any documentation that it was introduced.

The recordings of the 911 call indicate that the 911 operator had trouble understanding the manager. The operator did understand that the complaint was a man with a gun. The 911 operator asked for a description, and when not answered, the 911 operator asked if the subject was Spanish, if he was white, or if he was black, with no response to the question. The 911 operator also asked for a description of the subject's clothing. Rather than respond to the question the manager kept saying, "Send the police." The description that was eventually given was a "Spanish guy in a black shirt."

During the conversation between the manager and the 911 operator, when the operator was having a problem hearing or understanding Mr. Viricochea, Mr. Viricochea handed his telephone to someone else. The 911 operator asked who they were. The person responded, "My name is Alex."⁷ Alex told the 911 operator that the police had

---

⁵ Governments Exhibit 14, Case No. 2010 CF3 016079, Old Glory Credit card receipt.

⁶ According to Google maps, from Old Glory to The Guards, is around one thousand feet, or 1/5 of a mile.

⁷ Recordings of a CD and labeled: "United States v. Heath Thomas, 2010 – CF3 – 16079, Radio Run, Tac Radio run and 911 Call.

arrived. No one with the name of Alex was listed as a witness or summoned to testify at the grand jury or the trial.

The dispatching call recordings clearly stated, "Man with a Gun" at "2915 M Street NW" at 2358 hours."[8] The dispatcher later gave the time of 2359 hours and then later 2400 hours. The recordings indicate that the officers arrived in less than two minutes, and the responding officers informed the dispatcher that they had someone in custody.

The fact that the time when the incident occurred was known and was reported should not be in dispute. And yet, throughout the grand jury testimony, the ABRA investigation and Alcoholic Beverage Control Board Fact-Finding Hearing, and the court proceedings, the wrong times were used and used frequently. Why would the wrong times be used? Either it was accidental, or it was intentional. In a court of law where everything is examined and scrutinized, why was it not questioned? Was there a motivation to use the wrong times?

An argument could be made that Heath received a fair trial; they just got the time of the incident wrong. But, without a complete understanding of why the wrong time was used, how would you know the trial was fair? Also, if the court was misled or misinformed with something as simple as the time something happened, what else was left out, changed, or misstated, whether unintentionally or intentionally?

It may be significant that the individual who most frequently gave the wrong time of the incident, the manager, is the one who had Heath removed from the premises. It could also be important that the prosecution knew the correct time, but in both the grand jury and the trial, the prosecution allowed the wrong time to be used. On day two of the trial, Ms. Sawyer specifically asked the manager, "And at some point in time in the evening of August 28, 2010, around 10:30 p.m., did a verbal altercation take place at the Guards Restaurant?"[9]

Could there be a motivation for Mr. Viricochea to give the wrong time? When giving the time, he frequently remarked that the cameras were not on yet because he usually turned them on at 10:30. He stated that he was too busy to turn them on because of the number of customers in the restaurant, and he forgot to turn them on.[10]

Hypothetically, let us say you have a business. A government entity regulates the business, and the entity requires the business to have an approved security plan. The security plan requires the business to have security guards and video cameras working when the business has entertainment. The business has entertainment during a weekend evening, an incident occurs at 11:58 p.m., and the required contract off-duty police

---

[8] Recordings of a CD and labeled: "United States v. Heath Thomas, 2010 – CF3 – 16079, Radio Run, Tac Radio run and 911 Call.

[9] Information from the trial transcript, Criminal Action Number 2010-CF3-16079, dated August 16, 2011, p 117-118

[10] Information from the trial transcript, Criminal Action Number 2010-CF3-16079, dated August 16, 2011, p 142

officers are not present. In this scenario, you are the manager, and you believe you may be in some trouble with the regulatory government entity that approved the security plan. Additionally, the business has a poor record with the regulatory entity.

To correct this issue, you might consider going as far as to change the time of the incident to cover up the fact that you did not have the required security police officers working. And, if the camera system were on, you might turn it off to further cover up the time of the incident. Furthermore, if the incident were instigated by the business and not by a customer, turning off the cameras could also hide that fact. Of course, this is hypothetical.

In this case, why would someone change the time of the incident, and what would be his or her motivation to do so? The question was not answered nor even asked in court.

10A

Kristine Bunch: Fabricated Evidence

On June 30, 1995, Kristine Bunch woke up and found her mobile home residence was on fire. Her 3-year-old son, Anthony, was sleeping in the back bedroom, and she was unable to reach him. She immediately went outside, calling for help, as she used a bicycle to break through a window where the child was sleeping.

The fire department arrived quickly, but it was too late to save the child. Kristine told the authorities she awoke to the fire and did not know how it started. Arson investigators said they found accelerant not unlike kerosene in the boy's bedroom and the living room. She was later arrested and charged with arson and felony murder.

Eight months later, the case went to trial. The critical testimony from the prosecution came from two arson investigators. Mr. Brian Frank, a state arson investigator, and Mr. William Kinard, a forensic analyst with the Bureau of Alcohol, Tobacco, and Firearms (ATF). Mr. Frank testified that the fire started in two different places, and Mr. Kinard testified there was "*a heavy petroleum distillate*"[1] in the samples he tested.

The expert for the defense, Mr. Tom Hulse, testified that kerosene would be found in the living room in the vicinity of a kerosene heater, but the cause of the fire was undetermined and that the fire could have been accidental.

On March 4, 1996, Ms. Kristine Bunch was found guilty, and on April 1, 1996, she was sentenced to 60 years for murder and 50 years for arson, the terms to be served concurrently. An appeal was filed on June 9, 1998, which was denied. The Indiana Supreme Court affirmed the conviction citing the testimony of the experts identifying the presence of a "heavy petroleum distillate."

Kristine Bunch knew she was innocent and continued looking for attorneys that would take her case. She eventually hired Hilary Bowe Ricks, an Indianapolis attorney. Ricks enlisted the help of other attorneys along with the Center for Wrongful Convictions at Northwestern University School of Law.

The new legal team subpoenaed and obtained the data from the original investigation from the ATF. According to the documents, the only accelerant found in the home

---

[1] The National Registry of Exonerations, Kristine Bunch case 12-31-2012 www.law.umich.edu/special/exoneration/page

was in the living room in the area of a kerosene heater. The sample in the child's room was negative, contradicting the testimony given at trial.

The defense team filed a petition for post-conviction relief. The petition argued that Ms. Bunch's rights were violated because the evidence in the ATF documents was not available to her. The experts lied when testifying in the trial. This was in 2009. Eight months later, in 2010, the petition was denied.

The defense then filed an appeal to the Court of Appeals in July 2011. In March 2012, the court reversed the conviction saying Bunch was entitled to a new trial, citing the undisclosed ATF evidence contradicting the trial testimony. In August 2012, the Indiana Supreme Court upheld the findings from the Court of Appeals. Ms. Bunch was released after being incarcerated for over 16 years. Later that year, the prosecution declined to re-try her.

Unfortunately, we hear of cases where exculpatory evidence is withheld from defendants. In this case, they did not just withhold evidence that could have impacted the outcome; they created evidence that did not exist. The evidence from the trial that an accelerant was found in the child's room was not true. Giving known false testimony, lying under oath is perjury, and yet I found nothing about the expert(s) being held accountable.

The National Registry of Exonerations, "*University of Michigan Law School database that has cataloged information on more than 1,600 exonerations nationwide since 1989, includes just 148 women.*"[2]

References

Johnny Magdaleno, "She was wrongfully convicted and imprisoned", The Indianapolis Star, October 15, 2020.

Bluhm Legal Clinic Center on Wrongful Conviction, "Kristine Bunch," Northwestern Pritzker School of Law, www.law.northwestern.edu/legalclinic/wrongfulconvictions/exonerations/in/kristine-bunch.html.

---

[2] Bluhm Legal Clinic Center on Wrongful Conviction, "Kristine Bunch," Northwestern Pritzker School of Law, www.law.northwestern.edu/legalclinic/wrongfulconvictions/exonerations/in/kristine-bunch.html.

11

Day 4: An Uphill Battle, an Apology, and Witnesses
AUGUST 18, 2011

"Facts are stubborn things; and whatever may be our wishes, our inclination, or the dictates of our passions, they cannot alter the state of facts and evidence."

—John Adams

Before continuing the trial, Judge Dixon proceeded with the motion for acquittal that Mr. Hannon had submitted on behalf of the defendant. There were two counts of assault with a deadly weapon—the victims being Mr. Marshall Brackett and Cpl. Brandon Holubar. The judge, referring to the motion, counseled Mr. Hannon, "May I suggest to you that you have an uphill battle trying to convince me that the government was required to present some type of expert testimony to prove that – that Mr. Heath was not acting in accordance with his position as a law enforcement officer. And you have an uphill battle to convince me that notwithstanding a claim of – of self-defense, there isn't sufficient evidence of which if I end up believing it, I can conclude that the government has proven beyond a reasonable doubt that the defendant did not act in self-defense."[1]

Before responding to the judge's remarks, Mr. Hannon talked about the day before. He stated, "First, … after 4:45 yesterday, I lost my decorum a bit and I made a comment regarding your request to have us provide notice of our experts … that I think was rude and inappropriate and I apologize for that."[2] Judge Dixon said that an apology was not required.

Mr. Hannon continued, telling the Court that, on the previous evening, he sent reports to the prosecutor's office about the experts and arranged for two of the experts, myself and one other, to meet with the prosecution. He said a re-creation of the incident had been produced on a CD (the re-creation we filmed October 7, 2010), and he would

---

[1] Information from the trial transcript, Criminal Action Number 2010-CF3-16079, dated August 18, 2011, p 4
[2] Ibid

be seeking to have it introduced into evidence. Because the prosecution had not seen the film, he would show it to them during a noon break. He added that he also gave the prosecution copies of the defense attorney's notes.

As he told the judge, Mr. Hannon had called me the night before and said he had arranged for me to meet with the prosecutors at the courthouse so they could learn more about what I might testify to. The meeting was to take place early the following day. I arrived before the meeting time and waited, but the prosecutors never appeared.

Mr. Hannon seemed to be complying with the Court's view of evidentiary rules and judicial regulations for having the video admitted into evidence, although from his arguments the previous day, he believed he was already in compliance. The judge's opinion on the matter was as yet unknown.

The Defense Argues for Acquittal

Mr. Hannon began the argument for acquittal by stating, "Agent Thomas was carrying a weapon. He was authorized to carry a weapon. He became drunk. He went to the bar. He was loud and obnoxious. He used cuss words. Many people heard that."[3] He then explained the surrounding circumstances; Heath was asked to leave, the bar was busy, and he was carried out.

But several facts were still in question, Mr. Hannon argued. One issue was where the bouncer released Heath. Was it at the bottom of the steps, as Mr. Brackett claimed, or in the street, as the other witnesses had described? Another issue was what Corporal Holubar observed in just a fraction of a second when he said he saw Heath's finger on the trigger. Could he have really seen such fine detail in such a short amount of time? Hannon further noted that since the bouncer was also holding or controlling the gun, Heath was not in control of where the gun was pointed. "If one doesn't have control over the weapon, then one can't act on purpose, which is part of the count."[4] Hannon said no one saw Heath draw the weapon, arguing that Heath drawing the weapon was speculation. The weapon could have fallen to the ground or on the hood of a car or could have been tangled in his shirt. He also discussed the officer who testified that he had seen a holster that no one else saw.

While Mr. Hannon was talking, Ms. Sawyer interrupted and apologized, saying, "I think it would be appropriate to have the expert witnesses step out, particularly to the extent that these legal arguments are going to concern what they may say, what the testimony is going to be about."[5] Judge Dixon agreed, and the experts, including me, left the courtroom.[6] At that point Mr. Hannon said the government should have an expert tell the Court what Heath

---

[3] Ibid, 6
[4] Ibid, 7
[5] Ibid, 10
[6] Ibid

was permitted to do to protect his weapon. He also repeated that Mr. Brackett did not have the right to pick Heath up and, in doing so, had assaulted Heath. He said, "And the government said to all restauranteurs and bar owners that if someone is disrupting your premises without otherwise calling the police or engaging any other efforts, you can have someone assault them. With other elements, it could be a kidnapping."[7]

Continuing, he said, "The government has to disprove, as indicated in our pleading, that Agent Thomas believed that he was in imminent danger of bodily harm."[8] He added, if Heath did not believe he was in danger, that would change things, but also, "because a weapon is deadly and he has it on his person and there's someone within hand's reach of that weapon."[9] Essentially, he said the danger existed because there was always danger of losing the gun and having it used against him.

The Prosecution Responds

Mr. Rickard: "Mr. Hannon's argument, again, is kind of advancing two defenses again, which is why we filed a motion in limine in the first place. Either this was a deliberate decision by Mr. Thomas to draw the weapon in some kind of law enforcement role, in which case we can hear from these experts, or it came out accidentally… And, at this time, Your Honor would have sufficient evidence to find beyond a reasonable doubt that the weapon came out deliberately and there's not even self-defense at issue at this point."[10] He continued, "And it's not just me who says that an agent of the premises can remove – use reasonable non-deadly force to remove someone. That's what the jury instructions say."[11] He went on to say that the bouncer first asked Heath to leave, then used a "soft control"—tapping Heath on the shoulder—and only afterward did he pick him up and carry him out. "And once he carried him out, he stepped away from the defendant. That's the record testimony and that's the evidence."[12]

Limine is Latin, meaning "at the threshold," referring to a motion before a trial begins.[13]

This line of argument brings up an important question. If jury instructions allow a bouncer to pick someone up and carry them outside, would not they explicitly define the behavior that would enable those actions? According to the bouncer, he said he did not know why he removed Heath and did not identify himself to Heath.

Following Mr. Rickard's statement, the Court gave its opinion, summarizing the incident as described by the prosecution. Judge Dixon denied the motion to acquit for the first count—the assault against Mr. Brackett—but granted the dismissal on the sec-

---

[7] Ibid, 12
[8] Ibid
[9] Ibid
[10] Ibid, 14
[11] Information from the trial transcript, Criminal Action Number 2010-CF3-16079, dated August 18, 2011, p 14
[12] Ibid, 15
[13] https://legal-dictionary.thefreedictionary.com/Limine

ond count—Corporal Holubar.[14] The judge agreed with Mr. Hannon's argument that Heath did not have complete control of where the gun was pointed, with two people trying to control the weapon.

My perception was that the dismissal of one charge sounded like good news for Heath, it was also a foreboding of the judge's assessment of Heaths guilt on the remaining charge.

Expert Witnesses
With the motion for acquittal decided, Judge Dixon asked whether there were any issues with the experts. Mr. Hannon said that the experts had been available at 10 a.m., but the prosecutors had not had time to talk to them. He said he would not call the experts until after lunch, and the prosecution could speak with the experts during the lunch break.[15]

Ms. Sawyer said that she might have some objections related to the experts and "the timing of that testimony."[16] The judge asked if she meant "whether or not it comes before Mr. Thomas's testimony." Ms. Sawyer answered, "Precisely," and the judge countered, "I foresaw that as one of the issues."[17]

Reading the judge's words after the fact, I found them disturbing. Did Judge Dixon believe that Heath and I would be collaborating in some fashion? If that was his meaning, I should be offended. As a Maryland State Police Officer, if you lie on a police report, you can be fired and for good reason. How can someone believe the testimony of an officer if he or she has lied? Another thought I had was that if Heath did not testify, which was his right, would that mean that I could not testify? I had never heard of an expert in a trial not being allowed to testify until the defendant testifies.

The experts were allowed to re-enter the courtroom and the trial continued. Officer Cadle, one of the MPD officers to respond to the scene, had testified the day before as a witness for the prosecution; he was now called by the defense. His testimony was expected to refute some prosecution testimony.

The second witness the defense planned to call was Ms. Jane Jones, who was with Heath's party on the night of the incident. Agent John Eisert, Heath's supervisor, was also scheduled to testify, followed by Mr. Stanley Huff, a former co-worker of Heath's, and Mr. Anthony Gordon, both as character witnesses.

Officer Jeffrey Cadle
Mr. Hannon asked Officer Cadle if he was the first officer on the scene; he was not sure. When questioned about the broadcast (the radio lookout), he said, "For a man with a gun with a black top."[18] Mr. Hannon asked when and where he first observed Mr. Brack-

---

[14] Ibid, 22
[15] Ibid, 24
[16] Ibid, 25
[17] Ibid
[18] Ibid, 28

ett and Heath. Officer Cadle said he "had a visual of the two gentlemen struggling... in between this vehicle in the street area."[19]

Mr. Hannon asked if the two gentlemen were against or making contact with a vehicle, and Officer Cadle said "no." He said, "They were right in the middle of the vehicles. They were struggling with all their arms in the air. At some point, their arms are pinned against the hood of the car with the hands over the car in that nature."[20] When asked when he first observed the gun, he said, "I observed the weapon as it was on the ground."[21] He did not see the weapon when the arms were in the air or when the arms were pinned against a vehicle.

Officer Cadle said that he never lost sight of the two subjects. Officer Andelman was in front of him, and he heard him say, "Drop the weapon,"[22] after which, he saw the weapon on the ground and then handcuffed the man in the black shirt.

According to Officer Cadle, Sergeant Benton requested Heath's credentials, and because Heath was handcuffed, Officer Cadle removed the credentials from Heath's back pocket. Officer Cadle also said he never saw the credentials on the hood of a car or in the street. Mr. Brackett had testified that Heath took his credentials out of his pocket and showed them to him, but nobody else observed that behavior.

Mr. Rickard had just one question on cross-examination. He asked Officer Cadle, "You don't know what happened to those credentials before you saw them in the defendant's pocket, right?"[23] Officer Cadle answered, "I do not."[24]

Mr. Hannon then stood for redirect. "Did you ever see the man in the black shirt retrieve something from the hood of the Suburban and put it in his cargo pants?" he asked. Officer Cadle answered, "I did not."[25]

The judge asked Officer Cadle about how he looked for or located the credentials. Officer Cadle replied, "I believe he [Heath] said they were in my left rear pocket."[26]

Assuming Mr. Cadle recalled this scene correctly, the fact that Heath's credentials were still in his pocket refutes the statement from Mr. Brackett that Heath had somehow, in the midst of their struggle, shown him is credentials. This question of Mr. Brackett's credibility again went unnoticed.

Ms. Jane Jones

On the night of the incident, Ms. Jane Jones and her husband were one of the couples in the group with Heath. Ms. Jones had worked with Carole O'Connor, but she had never met Heath before that evening.

---

[19] Ibid
[20] Ibid, 29
[21] Ibid
[22] Ibid, 30
[23] Ibid, 32-33
[24] Ibid, 33
[25] Ibid, 34
[26] Ibid, 35

Ms. Jones said that she and her husband had been with Carole, Heath, Terry Spradlin, and his wife, Vicki. She and her husband drove to Georgetown and met the other couples at a restaurant, Old Glory. Her husband drove to the restaurant, and she was to be the designated driver going home. They had dinner, then left the restaurant and were walking down the street. The group did not have any specific plans after leaving the restaurant; at least, that was her belief.

The group stopped at The Guards; she had never been there before. When they entered, they went to the bar. She believed drinks were ordered, and she thought that Mr. Spradlin had a birthday drink. They were only at the bar a few minutes before they moved to an open table directly behind them. Nobody directed them to the table.

Asked about the drinks, she remembered that they had ordered martinis. There were problems with the drinks, and she said that there was an issue with what liquor was in the beverages, vodka, or gin; that the waitress believed they were made correctly, and there was a discussion about it. The waitress reached over her husband to take a drink back, and while taking it from her husband's hand, the drink spilled in his lap.

Mr. Hannon asked what happened after the drink spilled. Ms. Jones answered, "I don't remember how it got – I don't know that it got resolved. She spilled the drink. I can't remember if they brought a fresh drink back. I don't remember."[27] When questioned about her husband's reaction, she said that he was irritated. "There wasn't any anger or yelling. It was irritation because of miscommunication."[28]

Mr. Hannon: *At some point in time, you got up and went outside; is that right?*
Ms. Jones: *Yes.*
Mr. Hannon: *Could you tell the Judge why you did that?*
Ms. Jones: *I saw Carole get up from the table and she ran outside, and so I followed her to see why she ran outside.*
Mr. Hannon: *And when you saw her get up and go out, had you heard any commotion?*
Ms. Jones: *No. I just saw Carole get up.*
Mr. Hannon: *Why did you follow her?*
Ms. Jones: *Because she got up in such a rush. She didn't say anything. She just got up and left.*[29]

Continuing to describe the course of events, she said, "I followed her, my husband followed me, and we stood in the alcove. And once we realized what was going on, my husband said to go back inside."[30]

---

[27] Ibid, 45
[28] Ibid
[29] Ibid, 45-46
[30] Ibid

Mr. Hannon asked about the number of doors at The Guards; she remembered two, with an alcove in between. She remembered the door or doors to the street were open because they had a view of the street. She could not remember if anyone was between her and Carole when she followed her. Once at the second doorway, she could see Heath was against a vehicle with someone behind him.

Mr. Hannon asked about Heath's "mood and demeanor up to that point in the evening when Carole jumped up?"[31] Ms. Jones answered, "He was fine. It was nothing out of the ordinary. We weren't – I mean, we were having a nice night celebrating Terry's birthday. Nobody was belligerent. Nobody was rude. Nobody was…nobody was in bad spirits."[32]

> Mr. Hannon: *Were you in a position to reach an opinion as to whether Agent Thomas was intoxicated when Carole jumped up?*
> Ms. Jones: *No.*
> Mr. Hannon: *Did he appear intoxicated to you?*
> Ms. Jones: *I can't remember.*[33]

Mr. Hannon then asked, "During that evening, did you ever see…a young man, close-cropped hair, about 5' 8", 155, wearing a teal-colored shirt?"[34] The description was of Corporal Holubar. Ms. Jones said that she did; she saw him in the street close to a police car. This was after the police arrived. When questioned if she remembered seeing him earlier, she said "No."

Mr. Hannon asked, "how long approximately did you stay in the alcove observing Agent Thomas?" Ms. Jones answered, "It was a matter of seconds, ten seconds maybe."[35]

Mr. Hannon asked if she heard anyone say anything while she was in the alcove, and she answered, "I can't remember."[36] He asked whether she met or remembered anyone who could have been the manager, and she said that she might have observed him later, standing in the street. After she saw Heath and Mr. Brackett in the street, she went back inside, and she said, "I think we went back to our seat and paid our bill."[37]

Did Ms. Jones and her husband arrive in the doorway to the street before Cpl. Holubar or after Cpl. Holubar? They both said that they stood in the same location.

On cross, Mr. Rickard asked Ms. Jones about her relationship with Carole O'Connor, and she responded that they were not best friends, but they were more than just casual.

---

[31] Ibid
[32] Ibid
[33] Ibid, 48-49
[34] Ibid
[35] Ibid, 50
[36] Ibid
[37] Ibid, 51

Mr. Rickard continued, asking, "Ms. O'Connor had two Maker's Marks at Old Glory, right?" Ms. Jones answered, "I can't remember what she drank."[38]

Mr. Rickard read from her grand jury transcript: "There are two Maker's Marks. Do you recall who was drinking those?"[39] He then read the answer she gave: "I believe that was Carole."[40] He then asked her, "Is that correct?"[41] She responded it was correct.

Mr. Rickard asked about drinks they had at The Guards. Again, she said she did not remember, so he read from her grand jury testimony: "do you recall who was drinking the four Bombay Sapphires?" Answer: "So that would have been my husband and Heath."[42] He asked if that had been her answer, and she said "yes."

Mr. Rickard questioned her about the issues with the drink orders that Mr. Hannon had raised. Was there another problem before the drinks that were made with the wrong liquor? Again, Ms. Jones could not remember. Mr. Rickard asked, "Isn't it true that they both ordered dirty martinis, but the martinis came without olives?"[43] When she answered that she couldn't remember, Mr. Rickard again referred to her grand jury testimony, reading her response: "The first set of martinis that came out were not dirty...so the waitress brought back a glass of olives."[44] She agreed that she had given that answer.

After this exchange, Judge Dixon asked Ms. Jones, "Does that help you remember that that's what happened or you just don't remember now what happened?"[45] She answered, "I don't remember now what happened. This is helpful."[46]

It was clear to me throughout the trial that Mr. Rickard had prepared well, but from my perspective, at times he was overly aggressive in dealing with the defense. The forcefulness of his questions regarding dirty martinis is one example.

Returning to the issue of the drinks made with the wrong alcohol, Mr. Rickard noted that the issue was whether the drinks were made with gin or vodka; he asked her if she remembered which alcohol was supposed to be in the drink. She answered, "I would have to refer back to what I said to the grand jury. I can't remember at this point."[47] After allowing Ms. Jones to review her grand jury transcript, she said, "So they wanted to order gin martinis, but they didn't come out gin martinis. They thought they came out vodka martinis."[48]

---

[38] Ibid, 52
[39] Ibid, 53 and information from grand jury transcript of Ms. Jane Jones, October 22, 2010, p 34-35
[40] Ibid
[41] Information from the trial transcript, Criminal Action Number 2010-CF3-16079, dated August 18, 2011, p 53
[42] Ibid, 54
[43] Ibid, 55
[44] Ibid
[45] Ibid, 55-56
[46] Ibid, 56
[47] Ibid, 57
[48] Ibid

Mr. Rickard then asked about the incident with the spilled drink.

Mr. Rickard: *And you described that process whereby your husband was holding up the drink and the waitress reached for it and it spilled?*

Ms. Jones: *Yeah. He had the drink in his hand…And so she kind of reached over his shoulder and … – it wasn't in his line of sight. … she kind of took it. He didn't realize she was going to take it, and so it kind of dumped in his lap.*

Mr. Rickard: *And you don't know who all it spilled on, correct?*

Ms. Jones: *I couldn't tell you for sure.*[49]

Table is behind the pillar.

At that point Mr. Rickard moved on to ask about the seating at the table. Had she been facing Heath? She answered that she was across the table from him, not directly, but diagonally. He asked, "Do you recall that there was a pillar right here to your right?" And she said, "No. I don't recall one way or the other."[50]

Mr. Rickard: *You followed Ms. O'Connor seconds behind her?*
Ms. Jones: *Yes.*
Mr. Rickard: *And when you came out, you saw the defendant laid out on the hood of the car with someone on top of him and behind him?*
Ms. Jones: *Correct.*[51]

Ms. Jones testified she saw a gun pointing in the air, but she did not hear anyone say anything. She was in the alcove between the two sets of doors (in The Guards' entrance), and she saw Carole in front of her, to her left.

---

[49] Ibid
[50] Ibid, 59
[51] Ibid.

She was asked if she remembered Carole "talking to an older light-skinned white male?"[52] She could not remember and said, "I would have to refresh my memory through the grand jury testimony. I can't recall at this point."[53] After being shown her grand jury testimony, page 19, she remembered that Carole did talk to a light-skinned, older person.

> Mr. Rickard: *After the police were there and the scene was clearing, you asked Ms. O'Connor if she knew what happened that night, didn't you?*
> Ms. Jones: *That night? Yeah, I asked her.*
> Mr. Rickard: *And she said she didn't know what happened, right?*
> Ms. Jones: *I can't remember how she answered.*[54]

Again, the prosecutor used her grand jury testimony, and after doing so, Ms. Jones answered, "She [Ms. O'Connor] didn't know what happened."[55]

Mr. Rickard asked her if Carole had called her the evening before she testified to the grand jury. He also asked if Carole had told her what questions she was asked, the answers she had given, and what questions she should expect. Ms. Jones remembered that Carole did call her and told her about what she was asked, but she did not remember exactly what they talked about. That concluded Mr. Rickard's questioning.

Mr. Hannon, beginning his redirect, asked Ms. Jones to look at page 19 of her grand jury transcript. Mr. Rickard objected, and a bench conference was held. Mr. Hannon said that he was just clarifying a question from the prosecution. Mr. Hannon stated, "Mr. Rickard asserted that she told the grand jury that the man that she saw standing next to her was an older gentleman with light skin. Actually, she was asked, 'Black, white or some other race.'"[56] Mr. Hannon then read her response at the grand jury, "Answer, I would say white. He had light skin."[57] The judge overruled the objection. When Mr. Hannon repeated this to Ms. Jones, she recalled being asked the question and her answer.

Judge Dixon then asked how much time passed between Heath getting up from the table and Carole getting up. Ms. Jones answered, "Five minutes, ten – between five and ten minutes maybe. It wasn't long."[58]

---

[52] Ibid, 60
[53] Ibid.
[54] Ibid, 61
[55] Ibid
[56] Ibid, 63-64
[57] Ibid, 64
[58] Ibid

Judge Dixon: *When you were at the door...looking outside...Did you hear anyone say anything?*
Ms. Jones: *I can't remember, sir.*[59]
Ms. Jones was excused.

Special Agent John Eisert
Before Agent Eisert was sworn in, Ms. Sawyer raised the issue of an agreement. She said that Agent Eisert could testify to certain matters related "to his personal observations the night of the event and not anything – opinions on policy or other policy matters, which he's been expressly precluded by TSA from testifying about."[60] Agent Eisert did not work for TSA, so I assume that was just an error. Like Heath, he worked for the U.S. Immigration and Customs Enforcement (ICE).

The discussion of restrictions on what Agent Eisert could testify to went back and forth for some time, covering multiple pages of the transcript. Judge Dixon finally said, "Let's go ahead and proceed. And if you end up having an objection as we proceed or if the agent raises an objection, we'll stop, and that'll be a good time to recess for lunch."[61]

Mr. Hannon asserted, "While the agent is coming, since we're having this anticipatory discussion, Agent Eisert was asked policy questions and expert questions by government counsel in its prosecution case, which I'm explicitly forbidden to ask him in this courtroom. I just wanted to make that point."[62]

Once sworn in, Agent Eisert introduced himself and gave his current position as the National Security Chief for U.S. Immigration and Customs Enforcement.[63] He had been an agent since 1996, and Heath worked for him in an acting supervisory position.

On the night of the incident, Agent Eisert responded to a notification by the Second District of the Metropolitan Police Department. He had received a call from the ICE Duty Agent, saying that Heath was involved in something and was being held at the police station. He said that he was not on official business, he was not ordered to go, and he volunteered to go. He responded as a co-worker and supervisor, not as an investigator. He arrived at the police station shortly before 2:00 a.m.

When he arrived, he met several officers whom he believed included the arresting officer, the incident commander, and the detective investigating the incident. He asked to see Heath, and the request was granted.

He saw Heath twice that night, the first time for an estimated 30 minutes and the second time for just a few minutes. During the first meeting, Heath was in a cell, seated on a bench, facing the opposite cell wall. Agent Eisert was three or four feet away, standing and facing Heath's left side.

---
[59] Ibid, 66
[60] Ibid, 67
[61] Ibid, 70
[62] Ibid
[63] Ibid, 71

> Mr. Hannon: ... *Now, during that 30 minute time period did you have an opportunity to form an opinion as to whether Agent Thomas was intoxicated?*
> Agent Eisert: *I had formed my own opinion, sure.*
> Mr. Hannon: *And what was that opinion?*
> Agent Eisert: *He did not appear to be intoxicated.*
> Mr. Hannon: *And did – in assessing Agent Thomas at the time…was there anything about his articulation, anything about the coherence of his sentences or grammar or anything else that suggested to you he might be intoxicated?*
> Agent Eisert: *No.*[64]

Ms. Sawyer, on cross-examination, asked if Heath had been on duty that day, and Agent Eisert said "no." Mr. Hannon objected, and the judge overruled the objection.

Ms. Sawyer asked about the physical positions of Agent Eisert and Heath while they were meeting. Agent Eisert said he was standing outside of the cell. Heath was seated on a bench in the cell next to the cell bars but was facing the opposite cell wall. So, Agent Eisert was looking at the left side of Heath's face as Heath was looking forward. Ms. Sawyer also asked when Agent Eisert first saw Heath; it was "sometime around 1:30 a.m. on August 29; is that right?"[65] Agent Eisert agreed.

> Ms. Sawyer: *And so given that physical positioning, you weren't in a very good spot to detect whether he had any alcohol on his breath at that point, were you?*
> Agent Eisert: *I guess it would depend how strong the smell would have been, but I can tell you I did not smell any alcohol.*
> Ms. Sawyer: *Okay. And so the whole time that you were talking to him, he's looking ahead and you're looking at his profile?*
> Agent Eisert: *Correct.*
> Ms. Sawyer: *Okay. And, again, he remained seated the entire time. You never saw him walking around at all?*
> Agent Eisert: *That's correct.*
> Ms. Sawyer: *And the – the meeting that you had with him the first one, didn't last really any longer than 20 minutes, did it?*
> Agent Eisert: *I had just said a half-hour, 20 minutes to a half-hour. I couldn't be – on exact time.*[66]

Ms. Sawyer, with permission from the Court, approached the witness and handed him his transcript from his grand jury testimony.[67] Agent Eisert was directed to page

---

[64] Ibid, 76
[65] Ibid, 78
[66] Ibid, 79-80
[67] Ibid, 81 and information from grand jury transcript of Agent Eisert, March 11, 2011, p 21

21 and said, "I testified in the grand jury to 20 minutes, so I would say that's about accurate."[68]

> Ms. Sawyer: . . . And it's true that you did most of the talking during that meeting, right?
> Agent Eisert: I did.
> Ms. Sawyer: He didn't say a whole lot to you, did he?
> Agent Eisert: He didn't say a whole lot, no.
> Ms. Sawyer: But you did note something special about his demeanor, didn't you, that night?
> Agent Eisert: Yes.
> Ms. Sawyer: And you noted that it was – that it was somehow abnormal, it wasn't right?
> Agent Eisert: I think I described it as stone face.
> Ms. Sawyer: And it wasn't what you were accustomed to seeing from him; is that right?
> Agent Eisert: That is correct.
> Ms. Sawyer: And that he seemed kind of out of it?
> Agent Eisert: Yes.[69]

With the cross-examination concluded, the Court recessed for lunch.

* * *

After the break, before the testimony resumed, Mr. Rickard addressed the Court: "for the record, Mr. Hannon provided us with his laptop over the lunch break and has asked us not to – to leave the sound off while we watched the video at issue, which we did."[70]

This was the video to which Mr. Hannon had referred that morning. The video, made on October 7, 2010, included a demonstration and an explanation of how Heath's gun could have been dislodged when the event occurred.[71]

The proceedings returned to Agent Eisert's testimony.

Agent Eisert's Redirect

Mr. Hannon began by asking about Agent Eisert's impressions on the night of the incident, specifically of Heath's demeanor, that was in his grand jury testimony.

> Mr. Hannon: Were you asked other demeanor questions [at the grand jury]?
> Agent Eisert: Yes.

---

[68] Information from the trial transcript, Criminal Action Number 2010-CF3-16079, dated August 18, 2011, p 81
[69] Ibid, 81-82
[70] Ibid, 86
[71] Chapter 1, Demonstration video, Alexandria, VA, October 7, 2010

> Mr. Hannon: *And are you refreshed as to what other testimony you gave regarding Agent Thomas's demeanor?*
>
> Agent Eisert: *Yes.*
>
> Mr. Hannon: *And could you tell the Court what that testimony was?*
>
> Agent Eisert: *I testified what Heath looked like to me and the brief conversation that we had. And that demeanor was, one, that Heath was a little concerned about his job at the time.*
>
> Mr. Hannon: *And, specifically, with respect to the section of the transcript that I showed you, did you use a euphemism to describe what you thought his mental processes were in that testimony?*
>
> Agent Eisert: *Yeah. I could almost see a thousand thoughts running through Heath's mind and even made an action that he—*[72]

Before he could complete his response, the prosecution objected. Mr. Hannon said to Agent Eisert, "I don't want to hear the action. I want to know what your metaphor was for what you thought was his mental process?" Agent Eisert answered, "That he thought his career was going poof."[73]

Mr. Hannon directed Agent Eisert to the first three lines on page 21, asking, "And what was the metaphor that you used for what you thought his demeanor was?" Agent Eisert answered, "His wheels were turning in his head." Mr. Hannon continued, "Meaning that he was thinking?" Agent Eisert answered, "Correct."[74]

Mr. Hannon continued, "In your grand jury testimony, were you asked questions about the ICE firearms policy?"[75] Ms. Sawyer objected. Mr. Hannon argued that he wanted to know if Agent Eisert had been asked, hypothetically in the grand jury, "what he would have done in the same circumstance that Agent Thomas found himself in in this case."[76] The judge asked if this would end his questioning. Mr. Hannon answered, "It would because I'm prevented by the instructions of Homeland Security to elicit the testimony that he gave in the grand jury and to elicit from him what he told the prosecutors." Judge Dixon answered, "I think the record will reflect that to the extent you want to litigate it in any other form."[77] That ended the redirect questions from the defense.

Next, Judge Dixon asked Agent Eisert some questions about his description of the physical setting when he saw Heath on the night of the arrest. He asked, "You said… when you spoke to Mr. Thomas you were viewing him from the side?" Agent Eisert answered, "Yes, sir." The Judge continued, "That seems a little odd to me, did it seem

---

[72] Information from the trial transcript, Criminal Action Number 2010-CF3-16079, dated August 18, 2011, p 89-90
[73] Ibid, 90
[74] Ibid
[75] Ibid, 92
[76] Ibid, 92-93
[77] Ibid, 93

odd to you at that time?"[78] Agent Eisert responded, "No," and explained how the bench in the cell was positioned, continuing with, "if Heath wanted to see me face-to-face, he would have to turn his head to view me...I just saw the wheels turning, his thought process, and that was my assumption of his demeanor."[79]

Before Agent Eisert stepped down, Mr. Hannon asked if he could follow up on the judge's questions, and it was permitted. Mr. Hannon asked Agent Eisert, "Is it fair to say that you were giving Agent Thomas personal advice?" Agent Eisert answered, "Yes." Mr. Hannon continued, "And that he was thinking about it?" Agent Eisert again answered, "Yes."[80]

Special Agent Stanley Huff
The next witness for the defense was Special Agent Stanley Huff. Agent Huff worked for U.S. Customs and Border Protection; he was assigned to the Internal Affairs Office. Agent Huff's law enforcement career started in Arizona as a deputy sheriff. In 1995, he became a federal law enforcement officer, and a short time later, he met Heath. They worked together for the former Immigration and Naturalization Service and were assigned to the violent gang task force in Los Angeles.

Mr. Hannon asked, "Did circumstances arise in your professional relationship with Heath Thomas where you had an opportunity to form an opinion as to his character for peace and good order...?" Agent Huff answered, "Yes, on several occasions."[81]

Agent Huff said working for the violent gang task force, he and Heath coordinated their activities with the Los Angeles Police Department. They often encountered armed gang members, and they participated in a lot of foot chases. Agent Huff added, "I quickly determined that he ... had uniformed law enforcement experience before and that he was always very calm. And that's why I wanted to work with him because he would inject that calm into very tense situations ... So I could count on – on his reactions."[82]

Mr. Hannon asked, "And what is your opinion as to Heath Thomas's character for peace and good order?"[83] Mr. Rickard objected, and it was overruled. Agent Huff responded, "Well, I'd say that he acts appropriately. He's very stoic...And so a lot of the newer folks looked to him for guidance. And he would ... instead of retching up verbally or things of that nature that would increase the potential reactions of a suspect, he would just engage them, control the situation, and talk to them just like a human being. And it was ... a calming effect."[84]

---

[78] Ibid
[79] Ibid, 93-94
[80] Ibid, 95
[81] Ibid, 98
[82] Ibid, 99
[83] Ibid, 100
[84] Ibid, 100

Mr. Hannon continued, "In the course of your professional relationship with Heath Thomas, have you been able to form a personal opinion as to his character for truthfulness?"[85] Ms. Sawyer objected, and it was overruled. Agent Huff answered, "Well, based on my experience with Mr. Thomas, he's – he's very honest."[86]

Ms. Sawyer objected again, and it was again overruled. Agent Huff continued, "And there's never been any sort of — not even a rumor or anything I've heard of where it would question the veracity of his testimony."[87]

Mr. Hannon asked, "And are you in a position to have an opinion as to his character for sobriety?"[88] Ms. Sawyer objected, it was overruled, and Mr. Hannon repeated the question. Agent Huff said he did have an opinion and that he had been out with Heath on several occasions, stating, "I have had on a couple of occasions when we were out of state in Georgia and in a controlled environment, yes, we imbibed in alcoholic beverages. But it's – like I said, he's so stoic I – I've never noticed him to lose control or, you know, anything like that."[89]

Ms. Sawyer's cross-examination was brief. She noted that Agent Huff and Heath had only worked together for about a year and a half and that most of their contact was work-related. She asked, "And you didn't go out a whole lot during that period, so you only drank with him on a few occasions?" And he answered, "That's correct." She then asked, "Did you ever see him drink with his weapon?" He answered, "No."[90]

Mr. Hannon, standing for redirect, asked Agent Huff, when they were out and had drinks, did he ever ask Heath if he were carrying a gun, and Agent Huff said, "No."[91]

Agent Anthony Gordon

The next defense witness called was Mr. Anthony Gordon. Agent Gordon was a detention and deportation officer with U.S. Immigration and Customs Enforcement. He was assigned to the national Joint Terrorism Task Force (JTTF). Agent Gordon had been in law enforcement for almost 14 years, and he worked with Heath in several different areas. He had remarkably high regard for him.

> Mr. Hannon: ... *In the circle in which you've gotten to know Agent Thomas, have you been able to form a personal opinion as to his character for truthfulness?*
> Agent Gordon: *Yes, I have.*
> Mr. Hannon: *And what's your opinion?*

---

[85] Ibid
[86] Ibid, 101
[87] Ibid
[88] Ibid.
[89] Ibid, 102
[90] Ibid, 104
[91] Ibid, 105

Agent Gordon: *I believe that Agent Thomas has incredibly high integrity and character. I've never had any issues with his – him being untruthful.*[92]

Mr. Hannon: *Have you been able to observe whether Agent Thomas has a character for a temper?*

Agent Gordon: *I've never seen Agent Thomas have any temper. ... we've been in some incredibly stressful situations. It's not life or death, but working inner agency missions can be pretty difficult, being pushed and pulled either way. I've never seen Heath lose his temper. When a friend of ours died in Pakistan, he was not –*[93]

Ms. Sawyer objected, and it was overruled. Agent Gordon continued, "When a friend of ours passed away in Pakistan, Heath wasn't mad. He didn't focus his energy in that direction. He goes into problem solving mode trying to get people together. So, no, I've never seen him mad."[94]

Ms. Sawyer stood for her cross-examination. Although she appeared to be a relatively new lawyer, Ms. Sawyer's presentations were respectable, and she carried herself well. To begin the questioning, she reviewed Agent Gordon's work history and then focused on the nature of his relationship with Heath.

Ms. Sawyer: *... And you'd classify your relationship with him largely professional, right?*

Agent Gordon: *I would – I would consider him a friend but I —*

Ms. Sawyer (interrupting): *But you don't socialize with him extensively outside of work?*

Agent Gordon: *Not extensively outside, no.*

Ms. Sawyer: *... So you haven't been in a position to see him, for example, in a bar on a weekend?*

Agent Gordon: *I've been to social occasions... international affairs where there are beverages — alcoholic beverages served through work function.*[95]

Agent Gordon stepped down.

The character witnesses for Heath seemed to be effective in portraying Heath in a positive light. As strange as it may sound, although Heath was later found guilty, I think Judge Dixon believed the witnesses' descriptions of his character.

---

[92] Ibid, 109
[93] Ibid, 110
[94] Ibid.
[95] Ibid, 111-112

11A

A Dangerous Situation

While writing this book, I recalled an event from many years ago that was like Heath's case. A former state trooper and coworker of mine, Dan Seiler, experienced losing his off-duty gun while out at a restaurant. He writes the story.

* * *

My Encounter with the Pagan Motorcycle Club
By Dan Seiler
What started out as a birthday celebration for my wife, Peggy, turned into a shooting incident with a member of the Pagan Motorcycle Club. I had recently graduated from the Maryland State Police Academy and was enjoying some time off duty between Christmas and New Year's. I was a rookie with the Maryland State Police and had not even checked into my first duty assignment. Although a new trooper, I had several years of law enforcement experience. I had previously worked for the Baltimore City Police Department for about 13 months. I was also a former decorated combat-tested Marine. I served my country for 13 months in Vietnam. In my last year in the United States Marine Corps, I was assigned as a military police officer stationed at Andrews Air Force Base. I received firearms training in all of my current and previous positions. I carried an off-duty weapon, a Colt Cobra five-shot .38-caliber revolver, with me just about everywhere I went. I holstered the weapon with an inside-the-belt, clip-on type of holster.

My evening began peacefully but would turn tragically dangerous before the night was over. That January 29 we were celebrating my wife's 21st birthday, and as a birthday gift to her, we went to the Mechanic Theater in Baltimore City to see a musical play. We were joined by two close friends, Marty and Christine Scutt. Marty and I had become good friends while we were in Baltimore City Police Academy. We lived within a couple of blocks of each other. Marty was at the time a uniformed Baltimore police officer.

After the theater, on our way home, we decided to stop at the Patapsco Inn for a beer and pizza. The Patapsco Inn was located on Route 648 just inside the Baltimore County line. I had been inside the establishment two or three times in the past. The bar was known as a safe police bar and a place where a lot of off-duty police officers frequented.

As we entered the bar, we noticed that it was extremely crowded, but there was one table near the back of the establishment available. Our eyes took a few minutes to adjust to the dark lighting. This made it slightly difficult to make our way through the crowd to the empty table. Peggy and I followed Marty and Christine to the table. After the ladies were seated Marty and I went to the bar to get a couple of draft beers. This couldn't have taken more than about five minutes. Marty got his beers first and disappeared into the crowd as he returned to our table. I got my two draft beers, and as I returned to our table, I noticed that Christine and Marty were not there, and Peggy was standing next to her chair. I set the beers on the table and asked Peggy where Marty and Christine went to. The music was very loud and it was difficult to communicate. As I talked with Peggy, I became aware of my surroundings and noticed that there was a large group of unruly male individuals seated close to our table. I could clearly see that they were members of the Pagan Motorcycle Club, an outlaw motorcycle gang, because they were wearing the gang's colors.

Suddenly, I saw my wife push a hand away from her body. The hand belonged to one of the Pagans seated at the table next to ours. After Peggy rebuffed the individual, he stood up quickly. With interlaced strong profanity he stated, "if I wanted to fuck you, bitch, I'd do it right here on the table." I immediately stepped between the individual and Peggy, advising the person that I was a police officer. I warned him that if he continued his behavior, I would arrest him. Without warning, the individual took a roundhouse swing at me, which I avoided easily. I countered his assault with a sharp jab to his jaw, knocking him to the floor. Almost instantaneously, I found myself in a fight with five or six Pagans. I was able to defend myself until I was struck on the back of my head with a bottle. This blow caused me to drop to the floor on my knees. I could feel my off-duty weapon fall from my waist holster. I looked down and saw my gun on the floor within reach. By this time, I had suffered several major blows and was concerned that I would not survive many more. I dove for my weapon, turned, and noticed an individual standing about a foot or two from me with his hand in his pocket. In my mind it could only have been a weapon he was trying to pull from his pocket. From the floor shooting up at a sharp angle, I discharge one round that I thought struck the individual directly in the center of his chest. The blast knocked the individual down, and I could clearly see that he was holding a pistol. Without much thought, I used a pistol take-away maneuver, secured the weapon, and handcuffed the individual. I did not see any signs of injury as I stood him up from the floor. I later learned that my bullet went through his jacket but never hit his body.

As I began to walk the arrested individual out of the establishment, I saw Marty return with his weapon drawn. I told the bartender that I was a Maryland State Police

Officer and requested that he call the police. I took the individual outside and waited for the police to arrive. While we waited outside, one of the other Pagans who had assaulted me approached and objected to the arrest of his friend. I later learned that his friend was the president of the local Pagan Motorcycle Club. This person doing the objecting was the club's sergeant-at-arms. Without hesitation, I arrested the second individual and by the time a uniformed police officer arrived, I had two people in custody.

One thing I learned from this ordeal was that I would never again use a clip-on, inside-the-belt holster. I learned the hard way that my gun was not going to stay in this holster in a physical struggle. Had I not quickly recovered my weapon the outcome of my story might have been very different.

*   *   *

As a firearms instructor, I have heard numerous stories of problems with holsters and weapon retention. The concealable holster worn by Dan Seiler was not that different from the one worn by Heath, with the exception that the one Heath was wearing had a snap closure to keep it attached to his belt.

Dan's story is not unique because his gun came out. It is unique because he had to use it.

Shannon Bohrer

12

Day 4, Continued:
Not Trusted Before You Testify
AUGUST 18, 2011

The first half of day four had mixed results. The charges related to Corporal Holubar were dismissed, and the judge heard positive comments about Heath from character witnesses, but I had a feeling that no matter what I said as Heath's expert witness, Judge Dixon's decision was already made. As it turned out, my testimony was postponed, and the reason given was not good.

The Next Witness
Mr. Hannon told the Court that he was calling Shannon Bohrer (me) as the next witness. However, Ms. Sawyer said, "Your Honor, I think we need some discussion before we get to this witness."[1] I was asked to leave the courtroom.

The next *fourteen pages* of the trial transcript were devoted to the courtroom discussion of why I should or should not testify at that time. Ms. Sawyer said that the prosecution was not ready. She noted that Mr. Hannon had given the prosecution reports on the experts at 9 p.m. on the previous evening. She expected to have some objections to testimony on various subjects. She also mentioned the timing of my testimony, as Heath had not yet testified.

In addition, Ms. Sawyer was concerned about the video Mr. Hannon had provided, which the prosecution had viewed only that day. She said that they had not had time for their potential expert to review it. She said, "So I think that that's even a threshold matter before we get into arguments about excluding experts and excluding areas of testimony."[2]

Judge Dixon voiced his concern that Heath might not testify, noting, "And so your threshold issue has to do with the timing of their testimony."[3]

Mr. Hannon countered, "The government had no right to any of the information that was provided to them."[4] The Court did not order him to share the materials with the prosecution, he said, and the experts had been made available to the prosecutors that morning before the

---
[1] Ibid
[2] Ibid, 114
[3] Ibid
[4] Ibid, 116

trial started. He added that the prosecutors did not take the time to meet with the experts.

Judge Dixon reiterated his concern that Heath, although scheduled to testify, could also decide not to testify.

> Judge Dixon: ... *In the absence of his testimony, I cannot conceive at the moment how these expert witnesses are going to be of assistance to me based on the record that's developed so far.*
>
> Mr. Hannon: *The foundation* [of the expert's testimony] *is what they have viewed in the case plus the testimony —, what he told them—*
>
> Judge Dixon: ... *That's my point, what he told them. It's not in this record.*
>
> Mr. Hannon: ... *There is no grounds to prevent in limine an expert for — who's testifying in a criminal case who has interviewed the defendant ...*
>
> Judge Dixon: *Here's my concern, this witness is going to be offering exculpatory testimony from your client, which you know is not permissible at this point.*
>
> Mr. Hannon: *I'm sorry, Your Honor. He's going to be rendering an opinion. And his opinion is going to be based in part – in part on information that he has received from Agent Thomas. And he will illustrate that with Agent Thomas in a video that we've made available to the government.*[5]

Mr. Hannon continued, "Now, I – from a conceptual standpoint, Your Honor, you know that the information upon which an expert relies doesn't have to be evidence in the case. You also know that evidence which an expert relies, which is evidence in the case, doesn't have to be presented. It can be presented by hypothetical. Or if it's documentary evidence, it can be given to the expert ahead of time and the fact finder gives it such weight as it deems appropriate. But the information upon which the expert relies doesn't have to be in evidence at all."[6]

Judge Dixon responded, "I'm not going to allow these witnesses to testify before the foundation is presented through your witness ... You're going to have to present him first before I hear from those other witnesses."[7]

Although these are only excerpts from the fourteen pages, from my perspective, it is a fair account of the full breadth of the discussion.

I was not called to testify on that day.

The last two witnesses for the defense to be called this day were Detective Keith Tabron and Lieutenant Antonio Charland, both MPD officers. At the end of the day, I believed the testimony of both officers was helpful to the defense.

Detective Keith Tabron

The next defense witness called was Detective Keith Tabron. Detective Tabron was assigned to the Second District in Washington. He responded to the scene on the night

---

[5] Ibid, 117-118
[6] Ibid, 119
[7] Ibid, 121

of the incident and was responsible for the investigation. He said, "My role was to investigate an assault that just took place at that location."[8]

Detective Tabron said he was with Heath at the Second District police station for about 15 to 20 minutes that evening, "To attempt to interview with him in reference to the event that had taken place earlier."[9]

> Mr. Hannon: ... *During the course of that interview, did you observe any evidence that Agent Thomas was previously drinking alcohol?*
> Detective Tabron: *Not to my knowledge.*
> Mr. Hannon: *During that interview, did you smell alcohol?*
> Detective Tabron: *No I didn't.* [10]

Mr. Hannon offered the video (a DVD) of the interview with Heath at the police station, as Exhibit 100, and he provided a transcript of the interview. He said that the transcript of the interview was being offered "for the purpose of simply of allowing the Court to follow it because of the sound...to assist the listener in following it."[11] Mr. Rickard objected.

> Mr. Rickard: *Your Honor, this is another attempt to get the defendant's statements into evidence without him testifying. They are not admissible to hearsay.*
> Mr. Hannon: ... *The purpose of our presenting this is to allow the Court to see the same thing that Detective Tabron saw when he did not see any evidence of alcohol ingestion by ... Agent Thomas and for the Court to ascertain what his demeanor was shortly after this incident. We're not presenting this for the Court to rely upon any of his statements made. In fact...Mr. Rickard, I think, is aware that there was nothing in there either exculpatory or inculpatory.*
> Judge Dixon: *Is the event discussed?*
> Mr. Hannon: *No.*
> Mr. Rickard: *I disagree with that assertion.*
> Judge Dixon: *Is there a portion of the interview where just personal information is being obtained?*
> Mr. Hannon: *It's a discussion back and forth as to whether he's going to make a statement about the incident, whether he's going to assert his rights under Miranda. And, to us, it's very important for the Court to be able to see the demeanor of the defendant very shortly after this incident.* [12]

---

[8] Ibid, 127
[9] Ibid, 128
[10] Ibid, 128-129
[11] Ibid, 129
[12] Ibid, 130-131

Mr. Rickard explained why the transcript should not be used, and since the interview took place later in the night, he objected to the relevance. After some discussion, Mr. Rickard finally conceded: "I think up to the point where there's the advice of rights, that would be fine."[13]

Mr. Hannon said, "Judge, I'll sit down and let him [Mr. Rickard] read the transcript because the Court asked him to point out specifically what he is concerned about."[14]

The back and forth continued (covering more than seven pages of transcript) between the prosecution and defense without reaching any agreement on the film or transcript.

Judge Dixon finally said, "All right. Let me take a look at the transcript. I'll tell you what I'll permit you to play."[15] Ms. Sawyer asked to be heard, saying, "There does… come a point where there's some discussion about experience training, et cetera, that I don't think we need to get into. … I don't think that the Court needs much of this, honestly, to see demeanor and hear voice and tone and whether he's slurring or not."[16]

The exchange continued, with the prosecution relenting to allow the tape to play until the fourth question.

Mr. Hannon: *Your Honor, I just wanted to let Your Honor know where you needed to begin to determine what part of the video is acceptable to the Court. I believe it's all acceptable after that, and I've asked the government to try and point out specific things and they just say it's the whole thing.*

Mr. Rickard: *And also, for the record Exhibit 99 [the transcript] is the first time I've seen it. I've watched the tape. I didn't notice anything inaccurate but… I will accept defense counsel's transcript for now. But I reserve the right to examine it and would ask for a copy of it later.* [17]

Judge Dixon responded, "All right. I'm going to listen and watch the whole video. Go ahead and play it."[18]

The video, which was about 20 minutes long, began with Heath coming into the interview room, followed by Detective Tabron entering the room. They both sat at a small table. There was some small talk between the two, and Detective Tabron then read Heath his rights. When asked if he wished to answer questions without a lawyer, Heath said, "No." But Heath also added that he wanted to talk. At one point Heath said, "Part

---

[13] Ibid, 132
[14] Ibid
[15] Ibid
[16] Ibid, 134
[17] Ibid, 135-136
[18] Ibid, 136

of me is like; you know you were just trying to do the right thing. The other part of me knows that certain things have to be done in a certain way, so…a bit of confliction."[19]

On the tape, Heath displayed good behavior; he was not fidgety, appeared calm, was polite, and appeared to be sober. At one point during the interview, Heath said, "I will say this, I have been a lot of places, done a lot of things, this, where I showed restraint … Interesting."[20]

Detective Tabron said, "I suggest you make whatever decision you want, but we don't have to have this conversation." Heath replied, "Should not have had this meeting at all."[21]

The argument for not showing the tape was to prevent statements about the incident from being entered into evidence without testimony, and yet the incident was not discussed. I expected Judge Dixon to say something to the prosecuting attorneys, but he was silent. If Hannon had misled the court, I would have expected Judge Dixon to have admonished him in some way.

Following the airing of the video, Mr. Rickard took up his cross-examination, asking, "What was the time of the offense?" Detective Tabron answered, "I have that at 23:58 hours."[22]

It was nice to hear the prosecution ask a witness what time the crime occurred and hear a witness give the correct time.

Lieutenant Antonio Charland
At the time of the incident, Lt. Charland was assigned to the Second District, and he responded to the scene at The Guards Restaurant.

> Lt. Charland: *There was a request from Sergeant Benton that they had an individual there for an assault with a deadly weapon. And there was a law enforcement officer as one of the suspects. The seriousness of the case, I responded to the scene.*
> Mr. Hannon: *… what was your purpose for being there?*
> Lt. Charland: *Overall supervision, ascertaining the facts of the case, make sure everything was handled detective-wise. Certain things happen with clubs in the Second District that we do have an ABRA investigator respond, look for videotape of anything that may have happened just to make sure that everything was overseen and taken care of.*[23]

---

[19] Transcript of Agent Thomas Interrogation, August 29, 2010, 0242 hours, 2nd district DC Metro Police Station, U. S Government Exhibit 99 Case No, 2010, CF1 018988, U. S. v. Heath Thomas.
[20] Ibid
[21] Ibid
[22] Information from the trial transcript, Criminal Action Number 2010-CF3-16079, dated August 18, 2011, p 142
[23] Ibid, 144

Lt. Charland said that there were obligations and procedures when investigating an offense at ABC-licensed establishments like The Guards.

> Mr. Hannon: *And what are those procedures?*
> Lt. Charland: *Well if there's a bouncer involved or an employee or management of a club, we respond to the scene and see if, one, if there's videotape surveillance, try to get witness investigation; get an ABRA investigator to the scene depending on the type of offense or incident. It depends on whether the ABRA investigator responds. This being an assault with a weapon, the ABRA investigator did respond. And I just more oversee the operation. I don't particularly talk to the ABRA investigator or the people involved. I just make sure that those proper people are notified.* [24]
> Mr. Hannon: *Did you ask about the conduct of the bouncer?*
> Lt. Charland: *I attempted to, yes.*
> Mr. Hannon: *What do you mean "attempted to"?*
> Lt. Charland: *I attempted to interview the defendant in this case and his girlfriend about the conduct and other witnesses about the conduct of the bouncer to no avail.*
> Mr. Hannon: *Lieutenant, did you also inquire of your officer regarding the conduct of the bouncer?*
> Lt. Charland: *I don't recall who I spoke with in reference to the actions of the bouncer, but I was informed of actions the bouncer did take.* [25]

Mr. Hannon asked several questions about the conduct of the bouncer, what Lieutenant Charland learned from sources, and the conduct itself. After each question, there was an objection from the prosecution, and each was sustained. The prosecution gave no explanation for the objections, nor did the court offer any explanation each being sustained.

Mr. Rickard began the cross-examination. "Did the defendant's girlfriend give you a statement on the scene?" Lt. Charland answered, "No, she didn't." "Did you make any observations with respect to the defendant's appearance and demeanor?"[26] Mr. Hannon objected, and it was overruled. Lt Charland responded, "I observed that, one, he wasn't speaking to me. I asked him some questions and he didn't respond to the questions regarding the seriousness of the matter, which I explained to him. I explained to him that I was the ranking official in charge of the scene."[27]

Mr. Hannon objected, saying, "This is beyond the scope of the question."[28]

---

[24] Ibid, 148
[25] Ibid, 150-151
[26] Ibid.
[27] Ibid, 152 - 153
[28] Ibid, 153

Judge Dixon said, "Okay. I think the ultimate question that I believe Mr. Rickard is getting to, if I'm not incorrectly predicting you, Mr. Rickard, is he's trying to find out whether or not there was any appearance of inebriation with respect to the defendant."[29] Addressing Mr. Rickard, the judge asked, "Is that what you're getting to, sir?"[30]

Mr. Rickard: *Yes. Thank you.*
Lt. Charland: *Yes, there was.*
Mr. Rickard: *And what did you observe in that regard?*
Lt. Charland: *I was standing closely to him. I smelled alcohol from his person. His eyes were a little glassy. Those are my only observations that I could take from just standing next to him. He wasn't speaking to me so I couldn't ascertain from speech or anything else if there was anything further.*[31]

The lieutenant testified that the defendant did not speak to him; however, the memorandum (discussed in Chapter 9) from the U. S. Attorney's office said that Heath did talk to him. Included in the letter, "Lt Charland later asked your client if there was an official he should notify, and your client provided contact information."[32] Remember, Mr. Hannon had requested time to review the document and it was denied. Since the document was not introduced as evidence, the contradiction could not be raised. It is my belief that if Mr. Hannon countered this, the prosecution would have objected, and it would have been sustained.

Mr. Hannon on his second redirect asked, "Lieutenant, when you attempted to speak to Agent Thomas and observed him, you recall that you said to him, 'Why did you draw your gun on the bouncer?' You remember telling – remember saying that to him?"[33] Mr. Rickard objected, but the Court allowed it.

Lt. Charland: *No, I did not. That's false.*
Mr. Hannon: *Do you know whether when you attempted to speak to …Agent Thomas anyone else was present beside just you and him?*
Lt. Charland: *No. There were officers… around. I'm not sure which officers were there.*
Mr. Hannon: *So they would have heard what you said to him; is that right?*
Lt. Charland: *Yes.* [34]

---

[29] Ibid
[30] Ibid
[31] Ibid, 153 - 154.
[32] Letter to Hannon Law Group ref., Heath Thomas case, 2010-CF3-106079, by the U. S. Attorney's Office, responding to three inquiries', dated July 5, 2011, Appendix F
[33] Information from the trial transcript, Criminal Action Number 2010-CF3-16079, dated August 18, 2011, p 154
[34] Ibid, 155

Mr. Hannon then asked if a breathalyzer had been offered. The prosecution objected but was overruled. Lt. Charland answered, "I asked his [Heath's] supervisor if he wanted the test conducted."[35] Mr. Hannon noted that Heath's supervisor was not investigating the incident, and Mr. Rickard objected.

> Judge Dixon: *Mr. Hannon, this is what happens when you go off into those kinds of questions …*
> Mr. Hannon: *Did you and the Metropolitan Police Department take any steps to have Agent Thomas to submit to a Breathalyzer?*
> Mr. Rickard: *Asked and answered.*
> Judge Dixon: *Overruled.*
> Lt. Charland: *No. I didn't take any — I asked — I offered his supervisor the opportunity—*
> Mr. Hannon: *Lieutenant, the answer's no; is that right?*
> Lt. Charland: *Yes.*[36]

On re-cross-examination, Mr. Rickard asked, "Why is that you didn't have Agent Thomas tested on the Breathalyzer?" Lt. Charland answered, "It was the request of his supervisor that he did not want the test performed."[37]

> Mr. Hannon, speaking on additional redirect: *I don't know who he is. You mean the supervisor didn't want the test performed?*
> Lt. Charland: *Correct, from ICE.*
> Mr. Hannon: *So the Metropolitan Police Department was deferring to his supervisor as to whether it's going to collect evidence, as to whether this individual was intoxicated, is that what you're telling us?*[38]

Mr. Rickard objected, and it was sustained.

The lieutenant's testimony—that he offered the breathalyzer to Heath's supervisor and the supervisor declined—is difficult to believe, and that's being kind. Agent Eisert responded to the police station as a friend. He was not investigating the incident.

It appeared to me that the testimony, from both Detective Tabron and Lt. Charland, was favorable to the defense. While I had mixed feelings about the first half of day four, I was optimistic about the second half.

That concluded day four of the trial.

---

[35] Ibid, 156
[36] Ibid
[37] Ibid, 157
[38] Ibid,

12A

Anthony Ray Hinton: Bad Science and a Gun

In 1985 Mr. Anthony Ray Hinton was charged, tried, and convicted of two murders in Birmingham, Alabama. For these alleged crimes he was given a death sentence. After spending almost three decades on death row, he was released in 2015.

The evidence that convicted Mr. Hinton came from the testimony of a ballistics expert. The expert testified that bullets recovered from the bodies of the homicide victims were from a gun that was found in Mr. Hinton's mother's home. According to the reporting, the ballistics was the determinant evidence presented by the prosecution at the trial. Mr. Hinton's employer testified for the defense that Mr. Hinton was at work when the crime occurred, but he was not believed.

In 2002, Mr. Bryan Stevenson, Hinton's attorney, hired three ballistics experts to examine the gun and the bullets. The experts said the bullets did not come from the weapon that was recovered in Mr. Hinton's mother's home. Additionally, the bullets were not all from one gun.

Nevertheless, even after the ballistics retesting in 2002, which proved the gun did not fire the bullets, the state refused to release Mr. Hinton or even give him a new trial. Mr. Hinton's attorney appealed to the U.S. Supreme Court, and in 2014, 12 years after the new ballistics test, the Court ruled in his favor. Mr. Hinton was entitled to a new trial. A new trial never occurred, however, and in 2015, he was finally released.

Bryan Stevenson, Hinton's attorney, said, "Every day, every month, every year that the state took from him, they took something that they don't have the power to give back. While this moment is quite joyous and is quite wonderful, this case is quite tragic." He also said, "He was a poor person who was convicted because he didn't have the money to prove his innocence at trial. He was unable to get the legal help he needed for years. He was convicted based on bad science."[1] Mr. Stevenson worked on the case for sixteen years.

At the time Mr. Hinton was released, on April 3, 2015, he was one of the 152 persons who had been exonerated while on death row, in the United States, since 1983. He was the sixth person exonerated from death row in Alabama.

---

[1] AP report, "Alabama inmate freed after nearly 30 years on death row", April 3, 2015

"Race, poverty, inadequate legal assistance, and prosecutorial indifference to innocence conspired to create a textbook example of injustice. I can't think of a case that more urgently dramatizes the need for reform than what has happened to Anthony Ray Hinton."[2]

Did the state's expert testify at other trials, before or after this case? If so, were the other cases re-examined? After the ballistics testing, why did the state continue to hold Mr. Hinton if the ballistics was the principal evidence and crucial to their case? Holding someone for 13 years after the central evidence used to convict them was proven false should be a crime itself.

References

Jason Hanna and Ed Payne, "Alabama inmate freed after nearly 30 years on death row", Associated Press, April 3, 2015

The Equal Justice Initiative https://eji.org/cases/anthony-ray-hinton, April 3, 2015, no author given.

Bryan Stevenson, The Milbank Tweed Forum, https://www.law.nyu.edu/news/bryan-stevenson, April 3, 2015

---

[2] https://www.law.nyu.edu/news/bryan-stevenson, "The Milbank Tweed Forum", posted April 3, 2015

13

Day 5: Is Carole on Trial?
MONDAY, AUGUST 22, 2011

"To be persuasive we must be believable; to be believable we must be credible; to be credible we must be truthful."
—Edward R. Murrow

I was not in the courtroom on day 5, but I was told that before the trial began the courtroom was quiet. Were Heath's friends, and others in the courtroom concerned? The trial seemed to be moving in slow motion, traveling in the wrong direction.[1]

Two key witnesses would testify for the defense that day. The first to be called was Ms. Carole O'Connor, and the second was the defendant, Mr. Heath Thomas. While the story being presented to the court, at times, seemed to be moving in the wrong direction, I was hopeful that both witnesses could change the direction.

Ms. Carole O'Connor

At the time of the incident, Heath and Carole were in a relationship. Carole was employed by a contractor for the Navy, working on a submarine program. Altogether, she had worked for the Department of Homeland Security with various companies for about seven years in project management. Her formal education included a bachelor's degree in political science and international studies and a master's in international business. As a requirement of her employment, she had a government security clearance.

She testified that the evening dinner was a planned event. A former co-worker, Mr. Terry Spradlin, was in town, so she and Ms. Jane Jones—also a former co-worker—planned a night out. Carole and Heath left her home, taking a cab into Georgetown. She was asked if she knew that Heath was armed; she replied that she was aware that he was and added, "I had always assumed that he carried it."[2] She was also asked if she had been out with him before when he had consumed alcoholic beverages, and she said yes.

---

[1] I was not present for the trial for August 22, and 23. I was out of state for both days. Mr. Hannon provided me the transcripts for both days and conversations with other witnesses and persons attending the trial gave me additional information.

[2] Information from the trial transcript, Criminal Action Number 2010-CF3-16079, dated August 22, 2011, p 8

The plan that evening was to meet the two other couples at Old Glory for dinner. They arrived at the restaurant around 7 p.m., and they were there for several hours. When asked what time she left, Carole said 11 p.m. or a little after. When questioned about the drinks, she said that they had three rounds of drinks. She had two ciders and one Maker's Mark and 7Up. The group ordered another round, but by the time it came to the table, they were ready to leave, so not everyone drank their last orders. She said she had maybe half of that drink. The group had no plans after leaving Old Glory, but once outside, they decided to stop for one more drink.

Carole was then asked to describe Heath's demeanor that evening as they left the restaurant. She said, "Good. Good. Everybody was in a good mood. We had a nice time."[3] Mr. Hannon asked, "At that moment did it appear to you that Agent Thomas was intoxicated," to which Carole replied, "No."[4]

Answering questions about The Guards, Carole said that they had not made any plans to stop there; they were just in the area. When they decided to stop, they met a bouncer at the door. She remembered the bouncer because she made a joke about not being carded, "And he just kind of gave me this stone-faced look like I don't care."[5] When asked about the bouncer's attire, she said the bouncer was wearing a dark shirt.

After entering The Guards, the group went to the bar and ordered drinks. She ordered special drinks for Terry and his wife; they both had a birthday that week. They were at the bar a short while and then moved to a table. She remembered the whole front area as empty, with three tables across from the bar.

Mr. Hannon showed Carole Exhibit 15—a check from The Guards—and asked her if she recognized it. She did not recognize the check, but she remembered the amount; she said she never saw the bill. The check had been opened at 10:17 p.m. and closed at 11:57 p.m. in the amount of $13.15, with the name of O'CONNOR/CAROLE on it.[6] Mr. Hannon then showed her Exhibit 16, which was the merchant's copy of the credit card receipt in the amount of $13.15, time-stamped 11:47 p.m., with the Check ID name of O'CONNOR/CAROLE, signed by Carole.[7] She recognized the credit card receipt, and when questioned, said, "it was the bill I paid at The Guards after the incident outside after everything happened."[8] When asked about the time (11:47) on the receipt, Carole said, "It would seem to be the time they printed out the bill, but it doesn't make sense because it wasn't until a long time after the incident that I wanted to pay the tab. And the stamp on this is before."[9]

---

[3] Ibid, 10
[4] Ibid
[5] Ibid, 11
[6] U.S. v. Heath Thomas, U.S. Government's Exhibits 15, Case No. 2010 CF3 016079
[7] U.S. v. Heath Thomas, U.S. Government's Exhibit 16, Case No. 2010 CF3 016079.
[8] Information from the trial transcript, Criminal Action Number 2010-CF3-16079, dated August 22, 2011, p 13
[9] Ibid, 14

```
      The Guards                              The Guards Restaurant
   2915 M St. NW                       Date:         Aug28'10 11:47PM
   Washington, DC-20007                 Card Type:    Amex
                                        Acct #:       XXXXXXXXXXXX4007
213 Xan X                               Exp Date:     03/12
                                        Auth Code:    545599
  Chk 2146   O'CONNOR/CAROLE   Gst 0    Check:        2146
             Aug28'10 10:17PM           Check ID:     O'CONNOR/CAROLE
                                        Server:       213 Xan X

   1 PREMIUM BEER          5.45         Subtotal:           13.15
   1 Call                  6.50
   XXXXXXXXXX4007 03/12                 Tip:_____
             Amex         13.15
                                        Total:_____
   Subtotal               11.95
   Sales Tax               1.20         Signature
   Payment                13.15         I agree to pay above total
   ---------213 Check Closed---------   according to my card issuer
   -----------Aug28'10 11:57PM--------  agreement.

                                          * * * * Merchant Copy * * * *
```

Exhibit 15   Exhibit 16

When Mr. Hannon asked Carole about the time of 10:17 being on Exhibit 15, she responded that the time was incorrect. She explained, "My guess is that they never reset their computers for Daylight Savings, which would explain why everything is an hour off."[10] She believed that they arrived at The Guards one hour later. When asked about the time of the incident, she said, "Around midnight."[11]

Mr. Hannon asked Carole to recount the problems with the drinks, and she did so, corroborating the previous testimony on the subject. The questions then returned to the critical events. Mr. Hannon asked, "After he [Heath] got up to leave the table, when did you next see him?" Carole said, "Being carried out."[12] She said that Heath had been gone maybe three to five minutes when she saw him being carried out, and during that time, she did not hear anything from the bar area.

> Mr. Hannon: *Could you tell the Court what you saw when you first noticed Agent Thomas being carried out?*
> Carole: *… the first thing I saw was somebody's feet off the ground … And then I'm like, oh my gosh, those are Heath's feet. And I look up and the bouncer has him kind of grabbed in a bear hug around the waist… And I remember thinking he [Heath] looked like a doll.*[13]
> Mr. Hannon: *What did you do when you saw him?*
> Carole: *I jumped up.*
> Mr. Hannon: *And then what?*

---

[10] Ibid
[11] Ibid, 15
[12] Ibid
[13] Ibid, 20

> Carole: *... And then I said to Jane and Dennis at the end of the table – I am like, oh, my gosh, that is Heath and I jumped up and I ran out.*
>
> Mr. Hannon: *Where was Agent Thomas once you got up and headed out of the bar?*
>
> Carole: *... I ran out behind them as fast as I could. It was the bouncer carrying Heath and then the bar manager ... you have got to make a right and then a left and go through the vestibule.*[14]

She said the manager was following the bouncer carrying Heath, and she could not see the bouncer while following them because the manager was blocking her view.

> Mr. Hannon: *Do you know at that moment [when she is following the manager] whether the bouncer had already gone out the first set of doors?*[15]
>
> Carole: *I am not sure, because he was in front of the manager. I just know they walked by. The manager walked by and then I jumped up and ran behind him.*[16]

Carole said that there was no one except the manager between her and the bouncer. As she exited the bar through the vestibule, she stood on the top step, and the manager was standing next to her, to her left.

> Mr. Hannon: *And what did you see?*
>
> Carole: *I saw the bouncer trying to take Heath's gun.*
>
> Mr. Hannon: *Where were the two of them?*
>
> Carole: *They were ... on the sidewalk right before the curb, right at the curb.*
>
> Mr. Hannon: *And was there anyone else that you saw in the front of the entrance at that time?*
>
> Carole: *No. No. It was pretty quiet on the sidewalk.*
>
> Mr. Hannon: *And did you say anything once you saw what was going on?*
>
> Carole: *I said, stop, what are you doing? He is a federal police officer.*
>
> Mr. Hannon: *Was there a response that you could hear from the bouncer?*
>
> Carole: *The bouncer ... was loud. He was angry. He said, I don't care. I don't care. He has got a gun. Nobody waves a gun at me. I am going to get it and I am going to take it from him.*[17]

When questioned about other people being in the area, Carole said the manager was standing nearby when she told the bouncer that Heath was a police officer. She said,

---

[14] Ibid, 21
[15] Ibid, 22
[16] Ibid
[17] Ibid, 23

"it was just before then he [the manager] opened his phone and I knew he was calling the police. And I said, wait, wait, can we calm down? Can we just take a minute? Can everybody just calm down?"[18] She said the manager ignored her while moving to the curb area, about ten feet from her and to the right of the struggle.

Carole was still watching the struggle, and after the manager moved away, she heard, "hey, lady, look out, he has a gun, I remember thinking where is that coming from because there is nobody else there."[19] She turned around and saw Corporal Holubar—although she did not know him at that time—standing behind her. Describing Corporal Holubar's attire, she said he was wearing trousers and a light-colored shirt. "It was like a light-faded teal."[20]

Carole said that after Corporal Holubar warned her, she said to him, "he is a federal police officer. He is my boyfriend. Go back inside."[21] She added, "My thought at that point was … he was kind of standing there like Chicken Little and, you know, he wasn't helping."[22]

After talking to Corporal Holubar, she turned her attention back to the bouncer and Heath. The struggle seemed to be at a stalemate, with the bouncer pushing Heath against a vehicle. Mr. Hannon asked about the arrival of the police. She said they arrived, but only after she had gone back inside to tell her friends what was going on. When she returned outside, the police were there. There were numerous officers; one was with Heath, next to a police car, and "there were other police talking to the manager and the bouncer."[23]

Mr. Hannon asked Carole to identify a photograph of the front steps at The Guards, that she had taken. Using a monitor to display the photograph, Mr. Hannon asked Carole to use a laser pointer to show where she was standing on the steps. She pointed to the right side of the second step as her location. When asked to point where the manager was standing, she did so, stating, "I am not sure if he was standing on this step or the sidewalk."[24]

Mr. Hannon asked, "And when you first observed the gentleman in the teal shirt, where was he standing?"[25] Carole said he was behind her, and she had to turn her head around to see, over her right shoulder. Mr. Hannon showed her Exhibit 92; she identified it, saying, "It is a picture from behind me as I think roughly where the man in the teal shirt would have been standing."[26] Exhibit 92 was a photograph of Carole standing inside the doorframe area of the doorway.

---

[18] Ibid, 24
[19] Ibid
[20] Ibid
[21] Ibid, 25
[22] Ibid
[23] Ibid, 26
[24] Ibid, 28
[25] Ibid, 29
[26] Ibid, 30

Photo viewing the front steps from the sidewalk.   Photo of Carole standing in doorway.

Mr. Hannon concluded his questions and Mr. Rickard began his cross-examination. He asked Carole if the group had gone out that evening to celebrate Mr. Spradlin's birthday. Carole said no, the reason they went out was "I used to work with both of them and he [Mr. Spadlin] was going to be in town… we went out just to see each other."²⁷ Carole said that she had only learned that it was his birthday that evening.

Mr. Rickard went over the drinks Carole had while having dinner at Old Glory. She repeated that she had two ciders and a Maker's Mark with 7Up and that the group had ordered another round. However, the service was slow, and the drinks arrived as they got the check and were leaving.

> Carole: *… So we pretty much got our drink as we got the check, so I don't know that everybody finished their last drink.*²⁸
> Mr. Rickard: *At Old Glory, the defendant, Mr. Thomas, was drinking beers; correct?*
> Carole: *Yes.*
> Mr. Rickard: *And then you think that he also had a beer that he purchased but didn't finish?*
> Carole: *… I don't think anybody finished their drink.*²⁹

At Old Glory, she said, the group collectively ordered four rounds of drinks.

Mr. Rickard asked Carole if Heath ordered a beer at the bar when they first arrived at The Guards. Carole said, "Yes. But he – he only took a couple of sips. He didn't like it. He gave it back."³⁰ Mr. Rickard questioned her further about her memory of this, and Carole answered, "He said he didn't like it. And I said, well, then don't drink it."³¹

---

²⁷ Ibid, 32
²⁸ Ibid, 33
²⁹ Ibid, 34
³⁰ Ibid, 35
³¹ Ibid

Mr. Rickard questioned Carole about the receipts, Exhibits 15 and 16. He specifically asked about Exhibit 15, which listed a premium beer and a call (a mixed drink). The only thing Carole saw was the credit card slip (Exhibit 16) for $13.15. Carole said, "I did not see the check for one beer and one call. Had I seen it, I would have said something because I know he didn't drink his beer. I assumed it was for the two shots [that she had purchased for the Spradlins]."[32] The two shots were not on the bill.

Mr. Rickard asked Carole if she remembered her grand jury testimony, reminding her that she was under oath, and she agreed. He introduced Exhibit 33, which was her grand jury transcript. She was directed to page 36, the question, "And how about Mr. Thomas? What had he had to drink?"[33] Her answer was, "He had one beer."[34]

Mr. Rickard asked, "You didn't tell the grand jury that he had a few sips and gave it back?"[35] Carole answered, "That – I don't know. That is what I said."[36]

Carole was questioned about seeing the bouncer carrying Heath; she recognized him as the person she saw when entering The Guards. Mr. Rickard asked, "When you saw them go by, Mr. Thomas didn't say anything, did he?"[37] Carole agreed.

Judge Dixon interjected and asked if the bouncer carrying Heath walked right past the table where the group was seated. Carole said, "Yes." The judge asked, if everyone had still been at the table at that point, why was she the only one who saw the bouncer carry Heath out. Carole replied, "Because everybody else was still kind of chitchatting ... I was the only one facing directly at the aisle. So they walked by... and I jumped up as fast as I could."[38]

Mr. Rickard then asked if, when she testified at the grand jury, she said anything about changing seats, and she answered, "I don't know if I was asked."[39] Mr. Rickard stated as a question that when she testified today, she said the bouncer carried Heath from his waist area, and she agreed.

Mr. Rickard: *You didn't tell the grand jury that, either, did you?*
Carole: *I don't remember. They had him in a bear hug. I actually demonstrated it.*
Mr. Rickard: *You demonstrated a bear hug; correct?*
Carole: *... I stood up. I demonstrated... how Heath was positioned that his arms were pinned down and the bouncer grabbed him around here (indicating)* [her waist]. *That he was grabbed in a bear hug from behind, picked up and carried out.*
Mr. Rickard: *... Now, you didn't actually see the bouncer pick up Mr. Thomas, did you?*[40]

---

[32] Ibid 36
[33] Ibid, 37-38 and information from grand jury transcript of Ms. O'Conner, October 2010, p 36
[34] Ibid, 38 and information from grand jury transcript of Ms. O'Conner, October 2010, p 36
[35] Information from the trial transcript, Criminal Action Number 2010-CF3-16079, dated August 22, 2011, p 38
[36] Ibid
[37] Ibid, 40
[38] Ibid, 40-41
[39] Ibid, 41
[40] Ibid, 41-42

She answered no.

Continuing, Mr. Rickard asked Carole about the distance the bouncer and Heath were from her when they moved past her. Carole said she believed the distance to be "at least 5 feet, 6 feet."[41] Her estimate of the distance was from where she was sitting in the courtroom to the end of a table. Mr. Rickard continued, "In the grand jury when you demonstrated it was 7 or 8 feet, wasn't it?"[42] Carole answered, "That was Sean Lewis's assessment."[43]

During her grand jury testimony, she had estimated the distance from her seated position to a coffee cup in the room.

Mr. Rickard asked, "When Sean Lewis made his assessment of 7 or 8 feet, you didn't correct him, did you?"[44] Carole answered, "I thought it more or less."[45]

In both instances, Carole estimated a distance between her and when she saw the bouncer carrying Heath. The first estimate was given at the grand jury, and the second was given at the trial. Both estimates used objects as a reference from her seated position. In both instances, the prosecution—using the same objects—made their own estimates, which were different by a foot or two. The importance of a foot or two, or lack of importance, was not said. If the prosecution believed the distance to be so critical, why not measure the distance?

Mr. Rickard next asked about the struggle between the bouncer and Heath. Were they on the sidewalk when she first saw them? Carole answered yes.

Mr. Rickard: *You saw them struggling…?*
Carole: *Yes.*
Mr. Rickard: *But isn't it true that you say when you saw them struggling you always saw the gun pointing at the ground?*
Carole: *It was always angled down, yes.*
Mr. Rickard: *And you said they were just kind of – it wasn't anything dramatic, they were just pulling it back and forth as it continued to point at the ground?*
Carole: *Yes … like small wiggles I believe I said.*[46]

Mr. Rickard stated that during the struggle, Carole was the first person to identify Heath as a police officer, and she agreed. When she was inside the bar, she did not hear anyone in the bar identify Heath as a police officer. As she said, "I didn't hear the conversation at the bar that he had. We didn't hear anything from our table."[47]

---

[41] Ibid, 43
[42] Ibid, 43
[43] Ibid
[44] Ibid, 44
[45] Ibid
[46] Ibid, 44
[47] Ibid, 45

> Mr. Rickard: *During the struggle that you saw, Mr. Thomas was very quiet. He was quiet the whole time, wasn't he?*
>
> Carole: *Yeah, he was very quiet.*
>
> Mr. Rickard: *And quiet, he didn't say anything?*
>
> Carole: *I don't know that he said nothing. He might have… identified himself as a police officer when we were outside. But he wasn't yelling, he wasn't creating a fuss…*[48]

Mr. Rickard read a question from Carole's grand jury testimony: "At that moment when you first come out and see two men down by the curb, is Mr. Thomas saying anything?"[49] Then reading the answer she gave, "He might have. He might have been saying I am a federal police officer. I am a federal police officer. But, no, it was – he was very quiet."[50] Mr. Rickard, still reading from the transcript: "And I vividly recall the first thing the bouncer said when I said he is a federal police officer, the bouncer said, I don't care."[51]

Mr. Rickard asked, "Were you asked that question and did you give that answer?"[52] Carole answered, "Yes, that's what I just said a few minutes ago. He was quiet meaning he wasn't yelling and screaming, but —"[53] Mr. Rickard stopped her, saying she had answered the question.

> Mr. Rickard: *And it is your testimony, too, that no one was really on the street at the time?*[54] Carole: *I don't recall anybody else being there.*[55]

Mr. Rickard reviewed her previous testimony about going back inside to the table and informing her friends of the situation, after which she grabbed her purse and went back outside. Carole agreed with Mr. Rickard's review.

> Mr. Rickard: *And before you did that, that is when you told the manager not to call the police?*
>
> Carole: *I'm not sure what point in time you are referring to.*
>
> Mr. Rickard: *You said you told the manager just calm down. You said he started to call the police and you said don't worry about it, just calm down?*

---

[48] Ibid, 46
[49] Ibid, 47 and information from grand jury transcript of Ms. O'Conner, October 2010, p 20
[50] Ibid
[51] Ibid
[52] Ibid
[53] Information from the trial transcript, Criminal Action Number 2010-CF3-16079, dated August 22, 2011, p 47
[54] Ibid, 47-48
[55] Ibid, 48

> Carole: *I didn't say don't worry about it. I said when I first walked out the door when initially the bouncer carried Heath and the manager followed them and I followed the manager, the first thing I saw was the two of them on the sidewalk, you know, just off the curb struggling over the gun. And when then the manager opened up his phone and I said, wait a minute, wait a minute. Can we just calm down? Can we just take a minute and just calm down? I did not say don't call the police.*
>
> Mr. Rickard: *But you knew he was calling the police when he opened his phone?*
>
> Carole: *I assumed.*
>
> Mr. Rickard: *And you told him to wait a minute?*
>
> Carole: *Yes.*
>
> Mr. Rickard: *And you wanted everyone to just calm down.*
>
> Carole: *… I asked him. I didn't tell him, I asked him. I said can we just take a minute. Can we just calm down?*
>
> Mr. Rickard: *So even though there was this bouncer here struggling with a weapon that he and Mr. Thomas were both wiggling over, you advised the manager not to call the police?*
>
> Carole: *I did. Again, I did not say…*

Mr. Rickard interrupted.

> Mr. Rickard: *By the wait a minute, you advised him to wait.*[56]

The court reporter asked for a moment, after which the judge asked, "Where are we? Did you finish your question?"[57] Mr. Rickard said he would revise his question and said, "You advised him to wait a minute when you assumed that he was calling the police and had his phone out."[58] Carole answered, "I asked him to wait a minute."[59]

> Mr. Rickard: *Later on when the police were there and other people gathered in the street —you told people it was none of their business what was going on; correct?*
>
> Carole: *I did. The police were not controlling the scene at all at that point. And there were people all over the sidewalk everywhere wanting to know what is going on. I am a citizen, it is my business. And I said, no, it is not, it is a police matter.*
>
> Mr. Rickard: *All right. It was a police matter; right? The police were there to investigate?*[60]

---

[56] Ibid, 48 - 50
[57] Ibid, 50
[58] Ibid
[59] Ibid
[60] Ibid

Mr. Rickard mentioned the lieutenant from the Metropolitan Police Department that was at the scene.

Carole: *He showed up very late.*

Mr. Rickard: *And you wouldn't give him a statement, would you?*

Carole: *He wouldn't give me the time of day.*

Mr. Rickard: *Well, he wanted a statement from you and you wouldn't give him one, would you?*

Carole: *... initially when the incident happened, the police were very concerned in talking to the bouncer, talking to the manager and no one came up to me or my party at any point. I came forward, walked up to the patrolman and said, is anybody going to talk to me? And at that point he said who are you? ... and I said, I am his girlfriend. And I gave him my name and he said, well, did you see the gun come out? And I am like, no. And he is like okay. And then he turned his back and started walking away. And I am like, are you going to write anything down? And he scribbled – he scribbled a couple of things. And that is it. I got all of 30 seconds from him. And then about an hour, maybe 45 minutes later, he came back, handed me a form and said, here, fill this out. I said, what is that? And he said it is your statement.*

Mr. Rickard: *... so you were given a form to write a statement on and you didn't? That was my question.*

Carole: *He handed me a form and walked away.*

Mr. Rickard: *... It was a yes-or-no question. You were given a form.*

Carole: *I was given a form.*

Mr. Rickard: *And you did not write a statement.*

Carole: *I got no instructions.*

Mr. Rickard: *You didn't know what this form was?*

Carole: *I didn't know what this form was. I had never been in that situation.*[61]

Mr. Rickard continued discussing her previous testimony. He repeated that the first time she saw the man in the teal shirt (Corporal Holubar), he had been behind her and said something about a gun. Mr. Rickard asked if she saw him before the incident, and she said she noticed him in the bar area. So, the record was corrected; the first time she observed him and heard him speak was while she was on the steps outside. She had observed him earlier but had not heard him speak. She also referred to him earlier as a Marine, but when questioned, she said she did not know he was a Marine on the evening of the incident.

Mr. Rickard clarified, "You have learned he is a Marine because you have been involved in this case; correct?" Carole answered, "Because I have been asked questions, yes."[62]

---

[61] Ibid, 51-52
[62] Ibid, 54

Mr. Rickard asked Carole about a message on Facebook that she had sent to Corporal Holubar before the trial.

> Carole: *Yes, I was asked by the defense to send him a message asking him to contact them.*
> Mr. Rickard: *You introduced yourself as the person from that night and asked Corporal Holubar to contact the defense?*
> Carole: *Yes.*[63]

Moving on, Mr. Rickard asked if she had contacted Ms. Jones the evening before Ms. Jones was to testify at the Grand Jury.

> Carole: *We had exchanged emails and we might have talked the day before. I don't remember.*
> Mr. Rickard: *Do you recall telling her the questions you were asked and the substance of the answers you gave to the grand jury?*
> Carole: *I did share my grand jury testimony… because Sean Lewis and Detective Tabron said I could.*
> Mr. Rickard: *So you learned that you were permitted to talk about what you told the grand jury with other people; correct?*
> Carole: *Yes. From your office.*
> Mr. Rickard: *But no one told you that you needed to tell Ms. Jones what you said in the grand jury. That was a decision you made after you learn it was permissible; correct?*
> Carole: *I was told by my lawyer, again, in front of Sean Lewis and Detective Tabron that my testimony was my testimony and I could share it.*
> Mr. Rickard: *You were told you were permitted to share it; correct?*
> Carole: *Yes, I think he said you could put it in the front page of the newspaper if you wanted to.*
> Mr. Rickard: *But you chose to tell Ms. Jones the night before she testified about your testimony; correct?*
> Carole: *Yes. Because she had also asked, what it is like.*
> Mr. Rickard: *And you did the same for Mr. Spradlin, didn't you?*
> Carole: *Yes.*[64]
> Mr. Rickard: *And you have been present at a lot of the court proceeding in this case; correct?*[65]

---

[63] Ibid, 55 also Appendix Exhibit F, Email from Carole O'Connor to the writer.
[64] Information from the trial transcript, Criminal Action Number 2010-CF3-16079, dated August 22, 2011, p 56-57
[65] Ibid, 57

Mr. Hannon objected, and Mr. Rickard changed his question.

Mr. Rickard: ...*You were present at the hearing on the motion to compel in the beginning of August of this year; correct?*
Carole: *I don't remember specifically what the date was but, yes. I have been at a lot of the – I don't know what they are called ...*
Mr. Rickard: *You heard Mr. Hannon's arguments about the motion?*
Carole: *I really don't remember what motion to compel is.*[66]

Mr. Rickard reminded her that he had asked her to be excused from the room during the motion and before his arguments. As she said, "Nobody told me I couldn't be in there."[67]

Mr. Rickard asked, "So you talked to all of these witnesses, but you hadn't had any conversations with the defendant about what happened that night, have you?"[68] Carole answered, "No. No."[69] Carole was adamant that she had not talked to Heath about the incident. When asked the same question again, she answered, "No. We have actually avoided that."[70]

Mr. Hannon's first and only question on redirect was why she did not talk to Heath about the incident. Carole answered, "Because very early on I think the first time I met with Charles Cate, who was my first lawyer, he said not to."[71]

Judge Dixon, following up, asked Carole when she had realized that there was a gun involved. Carole said that she noticed the gun right away; it was low, and the bouncer was trying to take it away.

He also asked about any conversations she heard during the struggle. She repeated that she believed Heath said he was a police officer, but he did not say it loudly and was not yelling. The question was repeated about the specific words that Heath used, and Carole said she believed he said, "I am a federal police officer."[72]

The next question was about how long she was outside; she said it was several minutes. It was after she talked to Corporal Holubar that she went back into the bar. She described the struggle before she reentered the bar, saying, "It was like a stalemate, you know, like two kids on the playground fighting over a ball, it is going no place."[73] Did she hear the bouncer say anything? She replied yes, when she first witnessed the

---

[66] Ibid
[67] Ibid
[68] Ibid
[69] Ibid, 58
[70] Ibid
[71] Ibid
[72] Ibid, 60
[73] Ibid

struggle, she said something like "stop" to the bouncer, "He is a federal police officer." She said that the bouncer answered her, saying, "'I don't care. I don't care.' And he was angry. His tone was 'I don't care, he has got a gun. Nobody waives a gun at me. He has got a gun and I am going to get it and I am going to take it from him.'"[74] She believed it was after this that Heath identified himself as a federal police officer.

> Judge Dixon: *Did you notice any other person in the vicinity?*
> Carole: *No I really didn't. Which is why when I heard the guy in the teal shirt behind me, that's like … where is that coming from? Because there was nobody in my line of sight other than them and that's when I turned completely around.*
> Judge Dixon: *… even though you didn't see anyone else out there, did you hear anyone else say anything about the presence of a gun?*
> Carole: *No. No. I don't remember hearing anybody else, seeing anybody else.*[75]
> Judge Dixon: *… And I take it as far as Corporal Holubar, you didn't know him before that evening?*
> Carole: *No. No. He just stood out because of the color of his shirt.*
> Judge Dixon: *And you learned his name about the same time or just before you contacted him through Facebook to ask him to contact the defense?*
> Carole: *I can't remember exactly when, but it was through Mr. Hannon's office. And he asked me to send an email or a message and so that's what I did.*[76]

Judge Dixon asked if she had to "friend" him to send the message, and she said "no." She also said she was not sure of the rules for Facebook.[77] That concluded her testimony.

Carole's testimony at trial, like her grand jury testimony, was lengthy. In both instances, the prosecution seemed to be focused on her actions before and after the incident. Mr. Rickard continued his aggressive manner with the defense, and anyone witnessing the questioning who was not involved with the case might conclude that it was Carole who was on trial.

Following Carole's testimony, the Court intended to break for lunch, but the prosecution asked the Court about a motion that had been filed. The motion concerned the DVD demonstrating how Heath's weapon became dislodged during the incident. The prosecution had watched the video but with no sound. Mr. Hannon agreed to allow the prosecution to view the DVD with sound during the lunch break.

After lunch the trial resumed, and Ms. Sawyer informed the Court that Mr. Hannon had provided the DVD with sound, and the prosecution now possessed a copy of it.

---

[74] Ibid, 61
[75] Ibid, 62
[76] Ibid, 63
[77] Ibid, 103, also Appendix Exhibit H, email from Carole O'Connor to the writer. The email was originally from Mr. Hannon's Office asking her to contact Mr. Holubar, dated August 12, 2011

After some discussion, Ms. Sawyer asked, "Your Honor, may I just make one request: I can't say with certainty that we will do this, but just in the event that we do want to call Ms. O'Connor for rebuttal, we would ask that she not be present for the testimony."[78]

Judge Dixon turned to Mr. Hannon for comment, and Mr. Hannon asked, "Well, do they plan to call her for rebuttal?"

Judge Dixon had the parties approach the bench. Ms. Sawyer began her argument with, "I can't say with certainty, Your Honor. But we would like to preserve it as an option."[79] The judge asked, "Can you proffer to me even ex parte some basis on which you believe there is reasonable prospect you will call her as a rebuttal witness, even an ex parte proffer?"[80] Ms. Sawyer responded, "Sure. I could do an ex parte proffer."[81] The judge said, "Okay. Step back."[82]

> Ms. Sawyer: *And honestly, Your Honor, I haven't given it a great deal of thought. It is just when I saw her sitting there, it is sort of – it crossed my mind. But to the extent, I suppose, that Agent Thomas says anything that conflicts with something that we know she said in the grand jury or—*[83]
>
> Judge Dixon: *Well, if it conflicts with something she said in the grand jury, it is in the grand jury transcript. You will still be able to introduce them even if she doesn't admit them. Anything else?*
>
> Ms. Sawyer: *No. I just sort of was trying to take precaution, that is all. But, no.*[84]

Judge Dixon said he would allow Ms. O'Connor to remain in the courtroom, and the bench conference ended. As in other instances, the judge seemed to give the prosecution a pass, perhaps due to their youth or other unknown reasons; I don't believe Mr. Hannon would have received the same consideration.

Before moving on, Judge Dixon said to Mr. Hannon, "I really neglected to ask you, what is your position with respect to whether to or not Ms. O'Connor should remain in the courtroom?"[85] Mr. Hannon said that he did not see a reason she would be re-called for a rebuttal. Judge Dixon interpreted Mr. Hannon's response as an objection, and he sustained the objection.

Heath would testify next.

---

[78] Ibid
[79] Ibid
[80] Ibid
[81] Ibid
[82] Ibid
[83] Ibid, 67-68
[84] Ibid, 68
[85] Ibid

13A

Joyce Ann Brown: The Wrong Joyce Brown

On May 6, 1980, two African American women robbed Fine Furs by Rubin, a fur store in Dallas, Texas. During the robbery, the owner, Rubin Danziger, was shot and killed. His wife was shot at but was not hit. The two robbers escaped in a vehicle that was later determined to be a rental car.

The rental car was located the following day, and it was determined that a Joyce Ann Brown rented the vehicle. The police found Joyce Ann Brown, who lived in Dallas and worked at another fur store, just several miles from the crime scene. The police showed Ms. Danziger, the victim's wife, a photo of Ms. Brown, and she identified the photo as the accomplice in the robbery, but not the person who shot her husband.

Ms. Brown was arrested and charged with the crime; her home was searched, but nothing was found. Prior to her arrest, Ms. Brown had gone to the police station because her name was in the paper as a suspect. She was attempting to clear her name.

In the interim, the police learned that the Joyce Ann Brown who rented the vehicle was from Denver, while the Joyce Ann Brown they had in custody was not. The Joyce Ann Brown from Denver was questioned about the robbery. She denied any involvement with the crime, and she said she loaned the rental car, meaning she rented it, to a friend, Renee Michelle Taylor.

The police failed to locate Ms. Taylor, but they obtained a search warrant and searched her apartment. The search revealed the stolen furs and clothing that matched the clothing worn by one suspect during the robbery, along with a .22-caliber pistol.

Joyce Ann Brown—not the one who rented the car, but the one who was arrested—was tried, found guilty, and sentenced to life in prison. The evidence against her included the testimony of Ms. Danziger and the testimony of a jailhouse informant. The jailhouse informant, Martha Bruce, said Ms. Brown told her of her involvement in the crime. At trial, Ms. Bruce was questioned about her criminal record. She related that she was recently convicted of attempted murder, but she failed to disclose her conviction of making a false statement to the police. She also refuted a claim that she was promised any leniency in exchange for her testimony.

The defense presented several witnesses as well as a timecard, which showed Ms. Brown was at work on the date of the crime, except for 36 minutes during her lunch break. The prosecution argued that Ms. Brown had time to change clothes, meet her accomplice, commit the crime, change clothes again, and return to work.

One month after Ms. Brown's conviction, the Dallas district attorney, Henry Wade, wrote the Board of Pardons and Paroles, requesting a reduced sentence for Martha Bruce, the jailhouse informant. She was released.

Six months later, Ms. Renee Taylor was arrested and charged with the crime. She accepted a plea agreement and pleaded guilty to the murder of Mr. Danziger. She refused to identify the second woman who participated in the robbery.

In 1989, the case against Ms. Joyce Ann Brown was appealed to the Texas Court of Appeals, and her conviction was reversed. It was concluded that Ms. Martha Jean Bruce, the jailhouse informant, had perjured herself during the trial of Ms. Brown. It was also disclosed that "the prosecutors failed to disclose that Bruce was in fact a convicted liar."[1] The prosecutors chose not to retry Ms. Joyce Brown. She served nine years and five months for a crime she did not commit.

The prosecution knew the Joyce Ann Brown they had in custody was not the person who rented the vehicle used in the crime. The only evidence they had was the victim identifying a photograph. To ensure a conviction, they used the testimony of a jailhouse informant who had been convicted of lying. Was there collusion between the prosecution and the jailhouse informant?

References

Deborah Fleck, "Joyce **Ann Brown**, a longtime advocate for the wrongly convicted, has died," The Dallas Moring News, June 13, 2015. www.innocenceporject.org, posting date before June 2012, updated: 6/13/2015

Bluhm Legal Clinic Center on Wrongful Convictions, "Joyce Ann Brown," Northwestern Pritzker School of Law, www.law.northwestern.edu/legalclinic/wrongfulconvictions/exonerations/tx/joyce-ann-brown.html, no date or author given.

---

[1] Bluhm Legal Clinic Center on Wrongful Convictions, "Joyce Ann Brown," Northwestern Pritzker School of Law www.law.northwestern.edu/legalclinic/wrongfulconvictions/exonerations/tx/joyce-ann-brown.html

14

Heath Testifies

MONDAY, AUGUST 22, 2011

"When you have eliminated the impossible, whatever remains, however improbable, must be the truth."

—Sherlock Holmes

On day five of the trial, there were only two witnesses, Ms. Carole O'Connor and Mr. Heath Thomas. Ms. O'Connor's testimony ended around 1 p.m. The Court adjourned for lunch and in the afternoon session, Heath testified in his defense. I was not in the courtroom that day, but my perspective was that the trial was not going well for Heath, so this was an important day for the defense.

Direct Examination

After Heath was sworn in, Mr. Hannon requested permission from the judge to show the defendant Exhibit 32, Heath's résumé, and Heath identified it. Mr. Hannon said, "I move 32 for the purpose of use by the witness in describing his professional background."[1] Mr. Rickard objected. Judge Dixon said, "I have the discretion to admit this document. So over your objection, it is admitted."[2]

Heath began by describing his work experience, starting with his government service at the age of 18 when he was in the U. S. Navy. After leaving the Navy, he joined the U. S. Border Patrol and was deployed to San Diego. In 1997 Heath became a criminal investigator with the Immigration and Naturalization Service (the predecessor of ICE, Immigration and Customs Enforcement). Four years later he was placed on long-term temporary duty overseas in Bosnia Herzegovina. Finally, in 2006 Heath was reassigned to agency headquarters in Washington, D.C.

Heath holds a Bachelor's in Education from Southern Illinois University in Carbondale. He completed his classes (distance learning program) in 2006 and graduated with honors.

Having established Heath's background, Mr. Hannon questioned him about Exhibit 37, a policy that covered firearms and holster use. Heath said the policies in Exhibit 37 included guidance for primary holster use. Mr. Hannon also introduced Exhibit 102,

---

[1] Information from the trial transcript, Criminal Action Number 2010-CF3-16079, dated August 22, 2011, p 69
[2] Ibid, 70

which was the holster Heath was wearing on the night of the incident. When questioned, he identified it as his holster. Mr. Hannon asked, "And were you authorized by ICE to wear that holster?"[3] Heath answered, "It is an authorized holster."[4]

"And what kind of gun were you carrying on August 28th?" Mr. Hannon asked. Heath answered, "A Sig 229R DAK."

Mr. Hannon introduced a plastic replica of the gun Heath was carrying on the evening of the incident. He requested permission from the Court to have Heath demonstrate how he wore the holster with his weapon, and the judge granted the request.

Heath stepped into the well of the court (an open space) and demonstrated the holster use. The holster is worn inside the pants, partially concealed, and affixed to the user's belt with a single snap loop. The snap loop is attached to the holster with a single screw-type rivet that allows the holster to cant in either direction.[5] The holster itself was molded plastic (Kydex type) and retained the weapon with friction.

Mr. Hannon asked if the holster was designed for the weapon he was wearing, and Heath said, "This is molded for this weapon."[6] Demonstrating the retention value of the holster, with the plastic gun replica in the holster, Heath held the holster upside down. The replica weapon did not fall out. He then moved the holster up and down, shaking it, which caused the replica weapon to fall out.

Mr. Hannon asked, "Did you customarily carry that weapon when you were outside working hours?" Heath said "No" and explained that he normally carried an H&K P2000 SK, which is smaller and lighter. He was not carrying the H&K, because it was in the repair shop.[7]

> Mr. Hannon: *Under ICE firearms policy, is there a restriction on ICE agents carrying weapons ... while drinking alcohol?*
> Heath: *Yes.*
> Mr. Hannon: *Could you tell the Court what that restriction is?*
> Heath: *We're not supposed to drink alcohol while carrying a weapon.*[8]
> Mr. Hannon: *Could you tell the Court why it is that you carry your weapon even when you may be drinking alcohol?*[9]

Heath explained that early in his career with the Border Patrol, his supervisor, Agent Lawrence B. Pierce, was involved in an off-duty incident. He was unarmed, and he was killed.[10]

---

[3] Ibid, 90
[4] Ibid
[5] Canting is tilting the gun and the holster forward or rearward, allowing the user to adjust the angle.
[6] Ibid
[7] Ibid, 93-94
[8] Ibid, 97
[9] Ibid, 98-99
[10] Ibid, 99 and information from the Officer Down Memorial Page, end of watch August 17, 1995, Appendix G

Left to Right: Photo of Holster taken by Adam Enatsky; photo of plastic insert gun and holster, taken by Adam Enatsky; and photo of holster on belt with plastic insert gun in holster taken bby Adam Enatsky.

Mr. Hannon continued, "So what is your personal and professional rule of the thumb when you are carrying your weapon and drinking alcohol?"[11]

Heath explained that if he were to drink, he did so in moderation by having only one drink an hour.

Mr. Hannon asked about the training he received on gun retention, and Heath responded, "It is training so that a law enforcement official maintains positive control over the weapon."[12] He said he received weapon retention training in his basic academy, in transition classes, and in conjunction with his martial arts training.

Heath then explained the plans for the evening of the incident. He said they were going out to dinner with Carole's former colleagues and their spouses. The group was expected to include six people. He and Carole took a cab to Georgetown, where they joined the rest of the group and had dinner. He did not have anything alcoholic to drink before arriving at the restaurant. While at dinner, he drank three and a half Red Hook beers in plastic cups. He said they left the restaurant "After 11:00."[13]

After leaving Old Glory, the group walked a short distance and entered The Guards, which was down the street from the restaurant. Mr. Hannon asked how Mr. Brackett, the bouncer, was dressed. Heath said he was wearing a dark-colored shirt; "Actually, I more remember his affect than anything else."[14] Mr. Hannon asked, "Why?" Heath answered, "Carole tried to make a joke with him and he was more standoffish. … he was kind of rude."[15]

When they entered The Guards, the group went to the bar area. Heath remembered the bartender, Ms. Marina Yudina, who had testified on August 15, 2011. He said that he ordered a beer, and after tasting it, he returned it because it tasted so bad. He told the bartender to "just leave it on the tab. And she said no, no, don't worry about it, you haven't drank [sic] any of it."[16]

---

[11] Information from the trial transcript, Criminal Action Number 2010-CF3-16079, dated August 22, 2011, p 99
[12] Ibid, 101
[13] Ibid, 106
[14] Ibid, 107
[15] Ibid
[16] Ibid, 107-108

After returning the beer, the group moved to a table, which was more conducive to conversation. Heath was asked if he recognized Ms. Perez, the waitress, who also testified on the first day of the trial. He answered, "She looked familiar to me … she appeared to be the waitress that served us."[17]

When asked about the drink service, he said the waitress came over to the table and asked if they needed drinks; Mr. Jones ordered a "Bombay sapphire martini."[18] Mr. Jones had already bought one at the bar, so this was his second. Heath asked about the drink, saying, "Are those any good?"[19] Mr. Jones said yes, so he ordered one.

When the waitress returned with the drinks, Mr. Jones "held his up and sniffed it and said, 'This isn't gin.'" The waitress and Mr. Jones had a discussion, "and she [the waitress] seemed to be flustered."[20]

The waitress took the drinks back to the bar. When she returned, she said "that the bartender said that he had made us gin martinis and they were gin martinis."[21] The waitress put a drink in front of Heath and started to put a drink in front of Mr. Jones. Mr. Jones moved, and "she dropped or spilled almost all of his martini on him in the process."[22] Heath said he was not sure who hit the table or if the waitress did something, but the table moved, and his glass tipped over. He added, "I caught the glass, but there was only a small amount left in it. I kind of slid back a little bit, but I got martini on my shirt and arm."[23]

Mr. Hannon: "does that take care of the events regarding the service of alcohol that evening that you found unusual?"[24] Heath added that Mr. Jones and the waitress discussed the service, and he told Mr. Jones, "it is no big deal … we'll just get another round … And I looked at her [the waitress] like, obviously, you are not going to charge us for these."[25]

The group had to wait for some time for the waitress to return. When she did return with the drinks, Carole told him that the Spradlins needed to leave. Heath took a sip from his drink and went to the bar to pay the tab.

> Mr. Hannon: *So what did you do?*
> Heath: *I got up from the table and I walked directly to the bar, probably at the midpoint of the bar and engaged the blond bartender. At that point the waitress* [that served them at the table] *came up and was very excited about wanting to take care of the tab. I said no, no, don't worry about it. I will take care of it at the bar. We wanted to leave.*

---

[17] Ibid, 108
[18] Ibid
[19] Ibid
[20] Ibid, 109
[21] Ibid
[22] Ibid
[23] Ibid, 109
[24] Ibid
[25] Ibid, 110

> Mr. Hannon: *Now, did you go up there with the intention of not leaving a tip?*
> Heath: *No. I wanted — I just wanted to pay the tab.*[26]

The bartender asked Heath for the names on the tab, and he told her, "O'Connor and [Jones]" and, "she seemed kind of confused. And I said I am right at this table right behind me. And she just looked at me confused again. And I said the tab is O'Connor and Jones. And she says, well – I don't remember exactly what she said but something to the effect that I need the names. I said, I gave you all of the names. And she says, 'no, you didn't.'"[27]

As the conversation continued, the bartender said, "there has to be other names." Heath answered that he did not know. He explained, "I was assuming that they … identified the tables in a way that they would know what tabs were at the table."[28]

He continued, "And right around that point, a male bartender came from the back of the bar and engaged. And he says, sir, you have to give us the names. And I said, I just gave you all of the names. And I said O'Connor and Jones. And he wasn't – he actually seemed perturbed with me more so than anything else. I kind of was not – I was feeling exasperated because all I wanted to do was pay the bill."[29]

Mr. Hannon asked, "So what did you do?"[30] He said that he noticed an older Hispanic gentleman who looked like the Manager; he was wearing a tie and standing at the bar by the brass railing.

> Heath: *…So I walked up to him. And I remember watching the bartender follow us on the other side of the bar. He had something in his hands. I don't remember what it was. … as I walked up to Oscar* [Viricochea, the manager], *he looked surprised and kind of perturbed that I was engaging him. And I asked him in English, are you the Manager? And he says yes. And I said do you speak Spanish? And he said yes. So I then proceed to engage him in Spanish.*
> Mr. Hannon: *Why?*
> Heath: *I wanted to have a private conversation with him. Mr. Fleming was – or what I later found out … the male bartender – seemed to be just hanging about. And I wanted to discuss this with the Manager.*[31]

When conversing with Mr. Viricochea, he and the manager were to the right of the brass rail, outside of the serving area.

---

[26] Ibid
[27] Ibid, 111
[28] Ibid
[29] Ibid, 111-112
[30] Ibid, 112
[31] Ibid

> Mr. Hannon: *What did you say to him in Spanish?*
> Heath: *Basically, what I told him was that all I want to do is pay the tab, but this lack of consideration from your staff: One, being rude; and, two, they can't seem to find my tab. And we haven't been getting very good service. ... and all I really wanted to do is just take care of the tab and tell him that he needs to work on it. And I wanted to leave. My party wanted to leave.*
> Mr. Hannon: *Did he speak to you in Spanish?*
> Heath: *No. He actually only made one comment to me.*
> Mr. Hannon: *What was that?*
> Heath: *If you don't like it, you can call the police.*
> Mr. Hannon: *Was that in English or Spanish?*
> Heath: *In English.*
> Mr. Hannon: *What did you hear next?*
> Heath: *I didn't hear anything next because what I did was raised my hand to go – to kind of like, okay, I am not getting anywhere. I turned to face the bar and reached into my cargo pocket, my left cargo pocket because that is where my wallet was at, to try and engage the bartender – okay, look, how much is it? So I can pay. And next is when I felt a hit.*[32]

Mr. Hannon asked, "Prior to that, had you said anything about being a police officer?" Heath explained that after the manager told him that he could call the police, "I was a bit rude and exasperated and I said, 'I am the fucking police.'"[33] He said that in English, and that was the only profanity he used.

> Mr. Hannon: *Describe what you mean when you say you felt the hit?*
> Heath: *It was like playing football. It is like getting tackled. I felt someone hit me around the midsection. And I felt my head go back and I was wondering if I was going to hit the bar. And I felt my hands get pinned around my waist and then I was lifted up.*
> Mr. Hannon: *And what was your reaction to that?*
> Heath: *Surprised, a little bit of alarm – kind of wondering why is this happening ... I am trying to pay the bill ... I started thinking, okay, what do I need to do next?*
> Mr. Hannon: *Did you know who the person was that hit you from the rear?*
> Heath: *No.*[34]

Now, recall that the bouncer testified on August 16 that he said something to Heath and touched his arm several times before picking him up. If he did so, Heath would

---

[32] Ibid, 113-114
[33] Ibid, 114
[34] Ibid, 115

have been aware of his presence and his intent, and he would not have been surprised as he just described. Mr. Brackett saying something to Heath and touching his arm before picking him up has about the same probability as the bouncer picking Heath up around his shoulders.

Mr. Hannon asked Heath to demonstrate to the Court how his arms were positioned when he was in the bear hug. When he did so, his elbows were at his side. His hands were to his front, and his arms were pinned. Heath did not know who picked him up, but when talking to the manager, there was a person on his left side, possibly the doorman, but he did not see the person approach him.

> Mr. Hannon: *And so he picks you up and then what happens?*
> Heath: *We start to move relatively quickly to the front of the bar. I remember thinking, okay, should I do something? And I am thinking, no, because there is really no room — I need more information to process this. … I don't understand why this is happening. I remember getting to the doorway and thinking, you know, I could push off the doorway and escalate this, but I didn't think that was a good idea at that time either.*
> Mr. Hannon: *How would you push off the doorway?*
> Heath: *I could have put my foot out against the door jamb and created an off-balancing move. Whoever it was, you could tell that they were arched back and the way they were moving … they were having a little bit of problems with my weight.*[35]
> When asked, Heath said he weighed 190 pounds and was 5 feet 7 inches tall.
> Mr. Hannon: *And when you say you were trying to think of whether to do something, what else did you think of?*
> Heath: *I actually thought that it wasn't a good idea to do anything because at that point … I don't have enough information as to what is going on. I do feel threatened, but there are people around … it would exacerbate the situation.*
> Mr. Hannon: *Did you speak to the person who was carrying you?*
> Heath: *No. There wasn't much time to. And I didn't think he could hear me anyway, because their head was like in the middle of my back.*[36]
> Mr. Hannon asked what happened after they went through the inside doors.
> Heath: *We went out through the doors* [the second set to the street] *and then we started going down the steps and there everything seemed to speed up, because it was almost like we were falling … and as we were going down the stairs, what I noticed was I felt my gun dislodge in its holster. I felt it moving on its own, which was probably one of the most terrifying things I have ever felt, because I – I had no way to secure it. My arms were pinned and this thing feels like it is moving around on its own. So as we come down the stairs and we get to the stoop, it is almost like we*

---

[35] Ibid, 116
[36] Ibid, 117

launched off the stoop because we were moving pretty quickly. And I felt him release his grip. And I fell forward and I caught myself with my right foot forward. And the first thing that I thought of doing was I need to secure this gun before it falls out onto the street. I have had that happen before and it is not – is not a feel-good situation ...

Mr. Hannon: So what did you do?

Heath: *... the motion for securing the gun would be to go to it with both hands.*

Mr. Hannon: Why?

Heath: *Well, that is also the way we train. You always move with both hands. ... you want to retain it, so two hands are always better than one to keep it... — to make sure that it was pushed back in the holster... to do that, I had to get my shirt out of the way. Because my shirt is a cover article. So as I pull the shirt up ... get ahold of the grip and push it back in. ... At that time, I am kind of — I am stepping out on my right foot and I am turning my right shoulder going forward ... I never feel the individual come off of me. I just feel the release of the arms. And then I feel him kind of fall into me and grab at me again when I started moving. As I started moving, he grabs at me. He actually hits my right arm. And I am thinking now I am going to end up losing control of the gun so I grab it harder. And he actually forces it out of the holster. I try to pivot to go get away from that hit on the right arm and then I feel his left hand come around my left bicep and he grabs the muzzle of the weapon ...*

Mr. Hannon: *Where was your left hand when he grabbed the muzzle of the weapon?*

Heath: *It was almost touching my right hand.*[37]

Heath asked if he could demonstrate; the judge said yes and allowed Heath to move to the well. Mr. Hannon asked Heath to describe the movement and then present it.

Heath: *As I am trying to get both hands on the gun ... the individual* [the bouncer] *put his left hand around the — what would be the slide and muzzle of the weapon ...*

Mr. Hannon: *And when that occurred, your right hand was on the weapon?*

Heath: *My right hand was here* [on the grip] *and my left hand was coming up to the grip ...*

Judge Dixon: *Before you go forward, would you start again from reaching under your shirt to the gun and describe what happened ... you will get a chance to demonstrate it, but just describe what happened when the person grabbed you again because we started to do the demonstration then we came back to explain. I just want to hear the continuity of it.*

Heath: *... as I am dropped and I feel the release of the bear hug, I am off balance so I step out with my right foot to gain my balance and I start to make the motion to secure my weapon with both hands. I am bladed* [at an angle to the other party] *and*

---

[37] Ibid, 117-119

> then I feel the individual who I have never felt leave my back ... his chest has been to my back. I feel him grab at me again. And when he grabs at me again, he hits my right arm, which forces my hand up, because I am trying to secure this weapon. The weapon comes out of the holster. I try to turn more to my left. ... As I turn and I am trying to get a two-handed grip, another hand comes over and grabs the muzzle of the weapon.[38]
>
> ... At that point, I am trying to lower my center of gravity and step away, but this individual is still on my back. And what I feel at that point is a sharp pull that actually causes me to step back. And I feel the gun pull upward and I am trying to center my body and my weight to pull the gun down and keep it pointed downwards and in a safe direction.[39]

The demonstration concluded, Heath returned to the witness stand and the defense resumed direct examination.

Mr. Hannon asked, "Did you recognize the circumstances that you were in when he grabbed the muzzle from your training?"[40] He said, "Yes. This was serious – my life was in danger. Somebody was trying to take my gun away from me."[41]

Mr. Hannon asked Heath whether he had experienced someone grabbing the muzzle of his gun, and he said yes, it was part of his training. When asked about options a person has when someone grabs their gun, Heath said there were several de-escalation and defensive tactics the person could use. The purpose of these tactics is to have the offender release the weapon. Describing the defensive tactics, Heath said, "you can be offensive and either use empty-hand techniques like kicks, ... or you can turn into the individual and go offensive and you can shoot them off your gun."[42]

> Mr. Hannon asked what happened after the bouncer had his hand on the muzzle.
> Heath: *I pulled the weapon in close and tight ... you are getting as much of your body around the weapon and you are using your body... to give you as much leverage in retaining the weapon. I also ... centered my weight, lowered my center of gravity ... And at the same time I began to verbalize to this individual who I was.*
> Mr. Hannon: *What did you say?*
> Heath: *I am a federal police officer, let go of the gun.*
> Mr. Hannon: *What was his response?*
> Heath: *I don't care. I don't care. I am taking it away from you.*

---

[38] Ibid, 120-121
[39] Ibid, 121-122
[40] Ibid, 122
[41] Ibid
[42] Ibid, 123

Mr. Hannon: *Now, could you describe your tone of voice?*

Heath: *... we are pretty much very close, almost face to face. I was empathic ... but I was trying to be clear and concise and make the statement in such a way that it is not escalating. I am trying to get him to understand... I am not planning on hurting you; this is not my point.*

Mr. Hannon: *Did you verbalize anything like that to him?*

Heath: *Yes, I told him I wasn't going to shoot him.*

Mr. Hannon: *What was his response?*

Heath: *I don't care. I am taking the gun away.*[43]

Heath continued, "I heard him yell ... in the midst of the struggle, this time louder, that he didn't care, he was going to take the gun away from me."[44]

Mr. Hannon: *Now, what was the movement after he had the muzzle in his left hand?*

Heath: *... not very large movements until I think he was actually becoming much more agitated because he couldn't take the gun away from me. I think that was actually an anger point for the individual, because he seemed to be - he was escalating as opposed to trying to separate. His motions and mannerisms that I felt were becoming more violent. But he was starting to tire out...*[45]

Mr. Hannon: *Where did you move –... from the point that he had the handle (sic) on the muzzle?*

Heath: *We moved across the sidewalk. And I remember that at one point he seemed to – we both made the same motion and we ended up against a vehicle... And as we were up against the vehicle. ... I pulled the gun away and he pushes the gun away. And it seems at that point, we are both tiring. And without really saying anything, we were happy with the stalemate. I was happy I still had both hands on the gun. He had one hand around my waist, one hand on the gun. I keep telling him to let go. He wouldn't let go. And right around that point is when I heard sirens. And I was thinking to myself, okay, I am getting tired here, if we start up another bout of fighting, I am going to have to take another course.*

Mr. Hannon: *What effect did this struggle have on your strength to maintain control of the weapon?*

Heath: *I was starting to get pretty tired and I was thinking that ... this individual is pretty big. I am not really a big guy, but I am pretty strong. But this guy was – he is probably one of the biggest guys I have ever had to struggle with...*[46]

---

[43] Ibid, 123-124
[44] Ibid, 124
[45] Ibid, 124-125
[46] Ibid, 125-126

Mr. Hannon asked about the physical strength he was using to hold on to the weapon. Heath responded, "I was over 100 percent. I was giving everything to keep that weapon ... I was going to have to change tactics or do something else ... I knew I was going to be exhausted. This scene was life or death."[47]

Mr. Hannon asked, "Did you believe that you were capable of doing something else besides tiring in this stalemate?" Heath answered, "Yes."[48]

That answer led to questions about what he was capable of and what options he could have used.

> Heath: *I think if need be, I could have harmed the individual drastically.*
> Mr. Hannon: *... in what way?*
> Heath: *I probably could have turned the tables on him and shot him.*
> Mr. Hannon: *You described something earlier, 'shoot him off the gun.' What is that?*
> Heath: *It is an option that is taught in certain weapons retention courses that if it gets to a point where you think you are going to lose total control over the gun, you have to keep in mind that the individual is not trying to take the gun away to be nice to you... — and it is a deadly force issue at that point that you shoot them before you let them have control ...*
> Mr. Hannon: *Does the weapon have to be pointed at the individual before you would shoot?*
> Heath: *The training I have, yes...*[49]

Mr. Hannon asked what would happen if he could not point the gun at the bouncer, and Heath replied that if he could not point the gun at the bouncer, he would not shoot. He explained that he needed to know what was in front of the muzzle (the direction the bullet would travel).

> Mr. Hannon: *What happened when the police arrived?*
> Heath: *When the police arrived, the individual jumped off me and kind of made motions pointing at me. I don't remember what he said. I remember focusing on what the police were saying. The police said, drop the weapon ... I put my hands up and I dropped the weapon.*[50]
> At that point Mr. Hannon moved forward in time, asking about Heath's meeting with Agent John Eisert.
> Mr. Hannon: *... could you tell the Court what your demeanor was at that time?*

---

[47] Ibid, 126
[48] Ibid, 127
[49] Ibid, 127-128
[50] Ibid, 128-129

Heath: *I say my thoughts were racing. I was very concerned about the position I found myself in. I was trying to play out what different scenarios were as to what was going to happen to me.*

Mr. Hannon: *Is it correct that you did not make eye contact then?*

Heath: *I remembered looking at him. He may not have seen me when I did it. I was kind of leaning up against the back wall...*[51]

Mr. Hannon: *What was your goal in the conversation that you had with Detective Tabron ...?*

Heath: *I was trying to find out from him what exactly, if any, were avenues open to me ... were they actually interested in finding out what happened or were ... they were already down the road putting me in jail.*

Mr. Hannon: *Why did you decide not to talk to them?*

Heath: *It became pretty obvious to me that anything I said to him at that point wasn't going to change the outcome of that evening ... I felt that since the conduct of the police from the scene was prejudicial, I thought it best to wait until I could talk to an attorney.*[52]

Returning to the incident, Mr. Hannon asked Heath if he was intoxicated when Mr. Brackett picked him up. He answered, "No."[53]

Mr. Hannon requested the judge's permission to conduct a demonstration of the event, with Mr. Hannon playing the role of Mr. Brackett and Heath playing himself. The judge allowed the demonstration, and Heath used his holster (defense Exhibit 102) along with a molded plastic replica of the gun.

Heath went through the demonstration while describing his movements—going forward, lifting his shirt with his left hand, at the same time turning left to keep the gun away from whoever was behind him. He was reaching with his right hand for the pistol grip when something hit his right arm. He said he was not sure if it was Mr. Brackett's forearms, but since his hand was already on the pistol grip, "it dislodges the gun."[54] He described and demonstrated that he was trying to get his left hand to the gun when he felt another hand—Mr. Brackett's left hand—grab the muzzle of his gun. Almost at the same time, Heath's left hand reached the weapon, so he had two hands on the firearm's grip. He continued to demonstrate the pulling and pushing of the gun, a back-and-forth motion while keeping the muzzle pointed down.

Mr. Hannon asked about the placement of his right index finger (his trigger finger) when he was holding the gun. Heath explained that his right index finger was straight

---

[51] Ibid, 129-130
[52] Ibid, 130
[53] Ibid
[54] Ibid, 132

and along the right side of the frame. He said the trigger finger stays off the trigger until you are going to shoot.

> Mr. Hannon: *Did you ever have your finger in the trigger?*
> Heath: *No.*
> Mr. Hannon: *… did you ever attempt to or actually display your credentials to Marshall Brackett outside the bar?*
> Heath: *No.*
> Mr. Hannon: *Were your credentials on the hood of the vehicle when the police came?*
> Heath: *No.*
> Mr. Hannon: *Where were the credentials?*
> Heath: *They were in my left cargo pocket.*[55]

An officer asked Heath for his credentials after the incident, he said, but he was handcuffed, so he told the officer where the credentials were. Heath explained, "The officer reached into my cargo pocket, took them out, he opened them up and then he gave them to another officer."[56]

That concluded Mr. Hannon's questions.

Initiating his cross-examination, Mr. Rickard stated as a question that Heath was not on duty when the incident occurred and that he had no official responsibility at either establishment on the evening of occurrence. Heath agreed. Mr. Rickard went over some previous testimony affirming that Heath was with Carole, and they went out to see her friends. He said they took a taxi because he might be drinking and asked Heath if that was correct.

> Heath: *Potentially.*
> Mr. Rickard: *When you say potentially, that is because you are concerned about your ability to operate a vehicle when you have been drinking; correct?*
> Heath: *Yes.*
> Mr. Rickard: *At Old Glory you ordered at least four Red Hooks with dinner; correct?*
> Heath: *Yes.*[57]

Mr. Rickard showed Heath Government's Exhibit 14, which displays three tabs for Old Glory on the night of the incident. He had Heath identify his tab, which was one of the three.[58]

---

[55] Ibid, 136
[56] Ibid, 137
[57] Ibid, 140
[58] Ibid, 141 and U.S. v. Heath Thomas, Governments Exhibit 14 Case No. 2010 CF3 016079, Old Glory Restaurant Tab

Mr. Rickard said after leaving Old Glory, the group went to The Guards to buy more drinks. "You didn't go there for any reason other than to buy more alcoholic drinks; correct?"[59] Heath answered, "Actually, we went there to sit and chat some more. But it wasn't to just buy drinks, we were going to continue our discussions."[60]

Mr. Rickard noted that Heath ordered a beer at the bar when they first arrived and two martinis at the table, and Heath agreed. Mr. Rickard asked, "One of the martinis was spilled at some point?"[61] Heath answered, "Yes."[62]

Mr. Rickard went over other problems with the service at The Guards to which Heath and his companions had testified, including the dirty martinis that weren't dirty and the martinis not made from gin. Again, Heath agreed.

Mr. Rickard: *The waitress just couldn't get it right; correct?*
Heath: *I don't know if that was the issue or not.*
Mr. Rickard: *You thought she was annoyed at you and the table, correct?*
Heath: *I got that impression that ... she was overwhelmed.*
Mr. Rickard: *And you said the service was slow, right?*
Heath: *Yes.*[63]

Mr. Rickard went back to the service at Old Glory, where the group had dinner, saying that the service there was slow as well, and Heath agreed. He then repeated that the service at The Guards was also slow, and Heath agreed.

Mr. Rickard: *After all of those problems with the drinks, you went up to the bar to try and get the tab; right?*
Heath: *Yes.*
Mr. Rickard: *But even though you gave them the name, they just kept asking you, that's your testimony, isn't it?*
Heath: *They didn't seem to be able to produce a tab, yes.*[64]

Mr. Rickard talked about the wedding party coming in, noting that they were being served, while Heath was still waiting for his tab.

Heath: *I don't know what they were doing.*
Mr. Rickard: *You felt that they weren't paying attention to you, didn't you?*

---

[59] Information from the trial transcript, Criminal Action Number 2010-CF3-16079, dated August 22, 2011, p 141
[60] Ibid
[61] Ibid, 142
[62] Ibid
[63] Ibid, 142
[64] Ibid, 143

Heath: *I really hadn't looked at it that way, so –*

Mr. Rickard: *Then this bartender – male bartender came up and intervened in the situation: right?*

Heath: *Yes.*

Mr. Rickard: *And you felt he was disrespectful to you, didn't you?*

Heath: *No, I don't think he was disrespectful.*

Mr. Rickard: *Didn't you say something on direct, he was petulant or annoyed at you or something like that?*

Heath: *He seemed annoyed … he just seemed to interject himself into the situation.*

Mr. Rickard: *And he just kept asking you the same questions, right, the names on the tab?*

Heath: *He asked me one question which involved the names on the tab. And when I told him that I had given him the names, he answered that, no, I hadn't and that's when I went and talked to the Manager.*

Mr. Rickard: *So they just couldn't understand that you had given the names?*

Heath: *Apparently.*

Mr. Rickard: *And you were upset enough to swear at the bartender, weren't you?*

Heath: *Excuse me.*

Mr. Rickard: *You were upset enough to swear at the bartender.*

Heath: *I didn't swear at the bartender.*

Mr. Rickard: *And you were upset enough that you needed to go have a private conversation with the Manager in Spanish; right?*

Heath: *I was bothered enough by the situation that I sought out the Manager, yes.*

Mr. Rickard: *You got in his face; right?*

Heath: *No.*[65]

Mr. Rickard repeated previous testimony that Heath went to the service area.

Mr. Rickard: *It's easier for you to get attention when you are in the service area?*

Heath: *I actually went to the service area because the Manager was standing there.*

Mr. Rickard: *He [the Manager] told you to leave, didn't he?*

Heath: *No.*

Mr. Rickard: *… your testimony is that there was no mention of the bouncer or security before you were suddenly picked up?*

Heath: *That's correct.*

Mr. Rickard: *So it is your testimony that it was to Oscar [the Manager] that you said you "are the fucking police"?*

Heath: *Yes.*[66]

---

[65] Ibid, 144-145
[66] Ibid, 145-146

Mr. Rickard repeated Heath's testimony that he was picked up with no warning and that no one asked him to leave, and Heath agreed.

> Mr. Rickard: *You have no recollection of anyone coming up and asking you to leave?*
> Heath: *That is correct.*
> Mr. Rickard: *You are not able to recall anyone trying to pull you out of the bar; correct?*
> Heath: *No one did that.*
> Mr. Rickard: *At that time, other than saying, I am the F'ing police, you hadn't identified yourself as a police officer; correct?*
> Heath: *That's correct.*[67]
> Mr. Rickard: *You didn't want to be let* (sic; led) *out of by security, did you?*[68]
> Heath: *I wasn't expecting that.*[69]

Mr. Rickard questioned Heath about dropping his weight when he was picked up; Heath answered that did not happen. Mr. Rickard then asked why he did not do so if it could be done to resist. Heath said it could not be done once you are picked up; you need a warning that someone is about to pick you up.

Heath's response here is accurate. With a warning that you are about to be picked up, if you drop your weight, the person attempting to pick you up grabs you around your shoulders or above. When grabbed around the shoulders, raising the elbows prevents the grabber from holding you. This again challenges the bouncer's claim that he picked Heath up by the shoulders. Had he done so, Heath could have most likely slipped out of his grip.

Mr. Rickard asked Heath why he remained silent while being carried out. Heath repeated his testimony that he believed the bouncer could not hear him. According to Heath, he was grabbed around the waist, and the bouncer's head was in Heath's back.

> Mr. Rickard: *When you got outside, he put you down on your feet; right?*
> Heath: *– he dropped me.*
> Mr. Rickard: *You landed on your feet; right?*
> Heath: *Yes.*
> Mr. Rickard: *He released you?*
> Heath: *He dropped me is a better way to characterize it.*
> Mr. Rickard: *And at that time, you didn't identify yourself to him as a police officer?*
> Heath: *There wasn't a lot of time.*
> Mr. Rickard: *You didn't step forward, did you?*

---

[67] Ibid, 146-147
[68] Ibid, 147
[69] Ibid

Heath: *I did step forward.*
Mr. Rickard: *Just with your right foot?*
Heath: *That's all the time I had.*
Mr. Rickard: *You didn't create any distance?*
Heath: *slightly. ... But he was falling into me.*
Mr. Rickard: *You said that on direct, he was falling into you?*
Heath: *That's what it felt like.*
Mr. Rickard: *You didn't see or feel anyone behind him pushing him into you, did you?*
Heath: *No.*
Mr. Rickard: *Now, according to your training and experience, creating distance would have been the best thing to do in that situation, wouldn't it?*
Heath: *Yes. And I was attempting to.*
Mr. Rickard: *There was no one in front of you, was there?*
Heath: *No.*
Mr. Rickard: *You said that the bouncer put you down on the sidewalk?*
Heath: *Yes.*
Mr. Rickard: *So nothing was blocking the path in front of you; correct?*
Heath: *Not that I recall.*
Mr. Rickard: *You didn't identify yourself until after Ms. O'Connor came out and she said you were a federal police officer; right?*
Heath: *I don't know about the timing of that. I believe I was already talking to him when we were struggling.*[70]

Mr. Rickard asked about the wording Heath used and Heath replied that he used both, "a police officer and ... a federal agent."[71]

Mr. Rickard: *In fact you are a special agent with Immigration and Customs Enforcement; right?*
Heath: *Correct.*
Mr. Rickard: *You are not just a federal police officer?*
Heath: *But most people don't understand that, so usually a police officer seems to resonate with most people. That's why most raid gear says police on it as opposed to special agent.*
Mr. Rickard: *You didn't identify yourself as a police officer when you were released because you weren't acting as a police officer then, were you?*

---

[70] Ibid, 148-150
[71] Ibid, 150

Heath: *No.*

Mr. Rickard: *... you said there wasn't time to identify yourself as a police officer; correct?*

Heath: *This is correct.*

Mr. Rickard: *But nothing kept you from talking while you moved the rest of your body; right?*

Heath: *I was more focused on trying to retain my weapon ... and find out what this assault behavior ... was coming from. ... I don't know where it was coming from, so I didn't know who to verbalize it to.*

Mr. Rickard: *You didn't know who the pressure was coming from, is that what you just said?*

Heath: *I knew it was somebody behind me, but I didn't know exactly for sure who it was.*

Mr. Rickard: *You didn't know it was a person capable of hearing words, is that what you're saying?*

Heath: *I am saying I did not think of it in that point. What I was thinking about was mainly weapons retention.*[72]

Mr. Rickard: *Would you agree that giving verbal commands is one important part of weapons retention; right?*

Heath: *It's part of the use of force, yes.*

Mr. Rickard: *And the very first – according to this ICE policy that was marked as defense exhibit, the very first thing you would do in any use of force situation is to identify yourself as a police officer; right?*

Heath: *That is incorrect. Use of force continuum says that there is an action and then a response. So depending on what the perceptions of the officer are of what the action ... the officer chooses amongst a litany of responses.*[73]

Police policies contain language that tells officers to use verbal commands *when and where feasible.*

Mr. Rickard: *One thing you can do is identify yourself as a police officer; right?*

Heath: *And I eventually attempted to.*

Mr. Rickard: *Part of your identifying yourself as a police officer is having a courteous and professional demeanor according to ICE policy, isn't it?*

Heath: *Yes.*[74]

---

[72] Ibid, 150-152
[73] Ibid, 152
[74] Ibid, 152-153

Mr. Rickard reiterated that verbal commands were also an option, and Heath agreed.

> Mr. Rickard: *You should shout things like get off my gun, right? That would be something you could do?*
> Heath: *That is all in the realm of possible.*
> Mr. Rickard: *It is just not what is possible, it is what you are trained to do, right?*
> Heath: *Actually, I don't remember being in a training course where they told me to use that particular verbiage.*
> Mr. Rickard: *Are you familiar with ICE use of force policy from July 7, 2005?*
> Heath: *I don't know it verbatim.*
> Mr. Rickard: *But you have been trained on the idea that verbal commands should be in a professional and firm voice, right?*
> Heath: *Yes.*
> Mr. Rickard: *And that instructions should be simple, easy to understand and repeated as necessary?*
> Heath: *Yes.*
>
> Mr. Rickard: *But that is not what you're doing; right? You didn't give those commands?*
>
> Heath: *I did. I asked him to get off the gun.*
> Mr. Rickard: *That was later when he had his hand on the muzzle, correct?*
> Heath: *He had his hand on the muzzle the whole time.*
> Mr. Rickard: *But before he had his hand on the muzzle, you didn't give him any commands about you being a police officer?*
> Heath: *There wasn't any time. It was a pretty fluid situation. I didn't have time to talk to him.*
> Mr. Rickard: *You were outraged that he had carried you out; isn't that true?*
> Heath: *I was concerned.*
> Mr. Rickard: *And you never told any of the officers that you were trying to arrest Mr. Brackett, right?*
> Heath: *No.*[75]

Mr. Rickard repeated the same question in a different manner, and the judge asked counsel to approach the bench.

> Judge Dixon: *All right. Now in terms of what he told the officers when they arrived, once a person is taken into custody, they don't have any obligation to say anything to anybody. There were no objections [from defense counsel] so I don't know whether or not for strategy reasons you are deciding not to object or what. But I don't want*

---
[75] Ibid, 153-155

any issue of ineffectiveness of this hearing. Is there an objection to those statements, to those questions, that is what he told police officers after they arrived or not?

Mr. Hannon: *No, sir.*[76]

That ended the bench conference. Mr. Rickard then continued.

Mr. Rickard: *At the time that you were being carried out and you were released, you weren't in fear at all, were you?*
Heath: *Actually, I was.*
Mr. Rickard: *Isn't it true that you were amused by what had happened?*
Heath: *No.*[77]

Mr. Rickard referenced documents filed with the Court for the conditions of release when Heath was in custody. In the paperwork from Heath's attorney to the Court, it said, "However, Agent Thomas, somewhat amused by the doorman's actions allowed himself to be physically taken out of the front door of the restaurant."[78] Mr. Rickard read the passage from the documents, and Heath agreed that the quote had been in the paperwork.

Mr. Rickard: *So I am just trying to figure out what was going on here. You weren't making an arrest; correct?*
Heath: *Correct.*
Mr. Rickard: *And you were amused, not in fear?*
Heath: *That is not accurate.*
Mr. Rickard: *And you weren't identifying yourself like you have learned in your policy, correct?*
Heath: *Yes.*
Mr. Rickard: *That is because you were angry and outraged at what happened in the bar, isn't it?*
Heath: *No.*
Mr. Rickard: *And it is because you were drunk, isn't it?*
Heath: *No.*

Mr. Rickard then described Heath as a trained federal agent with a third-degree black belt in aikido, and Heath agreed.

---

[76] Ibid, 155
[77] Ibid, 156
[78] Ibid, 157 Governments Exhibit 26, Case No. 2010 CF3 016079, conditions of release from Heath's arrest

Mr. Rickard: *So if you were sober, it would have been no problem for you to disable Mr. Brackett, right?*

Heath: *I don't think that would have been a problem to do at the time. That is not what my goal was.*

Mr. Rickard: *You would have been able to disengage from him without pulling your gun, right?*

Heath: *I didn't need my gun. I was trying to retain my gun.*[79]

Mr. Rickard then changed the focus of his questioning, asking, "In fact, as you testified on direct, you made a conscious decision to go drinking with your firearm that night; right?"[80] Heath answered, "Yes."

Mr. Rickard repeated the ICE firearms policy, specifically, "ICE policy is that ICE officers are prohibited from consuming alcoholic beverages while carrying any firearms, except when engaged in operational activities necessitating the consumption of alcoholic beverages."[81] Heath agreed.

Mr. Rickard also quoted from the ICE policy for holsters.

Mr. Rickard: *'Handguns must be carried in a holster provided by ICE or in one that meets the same minimum standards as prescribed by the NFTTU [National Firearms and Tactical Training Unit]. Officers with ICE approved personally-owned handguns must provide their own holsters and related leather gear for their personally-owned weapon.'*[82] *Are you familiar with that policy?*

Heath: *Yes.*

Mr. Rickard: *And the policy regarding holsters, Government Exhibit 23 which defense counsel also showed you on direct, that says, 'Holsters must have at least one positive retention device that requires some deliberate actions by the wearer to release the weapon, such as a thumb brake.' Are you familiar with that policy?*

Heath: *It is not a policy; it is a guideline.*

Mr. Rickard: *That is a guideline that you are strongly encouraged to follow when off duty, isn't it?*

Heath: *Yes.*

Mr. Rickard: *Is it your testimony that friction is a positive retention device like a thumb break?*

Heath: *It is not similar to a thumb break, no.*[83]

---

[79] Information from the trial transcript, Criminal Action Number 2010-CF3-16079, dated August 22, 2011, p 158

[80] Ibid, 159

[81] Ibid, 160

[82] Ibid, 160-161 and U.S. Immigrations and Customs Enforcement, Guidance for Primary Firearms Holsters, December 2004, Government Exhibit 23

[83] Information from the trial transcript, Criminal Action Number 2010-CF3-16079, dated August 22, 2011, p 161-162

Contrary to Heath's statement, holster manufacturers consider friction a security level, just like a thumb break is a level. Since it holds the gun with friction, the holster Heath used would be viewed as a retention holster.

Moving to a new line of questioning, Mr. Rickard stated the police did not seize the holster Heath was wearing the night of the incident. The holster was found when Heath was at the police station; it was not found at the scene, nor was it displayed or taken from him at the scene. The police held the holster for a few days and then returned it to Mr. Hannon.

Mr. Rickard asked, "You testified on direct that the gun had bounced out before, that it wasn't a good thing when the gun hit the ground?"[84] Heath responded, "It has happened to me before, yes."[85] Mr. Rickard asked Heath if he was using a friction-type holster when it happened. Heath answered, "Actually, no. I was wearing a thumb break holster that time."[86]

> Mr. Rickard: *It was your testimony on direct that you tried to push the holster – I'm sorry – the gun — Well, actually, which was it, was it the gun or the holster that was coming up or both?*
>
> Heath: *The gun had actually dislodged partially from the holster. So I was trying to get… a grip on the weapon, my goal was to try and get it back into the holster.*
>
> Mr. Rickard: *So you were trying to push the gun back into the holster?*
>
> Heath: *That was my goal. I didn't get to that point.*
>
> Mr. Rickard: *And your testimony is that someone who you later learned was Mr. Brackett, someone reached around and pushed your arm up, right?*
>
> Heath: *Yes.*
>
> Mr. Rickard: *And your testimony was they were reaching around you and were able to lift your arm up, even though you were pushing it down into the holster?*
>
> Heath: *I didn't say lift. I said they hit my arm.*
>
> Mr. Rickard: *They hit your arm?*
>
> Heath: *Yes.*
>
> Mr. Rickard: *And your testimony is that caused your arm to come up?*
>
> Heath: *Yes.*
>
> Mr. Rickard: *You would agree that as a matter of, I would say physics, you might talk about some self-defense principle that you have more leverage when you are pushing in closer to your body, right, rather than if you are pushing something farther away from your body?*
>
> Heath: *Correct.*

---

[84] Ibid, 162
[85] Ibid
[86] Ibid

Mr. Rickard: *... So it is your testimony that Mr. Brackett reached around and came towards you trying to take the gun from you as you were trying to take a single step away?... Your testimony is you took a step forward with your right foot, but despite that step, Mr. Brackett was still reaching around you hitting your arm?*

Heath: *Well, you are showing me with your right hand that he was reaching around and that is not what happened.*

Mr. Rickard: *I'm sorry. It was his left hand that grabbed the muscle* [muzzle]*, right?*

Heath: *Correct.*

Mr. Rickard: *So when the hand knocked your arm up and caused you to draw your weapon, was that his left arm or his right arm?*

Heath: *It was his right arm. He fell into me and I felt something hit my right arm, which I would assume was his hand or some part of his arm. And I was bladed and he is right on top of me.*

Mr. Rickard: *So your testimony is when he hits you, that knocked your hand up?*

Heath: *It pushed my hand up, yes.*

Mr. Rickard: *And you sat and saw this whole trial; right?*

Heath: *Yes.*

Mr. Rickard: *And you agree, wouldn't you, that no one else saw what you just described?*[87]

The judge intervened, saying, "No. Huh-un. Do not ask him to comment on the testimony of any other witnesses."[88]

Some spectators may have expected Mr. Hannon to object during this exchange, but he may have wanted the prosecutor, with his questions to Heath, to open the door for previous statements. The prosecution was giving an opening to Heath to comment on the testimony of others, which would be good for Heath. However, the judge stepped in.

Changing topics, Mr. Rickard discussed Heath's interest in the outcome of the trial because of his employment with ICE. He noted that Heath could face disciplinary action, including losing his job. Mr. Rickard asked, "That is why you told Agent Eisert that you saw your career being poof, right?"[89] Heath answered, "Yes, I was concerned about my career – still am."[90]

That concluded the cross-examination and ended the trial for the day. Mr. Hannon's redirect would have to wait one more day.

In my review of the transcripts for day five of the trial, the questioning by the prosecution about verbal commands Heath gave or did not give seemed immaterial. During

---

[87] Ibid, 163-165
[88] Ibid, 165
[89] Ibid, 166
[90] Ibid

the struggle for control of the weapon, Mr. Brackett acknowledged, in his testimony, that Heath and Carole told him Heath was a police officer, and that did not change Mr. Brackett's behavior. Judge Dixon had already heard Mr. Brackett's testimony, so he should have known the questions being asked had already been answered. At this point, I believe Mr. Hannon wanted the questions to continue because they should have been helpful to the defense. However, it seems Judge Dixon did not connect the questions to the previous testimony. I wondered if he had already made his decision.

14A

Wilton Dedge: Questionable Identification by a Witness and a Dog

On December 8, 1981, in Brevard County, Florida, a woman was attacked in her home by a male subject with an edged weapon. She was raped and cut numerous times.

Several days after the crime, while out shopping, the victim saw a man who resembled her attacker. She contacted the police but said the man she observed was shorter than her assailant. The person she saw was Mr. Wilton Dedge. The authorities arranged a photographic lineup. The victim was asked to view the lineup and identified Mr. Dedge as her assailant. However, the victim also said her assailant was six feet tall, 160 pounds, and of muscular build. Mr. Dedge was five feet five inches and 125 pounds.

Nevertheless, Mr. Dedge was arrested, charged, and found guilty of this crime. The conviction was based on identification by the victim, snitch testimony, hair comparisons, and dog-sniffing evidence. The tracking dog evidence was from Mr. John Preston, a well-known dog handler and professional expert witness.

None of the evidence against Mr. Dedge was particularly strong. The victim's testimony was considered weak because of the physical differences between her description of the assailant and Dedge's physical size. The snitch testimony was from a known snitch named Zacke. He testified that Dedge confessed to him about committing the crime while they were both in jail. The snitch received a reduced sentence for his testimony. The testimony about hair comparisons was weak; the expert said he could not eliminate the comparison of one hair to Dedge. Hence, the hair could be from Dedge, or it could be from someone else. The dog handler testified that after the dog sniffed an item with Dedge's scent on it, the dog alerted to Dedge's presence at the crime scene. The tracking dog evidence was believed to be critical to the conviction.

Mr. Dedge's defense included family members who testified that he was not in town when the crime occurred. The alibi was not believed, and in 1982 Mr. Dedge was sentenced to two concurrent life terms in prison.

In 1996, Mr. Dedge requested DNA testing on the hair samples, and four years later, his motion was granted. In 2001 the DNA testing was completed and proved that the hair recovered at the crime scene was not his. His attorneys asked the court to overturn the conviction, but the prosecution objected. The state had passed a postconviction DNA testing law in 2001 and "argued that because Dedge had won access to DNA testing too early—before there was a law governing post-conviction DNA testing—he could not benefit from the new law or get into court with new evidence of innocence."[1]

The state knew that part of its evidence had been eliminated and yet they opposed any additional testing and appeals. Three years later, the courts allowed an appeal, and additional DNA testing was ordered using the evidence from the sexual assault. The results excluded Dedge as the contributor. The case was dismissed on August 12, 2004. Mr. Dedge was incarcerated for 22 years before being exonerated.

The tracking dog evidence that was believed to be critical to the conviction must have been flawed. Was this the dog's error, or the handler's mistake? If the prosecutor trusted the tracking dog evidence, would it not seem irrational to object to the request for a second DNA examination?

After Mr. Dedge's guilt was questioned with the first DNA testing, it took three more years to allow further testing that proved he was innocent. The behavior of prosecutors to argue against the testing of evidence seems at odds with the finding of truth.

References

The Wilton Dredge case, National Registry of Exonerations (umich.edu), no author listed, posting date: Before June 2012.

no author listed, and no date posted.

Kelly V. Landers, P.A. Criminal Law, "A Tale of Exoneration, Does Innocence Matter in Florida?", a blog post, November 9, 2015, kvlcriminallaw.com

---

[1] Wilton Dedge - National Registry of Exonerations (umich.edu), posted before June 2012

15

Day 6: Who Can Testify to What?
AUGUST 23, 2011

"Belief perseverance" – we look for what supports our positions and disregard information that challenges our positions.[1]

Day five of the trial had ended with Heath responding to the prosecution's cross-examination. Because of time constraints, the redirect examination for the defense was scheduled for the next day, August 23, 2011.

Also scheduled to testify that day was Donnell Butler. Mr. Butler was an investigator for the Alcoholic Beverage Regulations Administration and was expected to testify regarding the ABRA investigation and hearing. Significant discrepancies existed between the trial testimony and information from the ABRA documents, including the time of the incident, the time when Heath and his party arrived at the Guards, whether the downstairs was open when the incident occurred, and the number of security guards that were working at the time. Mr. Butler's testimony could bring some of those discrepancies to light.

To open the proceedings Heath was called to the witness stand, but before he could take any questions, Ms. Sawyer spoke to the Court about a potential problem. It was her understanding that Mr. Hannon would allow Heath to handle a real weapon in the courtroom. Judge Dixon said no to this, and Mr. Hannon reminded the judge that he had not requested permission to use a real gun. Judge Dixon concluded, "Okay. Very well, then that is just an advisory opinion then."[2]

Mr. Hannon, launching his redirect, introduced Defense's Exhibit 34, "The U.S. Immigration and Customs Enforcement Use of Force Policy." Mr. Hannon said to Heath, "You were asked about the use of force continuum on cross-examination. Is that addressed in the use of force policy?"[3] Heath answered yes.[4]

Mr. Hannon referred to page 4 of the policy, the general guidelines of the policy.

---

[1] The Journal of Experimental Social Psychology, Volume 44, Issue 3, May 2008, Pages 706 – 712
[2] Information from the trial transcript, Criminal Action Number 2010-CF3-16079, dated August 23, 2011, p 174
[3] Ibid, 175
[4] Ibid

Mr. Hannon: *... could you tell the Court which of those general guidelines you were relying upon in your testimony about the use of force continuum yesterday?*

Heath: *... It would be 2, 3, 4 and 5 ...*

Mr. Hannon: *And could you explain to the Court what your conduct on which of these – how it was that you relied on these guidelines on October 28, 2010?*

Heath: *... The way I was applying these guidelines was based on the situation and what was happening. I used the necessary force to maintain retention of my weapon.*[5]

When asked which guideline he used first, Heath said "number 4."

Heath: *... Individual officers will perceive things differently and your response on the force continuum – you pick the one that you think is going to work the best for that particular incident. There is no requirement to start with one over another.* [referring to number 4]

Mr. Hannon: *Could you read to the Court A3 and explain...what that means in your training?*

Heath: *In some situations the proper initial response might be the application of deadly force.*

Mr. Hannon: *What did that mean in terms of your training?*

Heath: *That would mean that based on the perception of action that is being taken against me... the appropriate response might be ... the application of deadly force.*[6]

In any situation, the officer's perception and assessment determine what level of force to use. A force continuum does not require the officer to use force in a stair step process, starting at a minimum level and moving up. In some situations, verbal warning and defensive tactics are bypassed. The officer's judgment determines what amount and level of force to use, and the officer is required to justify any level of force used, including deadly force.

Mr. Hannon continued, asking, "And on August 28, did you fear the use of deadly force by Marshall Brackett?"[7] Heath responded, "I feared the use of force by the person that was trying to take away my firearm. And later I found out that was Marshall Brackett."[8]

Judge Dixon interjected, "Mr. Thomas, let me just ask one question. Throughout this entire episode, was there any point along the way before the bouncer grabbed your gun ... that you saw the potential need for deadly force?"[9] Heath answered, "No, Your Honor ... I was concerned as to what was happening ... I knew I was being assaulted, but I didn't feel that at that point up to we got outside."[10]

---

[5] Ibid, 176-177
[6] Ibid, 177-178
[7] Ibid, 178
[8] Ibid
[9] Ibid
[10] Ibid, 178-179

Mr. Hannon: *... the fact that you were armed that evening, what did that contribute to your state of mind when Marshall Brackett had you in the air?*

Heath: *... it is always in my mind to maintain positive control of the weapon. When I was in the air, what I was thinking was why is this happening, what is going on and also I have to make sure that I maintain control of the weapon. When it started – it was dislodged, my total concern and focus was on maintaining control of my weapon.*

Mr. Hannon: *Why?*

Heath: *It is something that is ingrained from your very first days in the academy that losing positive control of your weapon basically escalates the situation to a deadly force encounter ... if you are losing control of your weapon, and you have no weapon, potentially you are going to be the focus of that weapon being used on you.*[11]

Mr. Hannon: *... What did your training in martial arts and your experience in other incidents of potential deadly force contribute to your subjective concerns that evening?*

Heath: *... it goes back to once we got to the point where he was trying to take away my weapon, all my training and focus was maintaining control of that so that it doesn't get into someone's hands who I felt was going to potentially use it against me or someone else.*

Mr. Hannon: *... did you believe during the entire continuum of that evening with all of your skills you were ever not going to be able to prevent Brackett from taking your weapon?*

Heath: *Toward the very end of the incident when ... I was tiring out. It was a very high-stress situation like a grappling match. I was beginning to get concerned that I was going to be too tired to just maintain the weapon that I was going to have to take a different action.*

Mr. Hannon: *... So at that point, you had a subjective belief that with your training and skills, if necessary, you could have taken other action?*[12]

Mr. Rickard objected, and the Court sustained it.

Mr. Hannon asked, "Did you ever lose confidence in your skills to be able to prevent Brackett from taking the weapon?"[13]

Mr. Rickard objected. The judge responded, "I am going to allow it, but I really would like you to remember this is redirect, not an additional opportunity for direct."[14]

Heath said, "I didn't lose confidence in my ability. I was just concerned as to my – that I was getting tired, yes."[15]

---

[11] Ibid, 179
[12] Ibid, 179-180
[13] Ibid, 180
[14] Ibid, 181
[15] Ibid

Mr. Hannon spoke to the Court, "Your Honor, I have no other questions except for I wanted to present to the Court one issue. I believe that the examination of Agent Thomas has leveled a claim of fabrication against him. And the video demonstration was done quite some time ago before he ever heard the testimony of Holubar and Brackett. And I would like to admit into evidence those portions of the video which demonstrate what Agent Thomas did at the time that Brackett grabbed the weapon. And I wish to introduce that as a prior consistent statement to rebut a claim of recent fabrication.

"And I will also say to the Court that in the event that the Court would choose not to put on expert testimony, I would like to present the video through Agent Thomas to explain to the Court other parts of the video in which he demonstrated the conduct he could have utilized during the course of this episode but chose not to keep it from escalating. But this is sort of a preliminary objection, I suppose – or preliminary request."[16]

Judge Dixon called for a bench conference, and Heath stepped down from the witness stand. The judge asked Mr. Hannon to explain what he meant by "a recent fabrication."

> Mr. Hannon: *The examination of — Mr. Rickard has the purpose of suggesting to the Court that based upon what he has heard now of the testimony of the two alleged victims here he has somewhat sort of tailored his testimony.*
>
> Judge Dixon: *... I don't see what you're pointing to in regards to a claim of recent fabrication.*
>
> Mr. Hannon: *Well, all I can say is that Brackett and Holubar, each of them testified to completely different things between ... themselves*
>
> Judge Dixon: *Right.*
>
> Mr. Hannon: *And, frankly, when Mr. Rickard said [to Mr. Thomas] well, you have heard the testimony of everybody else here—*
>
> Judge Dixon: *I stopped him with that question.*
>
> Mr. Hannon: *... it doesn't have to be overt and explicit, the allegations of recent fabrication... the significant differences among three witnesses, I suggest to the fact finder, and I — you're the fact finder, so we're sort of in a little bit of different position here – that his testimony about what occurred is unworthy of belief because he tailored it to fit the Government's evidence. And I think under those circumstances the evidentiary rule that permits introduction of a prior consistent statement to rebut the claim of recent fabrication would allow the introduction of his demonstration of what happened, which took place in 2010.*[17]
>
> Judge Dixon: *... it was a suggestion that it is a fabrication of his testimony after he has heard the other witnesses, but the question was not permitted.*

---

[16] Ibid, 183-184
[17] Ibid, 184-185

Mr. Hannon: *... I understand that ...*

Judge Dixon: *... therefore, the mere fact that they cross-examined your client, does not in and of itself support a claim of — support an argument that the Government is claiming recent fabrication.*

Mr. Hannon: *I think the evidentiary rules are much broader than that. There doesn't have to be the explicit type of you heard the other testimony here examination in order for the rule to be effective. If in essence the Government's cross-examination is suggesting that and there is a prior consistent statement, under liberal rules of evidence, that is anything that is remotely relevant, is admissible under those circumstances. It is a very broad rule of admissibility and doesn't require the type of explicit attack that Your Honor prohibited. That is my view of the rule of evidence.*[18]

Judge Dixon asked Mr. Rickard if he wished to speak. Mr. Rickard said, "I just maintain that I agree with what Your Honor said, and even the question that Your Honor caught me asking, my suggestion there was the contrary, was that his testimony was different than every other witness. It wasn't that he fabricated, in fact, there was an inherent bias and that there was certain parts of the testimony that were inherently incredible."[19]

Despite the judge's position, my perspective is that Mr. Hannon made a good argument about Mr. Rickard's words on the previous day. When Heath explained how he believed the gun became dislodged from the holster, Mr. Rickard said, "And you agree, wouldn't you, that no one else saw what you just described," implying that his explanation was difficult to believe. That, along with his just spoken words, "...that there was certain parts of the testimony that were inherently incredible," could easily be interpreted as a claim of fabrication.

In response, Mr. Hannon asked the Court to allow the video to be entered through Heath. As the video was made before any testimony was heard, it would refute any claim of fabrication. It was my belief that he was concerned that the judge may not allow an expert witness to testify to the film. His concern was valid, as the film was never entered and the expert testimony, as we will see, was also limited.

After sustaining the objection, Judge Dixon followed with, "I wasn't sure if we addressed everything, because here was a request with respect to going into the video for the purpose of demonstrating a prior consistent statement. Did that take care of all of your requests with respect to Agent Thomas at this time ... ?"[20]

---

[18] Ibid, 186
[19] Ibid, 187
[20] Ibid

Mr. Hannon: *Well I raised the issue about the hypothetical if the Court sustains the Governments objection to the experts, I would like him to sponsor the video where he shows the demonstration of what he did that evening and also what he could have done.*

Judge Dixon: *What he could have done at what point in the continuum? When he was being carried out?*

Mr. Hannon: *Correct.*

Judge Dixon: *When the gun was grabbed?*

Mr. Hannon: *Correct. Both …*

Judge Dixon: *… you are asking me to consider that after I hear the Government's objection to the expert witnesses?*

Mr. Hannon: *If Your Honor would not permit the experts, then I'd ask to bring it in through Agent Thomas.*[21]

Judge Dixon agreed to hold the questions. He said they would address them later, and he ended the bench conference.

Mr. Hannon said he had no further questions, and Judge Dixon then questioned Heath.

Judge Dixon: *Mr. Thomas, what time did you arrive at Old Glory?*
Heath: *About 7:00 p.m.*
Judge Dixon: *What time did you leave?*
Heath: *A little after 11:00.*
Judge Dixon: *How many and what type of drinks did you have at Old Glory?*
Heath: *Three and a half beers; they were Red Hook.*
Judge Dixon: *Approximately what time did you arrive at The Guards?*
Heath: *About 11:20.*
Judge Dixon: *And what was the approximate time that this incident with the bouncer started?*
Heath: *About 11:40.*
Judge Dixon: *And what did you drink upon your arrival at The Guards? What did you order? What did you finish? What did you not drink?*
Heath: *I ordered a bottle of beer. I took a sip of it, didn't like it, gave it back to the bartender. Then we sat down, I ordered a martini. We went through the whole thing with the martini phase. I finally got a martini. I had a sip of that before I got up to go pay the tab.*
Judge Dixon: *So other than a sip of the bottled beer and a sip of the martini, that is all you had to drink at The Guards?*

---
[21] Ibid, 188

Heath: *Yes, sir.*

Judge Dixon: *When the bouncer grabbed you, did he say anything?*

Heath: *No sir.*

Judge Dixon: *During the entire time that he walked you from the inside of the bar to the outside, did he say anything?*

Heath: *No, sir.*

Judge Dixon: *Did you say anything?*

Heath: *No, Sir.*

Judge Dixon: *Any reason for not saying anything?*

Heath: *My mind was trying to figure out why I was in that position. And I didn't think it was going to help me yelling and screaming or saying anything. I thought it would actually make me look more ridiculous.*[22]

Heath repeated that he did not know who grabbed him, and he did not consider that it was someone with the bar, until "Once we were going out and – toward the door and I saw the manager sort of along with us, that's when I kind of had a realization that maybe it had something to do with the bar."[23]

Judge Dixon: *So from the area of the bar where you were trying to pay the tab until you got out to the door, it didn't even cross your mind that this might have been someone associated with the bar who was putting you out of the bar?*

Heath: *Again, I was more trying to figure out why this was happening because I was just trying to pay the tab. I was reaching in my wallet to get it, so it wasn't a long period of time.*[24]

Judge Dixon asked Heath about the shirt he was wearing. Heath described the shirt as green in color and a little oversized.

Judge Dixon: *And the oversized nature of the shirt would assist when you keep the shirt out of your pants, to cover up the fact that you are wearing a weapon?*

Heath: *Yes, Your Honor.*

Judge Dixon: *When the guard grabbed you, can you give me an estimate of the placement of his arms or hands in front of you in terms of how high it was above the barrel of the gun or it was touching the barrel of the gun?*[25]

Heath requested to illustrate, and the judge allowed it. Heath stood up for the demonstration.

---

[22] Ibid, 189-191
[23] Ibid, 191
[24] Ibid, 191-192
[25] Ibid, 192

Heath: *My hands were here* (indicating the front of his body). *His [Mr. Brackett's] arms were approximately between my wrist and right here and my forearm, so right around my beltline. And I would say his hands were just below my beltline. So he potentially could have felt the butt of the gun on his forearm.*

Judge Dixon: *... is it equally within the realm of what happened that your arms may have... prevented him from feeling the gun?*

Heath: *My recollection, Your Honor, is that my forearm was actually lodged behind the gun, so the weapon was actually resting on my forearm. So I can't say for certain whether he felt it or he didn't feel it, but I don't think that – my arm was not blocking him from feeling it.*[26]

Judge Dixon said that he had no further questions, and Mr. Hannon asked if he could ask a few more questions related the Court's inquiry. The judge allowed it.

Mr. Hannon addressed Heath. "Judge Dixon asked a question about your frame of mind once Brackett picked you up. And in addition to what you relayed to the Judge, did you also have thoughts about what you would do?"[27]

Mr. Rickard objected; it was overruled. Heath answered, "I was trying to take into consideration should I act… and what my options are… and taking into account that there are other people around."[28]

Mr. Hannon asked, "And was it characteristic of you that during this moment when Brackett had you off of the ground in a bear hug that you remained quiet?"[29] Heath said it would be, and Mr. Hannon asked him to explain.

Heath continued, "At that point, there is already an action being taken and I am actually trying to process it and decide upon my action. … it is a very fluid situation. It [is] not happening is stair-step fashion of one, two, three, it is all very – it is very dynamic. So while it sounds like a long period of time, it is really not."[30]

Mr. Hannon: *And at any point did you verbalize a threat to Brackett?*
Heath: *No.*
Mr. Hannon: *Why not?*
Heath: *I had no intention of threatening him.*[31]

That ended the redirect examination.

Mr. Hannon's questions were discerning about Heath's thought process—what he could have done—which reflects that Heath thought about his actions and acted deliberately, rather than just reacting to the moment.

---

[26] Ibid, 193
[27] Ibid, 194
[28] Ibid
[29] Ibid
[30] Ibid, 194-195
[31] Ibid, 195

Heath stepped down, and Mr. Hannon told the judge that Darnell Butler was to be his next witness. Mr. Butler was an investigator for ABRA who investigated the incident. The Court took a short recess to locate Mr. Butler, as he was not in the courtroom or the hallway.

After the recess, Judge Dixon questioned Mr. Hannon about Mr. Butler. Mr. Hannon stated, "The witness has not appeared and is not answering his cell phone." Without his final witness, Mr. Hannon said, "So ... this concludes our evidence [for that day and before the motion for acquittal]. And I don't know if the Court wishes to hear my motion for judgement of acquittal now or—."[32]

The judge indicated they would go on with the motion.

Later I was told that Mr. Butler did eventually arrive at the Court, but he did not testify. I attempted to contact him in connection with this book, telephoning him on several occasions and leaving messages. He never returned the calls, so I sent him a letter explaining why I wished to interview him. He never responded to the letter.

Although the ABRA hearing documents were entered into evidence, only persons that testified or witnessed the hearing could testify in court about the hearing. In Mr. Butler's case, because he investigated the incident at The Guards, he could also testify about the ABRA investigation. Entering a document like the ABRA hearing transcript alone does not automatically enter its contents into evidence. That is why Mr. Butler was considered an important witness.

The Motion for Acquittal

Judge Dixon began by saying, "I have before me the defendant's motion to dismiss. I have the Government's objections with respect to the expert witnesses that defense intend to call. And to put me in a position where I can consider these various issues, would you proffer initially for me, Mr. Hannon, what these witnesses will testify to so I can put the Government's objections in perspective?"[33]

Mr. Hannon requested a moment, and Ms. Sawyer interjected. Ms. Sawyer produced a letter the prosecution had received from Mr. Hannon, detailing what the defense experts were expected to offer in Court. The letter was from the Hannon Law Group, addressed to the prosecution, and dated August 17, 2011.[34] (See Appendix J.)

Ms. Sawyer gave Judge Dixon the letter and he said, "That probably will answer my questions that I have."[35] After examining the letter, the judge said, "The correspondence that was provided. The letter dated August 17 by Mr. Hannon to Ms. Sawyer and Mr. Rickard gives me the proffer that I was asking for, Mr. Hannon, so there is no need for

---

[32] Ibid, 204-205

[33] Information from the trial transcript, Criminal Action Number 2010-CF3-16079, dated August 23, 2011, p 205

[34] Letter from the Hannon Law Group, addressed to the Stephen Rickard and Katherine Sawyer, dated August 17, 2011, proffering what the defense's expert witnesses will offer in Court. See Appendix H

[35] Information from the trial transcript, Criminal Action Number 2010-CF3-16079, dated August 23, 2011, p 206

the proffer. This letter adequately proffers what you anticipate the testimony to be. I will hear the Government's objections."[36]

Ms. Sawyer argued that the timing of the expert testimony was important "because the testimony is only relevant if Agent Thomas put certain things at issue. And, obviously, before he took the stand, that was unclear. Now, he has testified and the gravamen of his testimony is essentially that the gun came up by accident. It wasn't drawn in self-defense. It wasn't drawn as a use of force in his capacity as a law enforcement officer. He testified that when he was securing it, all he was doing was securing it and that Brackett hit his arm and that hit caused that gun to be drawn."[37]

Ms. Sawyers argued that since Heath said that it was an accident when the gun came out, any testimony about self-defense was not relevant to the case.

Judge Dixon stated, "It seems to me that a part of the Government's natural theory in the case is that during the struggle that ensued after the bouncer grabbed the weapon, that somehow I can consider that in the course of determining whether or not the gun came out by accident or Agent Thomas intentionally brought the weapon out."[38]

Ms. Sawyer agreed with Judge Dixon, but she also said the relevance was lessened with the dismissal of the charge with Holubar as a victim.

> Judge Dixon: *Let me hear the rest of your argument with respect to the other issues.*
> Ms. Sawyer: *... well, specifically at least with regard to the use of force testimony, use of force is somewhat a term of art and there is a whole field of law in the 1983 civil context that deals with the use of force. In fact, the case that was cited by Mr. Hannon in his argument ... a civil case... examining reasonable use of force... All of those standards ... and those analysis only come into play when an officer is acting in his capacity and under color of law in his capacity as a law enforcement officer. And there is no evidence on this record whatsoever and, in fact, the evidence to this record is to the contrary that he was not acting under color of law. ... And, again, we would argue that this use of force testimony isn't relevant in this context at all.*[39]

When someone tries to take a weapon from an officer who is off duty, the status of the officer changes to on duty. The officer is now a victim—and is on-duty. If a gun comes out by accident, that is not a crime. However, if someone has their hand(s) on the weapon and refuses to release the gun, the officer is being assaulted by someone trying to take the gun. In this case, the potential offender, Mr. Brackett, was unaware that Heath was a police officer before the struggle. However, after being told that Heath

---

[36] Ibid, 207
[37] Ibid, 207-208
[38] Ibid, 208-209
[39] Ibid, 209-210

was a police officer, he should have released the weapon.[40] An off-duty officer could not make this argument if they were committing a crime while off duty, and then having his or her weapon taken away.

> Ms. Sawyer: *I would then go to just the standard for admissibility of expert opinion testimony. That the subject has to be so distinctively related to some science, profession or occupation as to be beyond the ken of the average layman. And I would submit that almost all of this testimony isn't beyond the ken of this Court. … So Mr. Bohrer is offered in the use of force, off-duty carry and holsters. A lot of those are simply issue of fact that have been addressed by Mr. Thomas in his direct testimony. He proffered the specific holster that was being used. He did a demonstration with the holster that was being used. Those just aren't appropriate subjects, I think, of expert testimony.*[41]

Ms. Sawyer was correct when she said, "the subject has to be so distinctively related to some science, profession or occupation as to be beyond the ken of the average layman." And she was just as wrong when she said, "I would submit that almost all of this testimony isn't beyond the ken of this Court." It was and still is.

Judge Dixon thanked Ms. Sawyer and then allowed the defense to respond.

Defense's Response

> Mr. Hannon: *It is our position that, as Your Honor recalls, that the Government in order to carry its burden in this case had to present expert testimony to the Court. I understand Your Honor rejected it at the close of the Government's evidence… And, quite frankly, had the Government consulted with an expert, we might not be here. But with respect to the issues of the admissibility of the proposed experts, as Ms. Sawyer indicates, on this evening Agent Thomas was a federal law enforcement officer. And he, unlike anyone else that we're aware of at The Guards that was authorized both by federal law and by his agency to carry his weapon or an authorized weapon off duty. And that is what he was doing.*[42]

Mr. Hannon continued, "And Agent Thomas is entitled to have an expert tell you that he not only met the standard of his training but he exceeded the standard of his training in the restraint that he exercised that evening. The evidence of the need for an expert is I think from cross-examination by Mr. Rickard. Mr. Rickard interpreted the use of force continuum, which I know Your Honor is familiar with, as somehow

---

[40] The information presented is taught just about every police academy, related to the carrying of a weapon off duty. If an off-duty officer observes a crime and takes enforcement action, they are then; on-duty.
[41] Ibid, 210-211
[42] Ibid, 212

requiring Agent Thomas to have begun at the lowest level of the use of force continuum, which consist of four steps ..."[43]

Mr. Hannon argued that officers are not required to go from the first step, proceeding through each step as needed, until the final step, which is deadly force. He explained, "Agent Thomas never used deadly force in this incident. He certainly could have used deadly force. But the cross-examination suggesting to you that he did not meet the standards of his profession makes my point."[44]

The judge asked Ms. Sawyer if she had anything else to say before he ruled. She did.

> Ms. Sawyer: ... *I just want to highlight one flaw in Mr. Hannon's argument about the use of force situation. He has likened it to a case that could be brought in Federal Court. And I think that is wrong. The analysis under the 1983 case to be brought is that the officer has to be acting under the color of law. And I can provide authority, Your Honor. I have got case citations to the extent the Court wants to hear them. But they are cases where the Court as [sic] held that an officer assaulting a fellow bar patron, which couldn't really be a lot more on point, and in no ways identified himself as an officer or claimed to be exercising his authority as an officer, was not acting under color of law and that in those cases, this use of force analysis is simply not apposite.*[45]

Judge Dixon's Ruling

Judge Dixon concluded, "I have considered the proffer that is contained in this letter dated August 17. I have considered the Government's objections. I have considered the defense arguments in favor of the request to call an expert witness. ... I am going to allow the defense to call expert — one or more expert witnesses, up to two. But certain – the testimony is going to be limited. One of the issues that was raised during the course of this trial concerns the law enforcement officer's training to always resist the effort for someone to take their weapon. And so with respect to training and policy with respect to a law enforcement's actions at the time someone is attempting to take their weapon, provided the witness is qualified, I will permit expert witness testimony with respect to that effect. I will permit expert witness testimony ... to the effect of things that could have been done by a law enforcement officer after the weapon was grabbed. I will not permit any expert testimony to be offered with respect to what was done or what could have been done by Mr. Thomas from the point that the bear hug was put on him until the time the weapon was grabbed. I will allow the expert witness testimony from the point that the weapon was grabbed.

---

[43] Ibid, 214
[44] Ibid
[45] Ibid

"… Now, from the Government's perspective, I understand your theory of the case is that this was not an accidental pulling of the weapon. This – this was an intentional act by Agent Thomas. And from the defense perspective, I understand the argument that this was an accidental event where the gun came out. It seems to me that the Government in arguing their position will be able to make use of the events that occurred after the gun was grabbed and, therefore, I should allow Agent Thomas to present evidence that would put that type of evidence in context with respect to his training as a law enforcement officer to always resist the effort by someone outside – by someone to take the weapon."[46]

How the gun came out is the case: was it intentional or accidental? Arguing for the defense that the gun can be dislodged (or partially dislodged) under the circumstances supports the defense and adds to the credibility of Heath. The judge offered no rationale or reason for placing limits on the testimony of the expert. Not allowing the argument could infer that the gun was drawn intentionally. While writing the book, I contacted Judge Dixon and he agreed to be interviewed. Later, when the purpose of the interview was explained, the interview was cancelled.[47]

Judge Dixon continued, "There is one additional matter I will permit testimony on. And that is the opinion testimony if the witness is qualified, the opinion testimony that … That it was highly improbable that Agent Thomas had his finger on – in the trigger guard of the weapon at the time that the struggle was occurring. However, I will not permit these witnesses to offer their testimony with respect to whether there was or was not restraint in the context of the struggle that was going on. I am only permitting them to testify as to things that could have been done or would have been authorized for a law enforcement officer to take. I will not allow any testimony with respect to actions that Mr. Thomas did or did not take prior to the time that the guard attempted to grab the gun as it relates to the guard. I will permit testimony as it relates to if a gun is slipping out or falling out or something of that nature, what is appropriate for a law enforcement officer to do. But other than that, no opinion testimony with respect to what Agent Thomas did, didn't do, could have done, should have done, prior to the time the weapon was grabbed. Now, this is all dependent upon the witnesses demonstrating their qualifications to testify in these areas. I am not making an assessment on that."[48]

Judge Dixon asked if either side had comments about his instructions and neither the prosecution nor the defense had anything to add.

The prosecution's assertion that the experts had nothing to offer is revealing. Considerable resources were used in this trial to prevent the experts from testifying. If the

---

[46] Ibid, 217-218

[47] A telephone call was made to Judge Dixons office, and his office responded and requested that I send an email, along with the questions. The email, along with the questions was sent to the Judge on 05-08-15. A follow up call to the Judges Office was made on 05-14-15. The interview was later cancelled.

[48] Information from the trial transcript, Criminal Action Number 2010-CF3-16079, dated August 23, 2011, p 218-219

expert said that the incident could not have occurred in the manner the prosecution presented but could have happened the way Heath testified, would that have changed the trial's outcome? If the expert's expertise were insufficient, could not the prosecutors have challenged it while the expert was on the stand?

Motion to Dismiss

The judge then moved forward with the motion to dismiss.

> Mr. Hannon: *Ms. Sawyer has indicated that, from the Government's perspective, the assault with a deadly weapon occurred when Agent Thomas drew the gun or had the gun in his hands. The only evidence as to how the weapon got into his hands is that of Agent Thomas. At the end of the Government's case we asked the Court to consider that it would be speculative for you to determine how the weapon got into his hand and therefore requiring you to speculate would be contrary to the typical instructions of a fact finder.*[49]

Judge Dixon replied that there was testimony that Heath turned with the gun in his hand, so there was other evidence.

> Mr. Hannon: *…there are multiple ways in which he would have had the need to have the gun in his hand.*
> Judge Dixon: *And there are multiple ways the gun could have ended up in his hand, which gets to the defense theory as to how it came into his hands.*
> Mr. Hannon: *… but the mere fact that the weapon was in his hands according to the government's evidence, just means that, that it is in his hands.*[50]
>   *However, if the evidence then is that Agent Thomas has testified as to how it got in his hands, if you balance the absence of any evidence that existed at the end of the Government's case and the inference that you would give full play to at that point, and the only direct evidence as to how it got into his hand, then the full play that you give to the Government's evidence at the end of the Government's case has evaporated, that bubble has been burst.*[51]

Judge Dixon responded, "Is this your motion to dismiss or is this your motion for judgment of acquittal?"[52]

Mr. Hannon apologized for any confusion, saying he would argue the motion to dismiss.

---

[49] Ibid, 219-220
[50] Ibid, 220-221
[51] Ibid, 221
[52] Ibid

Mr. Hannon continued, in a slightly different direction, saying that federal agencies have rules that forbid employees from testifying in cases in both federal and state courts. He made an argument that Heath's supervisor, Agent John Eisert, gave critical information to the grand jury before the trial at the request of the prosecution.

Mr. Hannon stated, "If I were to hypothesize, it would be because they anticipated that he might be a witness for Agent Thomas and they wanted to see what he had to say and lock him into certain things. But now we get to the point at trial and we make the appropriate request under the federal regulations that Agent Eisert be able to testify regarding the very things that we now have learned the Government asked him in the grand jury. And the Government has forbidden him from doing that."[53]

Mr. Hannon said that it was the United States Attorney's Office that did this, and that Ms. Sawyer had argued about this information earlier. The bottom line of Mr. Hannon's argument was, "the refusal of the United States to produce this evidence is sufficiently damaging to the defense ... The United States has made that choice in this case and as a consequence we have been denied what we know is exculpatory testimony because we have a record of it. It is in the grand jury."[54]

> Judge Dixon: *"What is the exculpatory testimony that you have record of that you believe the Government has prevented you from producing?"*[55]
>
> Mr. Hannon: *Well, in addition to what is stated in the Grand Jury –*
>
> Judge Dixon: *You have to tell me, because I don't know what is there.*
>
> Mr. Hannon: *Well, I am just going to go to what Agent Eisert told and I believe he told Ms. Sawyer in preparation for this trial. He was presented with the hypothetical of what was confronting Agent Thomas in this case. And Agent Eisert told her that based on his training, he would have shot Marshall Brackett. And the testimony in the grand jury regarding the use of force continuum and responsibilities regarding weapons and the like is consistent with what Agent Thomas has testified to in terms of his own training.*
>
> Judge Dixon: *Isn't that some of the same testimony that I just told you I was going to allow from your expert witnesses?*
>
> Mr. Hannon: *Some of it. But the –*
>
> Judge Dixon: *What the law enforcement officer could have done while that gun was being grabbed. I said I would permit that.*
>
> Mr. Hannon: *Agent Eisert didn't testify to that.*
>
> Judge Dixon: *No. I said that I will permit your expert witness to testify.*
>
> Mr. Hannon: *I understand that.*

---

[53] Ibid, 222-223
[54] Ibid, 224
[55] Ibid, 225

Judge Dixon: *... just because you don't get your selected person to give that testimony, this is a basis to dismiss?*

Mr. Hannon: *Yes, Your Honor. Because Agent Eisert is his supervisor and is trained the same way that he has trained. And his evidence is far more powerful than my expert, we hope, is going to be a paid expert.*

Judge Dixon: *Is it your contention that absent this U.S. Attorney's Office interference, that this witness would have made himself available to give that testimony?*

Mr. Hannon: *Absolutely. Absolutely.*

Judge Dixon: *On what basis? Because I thought what you told me was that -*

Mr. Hannon: *My conversations with him ...*

Judge Dixon: *No. No. No. Not your conversations with him. This U.S. Attorney's Office and the Department of Homeland Security, is that where the witness is from? Where is the witness from?*

Mr. Hannon: *He is with ICE, which is under Homeland Security.*

Judge Dixon: *Now, if Homeland Security or ICE instructed this witness that he may not testify on these issues that you wish to call him for —*

Mr. Hannon: *Yes.*

Judge Dixon: *—and if they only did that because this U.S. Attorney's Office instructed them they needed to do it, then I would see the interference that you are talking about. But if that is their policy and if that is the policy that they would follow under all given circumstances, I don't see any interference by this U.S. Attorney's Office. The mere fact that they presented the testimony in grand jury does not prove that there was anything improper done by this U.S. Attorney's Office. There is no rule that says you can only present in the grand jury evidence that you know is admissible at trial.*

Mr. Hannon: *My argument does not depend upon a conclusion by the Court that the U.S. Attorney's Office has acted improperly.*

Judge Dixon: *Okay.*

Mr. Hannon: *The U.S. Attorney's Office, in my opinion and my experience, has acted improperly because and they are naïve and they are not experienced in this... The agency acts appropriately to balance the interest of the Unites States – the security interest of the United States, just like the Department of Homeland Security apparently has acted appropriately here to balance its interest to forbid Agent Eisert to answer these fundamental questions. The U.S. Attorney's Office has deferred to the Department of Homeland Security and has reported to the Court and in the light of most favorable to the U.S. Attorney's Office that Agent Eisert has this constraint imposed upon him which he knew full well was a constraint imposed upon him. And he knows full well there are people from OPR and OIG [Office of Inspector General] here in the courtroom. And he is going to comply with that constraint. We[']re therefore denied the opportunity to have him testify on these matters. For some reason, he was permitted by the Department of Homeland Security to answer the questions that we wished to ask him in Court before the grand jury. ... And the regulation says that the Government can call such people to provide the testimony – grand jury testimony on their behalf, but is silent with respect to what happens when the Government calls such a person in a grand jury setting in the very same case in which they then turn around and deny him the ability to testify in public in the courtroom on behalf of the defendant. Now, all we're asking the Court to do is to recognize his right to compel any witness, even a duplicative witness, if Your Honor doesn't see the strength of the testimony of an Ice Agent who has been trained the exact same way that he is over a paid expert. The Government is telling the Court, yes, it can go forward. We are telling Your Honor that this is the same as the Government suppressing a witness that has exculpatory evidence for a defendant in the case – the very same thing. That perhaps is pejorative, I suppose. But I think under these circumstances, I am not certain that, quite frankly, I am not certain that DHS has seen the grand jury testimony, the people that made the decision to forbid Agent Eisert to testify to these things in trial...*

Judge Dixon: *All right. Mr. Hannon, it seems to me you are going uphill, but let me see what Mr. Rickard says.*[56]

Prosecution's Response

Mr. Rickard stated, "Your Honor, the most telling in that argument was when you asked Mr. Hannon for what part of the grand jury testimony was exculpatory, Mr. Hannon would not answer your question and that is because Mr. Eisert's grand jury testimony is, if anything inculpatory. ... Mr. Hannon's characterization of our meeting with Mr. Eisert last week or two weeks ago is, again entirely inaccurate. Mr. Eisert did not express any exculpatory opinions that Mr. Hannon has stated. ... And this, Your Honor, is the third time that Mr. Hannon has made material factual misrepresentations in his pleadings to this Court. He stated in a motion to compel that Mr. Thomas repeatedly identified himself as a law enforcement officer as Mr. Brackett carried him out. You now know that is not true. He stated that I told a witness to leave the jurisdiction or implied it in another motion without any support. And now he has refused to provide the Court with any factual support for this allegation that the Government has conspired to conceal a material witness when there is no conspiracy and the witness is not material or exculpatory."[57]

The witness Mr. Rickard allegedly directed to leave the jurisdiction was Ms. Yuliga Vetlugeena. In a pretrial motion, Mr. Hannon had asked for any notes or written documents from any interviews with her. The defense did summons her, but she could not

---

[56] Ibid, 225-230
[57] Ibid, 230-231

be located. The judge said that he would not rule on the motion at that time, saying that the witness might still be located. We don't know what the witness would have said, and I do not know if the judge ever ruled on this matter.

Mr. Rickard's characterization of what Mr. Eisert said was not entirely inaccurate. Mr. Eisert did not speak the words attributed to him in the grand jury. He reportedly voiced them in a meeting with the U.S. Attorneys. According to Heath, Mr. Eisert met with the prosecution multiple times. According to Mr. Hannon, Mr. Eisert told him that if he were in the same situation as Heath had been, he would have shot the bouncer. I interviewed Mr. Hannon for this book, and I specifically asked him about this subject. In an email reply, he said, "My recollection is that it was contained in a letter from the prosecutor providing me with Brady information. If so, Heath would have the letter."[58] I never located the letter.

I contacted Agent Eisert and asked him about the incident and his involvement. Agent Eisert advised me that he had to check with his legal advisor before talking to me about the case. He later called and said he was still prohibited from discussing the case.

The Decision

> Judge Dixon: … *I have considered the defendant's motion to dismiss. On one hand, I have the defense arguing that exculpatory evidence has been suppressed by the fact that the witness from Homeland Security is not being permitted to testify. And, on the other hand, the Government is arguing to me that the testimony, even if it were permitted, is not exculpatory because based on what they saw in the grand jury, it is not exculpatory. I don't have any basis to conclude that the evidence is exculpatory, so I will just go no further. I do not find that here is anything improper with what I understand to have occurred. That is that Homeland Security has advised the witness that he may not testify to these issues in the trial. In the absence of finding that there was anything improper, I have to conclude that it was proper. I do not find that for – was any bad-faith action by the U.S. Attorney's Office in this case, specifically the attorneys in this case from the U.S. Attorney's Office that in any suppressed evidence to which the defense would have otherwise been entitled. And, lastly, even assuming—and I have no basis to reach the conclusion – but even assuming that the evidence that the Homeland Security witness would have testified to would not have been exculpatory to the defendant, the defendant is going to present similar evidence apparently through other witnesses who will testify with respect to the actions of Mr. Thomas after the weapon was grabbed in accordance with what I said that I would permit. Therefore, I find there is no basis to claim that Mr. Thomas has been denied the right to present his defense. I find no basis to conclude that Mr. Thomas has been denied exculpatory evidence that is in the possession of the Government and find no basis to conclude that there has been any bad-faith action by Government counsel in this case. The motion to dismiss is denied.*[59]

---

[58] Email from Mr. Hannon to the author dated, 9-27-2015

[59] Information from the trial transcript, Criminal Action Number 2010-CF3-16079, dated August 23, 2011, p 232-233

There were no questions about the ruling, so the judge asked if there were any questions about his decision concerning the expert witnesses.

> Mr. Hannon: *Well, you remember when we were here last week, Shannon Bohrer indicated that he was leaving for a conference in San Diego and would not return until Thursday. Ken Kelly is in town. I would not call him until after Shannon Bohrer, if I call him at all. And, therefore, I would ask that –*
>
> Judge Dixon: *We are wasting a half a day, Mr. Hannon. And this trial has gone longer than any of us originally predicted. … There is no suggestion there that the fact that it wasn't completed last week is anyone's fault. … Why can't you make a decision now if you are going to call Mr. Kelly and call him this afternoon?*
>
> Mr. Hannon: *… the events of last week interfered with our order of proof. We are not necessarily entitled to a certain order of proof and – but the reason for the interference with our order of proof is that Your Honor was exercising your discretion to hold us to a certain order.*[60]

The order of proof or reordering of events relates to day four of the trial. After I was called to the stand, the prosecution voiced concern, and Judge Dixon questioned the appropriateness of my testifying before Heath testified. The result was that Judge Dixon ruled that I could not testify until after Heath testified.

Judge Dixon agreed, and Mr. Hannon continued, saying that they ran up against scheduling problems. He said he did not want to call Mr. Kelly until after my testimony.

> Mr. Hannon: *… And if you're asking me to make that decision now, then Agent Thomas is becoming a little prejudiced by our cooperation with the reordering of events.*
>
> Judge Dixon: *Well, I don't know that you can label it cooperation. You were just following my ruling, that is, you were not permitted to present those witnesses before Mr. Thomas.*
>
> Mr. Hannon: *… The only point I am making was it was a matter of the Court's discretion … If your Honor were to require me to make a decision as to whether I am going to call him today or not call him at all, I would have to say that I am not going to call him. I would rather be able to make that decision after the testimony of Shannon Bohrer.*[61]

Judge Dixon said that the decision to call Mr. Kelly would be Mr. Hannon's. The judge then proceeded to lay out a schedule for the rest of the trial. The trial would resume on Thursday, the 25th, and would finish on the following Monday. Mr. Hannon advised the Court of his anticipated schedule, and the prosecutors said they had no issues or questions. Day 6 of the trial had come to a close.

---

[60] Ibid, 234
[61] Ibid, 235

15A

William Dillon: Dog Identification and Other Faulty Evidence

On August 17, 1981, a man was beaten to death in a small town in Florida. The crime occurred in a tourist area, and the body was found in a parking area close to the beach. Several days after the crime, police detectives approached and questioned Mr. William Dillon, who was at the beach in the vicinity of the crime. Mr. Dillon said he was aware of the crime from news reports, and he saw the police tape in the area, believing that it was the crime scene.

For unknown reasons, Mr. Dillon became a suspect, and he was later questioned at the police station. While at the station, the police gave him a piece of paper. They asked him to ball the paper up and throw it in a trash can. Mr. Dillon was later arrested and charged with homicide. When arrested, he was told he had been identified as the killer by a trained dog.

Meanwhile, a potential witness had come forth with a bloody T-shirt. The witness told the police that he picked up a hitchhiker after the crime occurred, and the person left the bloody shirt in his vehicle. He believed the hitchhiker was the murderer. The trained dog, under the guidance of its handler, Mr. John Preston, linked the bloody T-shirt to Mr. Dillon's scent from the paper he balled up in the police station. The dog then linked the T-shirt to the crime scene. The tests were conducted eight days after the crime occurred.

The potential witness described the hitchhiker as 5 feet 8 inches to 6 feet in height, with short hair and a mustache. Mr. Dillon was 6 feet 4 inches tall, with long hair and no mustache, yet the witness identified Mr. Dillon as the person he had picked up on the night of the crime. The bloody t-shirt left in the vehicle was a size medium, too small for Mr. Dillon.

While incarcerated, another inmate said Dillon told him about the crime. The cellmate was willing to testify in court. Dillon's girlfriend was also questioned. She began by saying he did not commit the crime but then changed to "I saw him standing over the body."[1]

On November 14, 2008, Mr. Dillon's conviction was vacated, when DNA proved he did not commit the crime. He had been found guilty of murder, sentenced to life, and

---

[1] Justice 27 Years Too Late: The William Dillon Story, by Terrie Sundquist, January 17, 2011

after being incarcerated for 27 years, he was released on November 18, 2008. The state declined to retry his case.

The wrongful conviction was attributed to poor eyewitness identification and unreliable testimony from both the dog handler and the informant. The eyewitness who said the suspect left a bloody shirt in his vehicle was blind in one eye and had questioned his own identification of Mr. Dillon. Further, the jailhouse informant's testimony was not corroborated by other inmates that were nearby, and his story had significant differences from the actual crime. At that time, the informant was charged with the rape of a 16-year-old girl. Surprisingly, with his testimony, the charges against him were dropped.

The dog handler, Mr. John Preston, also testified in the Wilton Dedge case (see previous chapter) several months after the Dillon trial. In 1986 John Preston's expertise was tested and he was shown to be a fraud. Mr. Preston was called a "charlatan"[2] by the Arizona Supreme Court. The State of Arizona overturned all of the cases in which Mr. Preston's testimony resulted in convictions. Mr. Preston had been involved in hundreds of cases, testifying for the prosecution. This was unknown to Mr. Dillion and his defense team for over 20 years.

Another witness, Mr. Dillon's ex-girlfriend, recanted her testimony, saying the police had threatened her. According to her, the police said if she did not testify, they would charge her with being an accessory to murder.

The state built a case with evidence and witnesses that folded with scrutiny. Apparently, the prosecutors used Mr. Preston and his psychic dog to confirm their beliefs. Did the police ever suspect the witness who was blind in one eye? The jailhouse informant, who lied, had his rape charges dropped, so was that his motivation? If Mr. Dillon's ex-girlfriend was threatened by the police, as she alleged, was there an investigation of her claim?

This case was from Brevard County, Florida, as was the Dedge case.

References

William Dillon, www.innocenceporject.org, no author listed, posting date: before June 2012, last updated: 2/21/2019

William Dillon, "Unlock the Truth", Innocence Project of Florida, https://www.floridainnocence.org/william-dillon

Terri Sundquist, "Justice 27 Years Too Late, The William Dillon Story," Promega, January 17, 2011,

www.promegaconnections.com/justice-27-years-too-late-the-william-dillon-story/

---

[2] William Dillon - National Registry of Exonerations (umich.edu)

16

Our Perceptions

"Our past influences our perception of the present."
—Anthony Pinizzotto, Ph.D.

Two individuals exposed to the same incident may have different opinions or perspectives about what they saw and heard. While this may not seem logical, it occurs frequently. The arrest and prosecution of Mr. Heath Thomas is and has been viewed differently by the various parties involved. The prosecution felt strongly about Heath's guilt, just as the defense felt strongly about his innocence. The witnesses also did not agree as to what happened even though they were at the scene as it occurred.

Differences between the grand jury and trial testimonies contributed to the varied perceptions. The ABRA investigative report and the testimony at the ABRA hearing had additional discrepancies, to which no one testified at the trial. Further, during the trial, certain witness testimony conflicted with others' eyewitness accounts, and some testimony conflicted with the physical laws of human performance. Many of these discrepancies, I believe, contributed to the ultimate outcome of Heath's trial.

Why Some of the Differences Exist
How can two people witnessing the same event have different perspectives of what they saw? It really starts with who we are. It sounds simple enough, but when we examine who we are, we find differences that affect our views and perceptions. We have different backgrounds, different experiences, different education, and socialization encounters, all of which contribute to variations in our perceptions. Even differences in gender and ethnicity can result in different perspectives regarding similar or almost identical experiences.

Start with the Schema
An explanation of why each of us perceives an event differently is based on the theory of *schema*.[1] According to social psychologists, each of us has a schema that consists of our beliefs, biases, differences, and past experiences. These are the foundation for how we

---

[1] Schemas, Frames, and Scripts in Cognitive Psychology, from the International Encyclopedia of the Social and Behavioral Sciences, 2001, pages 13522 – 13526

make sense of the information we receive, what we see, and what we hear. The schema is a cognitive process—how we think, how we organize and interpret information. The schema gives us a structure or foundation for understanding events and experiences.

An excellent way to think of a schema is like a screen that surrounds us and filters the information we receive.[2] Because of our schemas, we often unconsciously filter what we see and hear, often related to our biases. The filter process interprets or makes sense of the information around us, at least from our perspective.

Confirmation Bias

Biases in our schema can filter information to fit our beliefs. This is generally an unconscious cognitive process. Social psychologists call this a "confirmation bias."[3] A confirmation bias is just what it says—we confirm what we believe. With a confirmation bias, we sometimes look for information that supports our preexisting beliefs and ignore information that does not align with our beliefs.

Belief Perseverance

Building on confirmation bias, one's beliefs can be so strong that people sometimes hold tight to their beliefs even when confronted with facts that discredit their position. Social psychologists refer to this as "belief perseverance."[4] When individuals have firmly held views, information that challenges those views can be ignored. This phenomenon is not uncommon. Political debate is a good example, since both sides often deal with the same facts, but the information is filtered differently.

If you're exposed to a new idea or thought, it may be difficult to accept the new information if that information conflicts with your current beliefs. Sometimes, to accept new or different information, one must admit that one's existing beliefs may not be correct. From that perspective, a logical conclusion is that our firmly held ideas sometimes can prevent us from learning.

Heath's case demonstrated instances of belief perseverance, since both sides, for the most part, had access to the same evidence, yet each side maintained strong beliefs of guilt and innocence. Take, for example, the prosecution's failure to acknowledge the fact that Cpl. Holubar could not have witnessed the start of the event outside. Evidence showed that he was not there when it commenced. To believe he was there, the court would have to think that Carole was not truthful when she said she was directly behind the manager. One also would have to ignore Cpl. Holubar's testimony that Carole was already outside when he got there. Did the prosecution overlook this fact because it did not fit with their belief?

---

[2] The screen example used a class, "Perspectives of Use of Force in Law Enforcement," given to the U.S. Attorney's Office at the FBI Academy, January 19, 1999, March 10, 1999, and January 19, 2000, by Anthony Pinizzotto, Ph.D. Behavioral Science Unit, FBI Academy Quantico Virginia

[3] The web Psychologydictionary.org and Psychology Today, April 23, 2015

[4] The Journal of Experimental Social Psychology, Volume 44, Issue 3, May 2008, Pages 706 – 712

Our Physical Position

Where we stand and what we are doing when we witness an event can also lead to significant differences in how we see and interpret events. Both our physical location and the activity in which we are engaged when an event takes place can affect what we observe and hear. It can add to the context of our experience, which is important, but it can also skew our perceptions. An example:

A police officer is investigating an accident at a busy intersection. Each party in the two-car accident claims that they were in the right and the other party caused the accident. In attempting to locate witnesses other than the drivers of the vehicles involved, the officer finds an independent witness who says that he saw the whole thing. When interviewed, the independent witness states:

> "I was sitting at the intersection, and I heard tires screeching and a horrible crashing sound. I set my coffee down and told my wife I had to get off my phone because there was an accident. She asked me if I was involved, and I said no, but I witnessed it. I then turned to look over my left shoulder and saw the whole thing."

Being in the vicinity of an incident does not mean you saw what happened. As in the above example, it can mean that you saw the vehicles at rest, right after the accident and before they were moved. Also, in this example, you could confirm the time with your phone records. Just because the "witness" did not see the physical event does not mean that what they heard is unimportant. Sometimes not seeing or hearing an event can have meaning that adds substance to what others saw or heard. Sometimes not seeing or hearing an event can also discredit other witnesses. The witnesses who were with Heath when the incident occurred were only 10 to 15 feet from the bar, and none of them heard a disturbance at the bar. Did the prosecution ignore that because it did not fit with what they believed happened?

In Heath's case, he was at the bar for some time. What was occurring during that time influenced the witnesses' perspective. If a witness heard Heath use profanity, he might not have been cursing the entire time. Conversely, if a witness heard Heath talking to the manager in Spanish and explaining his problem of not being able to pay his bill, that would not indicate he was explaining his position the entire time. Observation of a sliver of time does not usually give one a complete picture, but the pieces can still be important in developing the larger view.

Confabulation and Memory

"Confabulation is a memory error defined as the production of fabricated, distorted, or misinterpreted memories about oneself or the world, without the conscious intention to deceive."[5] Confabulation can occur when we "fill in" our own memory gaps by

---
[5] WWW.Wikipedia/confabulation

inserting what makes sense to us, given what we have experienced. While people have a natural tendency to add meaning to actions, the meanings we attach are not always correct. These factors affect and influence our interpretation—the importance we attach to what we see and hear during an event. A good argument can be proffered that everyone, from time to time, applies intent and meaning to someone's behavior.

We see people and hear parts of a conversation and then add the meaning from our perspective and consistent with our own schema. For example, Cpl. Holubar said that Heath was arguing with the bartender because he wanted a bottle—the bottle the bartender had in his hands. The bartender and Heath spoke to each other, but the conversation had nothing to do with a bottle. Cpl. Holubar attached meaning to what he observed, as many people would.[6]

Another way missing parts can be filled in is with the memories of others. In some incidents, people get together and talk about what they witnessed. Sometimes the memory of others becomes our memory. The person does not believe they are lying because they come to think that it is their memory. There was testimony that the bar employees talked about the event several times; did that influence their memories?

If someone witnesses part of an event, they start with the details they saw and then fill in the missing pieces to develop a complete picture. With the missing parts filled in, they can interpret the event as to what they believed happened. If a witness saw the bouncer carrying Heath, even if they did not see the bouncer pick Heath up, they would know it must have occurred. So, it could be part of their beliefs.

The human mind is not a recorder; it does not attend to every detail, and not every detail attended to is placed into long-term memory. Therefore, we often cannot remember what we had for lunch the day before. Witnesses can also distort what they witnessed by omission—which is a non-deliberate leaving out of parts from the description of an event.[7] They are not lying or trying to be deceitful—they just leave parts out, perhaps because they did not attend to those specific aspects when the event occurred or did not think them relevant.

The business checks and times indicate that Heath and his party were at The Guards for about one and a half hours. Heath and Carole believed they arrived at the Guards after 11:00, possibly relying on the Old Glory tab being closed at 11:02 p.m. However, the last of the three separate checks from Old Glory, (Exhibit 14) was completed at 10:08 p.m. This information aligns with the tab opened at The Guards at 10:17 p.m. (Exhibit 15), meaning they were at The Guards for about one and a half hours. Heath and Carole were not being deceptive or dishonest; they relied on information from one piece of evidence and adjusted their memories to fit.

---

[6] This is referred to as "attribution theory." Anthony Pinizzotto, Ph.D.

[7] "Perspectives of Use of Force in Law Enforcement" and "HOW WE REMEMBER WHAT WE REMEMBER?" given to the U.S. Attorney's Office at the FBI Academy, January 19, 1999, March 10, 1999, and January 19, 2000, by Anthony Pinizzotto, Ph.D. Behavioral Science Unit, FBI Academy Quantico Virginia

The Law Enforcement Perspective
The fact that each person sees and recalls events differently is well known within the law enforcement community. If a crime occurs and there are three victims and one offender, the police often end up with three different offender descriptions. The same is true in many court cases. Listening to the testimony on both sides, one can sometimes wonder if they describe the same event, which was not unlike this case. What is occasionally unusual is that although this is well known in the law enforcement community, there are instances when the law enforcement community does not believe it applies to them.

As a retired police officer, I was very surprised that the responding police officers in this case never conducted an investigation. Instead, they only collected information to prove what they were told by the alleged victims.

An Assumption of Guilt
In Heath's case, the police immediately assumed he was guilty—or at least their actions conveyed that message. I make this statement for several reasons. One is that only Heath was handcuffed and taken into custody. Both Heath and Mr. Brackett should have been handcuffed and taken into custody—or at least temporarily detained while an initial investigation was conducted. Once in handcuffs and in custody, Heath was placed in the role of the offender.

Anyone seeing Heath in custody would think him an offender. A police supervisor responding to the scene of a reported incident observes one individual handcuffed and in the back seat of a patrol car. Another person is talking to a uniformed officer. The uniformed officer is taking a statement from the person not in custody—the supervisor assumes that person is probably the victim. So, what status is the supervisor likely to attribute to the person in the back seat of the patrol car?

As seen with belief perseverance, if we start with a premise that could be incorrect, sometimes we find what we need to support that assumption, ignoring other evidence that does not align with our belief. Ignoring information that does not fit with what you believe is not helpful to any investigation; additionally, it can take the investigation in the wrong direction.

In Heath's case, the assumption of guilt was compounded by a lack of investigation by the police. There were probably 75 to 100 people in the area at the time of the incident, and it appears that the police only interviewed persons associated with the bar and one witness who confirmed the bouncer's version of events. They did not interview Heath's party, any potential witnesses inside the bar, or pedestrians on the street. Without a preponderance of information contradicting an initial assumption, those beliefs go unchecked.

When Perception Skews Witness Testimony
We recognize that numerous internal factors can affect one's perception and retrieval of information. There are also numerous external factors that can affect what we see and

hear, so two people who witness the same event can have different perceptions. Time is one factor and can be important.

During the ten-minute-plus time that Heath was at the bar trying to pay his tab, we know he had contact with different people. We know of two witnesses who were bar employees who gave statements on the night of the incident but did not testify. One employee, Mr. Mark Fleming, the bartender, said that Heath "was calmly and firmly escorted to the door." Yet, we know that is not an accurate description of what occurred.[8] Since Heath and the bartender's interaction seemed critical to the case, I expected the bartender to have testified at both the grand jury and the trial. The defense did summons the bartender for the trial, but he did not appear. A note attached to the summons says: "to service processor 7/22."[9] The note indicates the service processor (the person serving the summons) received the summons July 22; the identity of the service processor is unknown. In 2014, I sent the bartender a letter asking him to contact me about this book, but he never responded. I also telephoned and left a message, but again, no response.[10]

The second witness—a waiter, Cesar Stiles—in his written statement on the night of the incident, wrote, "The security guy grabbed him from the waist lifted him up and took him outside." That might be a better description of what occurred when Heath was carried out.[11] I attempted to contact this witness but was unsuccessful.[12] I was told that the defense summonsed Mr. Stiles for the trial, but I never located a copy of the summons.

Both the bartender and the waiter, in their written statements, said that Heath did identify himself as a police officer. And neither witness said anything about Heath talking to the manager in Spanish. Since the bartender was in the area, shouldn't he have heard that conversation? Did he speak Spanish? Were there others who witnessed the conversation but were not interviewed?

Mr. Oscar Viricochea

Mr. Viricochea, the manager at The Guards, was the individual responsible for having Heath removed from the bar. Heath testified at the trial that he approached Mr. Viricochea to tell him about the service problems he was experiencing. Mr. Viricochea testified in the grand jury that Heath was argumentative and was using profanity. He said that Heath was trying to "jump him," and he was also trying to fight with the bouncer. However, when Mr. Viricochea testified at the trial, he said that he did not see

---

[8] Mr. Mark Fleming's written police statement, taken on the night of the incident, p 1
[9] See Appendix I, Copy of Summons
[10] Letter sent to Mark Fleming; dated September 2, 2014, and several telephone calls were made to Mr. Fleming with no response
[11] Cesar Stiles written statement, taken on the night of the incident, p 2
[12] Several telephone calls were made with no responses

any interaction between Heath and the bouncer. When Mr. Hannon brought up the discrepancies during the trial, the Judge failed to see the problem.

In his grand jury testimony, Mr. Viricochea testified that he did not know whether Heath was drunk, but in his initial police statement on the night of the incident, he reported that Heath was drunk. At the trial, he was not asked about Heath's sobriety.

Beyond these examples, there appears to be some significant discrepancies in Mr. Viricochea's recall. He reported that the incident occurred around 10:30 p.m., when in fact it occurred at 11:58 p.m. In a document for ABRA, he reportedly said that Heath entered the bar at 5 p.m. with his girlfriend, but we know they did not arrive until after 10 p.m. At the trial, Mr. Viricochea said that the downstairs area was closed when the incident occurred, and Mr. Brackett was the only bouncer working. However, Cpl. Holubar, a prosecution witness, testified at trial that the downstairs area was open; and the owner of the Guards testifying at the ABRA hearing said there were three bouncers working when the incident occurred.

Did the court ignore the testimony of Cpl. Holubar when he said he was downstairs and it was crowded, while Mr. Viricochea testified the downstairs area was closed?

Also of significance was Mr. Viricochea's testimony in court about the verbiage which Heath used when speaking to him in Spanish. What Mr. Viricochea reported is different from what Ms. Perez reported when she described the same conversation.

Mr. Viricochea's memory issues were a problem that was not acknowledged by the court but should have been. His memory resembled what some have called situational memory. Basically, his memory was determined not by what happened but by the situation he was experiencing when asked to recall what happened. Mr. Viricochea does have problems with the English language, which may have contributed to misunderstandings. Memories also can change, but sometimes the changes and differences can be attributed to motivations to present something to support a particular agenda.

Mr. Marshall Brackett

Mr. Brackett's testimony of picking up Heath by his shoulders is difficult to believe. When he demonstrated his purported actions in the courtroom, picking up Mr. Hannon, he did so by picking him up around his waist. Although Mr. Hannon described this to the court during the demonstration, the significance of it seemed to go by unnoticed.

Meanwhile, Mr. Brackett's description of what occurred outside—stepping back, Heath turning, and him grabbing the gun before it was pointed at him—is just not physically possible. Nonetheless, he may be convinced that is what happened.

Mr. Brackett also said that when he was struggling for the gun with Heath, Heath pulled out his identification and showed it to him. No one else saw this, and Heath told me that he would never have taken one hand off the gun to show his identification.

Perhaps Mr. Brackett is not dishonest; he may believe everything he said, but that does not make it an accurate recollection of what occurred.

Corporal Holubar

The prosecutors and the judge involved with this case believed that Cpl. Holubar was an instrumental witness to the prosecution. He was the only witness to corroborate the bouncer's version of events, even though the bouncer's version of events could not be duplicated in court.

As stated above, Cpl. Holubar testified that the downstairs was open at the time of the incident. Telephone interviews that I conducted for this book with two employees of The Guards confirmed that the downstairs was open on the night of the incident. Freddy Biloatoomez, a bouncer at The Guards, said that he was working the night of the incident in the downstairs area.[13] Ms. Tara Novotny, an employee at The Guards, said that she was working downstairs on the night of the incident.[14] The interviews confirmed the fact that the downstairs area was open around 11 p.m. and that the incident occurred after 11 p.m., not around 10:30.

As previously mentioned, Cpl. Holubar said that he witnessed a conversation between the bartender and Heath. He believed they were arguing over a bottle, and according to him, there came a time when the bartender said he would call the police unless Heath calmed down. That description is significantly different from Heath's recollection of events. According to Heath's testimony, it was the manager who said he was going to call the police. In a telephone interview, Cpl. Holubar was asked if he heard Heath speaking Spanish, and he said no.[15]

Cpl. Holubar, the bartender, and the waiter all heard Heath identify himself as a police officer. However, Mr. Viricochea and the bouncer did not hear it. Again, not everyone was in earshot when it was said. Why did the bartender and waiter—both of whom heard Heath identify himself as a police officer and gave a written statement on the night of the incident—not testify at the grand jury or the trial?

At the trial, neither the prosecution nor the defense ever questioned Cpl. Holubar about the fact that he was not directly behind the bouncer when leaving the bar, but then neither did the police. Judge Dixon even asked Cpl. Holubar if Carole followed him. He asked, "Was she behind you inside the bar or was she outside?" and he answered, "She was outside, to my right."[16]

In another instance, Cpl. Holubar testified that Heath had his finger on the trigger because his finger was not straight. However, Heath is right-handed, and Cpl. Holubar

---

[13] Mr. Biloatoomez, was interviewed by telephone on September 30, 2015
[14] Ms. Novonty was interviewed by telephone on October 21, 2015
[15] Telephone interview with Brandon Holubar on November 16, 2014
[16] Day three of the trial, page 90 in the transcript

only saw the left side of the gun. So, he could not have seen a straight finger from his viewing position.

Cpl. Holubar's testimony included deficiencies and problems that can be directly related to the fact that he did not witness everything to which he testified. Part of his testimony could be confabulation and embellishments of the story. It is also possible that his consumption of alcohol affected his observations. According to his testimony, Cpl. Holubar drank a Long Island Iced Tea and one beer within an hour before witnessing the event. If a person weighting 155 pounds—like Cpl. Holubar —drinks a beer and a Long Island Iced Tea within the previous hour, the *estimated* blood alcohol content (BAC) would be 0.120, which is intoxicated. I used the website www.thealcoholcalculator.com to calculate his BAC.

Different Perceptions and Interpretations of the Same Event
In addition to how we perceive things differently, we also attach different interpretations and meanings to the same observations and events. When Agent Eisert had a conversation with Heath while he was in a cell, for example, the prosecution and the judge thought it odd or strange that Heath did not turn and talk to Agent Eisert. Whereas the prosecution seemed to think it indicated Heath was intoxicated, that he was not being forthcoming, or that he was trying to cover up his drinking, Agent Eisert did not think it strange. Another explanation could be that Heath was embarrassed about the circumstances and did not want to look his supervisor in the face. Or one could say that Heath was not focused on the conversation but was focused on how the incident happened and how it would end. Perhaps he was distracted by his own thought processing of the events of that night.

The prosecution and the judge also thought it was strange that Heath said nothing when he was being carried out of the bar, and again, it was implied that his behavior was that of someone intoxicated. However, Carole as well as Heath's coworkers testified that he was unflappable under stress, and this reaction was in character. If Heath had said something—like yelling that he was a police officer—would the prosecution then have viewed that yelling as an intoxicated person's behavior?

Throughout the trial, the prosecution described and insinuated that Heath was intoxicated; whenever possible, there was an association of his behavior with that of an inebriated person. Heath testified that he had consumed 3.5 beers at dinner, and only had a sip of a beer at The Guards and a sip of one Bombay Sapphire martini. The first drink was spilled on the table, with much of it in Heath's lap. And when the second drink was served, he said he only took a sip and then went to pay the tab. Using the website www.thealcoholcalculator.com I entered 190-pound male into the BAC calculator and entered four 12-ounce beers (not 3 ½ but 4) and added 1 oz of 40 percent liquor (as if he drank most of a martini). All of this was consumed in a 5-hour period, with the drinks being somewhat equally spread out. That would mean he drank all four beers and most of the last martini set in front of him. The calculator showed his blood alcohol content at 0.037, which would not be intoxicated. Note: The beers were consumed between 7 pm and 10 pm with dinner, and the one mixed drink was consumed between 10:17 p.m. and 11:58 p.m.

> "Everything we hear is an opinion, not a fact. Everything we see
> is a perspective, not the truth."
> —Marcus Aurelius

We Find What We Seek
It was once said that if the president of the United States walked on the Potomac River, the opposition party would say that he could not swim. A prosecutor's job is to prosecute, so they naturally view their cases from that perspective. The defense attorney's duty is to defend, so they look for facts that support their position. It is the judge's responsibility to weigh both positions within the legal rules and standards. However, the judge's responsibility is not just constrained by the evidence that is brought into the courtroom but also by the interpretations of words and actions that are also brought into the courtroom. And, in this case, that was significant.

A courtroom is a place where we look for and find facts to determine what occurred, who did what, and why. To do so requires one to have an open mind. Conversely, in some trials it is not abnormal for the parties to have preconceived notions about who is guilty and who is credible. Looking for what we expect to find is not that uncommon, but it can have harmful and lasting ramifications.

16A

Henry McCollum and Leon Brown: False Confessions

In 1983, in Red Springs, North Carolina, the body of 11-year-old Sabrina Buie was found in a soybean field. Investigation revealed that she had been raped and murdered, and her underwear had been stuffed in her throat. This was the first murder in Red Springs in four years, and the residents' wanted answers.

The investigators questioned Rosco Artis, who lived in the home nearest the crime scene. After the interview, he was not considered a suspect, and no background check was conducted.

At the time, a young schoolchild reported that two young men, Henry McCollum, and Leon Brown, were "acting strangely." This was only a rumor, but the police interviewed them as well as numerous other people. Henry McCollum lived in New Jersey and was visiting his mother and his half-brother, Leon Brown, who lived in Red Springs. His mother's residence was not far from the crime scene. McCollum had only been there a few weeks when the crime occurred. He was 19 years old at the time and had the mental capacity of a 9-year-old. His half-brother, Leon, was 15 years old and was also mentally challenged.

The police picked up McCollum at his mother's home and transported him to the police station. At the station, he was interviewed for four and a half hours. Reportedly, he was told that if he gave the police the facts about the crime, he would be allowed to leave. McCollum eventually told the officer(s) about the crime, using the facts he was provided by the police, adding that his brother Leon and two other boys were present. The officer wrote up a confession, and McCollum signed it. After signing, he asked, "Can I go home now?"[1]

Late that night, McCollum's mother and her other son, Leon Brown, went to the police station looking for Henry. Officers took Leon from the waiting room into an interrogation room. After some time, Brown also confessed to the crime, again using facts given to him by the police.

In 1984, Henry McCollum and Leon Brown were convicted of murder and rape, and the jury sentenced both men to death. They had both signed confessions written by

---

[1] North Carolina Coalition for Alternatives to the Death Penalty, nccadp.org/henry-McCollum-Leon-brown/published 2018

the police but had quickly retracted them, claiming the police coerced them to confess, promising them they would be released. The false confessions were the basis for their convictions. In 2010, after being contacted by Leon Brown, the North Carolina Innocence Commission agreed to investigate the case. The commission found fingerprints in evidence that did not match McCollum or Brown. The fingerprints had never been compared to anyone.

A few weeks after this crime occurred in Red Springs, an 18-year-old woman was raped and murdered while Henry and Leon were in jail. Roscoe Artis committed that crime. He was the first person the police interviewed in the Sabrina Buie case. The commission also found that the physical evidence, the fingerprints, from the Buie case matched Roscoe Artis.

Although the prosecutor in the Buie case, Joe Freeman Britt, knew that Roscoe Artis was charged with a similar crime while McCollum and Brown were in jail, the defense attorneys were never given the information. McCollum and Brown were exonerated with DNA evidence and were released in 2014 after serving 30 years in prison.

While this case presents an unconscionable and immoral view of the justice system, what is not in the case is just as disturbing. In 2010, during North Carolina's legislative elections, political flyers with Henry's face on them were used in election materials. McCollum and Brown were touted as examples of people who should be executed. Also, "U.S. Supreme Court Justice Antonin Scalia pointed to the brutality of Henry's crime as a reason to support capital punishment."[2] With McCollum and Brown now exonerated, the case could rightly be used in an argument *against* capital punishment.

References

Henry McCollum and Leon Brown, North Carolina Coalition for Alternatives to the Death Penalty, nccadp.org/henry-McCollum-Leon-brown, published 2018.

Thomson Reuters," Henry McCollum, Leon Brown freed after 30 years in prison",

CBC News website, September 03, 2014, www.cbc.ca/news/world/henry-McCollum-Leon-brown-freed-after-30-years-in-prison-1.2753737

Bryan Pietsch, "Cleared of Murder," New York Times, May 17, 2021.

---

[2] North Carolina Coalition for Alternatives to the Death Penalty nccadp.org/henry-McCollum-Leon-brown/published 2018

17

Day 7: The Expert's Testimony is Limited
AUGUST 25, 2011

"This is a Court of Law, young man, not a Court of Justice."
—Oliver Wendell Holmes

The trial had now stretched long past the original estimate of three and half days, and the situation had not improved for Heath. Carole and Heath had both given exemplary testimony. However, Judge Dixon did not seem moved. Expert testimony, if allowed, would be the defense's next and possibly last opportunity to turn the tide in Heath's favor.

On day six of the trial two days earlier, the Court had heard arguments about potential experts and what testimony they might offer. Judge Dixon's decision to allow experts for the defense included that he would "not permit any expert testimony to be offered with respect to what was done or what could have been done by Mr. Thomas from the point that the bear hug was put on him until the time the weapon was grabbed. I will allow the expert witness testimony from the point that the weapon was grabbed."[1]

When Mr. Hannon informed me of Judge Dixon's instructions, I had never encountered restrictions like this before. How the gun was dislodged was critical to the case. While I was not at the scene and did not witness the event, I expected to testify hypothetically and to be able to use the film we made to demonstrate how the incident could have occurred. The Judge's instructions made much of what was expected and planned in my testimony no longer available.

Testimony of Shannon Bohrer
At the start of my testimony, I introduced myself, then gave an overview of my professional career and my formal education. Mr. Hannon asked to move Exhibit 21, my résumé,[2] into evidence. Ms. Sawyer objected and was overruled.[3] Mr. Hannon questioned me about training with the U.S. Attorney's Office in Washington D.C. The program was

---
[1] Information from the trial transcript, Criminal Action Number 2010-CF3-16079, dated August 23, 2011, p 217-18
[2] Appendix J, Exhibit 21
[3] Information from the trial transcript, Criminal Action Number 2010-CF3-16079, dated August 25, 2011, p 246

titled "Perspectives on the Use of Force." My background included teaching the use of force, off-duty safety, and additional related topics.

As part of that discussion, Mr. Hannon asked about Defense Exhibit 19.

> Me: *This is an article that I co-wrote on the training that I and others did with the United States Attorney's Office.*
> Mr. Hannon: *I want to show you Exhibit 20 from the FBI law enforcement bulletin ... entitled "Use of Deadly Force Investigations." Is that an article that you wrote?*
> Me: *Co-wrote, yes.* [4]
> Mr. Hannon showed me Exhibits 105 and 106, two additional articles.
> Mr. Hannon: *What is Exhibit 105?*
> Me: *"Unintentional Discharges, Finger Off the Trigger." It is about unintentional or what some people call accidental discharge of the weapon when the weapon goes off, and it is not intended to.*
> Mr. Hannon: *And number 106?*
> Me: *"Off Duty Training - What Constitutes a Threat?"* [5]

I authored Exhibit 105 and co-authored Exhibit 106. Mr. Hannon referenced each article, asking if the information was related to my expert testimony, and I answered, "Yes."[6]

> Mr. Hannon: *... have you ever been proffered and accepted as an expert in a court of law of law enforcement use of weapons and use of force?*
> Me: *Yes.*
> Mr. Hannon: *... how many times and in what courts?*
> Me: *Federal and state courts. And it would be eight, ten times maybe. Most of the time employed as an expert witness. You either give a deposition or go to trial, but not both.*[7]

I explained that there were also times when I had been retained as an expert but never gave a deposition or testified.

Following this exchange Mr. Hannon proffered me "as an expert in the field of law enforcement use of force and firearms training."[8] The Judge said, "That is kind of broad, Mr. Hannon. Remember the contours of my initial ruling in terms of what your witness

---

[4] Ibid, 252-253, Appendix K, exhibit 19 and Appendix L, Exhibit 20
[5] Ibid, 253-254, Appendix M, Exhibit 105 and Appendix N, Exhibit 106.
[6] Information from the trial transcript, Criminal Action Number 2010-CF3-16079, dated August 25, 2011, p 254
[7] Ibid
[8] Ibid

would be permitted to testify about."[9] The Judge then allowed Ms. Sawyer to ask questions related to my qualifications and expertise.

Ms. Sawyer stated, as a question, that I had never worked for ICE and Homeland Security, and I agreed.

"And you have no first-hand of how their policies, ICE and DHS respectively, are taught or enforced or interpreted; correct?"[10] I began to answer, "I have worked," but Ms. Sawyer stopped me and said, "First-hand knowledge."[11] I answered, "That is correct."[12]

Mr. Hannon objected and was told by the Judge that he would be able to re-direct.

> Ms. Sawyer: ... *And the civil rights division of the Department of Justice deals with cases in which officers are acting under color of law; correct?*
> Me: Yes.
> Ms. Sawyer: *In their capacity as law enforcement officers; correct?*
> Me: Yes.[13]

That concluded her questions, and Mr. Hannon had no further questions. Judge Dixon followed up with questions of his own.

> Judge Dixon: ... *One of the articles that you said you wrote concerned officers carrying weapons off duty; is that correct?*[14]
> Me: *That is part of the off-duty behavior, yes.*
> Judge Dixon: *And I think a part of what I heard you say when you were describing the article is that there is not very much written on that subject.*
> Me: *At that time, yes ...*
> Judge Dixon: ... *are there national guidelines now with respect to off-duty behavior and officers carrying weapons?*
> Me: *The only national guidelines ...is the IACP model polices. ... They have model policies on off-duty rules and regulations. That is the only ones I am aware of.*[15]
> Judge Dixon: *What is that organization?*[16]
> Me: *The International Association of Chiefs of Police.*[17]

---

[9] Ibid
[10] Ibid, 256
[11] Ibid, 257
[12] Ibid
[13] Ibid, 257-258
[14] Ibid, 258
[15] Ibid, 259
[16] Ibid
[17] Ibid, The IACP has model policies, but there are no national standards that require agencies to follow the policies.

At that point Judge Dixon called a conference at the bench, and I was asked to step down.

Judge Dixon said, "I know I haven't heard any argument yet. Is there going to be any objection to Mr. Bohrer – any additional objection to Mr. Bohrer being recognized as an expert witness?"[18] Ms. Sawyer answered that there would be.

The Judge said that he would hear the arguments in open court, noting, "then I will go through the contours of my rulings, if it is appropriate after I finish ruling on those objections."[19]

Judge Dixon then addressed me. "Mr. Bohrer, I was putting the cart before the horse. I need you to step outside while I hear arguments in open Court."[20] I left the courtroom.

> Ms. Sawyer: "Thank you, Your Honor. At this point, I would reiterate, to begin with, one of the arguments I made the other day regarding expert testimony … [21] And, Your Honor, that just goes to the run-of-the-mill standard that is applied as to whether or not this testimony is admissible to begin with. And I think the Court's question went to a fair point about off duty. And I don't know that it has all been established that that is a recognized field of science, profession or expertise that he can testify about. I think that is – it also somewhat goes beyond the scope of the Court's ruling from the other day regarding what the witness was going to be permitted to testify to. The other argument is that while he certainly has experience in law enforcement, he has none in the realm of Department of Homeland Security or ICE. He is not going to be speaking to training – the specific training that this defendant received. And so those would be my two objections at this point. And I do have concern about the scope of his testimony as well, but I think that is a separate issue.[22]

Ms. Sawyer seemed to be trying to block or even eliminate my testimony. At several other times during the trial, she made comments or motions that seemed odd or unconventional, such as when she wanted Carole excused from the courtroom, with no viable reason. Similarly, she did not want Judge Dixon to see and hear the interview tape from when Heath was interviewed on the night he was arrested. I don't think she wanted me to testify, which may have been why she did not meet with me. If we had met, that would have allowed Hannon to ask about the meeting and the conversation. Then again, even if a meeting had taken place, she may have objected, and Judge Dixon may have agreed with her.

---

[18] Information from the trial transcript, Criminal Action Number 2010-CF3-16079, dated August 25, 2011, p 259
[19] Ibid
[20] Ibid, 260
[21] Ibid
[22] Ibid, 260-61

In the end Judge Dixon ruled that I would be allowed to testify based on my experience, background, and education. He said he would go over "the contours of that ruling so that he [me] will know and that counsel will know the areas in which he will be permitted to testify so that it won't come as a surprise to him."[23] I was called back into the courtroom.

Judge Dixon stipulated, "Okay. As indicated, over objection, I am permitting Mr. Bohrer to testify as an expert witness within the contours of the ruling that I made in open Court when I ruled on the Government's various objections ... The witness may testify with respect to general standards governing officers carrying weapons while they are off duty... He may testify with respect to ... whether or not a particular holster is a proper type of device in which to hold the officer's weapon. He may testify with respect to general training of officers with respect to what they are permitted to do or not do, what they should do or should not do when there is an effort by any unauthorized person to obtain their weapon. The witness may not give us his own evaluation of the struggle between Mr. Thomas and the bouncer who had grabbed the particular weapon, but he may testify with respect to general standards and applicable standards, what the officer would have been permitted to do and not do under those circumstances. If there are any other areas in which this witness is being proffered, perhaps you should let me know, Mr. Hannon, so that I can give you an initial ruling whether or not it is going to be permitted."[24]

Mr. Hannon said that he would use the outline the Court proffered.

> Mr. Hannon: ... *So to the extent that I need to object, I am going to rely on that outline. I won't go into any other areas outside those that have been offered by the Court, based on your ruling.*
>
> Judge Dixon: ... *are there any particular areas in which you thought I ruled the testimony might be permitted, which I over looked in my ruling?*
>
> Mr. Hannon: *My notes indicate that you authorized him to opine as to whether he has an expert opinion from the information presented to him as to whether Agent Thomas had his finger on the trigger.*[25]

Judge Dixon agreed and told Mr. Hannon to proceed.

Mr. Hannon asked about my preparations for the case and how I came to my opinions. I testified that I read and reviewed the materials provided to me—the grand jury transcripts, the ABRA investigation and hearing report, a few police notes, along with some photographs. I discussed the case with Heath and assisted with a film that demonstrated how I

---

[23] Ibid, 261
[24] Ibid, 262-63
[25] Ibid, 263

believed the incident occurred. I had conversations with Mr. Hannon and with Heath on various occasions and witnessed the trial for all but two days. Mr. Hannon asked if I had reviewed Heath's testimony, and I said yes, from a transcript.

> Mr. Hannon: *Is there any information that you, in your professional opinion, are missing in order to be able to testify to the topics that the Court has discussed today?*
> Me: *No.*[26]

Mr. Hannon asked my opinion on the "level of training that Agent Thomas has achieved in firearms and use of force."[27] There was an objection from the prosecution, which was sustained. Mr. Hannon continued, "Could you tell the court what the training a federal law enforcement officer … would receive in terms of retaining control of his or her weapon?"[28] Ms. Sawyer objected; it was overruled.

> Me: *Weapon retention is taught in every academy,* [it is] *standard police training of how to retain your weapon primarily with a duty holster* [when some is trying to take the gun]. *Weapon retention started in the mid- '80s* [when it recognized as a problem] *… And it has continued and evolved because of the changes in the holsters …* [29]

I continued describing elements of the training involving gym activities where an officer is exposed to someone trying to take their gun. The officers are taught defensive tactics, to keep control of their weapon.

> Mr. Hannon: *And when does the – where does the continuum begin in an officer's training in terms of retention of his or her weapon?*
> Me: *I'm not sure of the question with continuum in there.*
> Mr. Hannon: *Is it fair to say there are different levels of threat to an officer's loss of his or her weapon?*
> Me: *Possibly.*[30]

I addressed the Court, for clarity purposes: "I have to clarify this, Your Honor, if I can. If somebody is trying to take the weapon, there is only one level: You keep it at all costs."[31]

---

[26] Ibid
[27] Ibid, 266
[28] Ibid
[29] Ibid, 266 - 267
[30] Ibid, 267
[31] Ibid

Mr. Hannon continued, "And in the training of the officer in weapon retention, how are they able to detect a threat to the retention of their weapon?"[32] I responded by explaining there are multiple elements, or pre-indicators, which include target glances (individuals looking at the officer's weapon), individuals who keep moving to the officer's weapon side, distraction while someone moves to the officer's weapon side, and others. These all are considered possible threats.

Mr. Hannon asked how officers are trained for these pre-indicators. Aside from knowing the indicators to look for, officers are trained to keep the weapon side away from persons, using a bladed stance. In some circumstances, if offenders escalate the situation, the officer can gain distance by backing up, giving verbal commands, and, when vehicles are involved, asking individuals to remain in their vehicles. I added, "It depends on the context of the situation. But the idea is you keep the weapon side away from them [offenders]."[33]

When asked what happens when offenders close the distance between themselves and the officer, I answered on the assumption he meant the offender was reaching for or grabbing the weapon. I replied, "Depending on the holster and situation, you can hold your weapon from the top with one hand and keep them from drawing it out. That gives you a free hand as long as it [the gun] is in the holster."[34]

> Mr. Hannon: *Once the offender has reached the point of having hands on the officer's weapon, what sort of procedure is the officer trained in at that point?*
> Me: *… you're either neutral, defensive, … or offensive … forward or back balance … The person is trying to pull the weapon, you basically turn to them and let them pull the weapon but you have both hands on it. It catches them off guard.*[35]
> Mr. Hannon: *And for what purpose is that taught?*
> Me: *If you are pulling on something and…it is released, you are going to fall backward.*
> Mr. Hannon: *If the officer doesn't succeed in that type of a maneuver, what is he or she taught?*
> Me: *They have … a last resort where you shoot them off the weapon.*[36]
> Mr. Hannon asked me to explain.
> Me: *The idea … is to fire the gun, because if they have their hand on the slide, most people are going to let go at that time. It doesn't mean that you have to shoot them, it just means that you fire the weapon. The difficulty there is the context of the situation you are in, the environment. If it is a … lonely highway and you are next to a field and you fire the weapon, the round goes into the field. If you are in an urban environment where there is a lot of concrete … you are taught that you are responsible for where the round goes …*

---

[32] Ibid
[33] Ibid, 268
[34] Ibid, 268 - 269
[35] Ibid, 269
[36] Ibid, 269 - 270

> Mr. Hannon: *And what is the officer trained in doing if the officer is uncertain about where the round might go in shooting the offender off of the gun?*
> Me: *That is the decision of the officer. The training only covers the parameters, the elements. … the officer has to make that decision. There are times when officers have made decisions … even in what would be considered a safe environment where someone unintentionally got hurt …*
> Mr. Hannon: *Why would an officer be trained to fire his weapon under those circumstances.*
> Me: *Well, I may have misspoken or been misunderstood … what I am saying is there are times when the environment would appear safe and the officer does fire the weapon but it does result in an unintentional injury, ricochet rounds…*
> Mr. Hannon: *When you talk about the judgement perspective of the officer, how does that play into the decision?*
> Me: *The decision to use force at any level is a decision of the officer at the scene. They [officers] cannot be trained on specific incidences when they can use it as much as they can staying within a parameter. Again the context of the situation when an officer can use force, including deadly force, is the officer's decision. They…have to justify it [the decision] after they have used it.*[37]

Mr. Hannon continued with questions about weapon retention. I responded that depending on the situation, the officer can maintain their position, back up, or move forward, and if needed they can fire the person off the weapon. When an officer fires a person off of their gun, the person holding the gun, will let go. Responding to another question, I said officers are taught to never release their gun. In every police academy the training standard is, "When somebody is going for your weapon, it is a given that their intention is to use the weapon against you."[38]

Responding to questions about the terms "offensive" and "neutral" that I used in my testimony, I explained that they related to defensive tactics and martial arts. A center, or neutral balance is, "low center of gravity, feet far apart, keep the weapon in close to you, that way you have the most muscle control on the weapon and it makes it harder for someone to pull the weapon away from you."[39] When in an offensive or front balance, you are moving forward, facing the offender, and, "you are just turning the weapon into the person and moving forward and that person while pulling the weapon is caught off balance."[40]

> Mr. Hannon: *Is there anything in the video that was made last October that would illustrate the testimony that you just provided to the Court?*

---

[37] Ibid, 270 - 271
[38] Ibid, 271- 272
[39] Ibid, 272- 273
[40] Ibid, 273

Me: *Yes…*

Mr. Hannon: *Can you tell the Court what is contained in the video?*[41]

Ms. Sawyer objected, but the Judge overruled the objection. I answered, "At the meeting I had with Agent Thomas, I asked him to demonstrate things that he could have done … I didn't tell him what to do, I just asked him to demonstrate things that he could have done."[42]

Mr. Hannon addressed the Judge, saying he wanted to play the video and to move it into evidence. The video was Defense Exhibit 107. Ms. Sawyer objected, and Judge Dixon heard her argument.

> Ms. Sawyer: *Well, in a few different respects, Your Honor. It is essentially hearsay. They are acting out a scenario to which – out of Court that could be testified to. I don't know what portion we're talking about. I don't think it is appropriate.*
>
> Judge Dixon: *Mr. Hannon, the way I have heard this testimony and you can reword it again if you like, but the way I heard it is that Agent Thomas was asked to demonstrate the things he could have done.*[43]

Mr. Hannon agreed, and the Judge said, "That is hearsay testimony from Agent Thomas."[44]

Mr. Hannon followed, "Mr. Bohrer, would this portion of the video illustrate the testimony that you just gave?"[45] Before I answered, Mr. Hannon addressed the Court, saying, "I only wish the Court to see it as an illustration."[46]

> Judge Dixon: *"An illustration of what?"*
>
> Mr. Hannon: *Of the techniques that Mr. Bohrer has testified to that an officer may utilize once he is in these circumstances.*
>
> Judge Dixon: *I mean, it was first introduced to me as Agent Thomas was asked to show things he could have done. And now you are trying to reintroduce it as, Mr. Bohrer, what are the things that an officer can do under these circumstances? I knew we were going to come to this rewording.*[47]

Mr. Hannon apologized to the Judge.

---

[41] Ibid
[42] Ibid
[43] Ibid, 274
[44] Ibid
[45] Ibid, 274 - 275
[46] Ibid, 275
[47] Ibid

> Mr. Hannon: *We used Mr. Thomas. But let me – as a predicate perhaps let me ask a different question ... [Speaking to me] The methods that Agent Thomas demonstrated to you as to the procedures he could have followed when his weapon was attacked, did you recognize those procedures? Did you recognize those moves?*
>
> Me: *Yes.*
>
> Mr. Hannon: *... what did you recognize them as?*
>
> Me: *Police training and defensive tactics and martial arts training for weapon* [retention] *defense.*
>
> Mr. Hannon: *And did Agent Thomas demonstrate the procedures you described earlier to the Court?*
>
> Me: *Yes, he did.*[48]

Mr. Hannon to Judge Dixon: "I understand Your Honor's concern. I will be happy to make Agent Thomas available for cross examination, but I think this is illustrative of his testimony. And if the Court feels it is inappropriate to see it, I think that is probably within your discretion. I think it is a discretionary call. I don't mean this to be testimony by Agent Thomas."[49] Judge Dixon responded, "Yes. And he even used one of the same phrases, so he has given his testimony about what he could have done and the things that he thought about."[50] The Judge sustained the objection.

I believed Judge Dixon was referring to the phrase "fire the person off the weapon" or "shooting a person off the gun," which are common terms that describe a tactic taught to police officers.

Mr. Hannon continued with his questions. He handed me Defense Exhibit 102, the holster that Heath was wearing when he was arrested, and he asked me about it. I told the Court that it was a current piece of equipment often referred to as a Kydex type holster—Kydex being a manufacturer of molded holsters.

Mr. Hannon asked, "Do you have an opinion as to whether that holster is appropriate for law enforcement officer in an off-duty capacity?"[51] Ms. Sawyer objected, and Judge Dixon overruled it. I said that I did have an opinion, and Mr. Hannon asked me to explain my opinion to the Court.

> Me: *This holster is very appropriate for wearing inside the pants and with a shirt on the outside. They make variations of this with thumb snaps, which is very appropriate when you are wearing a suit coat ... And it is ... a level II, because it has one restraint. In the literature on holsters, they use ... levels, even though there is no*

---

[48] Ibid, 275 - 276
[49] Ibid, 276
[50] Ibid
[51] Ibid, 277

national standard. A bucket is one. In other words, the gun just sits in it. This is a level two, because it is supposed to hold the gun if you turn the holster upside down. But if you shake it, it would fall out ...[52]

Judge Dixon: *What causes you to say that that is an appropriate holster if there are no national standards?*[53]

My answer, "Because it is used effectively."[54] I compared the holster to the earlier versions, with just clips to hold them to the belt, which often failed. Also, earlier inside-the-belt holsters were made of cloth type material or leather and did not provide the friction to hold in the weapon.

What the judge might not have known is that holster manufacturers advertise their standards, with each security device being a number (or level). In the advertising literature, there are no security levels listed for off-duty and/or concealable holsters.

Judge Dixon: *So, if Homeland Security had regulations that required a higher level of retention, that it required some type of hook over the gun, you're just giving us your opinion, that that is an unnecessary regulation, that what we have here in front of you is sufficient?*[55]

Me: *I wouldn't say it is unnecessary. I mean, that is their regulation. A lot of agencies have specific holsters rather than descriptors that are allowed. And other agencies have just descriptors ...*

Judge Dixon: *Okay. Now, I may hear from counsel later on this, but if – and we will just call it a hypothetical right now, if Homeland Security, that is the unit within Agent Thomas works, requires a holster off duty with a different level of security—is it your testimony that notwithstanding their regulation, this is an appropriate holster?*[56]

Me: *Your Honor, I don't want to say that – if that is their regulations, then it would only be appropriate for him to use their regulations.*[57]

Judge Dixon: *... I phrase it as if, because I am going by some things that I heard throughout the course of the trial, so I cannot tell you what their regulations are with any specificity at the moment.*

Mr. Hannon continued and showed me an ICE document titled "Guidance for Primary Firearm Holsters," December 2004. Mr. Hannon asked me if I had seen the document, and I replied that I had not; I did not remember it.

---

[52] Ibid, 278
[53] Ibid, 278
[54] Ibid, 278 - 279
[55] Ibid, 279
[56] Ibid, 279 - 280
[57] Ibid, 280

Mr. Hannon: *How common is that holster* [Mr. Thomas's holster] *among law enforcement officers?*
Me: *It is very common.*
Judge Dixon: *If there is no regulation that requires that higher level of security, then your testimony is that this is an appropriate holster for off-duty wear as long as – with that holster worn inside the pants clipped to the belt?*
Me: *Yes.*[58]

The purpose of any holster is to carry and secure the weapon, but if an officer is not in uniform, the holster conceals the weapon.

Mr. Hannon: *Assume for a moment that the offender has two hands on the weapon and the officer has one hand on the weapon. What is the training in terms of how to react to that circumstance?*
Me: *… your options are limited…the offender is eventually going to take the weapon.*
Mr. Hannon: *And so what is the officer trained to do under those circumstances?*
Me: *You* [the officer] *are going to have to use other force … you start with leg strikes or … leg sweeps … the … other option is to use the hand as a striking motion. But, if the weapon is taken away, it is taken away very quickly … you can't stand there and fight for a minute with a situation like that. You're already behind the curve.*[59]

Mr. Hannon asked about the use of force continuums. I explained that force continuums, in a stair-step fashion, were popular at one time, but many departments replaced them with force circles or wheels. With a circle, the officer does not have to climb a ladder of options. Describing the steps in a continuum, I said the least force is the presence of an officer at one end, and the other end would be the maximum use of force, or deadly force. I explained that the elements include "your presence and voice, hands on, resistance, batons, chemical agents, all the way up to the use of deadly force."[60]

Mr. Hannon: *What are law enforcement officers trained in terms where they begin on that use of force?*[61]
Me: *They are trained that they can begin at any level depending on the circumstance. You don't have to start at the beginning.*[62]

---

[58] Ibid, 280-81
[59] Ibid, 282-83
[60] Ibid, 283-84
[61] Ibid, 284
[62] Ibid, 284

Mr. Hannon asked about an article describing problems when officers have their finger on the trigger. He asked, "*Without comment on the credibility of any witnesses, do you have an opinion with your field of expertise as to whether, in this engagement, agent Thomas had his finger on the trigger of his Sig Sauer 229?*" [63] I answered, "*My opinion would be that there was a very high probability that his finger was not on the trigger.*"[64]

Explaining, I said that there are three instances in which an officer can have his or her finger on a trigger that could result in an unintentional discharge of a firearm. If an officer's finger is on a trigger and their balance is disturbed, the contraction of their hands can cause their finger to pull the trigger. If an officer's finger is on a trigger and they are startled, the trigger could be pulled. And if an officer's finger is on a trigger and the officer uses force with his or her free hand, the trigger could be pulled in the gun hand. If any or all three conditions exist, the probability is higher for an unintentional discharge. In all three instances, pulling the trigger can be involuntary and not a conscious act.

> Mr. Hannon: *And in reaching that opinion, have you relied upon any studies, surveys that have been done in connection with that phenomenon?* [65]
> Me: *Research from Dr. Enoka.*
> Mr. Hannon: *Can you describe that research to the Court?*
> Me: *Dr. Enoka published his research in 1991 at the University of Arizona. He is now at the University of Colorado. …he reviewed [the] article before it was sent for publishing.*
> Mr. Hannon: *Did you rely upon that expert's opinions in his field to reach your conclusions about this issue of finger in the trigger?*[66]
> Me: *I relied upon his [Dr. Enoka] expert opinions and the article was modified slightly, but had significant impact on the article because of his review.*
> Mr. Hannon: *And what did that expert's opinion contribute to your knowledge of this field?*[67] Me: *I did not realize that it was possible with your finger off the trigger, that during a struggle or an extreme incident, that your finger could go to the trigger without your knowledge.*[68]
> Mr. Hannon: *Well, are there circumstances under which a weapon can discharge without the holder of the weapon pulling the trigger?*[69]
> Me: *The modern day police firearm [handgun] can only go off if your finger is on the trigger and the trigger is pulled all of the way to the rear.*[70]

---

[63] Ibid
[64] Ibid
[65] Ibid, 285
[66] Ibid, 286
[67] Ibid
[68] Ibid, 287
[69] Ibid, 288
[70] Ibid

Mr. Hannon asked about my experience in this area as a subject matter expert. Ms. Sawyer objected, and it was sustained. That ended the direct questions from Mr. Hannon, and Ms. Sawyer stood for cross-examination.

> Ms. Sawyer: *I just want to briefly review so I can make sure I am clear on the materials you have relied on in preparation for your testimony today; all right?*
> Me: *Yes.*[71]

Ms. Sawyer went through a list of questions that included questions about my interview with Heath, watching portions of the trial, conducting a tour of the restaurant, examining government exhibits and review of grand jury transcripts, and discussion of some articles. In responding, I added some notes and papers which Mr. Hannon had sent me, but I forgot the ABRA materials.

She asked, "But you hadn't reviewed the ICE National Firearms and Tactical Training Unit guidance on holsters; correct?"[72] I answered, "No."

> Mrs. Sawyer: *You have used the term offender and officer, correct?*[73]
> Me: *Yes.*
> Ms. Sawyer: *"Well do you know whether he was on duty, whether he was at work that evening?*
> Me: *To qualify that, Your Honor, once somebody has your* [sic] *hand on your gun, then it is a…*[74]

Ms. Sawyer interjected, saying, "*I'm sorry, Mr. Bohrer, that wasn't my question. When Agent Thomas went out that evening, he was not on duty; correct?*" I answered, "Correct."[75]

She stated that Heath was not arresting or attempting to arrest or apprehending someone, and I agreed.

She asked about weapons retention, using an example that I had given with subjects in a vehicle. In that example, officers requested that the subjects remain in the vehicle as part of weapon retention and safety.

> Ms. Sawyer: *And that is because you want as much distance possible between you and a potential threat?*
> Me: *It is safety. It is harder for somebody to attack you from a seated position than outside of a vehicle.*[76]

---

[71] Ibid, 290
[72] Ibid, 291
[73] Ibid
[74] Ibid, 292
[75] Ibid
[76] Ibid, 293

She talked about the distance between the officer and the potential threat, as well as the officer backing up, both related to my testimony.

> Ms. Sawyer: *That is sort of the same vein that your objective there is to create distance between you and a potential threat?*
> Me: *Yes.*
> Ms. Sawyer: *Would you agree that the first objective is to keep that weapon in the holster; right?* [77]
> Me: *Yes.*
> Ms. Sawyer: *... you talked about shooting someone off of a weapon and how that is an option ...*
> Me: *Yes.*
> Ms. Sawyer: *And you also testified that the decision to use force in a shooting-off-the weapon scenario is going to be the decision of that officer in that situation at that moment ...* [78]
> Me: *Correct.* [79]
> Ms. Sawyer: *You testified that the goal, essentially, is that upon firing the weapon someone would release it, right?*
> Me: *Correct.*
> Ms. Sawyer: *So it's sort of to warn them, get out of here or the next one could be somewhere else?*
> Me: *Not necessarily to get out of here, but let go of the weapon.*
> Ms. Sawyer: *And are you aware that the ICE firearms policy specifically prohibits warning shots?* [80]
> Me: *No, I'm not.*
> Ms. Sawyer: *And you testified that there were, in fact, no national standards that regulate the use of holsters; right?*
> Me: *That is correct.*
> Ms. Sawyer: *But you weren't aware but now you are aware that there are at least guidelines issued by the National Firearms and Tactical Training Unit of ICE that regulate holster.*
> Me: *I am aware of that. I was aware of that before. I don't know what the guidelines are, but I am aware of that.*
> Ms. Sawyer: *Well, then you're not aware that level I retention holster should be designed so that when it is tipped upside down and shaken that the weapon is not going to come out of there?*
> Me: *I thought I testified to that.* [81]

---

[77] Ibid, 294
[78] Ibid, 295
[79] Ibid
[80] Ibid, 296
[81] Ibid, 296 - 297

Here Ms. Sawyer misconstrued what the National Firearms and Tactical Training Unit Guidance for Primary Firearms Holsters actually says. The guidance, Exhibit 37, has no mention of holding a holster upside-down and then shaking it, as a way of testing any holster. The guidelines mention a positive retention device, such as a thumb break, but do not address friction devices. Most manufacturers consider friction, for a specific weapon, to be a retention device.

Ms. Sawyer continued, "*Well, let me ask it this way: You classified Agent Thomas' holster as a level I retention device, right?*"[82] I answered "yes." (Meaning the friction is one level). Ms. Sawyer spoke about adding a thumb snap along with a friction holster and suggested it would be a level II, and I agreed.

The standards for holster security levels were created by holster manufacturers. Most agencies use the manufacturer standards. Each retention device adds one level. There is a difference between duty holsters and off-duty holsters. The differences exist because holster manufacturers label only the duty holsters with a security level. The off-duty holsters are not rated, although one could use the same standards.

> Ms. Sawyer: *And, again, the primary intention of a friction holster is concealment, correct, and not necessarily retention as much as a level two?*
> Me: *It is both ... even the duty holsters made today, the first level is the fact that the weapon can't come out by itself. It is no longer what they used to term a bucket. It is molded to the gun.*[83]

Ms. Sawyer asked if I was familiar with a use of force continuum and said that it has changed over the years, which it has.

> Ms. Sawyer: *And you used to have to start at level one and then proceed to level two and then three and that is no longer the case, right?* [84]
> Me: *No. You never had to start at level one. That is why it changed because people would interpret it in that way.*
> Ms. Sawyer: *All right. Now, an officer that is in a – let's just take the whole generic spectrum of threating encounters, the goal of that person is to get out of that threating encounter, correct?*[85]
> Me: *To survive it, yes.*
> Ms. Sawyer: *To get out of the threating encounter.*[86]

Mr. Hannon started to object but said the question was already answered.

---

[82] Ibid, 297
[83] Ibid
[84] Ibid, 298
[85] Ibid, 299
[86] Ibid

Ms. Sawyer: *And would you agree that an officer, for example, in a weapons-retention situation like you have been discussing on direct, that the ideal best-case scenario is to use the least amount of force possible to defuse that situation, correct?*

Me: *I would have to disagree with that.*

Ms. Sawyer: *Well, if you could get out of the scenario without harming the other person or yourself, is that not better?*

Me: *That is good.*

Ms. Sawyer: *Is that not the best-case scenario?*

Me: *I disagreed with the word[s] "the least amount of force."* [87]

Ms. Sawyer reworded the question, "*Let me say, causing the least amount of harm to all parties involved, is that not the best-case scenario?*"[88] I responded, "yes."

Ms. Sawyer said that verbal commands could be used in situations, and I agreed. She continued, saying that verbal commands can alert the culprit and the public, and I agreed.

Me: *Verbal commands where feasible should be given.*

Ms. Sawyer: *... one of the reasons for that, particularly if you are not wearing a uniform, is to let the person know who you are, correct?*

Me: *Yes.*

Ms. Sawyer: *... another sort of verbal cue training is essentially [to] narrate what is going on, right, give commands, drop my gun, drop the gun?*

Me: *It would depend on the context. But they do have other commands, yes, depending on what the situation is.*[89]

Ms. Sawyer: *And you testified to ... the issue with having your finger on the trigger ... I think you said that the gun could just as easily have gone off if your finger is on the trigger; right?*

Me: *... the person with their finger on the trigger under certain circumstances will pull the trigger involuntarily. It is not a conscious act. And that will make the gun go off, yes.*

Ms. Sawyer: *Well, shooting someone off your gun would also be a voluntary—*

Me: *Yes...*

Ms. Sawyer: *But these – particularly these involuntary reflexes are why that is such a dangerous situation ... to have your finger on the trigger if you don't actually intend to pull it?*

Me: *That is correct.* [90]

---

[87] Ibid, 299
[88] Ibid, 300
[89] Ibid, 300 - 301
[90] Ibid, 302

Ms. Sawyer again brought up ICE's firearms and use of force policies, saying "let me ask you, you are aware that the policy expressly prohibits agents from carrying a gun while consuming alcohol?"[91] I said, "Yes.,"

She continued with questions about how alcohol affects one's senses, physical abilities, and reactions, and I agreed with each question.

Ms. Sawyer: *And you are aware also the policy reflects – recognition that, in fact, that is so important that it can be used as a basis to revoke an officer's authority to ever carry a weapon?*

Me: *I am sure it could be, yes.* [92]

Ms. Sawyer: *Isn't it true that you refused to provide me with your resume until Mr. Hannon would approve you to do so?*

Me: *… yes.*

Ms. Sawyer: *You also refused to talk to me about your testimony until Mr. Hannon ordered to do so by the Court, is that correct?*

Me: *I wouldn't put it like that. I was working for him.*

Ms. Sawyer: *But you didn't want to share with me the subject of your testimony when—*[93]

Mr. Hannon interjected, "*Excuse me, Your Honor. I object. There are rules regarding each party's ability to discover the opinions of experts. And it is actually appropriate for a lawyer to ask a fact witness if they want to talk to them. But a lawyer for one party can't ask an expert for another party to tell them what their expert opinions are with following the rules.*"[94]

Judge Dixon: *Do you wish to be heard, Ms. Sawyer?*
Ms. Sawyer: *I'm sorry.*
Judge Dixon: *Do you wish to be heard?*
Ms. Sawyer: *Well I –*
Judge Dixon: *I think I agree with Mr. Hannon that the questions that you are asking about are more appropriately the guidelines with respect to fact witnesses. The objection is sustained.*[95]

Ms. Sawyer had no more questions.

During the trial Ms. Sawyer approached me and asked me if I would talk to her.

---

[91] Ibid, 303
[92] Ibid, 303 - 304
[93] Ibid, 304
[94] Ibid, 304 - 305
[95] Ibid, 305

I said I would if Mr. Hannon approved it; I do not know if she ever approached him. Additionally, on August 18, the fourth day of the trial I arrived early to meet the prosecutors at the courthouse, at Mr. Hannon's request, but they never appeared.

Judge Dixon asked Mr. Hannon if he wished to re-direct, and Mr. Hannon asked to approach the bench, at which point I was excused from the witness stand. According to the transcripts, Mr. Hannon said he "would like to ask Mr. Bohrer if he has an opinion as to whether alcohol adversely impacted Agent Thomas during the events of this event."[96] This was related to Ms. Sawyer's questions about the effects of alcohol. Judge Dixon said, "No, I will not permit that. I am assuming there is going to be an objection."[97]

Ms. Sawyer: *Yes, Your Honor.*
Judge Dixon: *I will not permit that.*[98]
Mr. Hannon: *Ms. Sawyer talked a lot about shooting off the gun, which, of course, was not what happened here. And I think that would allow me to ask him his opinion regarding whether Agent Thomas showed restraint.*[99]
Ms. Sawyer: *Well, I don't think I have opened the door to anything additional. I think that I simply asked follow-up question that were based exclusively on what Mr. Hannon asked on direct. And it was also simply to test the knowledge of the witness about the fact that those aren't even permitted by ICE.*

The Judge sustained the objection.

Mr. Hannon requested permission to question me about shooting a person off a gun and if it would be considered a warning shot. He also wanted to inquire about my objection to using the least amount of force when struggling to maintain your weapon. The Judge agreed to both questions.

Following the bench conference, I was called back to the stand.

Mr. Hannon: *You were asked about warning shots. Mr. Bohrer, do you – would you characterize the shot fired to shoot someone off your gun as a warning shot?*[100]
Me: *No.*
Mr. Hannon: *And what is a warning shot, to you?*
Me: *A warning shot is shooting over somebody's head... saying stop or I'll shoot ... warning them that you will shoot them the next time.*
Mr. Hannon: *And is that commonly prohibited by law enforcement?*
Me: *Today, yes sir.*

---
[96] Ibid, 306
[97] Ibid, 306
[98] Ibid
[99] Ibid, 307
[100] Ibid, 308

Mr. Hannon asked about my response to a question regarding an officer using the "least amount of force," with which I had disagreed. I explained, "You never know who your opponent is. And when you're in a situation … if you rely on a low level of force and then continually have to raise it, by the time you raise it, it might be too late. You want to use more than sufficient force to do what you have to do to maintain the weapon…"[101]

Following up after the redirect, Judge Dixon asked, "… the term shooting a person off the weapon … does the term suggest shooting the person off the weapon means that if a gun is fired, they are likely to release it?" I answered, "Yes, sir." [102]

Judge Dixon next asked about unintentional discharges—the three situations that I had described earlier that could cause an accidental discharge of a firearm. I repeated my earlier testimony referring to each one. Training literature uses the term "interlimb" to refer to using a fair amount of force with the free hand. The second, "startle response," means that the gun possessor is startled. The last one is "balance disturbance," implying that the person holding the gun loses their balance. In all three instances, if the officer's finger is on the trigger, the firing of a gun can be involuntary and unintentional.[103]

> Judge Dixon: *Would a situation such as an officer with his finger on the trigger and the assailant trying to pull the weapon away from the officer, does that fall into one of these categories?*
> Me: *It is a combination.* [balance and force with the free hand] *That is why I believe it would be a high probability the gun would have gone off if his* [Heath's] *finger was on the trigger.*[104]

I was excused, and Mr. Hannon asked the Judge if he could recall Heath to the stand. He said the purpose was to "testify about the authorization of this holster."[105] Judge Dixon agreed, and Heath was called to the stand.

> Mr. Hannon: *Agent Thomas, you previously testified that the holster you were wearing on the evening of this incident, Defendants Exhibit 102, is an ICE-authorized holster?*
> Heath: *Yes.*
> Mr. Hannon: *Could you tell the Court for the basis for that testimony?*[106]

Heath replied that he asked an ICE weapons instructor about the holster, and he had been using the holster at work for two years.

---

[101] Ibid, 308 - 309
[102] Ibid, 309
[103] Ibid, 310 - 311
[104] Ibid, 311
[105] Ibid, 312
[106] Ibid, 313

At that point Mr. Rickard took over from Ms. Sawyer for the re-cross examination. He asked, "When you testified on Monday, you were shown that Defense 37, which is that holster policy, right?"[107] Heath responded, "It is a guideline."

Mr. Rickard approached Heath and showed him Government Exhibit 23. He asked, "You recognize Government 23 as the holster guideline that we have been referring to, right?"[108] Heath answered, "Yes."

Mr. Rickard continued, "Is that the guideline that controls and recommends appropriate holsters for ICE officers on and off duty?"[109] Heath responded, "Yes. It strongly encourages ICE armed officers to adhere to these guidelines." Mr. Rickard then moved Government Exhibit 23 into evidence.

Mr. Hannon continued with his re-direct examination, referring to Governments Exhibit 23, asking Heath, "The first bullet point, could you read that to the Court?"[110]

Heath: *Holsters must have at least one positive retention device that requires some deliberate action by the wearer to release the weapons such as a thumb break.*
Mr. Hannon: *And does 102* [the holster] *have a retention device?*
Heath: *It is a tension retention device.*
Mr. Hannon: *And Mr. Bohrer was referring to a bucket holster. Do you know what a bucket holster is?*
Heath: *Yes. It is just a sheath.*
Mr. Hannon: *Does it have any retention devices?*
Heath: *No.*

Responding to a question from Mr. Hannon, Heath said, "My understanding is that this holster fell within the suggested guidelines." Mr. Hannon concluded, "We have no further evidence, Your Honor."[111]

The Court seemed concerned about the level of the holster that Heath was using, possibly because the gun came out. The holster type Heath was wearing—made of a hard plastic molded to fit a specific weapon—is popular and secure. However, when someone physically picks you up in a bear hug and carries you a distance and down a few steps, it does affect the effectiveness of the security of the holster. If Heath had been using the same style holster with a thumb strap, the same result could have occurred. If he had been using a holster that clipped to his belt, the holster and gun together probably would have been dislodged long before Heath was released.

---
[107] Ibid, 314
[108] Ibid, 314-15
[109] Ibid, 315
[110] Ibid, 315 - 316
[111] Ibid, 316

It is understandable that when examining the security issues related to law enforcement holsters, one would question why every holster does not possess every security device possible. The issue of the level of security needs to be balanced with the ability of the officer to draw the weapon if needed, which was one of the seventeen bullet points in Exhibit 23. It is my opinion that the holster Heath was wearing conformed to every point.

17A

Glenn Ford: The Witness Was the Girlfriend of Another Suspect

In 1984 Mr. Isadore Rozeman, a jeweler, was robbed and killed in his shop in Shreveport, Louisiana. Mr. Glenn Ford, who had done some yard work for Mr. Rozeman, was charged with robbery and murder. He was later tried, convicted, and sentenced to death. There were two other suspects in the case, Jake, and Henry Robinson. The Robinson brothers were also charged with the robbery and murder, but the charges against them were later dropped.

The evidence presented during the trial included items stolen from the victim's pawnshop. Mr. Ford admitted that he had pawned the items and that he had carried them in a brown paper bag. However, he also said the Robinson brothers gave him the bag with the items inside.

The critical evidence against Mr. Ford was the testimony of one woman, Ms. Marvella Brown, who told the police that on the day of the crime, she observed Ford carrying a brown paper bag, and he had a handgun on his person. During her cross-examination at the trial, she refuted some of her previous testimony, claiming the police told her what to say. Apparently, her contradicting statements did not convince the jury of Ford's innocence. What was not said in court was that Ms. Brown was the girlfriend of one of the Robinson brothers.

In 2012, new evidence about the case was filed in the District Attorney's Office in Caddo Parish, Louisiana. The information became known during the investigation of another homicide. An informant told the authorities that the Robinson brothers had committed the robbery and murdered Mr. Rozeman. Additional evidence revealed that detectives had lied about statements attributed to Mr. Ford during his interrogation. There were conflicting statements by the principal witness, Marvella Brown, along with the fact that she was the girlfriend of one of the suspects, all of which was not given to the defense.

Glenn Ford was on death row for almost 30 years before being released. Shortly after being exonerated in 2014, Mr. Ford, who was 65 years old, died of lung cancer. The lead prosecutor in Mr. Ford's case was Shreveport Attorney A. M. Stroud III. He publicly apologized for his role in the case and personally met with Mr. Ford before his death. Attorney Stroud also called for the abolishment of the death penalty. When Mr. Ford was released on March 12, 2014, he was "the 144th person [in the United States], since 1973 to be exonerated and freed after having been sentenced to death."[1] Mr. Ford was the 10th person released by exoneration from death row in the state of Louisiana.

When society experiences a vehicle crash, train wreck, or another preventable disaster that results in multiple injuries and/or deaths, we investigate these events to determine the cause(s) for the purpose of correcting human error and/or mechanical mistakes. Yet, our justice system has experienced problems that have resulted in numerous innocent individuals being incarcerated for many years, and the calls for reform are often ignored or seem to go unheard. Why do we not investigate these mistakes, at a minimum, to prevent the recurrence of the same problems and issues?

References

The Equal Justice Initiative, https://eji.org/news/glenn-ford-exonerated-released-after-30-years-louisiana-death-row, posted 03-18-14. The Death Penalty Information Center (www.deathpenaltyinfo.org) posted July 30, 2015

Alexandria Burris, "Glen Ford, Exonerated Death Row Inmate, Dies," *USA Today*, June 29, 2015. https://www.usatoday.com/story/news/nation/2015/06/29/glenn-ford-exonerated-death-row-inmate-dies/29489433/

---

[1] The Death Penalty Information Center (www.deathpenaltyinfo.org) is a non-profit organization serving the media and the public with analysis and information on issues concerning capital punishment.

18

Day 7, Continued: The End of the Line

"If the facts don't fit the theory, change the theory"[1]

The prosecution and the defense had concluded their arguments. The evidence was in, and the trial was almost over. In the second half of day seven, Judge Dixon heard the defense's motion for acquittal, followed by closing arguments for both sides. With the court assembled, Judge Dixon invited Mr. Hannon to proceed with his motion to acquit.

Defense Motion for Judgment of Acquittal

Mr. Hannon, addressing the court, opened his argument for acquittal by talking about three cases that had been overturned on appeal. With these cases, which he had presented in the written motion for acquittal, Mr. Hannon intended to show the court that there was just cause for acquittal in cases like Heath's. It was my thought that under the surface was Mr. Hannon's belief that no judge wants his or her ruling to ever be reversed.

The first case he discussed involved a robbery in which a wallet was found at the scene, but there was no evidence of how the wallet got there. Another case involved contraband (drugs) found in the back of a police vehicle, but how the contraband got there was not proven. The last case occurred in a commercial establishment when a product was moved but possession could not be established.

> Mr. Hannon: *And the facts in each of those cases that resulted in the Court of Appeals indicating that the Government's evidence was insufficient for the case to either go forward to a jury or for a judge at a bench trial.*[2]

Mr. Hannon continued, "And similarly here the Government has asserted that the assault with a deadly weapon took place when the weapon was viewed in Agent Thomas's hands. And the Court before hearing the testimony of Agent Thomas, I would submit, was in the same posture as the trial in each of those cases."[3]

---

[1] An age-old adage, attributed to Albert Einstein, printed in the journal *Product Engineering, 1958.*
[2] Information from the trial transcript, Criminal Action Number 2010-CF3-16079, dated August 25, 2011, p 321
[3] Ibid, 322

Mr. Hannon argued that similar to the wallet found on the ground, no one saw how the weapon came to be in Heath's hands. He then argued that the Government must prove its case; the defendant is not required to prove his innocence, and he again raised the issue of self-defense, saying it was the Government's burden to prove that Heath's actions had not been in self-defense.

> Mr. Hannon: ... *And I would suggest to the Court that if you look at the evidence and disbelieve Agent Thomas as to how the weapon got in his hand and assume, contrary to the cases that we have cited, that he intentionally drew the weapon in turn and the evidence is that Marshall Brackett said in the grand jury that "he tried to point it at me, but he wasn't going to, I never let him point it at me." But assume that that is the assault, he didn't fire the weapon. He didn't verbally threaten Brackett. The only surrounding circumstances that the Government point to suggest that he wasn't acting in self-defense is to say that he was drunk and that he was acting in retaliation for what occurred inside The Guards. That is simply insufficient. Because his conduct, once Brackett picked him up, is completely inconsistent with that theory. He did not continue to behave as the employees of The Guards allege he did, screaming and yelling.*[4]
>
> *I would also point out to the Court that there are three witnesses who are Guards employees who did not testify that he was using profanity and screaming and yelling, including Brackett and including Brandon Holubar – Corporal Holubar who was standing just a little bit away. So the behavior after that simply isn't sufficient to carry the weight that the Government is trying to place on what I am going to argue to the Court you can't believe.*[5]
>
> Judge Dixon: *At the risk of telegraphing my potential ruling before you finish your argument, you are going to be repeating yourself at closing argument.*[6]
>
> Mr. Hannon: *Yes, Your Honor. So that is why I want to stick with what I think the evidence in light most favorable to the Government is on the issue of self-defense. And that is that he intentionally pulled the weapon and he turned with the intent to point it at Brackett. We know that he didn't get to that point, because Brackett grabbed the weapon. And, Your Honor, to me that with the testimony of Shannon Bohrer establishes self-defense. I can't imagine other than what counsel said in their opening statement, that the explanation for his conduct was that he was acting intentionally in retaliation for what occurred inside The Guards is insufficient to establish that he did not act in self-defense beyond a reasonable doubt.*[7]

---

[4] Ibid, 322 - 323
[5] Ibid, 323
[6] Ibid, 324
[7] Ibid, 324 - 325

Judge Dixon thanked Mr. Hannon.

Judge Dixon: ... *There is no basis on which I intend to grant this motion, but the Government has the right to be heard.*[8]

Judge Dixon's words at this point tells me that he had already made his decision. While it may not seem logical, the court rules allow a defendant to make several arguments for their defense, and by claiming self-defense, Mr. Hannon started with the highest bar.

Mr. Rickard presented the government's opposition to the motion.

Mr. Rickard: *Your Honor ... I will just briefly respond to the points counsel made. Counsel said that Holubar – Corporal Holubar didn't see any cursing. That's – Your Honor's recollection will control, but that is not consistent with the evidence. ... And, of course, we maintain our argument that, in fact, the evidence in terms of self-defense is stronger – very strong at this point because self-defense wasn't even put at issue. That is what Agent Thomas testified to.*[9]

Judge Dixon summarized the evidence and concluded, "If I believe that evidence and if I believe it, it is sufficient to prove beyond a reasonable doubt an assault with a dangerous weapon, an intent to frighten offense; therefore, the renewed motion for judgement of acquittal is denied."[10]

Now all that was left was closing arguments.

The Prosecutor's Closing Statement

Ms. Sawyer started her presentation by quoting Mr. Rickard's opening statement on the first day of the trial. She said, "One man was able to do his job and another man who was hiding behind his."[11] She continued, "And that is what has continued to happen throughout the course of this trial. Mr. Hannon opened this case talking about lofty notions of self-defense and would be law enforcement privilege."

She said that this was a case of an individual who was intoxicated and frustrated. The defendant was drinking and became frustrated with poor service. He was then removed, and he was embarrassed. She said that at that point, "the defendant made a decision. And that decision had nothing to do with law enforcement privilege or self-defense. It had to do with a drunk, angry patron who was not going to be embarrassed the way that Mr. Brackett had embarrassed him. So he turns and pulls a weapon."[12]

---

[8] Ibid, 325
[9] Ibid, 325 - 326
[10] Ibid, 327
[11] Ibid, 328
[12] Ibid, 329

Ms. Sawyer summarized the Government's case, saying that Mr. Thomas took a cab, knowing he would be drinking, but still carried a firearm. The defendant admitted to consuming alcohol at two locations. She added, "The only people that tell the story about at least four drinks purchased but not consumed at The Guards are the defendant and Carole O'Connor, both of whom I would submit to Your Honor, are of doubtful credibility. And we'll get to that in a bit."[13]

She never did get to the point of doubtful credibility, for Heath and Carole. She continued, "Officers Cadle and Charland both testified that the defendant, at the point that they encountered him, smelled of alcohol, had affected speech, glassy eyes."[14] And Officer Cadle, she noted, testified that he would have requested or conducted a sobriety test if the encounter had been a traffic stop.

Ms. Sawyer then referred to Heath's actions while conversing with Agent Eisert in the lock-up, implying that Heath had been concealing something. She also implied that Heath was confused about the Miranda warnings during his taped interview with Detective Tabron.

> Ms. Sawyer: *You know he was angry and he got into an altercation – a verbal altercation with the bartender and Oscar. He gets inches away from Oscar's face and is cursing at him. You know through various witnesses, through Ms. Yudina, through Oscar who even testified that he thought that the defendant was going to attempt to fight with him.*[15]

She continued with testimony from Ms. Graciela Perez about the defendant being upset because he wasn't being helped and that the defendant himself said he was frustrated. Heath was so frustrated that he sought out the manager to complain and had a conversation in Spanish. She said, "It's corroborated by Corporal Holubar who confirms that the defendant was aggressively leaning toward the bartender, looking visibly irritated."[16]

She argued that Heath knew he was being picked up by the bouncer, saying it was "not some stranger who posed some sort of threat to him."[17] When Heath saw the manager, he knew why the event was occurring, that "This wasn't some random assailant."

> Ms. Sawyer: *So Mr. Brackett picks up the defendant – after he has been verbally abusive to the bar staff and resistant to any instructions from Mr. Brackett, he picks him up around his chest and ... walks him out. And that is corroborated by both*

---

[13] Ibid
[14] Ibid, 329 - 330
[15] Ibid, 330
[16] Ibid, 331
[17] Ibid

> Mr. Brackett and Corporal Holubar. Neither of them testified that Mr. Brackett is anywhere near the defendant's waist. ... He [Mr. Brackett] *puts him* [Heath] *down and he backs away.*[18]
>
> And that's important because those two stories, those two accounts from Mr. Brackett and from Corporal Holubar are entirely consistent on the point that they are very clear. Contrary to what the defense describes, Mr. Brackett releases him. And not only does he release him, he backs away one, if not two steps. And Corporal Holubar puts about three feet in between them, which is directly contrary to the description that only the defendant has provided. Because only the defendant has provided any testimony that Marshall Brackett was still on top of him when any of this happened. Ms. O'Connor couldn't even provide the Court with that because she didn't see it.[19]

Continuing, Ms. Sawyer described the event from the prosecution's perspective that the defendant turned with a gun in hand. She noted that, according to Corporal Holubar, if the weapon would have fired at that time, it would have struck Mr. Brackett. Mr. Brackett saw the gun and reached out to defend himself, and then the struggle for the gun occurred.

She discounted the defense's theory of self-defense, saying, "there is no evidence, even by the defendant's own admission of any fear that had arisen in the defendant until the struggle for the gun ensued. ... He testified that he never felt in fear for his safety or felt the need to use deadly force until that struggle for the weapon unfolded."[20]

Addressing the credibility issue she said, "how should the Court evaluate the credibility? Well, your Honor, the Court has the benefit, which it often does not, of having the testimony of a truly independent witness in Corporal Holubar."[21] She added, "the defendant is the only person who has testified to anything that makes this an accident. And Cpl. Holubar and Mr. Brackett are perfectly consistent on what that circumstance looked like when the gun came around."[22]

> Ms. Sawyer: ... *The entire basis for the defendant's accident testimony is that while he is reaching down, gripping the gun, securing it with an additional hand to simply re-holster it or secure it, here comes Marshall Brackett never backing off of his back ... somehow Marshall Brackett hits his arm with such force that out comes the weapon. Woops.*[23]

---

[18] Ibid, 332
[19] Ibid
[20] Ibid, 333
[21] Ibid, 333 - 334
[22] Ibid, 334
[23] Ibid, 335

> There are inherently inconsistent with the story the defendant is posing to the Court. And unlike the defendant, Corporal Holubar had two drinks all night. He has no dog in the fight. His recall on the details regarding the gun were extremely precise, which I think is worth noting. ... And he noted the presence of the defendant's [finger] on the trigger. In fact, corroboration for that is his own action or I guess in this case inaction based on that. So concerned was he that the defendant's finger was on the trigger as he turned that he failed to go and help the bouncer which is what he testified would have been his response in that scenario.[24]

She argued that Heath's finger was on the trigger when he pulled the gun, but not necessarily when the struggle ensued. She continued, "And the defendant's version is not credible; it is not reliable. His perception of the incident is clouded by alcohol, which is not what you have with Corporal Holubar, which is not what you have with Marshall Brackett. We also already know that the defendant was already in violation of ICE Policy the second he picked up the first drink."[25]

> Ms. Sawyer: ". . . *just the inherent implausibility of the story that the defendant is propounding to this Court is remarkable both by the defendant's own admission and his expert's own admission; he was in position of strength at the time that this gun allegedly came out ... It just doesn't make sense, Your Honor.*[26]
>
> *... It is not the only part of his story that doesn't make sense. He admits that he says inside the bar—he is getting irritated and he says, "I am a fucking cop." The interesting part is what that comes in response to. By the defendant's story, Oscar tells him, if you don't like the wait to pay the tab, then call the cops. Your Honor, that is not even a comment that makes sense to elicit that. It is not even a comment that makes sense in the context in which the defendant offers it. And the Court knows that is not the context that it was elicited in because Holubar confirms that the cop comment was in response to someone saying, sir, if you don't calm down, we are going to call the police.*[27]
>
> *He also wants you to believe that he was angry enough to need a private conversation with Oscar in Spanish. And he was upset enough to get rude with Oscar and curse at him. But somehow after being embarrassed and physically removed from a bar, all of a sudden he is a paragon of calmness outside exercising eminent reasonableness of an officer. That is not consistent with any evidence that is before this Court about what happened inside.*[28]

---

[24] Ibid, 335 - 336
[25] Ibid, 336
[26] Ibid, 336 - 337
[27] Ibid, 337 - 338
[28] Ibid, 338

Ms. Sawyer repeated that Heath never said anything while being carried out. She said, "I can't imagine how someone's face in your back could prevent them from hearing you shouting. So Your Honor, his explanation for his actions just don't make any sense."[29]

> Ms. Sawyer: *So Your Honor, if you resolve the issue of credibility in favor of the Government witnesses and the Court has to necessarily ask itself, why is the defendant telling the story he told? Well, because he is telling the only story that will protect him from criminal charges, that will protect his career as a federal agent, that will protect him from the situation that he put himself in that night. Because the fact of the matter remains once all of this evidence has now been presented that what the Court has in front of it was an intoxicated, angry, embarrassed individual who that night, unfortunately for everyone, happened to have a gun on him when he shouldn't. And he made a decision – he made a reasoned decision, not as a reasonable act of a law enforcement officer. He made a reasoned decision as a drunk citizen to get back at the bouncer who had embarrassed him in front of his friends. And, Your Honor, that is evidence beyond a reasonable doubt for assault with a dangerous weapon.*[30]

In sum, the prosecution's argument was that Mr. Thomas was drunk and made a bad decision. Ms. Sawyer took some liberties with some testimony, even saying that only Heath and Carole told the story of having just four drinks at the restaurant, then impugning the credibility of both, without the promised explanation. She did speak about the credibility of the independent witness, Cpl. Holubar. However, we know he did not see the beginning of the event as he claimed, since he was not directly behind the bouncer. Carole O'Connor was outside before him, and even Carole did not see how the gun came out. Ms. Sawyer also said that the independent witness only had two drinks, which was true. However, the two drinks, as explained in chapter 16, would mean that Cpl. Holubar's Blood Alcohol Content was estimated at 0.120, which is intoxicated.[31] Meanwhile, Ms. Sawyer stated that Heath was intoxicated, although, as explained in chapter 16, Heath's BAC was estimated to be 0.037, which is not intoxicated and not impaired. If Heath consumed three-and-a-half beers and only had a sip of a beer at the Guards and a sip of one Bombay Sapphire martini, his BAC would have been 0.021.

It was my impression in the courtroom that Ms. Sawyer's closing argument was compelling. Ms. Sawyer talked about the credibility of witnesses, and the Court seemed to be unaware of the lack of credibility of several prosecution witnesses, including Cpl.

---

[29] Ibid, 339
[30] Ibid, 340
[31] Information from the trial transcript, Criminal Action Number 2010-CF3-16079, dated August 16, 2011, p 278. The BAC calculation of Cpl. Holubar was estimated in chapter 15, p 8

Holubar and Mr. Viricochea. When I say unaware, the evidence was there, but maybe it was ignored because it would challenge what the court believed.

The Defense's Closing Statement

> Mr. Hannon: ... *The Court asked Mr. Thomas whether he feared deadly force at the time that Brackett carried him through the bar. I was actually surprised at his answer. He said, no, Your Honor. And you could tell from my questions following up on that I thought that is because he felt he was supremely able to protect himself and his weapon at that moment because of his martial art skills. I thought that, objectively speaking, any police officer would say at that moment, yes, because I had my weapon on me. ... the testimony of Agent Thomas was in response to Your Honor's question, when I felt my weapon moving and coming loose, at that point Your Honor, I felt the possibility of imminent deadly force, as well as the weapon coming out. But here is a man who is assaulting him. We're not talking about simply the inadvertent dropping of a weapon on a sidewalk.*[32]

Mr. Hannon repeated Mr. Brackett's testimony about how he had set Heath down, then stepped back and saw Heath turning with a weapon in his hand. He recounted that Mr. Brackett had said that he "grabbed it with both hands ... before it was pointed at him. And he said, I wasn't going to let it be pointed at me. So the question is, how far away was Brackett? ... So Brackett had to be close enough to be able to put both hands on the weapon in a moment – in an absolute moment, which Holubar described as a micro-portion of a second when he claimed to have seen the finger on the trigger."[33]

> Mr. Hannon: *At that moment, Agent Thomas subjectively believed he was at risk for deadly force. The use of his own weapon against him or someone else. That is undisputed testimony from his perspective ... And assuming Ms. Sawyer is correct and Your Honor wishes to believe that he turned with the weapon in his hand, until Brackett grabbed it, that is self-defense. That is also, according to Mr. Bohrer, an effort to retain his weapon. He didn't fire his weapon. He didn't shoot him off the gun.*[34]
> *And this man, in his police career, you have heard, has been in violent circumstances. Therefore, it is only fair for you to take into account what he was trained to do and determine whether his behavior after being grabbed by Marshall Brackett was the behavior of a highly trained law enforcement officer who exercised the height of*

---

[32] Information from the trial transcript, Criminal Action Number 2010-CF3-16079, dated August 25, 2011, p 340-341

[33] Ibid, 341 - 342

[34] Ibid, 342 - 343.

restraint and acted in the minimal way possible or whether it was reckless conduct of a drunk who was wearing a weapon and, apparently, was going to act out his embarrassment.[35]

The case is about character. And it is about a job, a career. The serpent in the Garden of Eden, a prosecutor once told me, could produce both character witnesses and alibi witnesses. What is important here in part is who those witnesses are. They were impressive in their own right. And the circumstances in which they knew Agent Thomas, was not just in his field of expertise but in times when he was exposed to violence and had to engage in violence.[36]

Character, ultimately, is what the fact finder believes it is. And character comes in part from the manner in which the witnesses handle himself on the witness stand. And the Government has told the Court that Agent Thomas is lying. And he is lying because the potential for conviction here and the risk to his job and career. And Your Honor knows that the Government is not aware of any conduct inconsistent with the opinions rendered that he is sober, law abiding, restrained, and has no temper, rather exercises stoicism, peace and becomes the cool head among the young agents. There is not one single incident in a career of 18 years that the Government has placed into the face –

Ms. Sawyer: *Objection.*

Mr. Hannon: *—of these people who have which come here to testify.*

Judge Dixon: *... The objection is overruled. Although the argument sounds like it is on the edge, those are issues that could have been brought up with character witnesses, if the Government had them. So I will allow Mr. Hannon to make that type of argument.*[37]

Mr. Hannon: *Not every agent is trained like Agent Thomas trained himself. ... But in contrast to the Government's theory of the case, one has to ask himself as a fact finder, how was he able to act with such restraint? Even assuming — ...that the truth of the event is that he intentionally pulled his gun and turned in an attempt to scare Brackett away from him and his weapon, but did not fire it.*[38]

In contrast, I would like to discuss the victims. I use the term loosely and in assessing the evidence in this case ... the sense of ... dignity of this place that they bring to the Court and the dignity and the significance of this place as being a place of justice ... I know that there are people who come to court and don't know better. Marshall Brackett knows better. He is involved in Law Enforcement as part of his profession. Officer Jeffrey Cadle knew him. In fact, that is why he didn't put handcuffs on him, because he knew him.[39]

---

[35] Ibid
[36] Ibid, 344 - 345
[37] Ibid, 345 - 346
[38] Ibid, 346
[39] Ibid, 346 - 347

Sitting in the courtroom at this time, I assumed Mr. Hannon was talking about the appearance of how the victims dressed when testifying in Court. When testifying, Mr. Brackett wore shorts, a pullover shirt, and flip-flops, and Cpl. Holubar wore slacks and a teal colored short-sleeve shirt.

> Mr. Hannon: *Marshall Bracket ... is a huge man. He is a weight lifter... in charge of all of the other bouncers, hiring and firing. And what is his job? He doesn't even know about the security plan. His job is violence when necessary. He testified that 80 percent of the people he decides to have leave, agree to leave and the 20 percent don't and he carries them out – just carries them out. That is an assault. It is a violation of the security plan. That is his job, though.*
>
> Ms. Sawyer: *Objection.*
>
> Mr. Hannon: *They haven't told him otherwise.*
>
> Judge Dixon: *What is your objection, Ms. Sawyer?*
>
> Ms. Sawyer: *Your Honor, it is a bench trial, I realize that. He is making legal assertions here at one point that are unfounded. I reserved on some objections because it is a bench trial. I don't think it is really all that important, but now we are talking about legal issues that I don't think, one, are relevant; or, two, even correct.*[40]
>
> Judge Dixon: *There was some testimony during the course of the trial about not – bouncers not putting their hands on patrons. And I assume that is what Mr. Hannon is alluding to.*[41]
>
> Ms. Sawyer: *Well, there was some testimony from the security plan. I don't think he is accurately characterizing it, but he is also making legal conclusions about it being an assault, which I also don't think I agree with. So that is my objection, Your Honor.*[42]

The objection was overruled, and Mr. Hannon continued.

> Mr. Hannon: *I won't comment on the objection. I can comment on the opening statement. It is shocking to believe that the Government is of the position that someone who engages in the most outrageous interpretation of Agent Thomas' conduct can be picked up by a 230 – pound man who has no training in weapons, who has no training in law enforcement and be carried 45 feet out in the street and deposited in the street. So let us examine that in a little bit more detail in connection with The Guards and Oscar, the manager whose testimony on direct and cross-examination was fluid, despite the language obstacles. ... He acknowledged that he knew me and I was on his side until the questions about ABRA and suddenly the veil fell and there*

---

[40] Ibid, 347 - 348
[41] Ibid, 348
[42] Ibid, 348

was something else going on in his mind. And what was going on in his mind is that their security plan prohibits the bouncers from touching a patron, unless the police are called or unless there is truly danger of an assault and one must come to the defense of another.[43]

And we know from the DC code that the Court took judicial notice of, that if you don't follow your security plan, you can have your license revoked. And then there was interesting testimony about whether there was entertainment going on downstairs. You remember Corporal Holubar said he went down with his Marine buddies and there was music playing and the place was packed. ... Why is that important? Oscar said this incident happened at 10:30. Why? Because the security plan says that when they have entertainment after 11:00, the police have to be there.[44]

So the assessment of that is as follows in my view: All of The Guards witnesses – and Graciela, by the way, did not testify to the spewing of profanities. Cpl. Holubar only heard the, "I am the fucking police" profanity. Brackett heard none of it. The table was maybe 15 feet away and this enormous hubbub wasn't heard by anyone at the table. But it is clear that Brackett is taught to take people out and make sure the police don't come ... Because if the police come, as you know from Lieutenant Charland, there needs to be a report to ABRA and ABRA is going to be there. And the risk is that they are going to discover that they don't have their cameras on. The cameras, which would have captured the truth of what really happened here inside the bar and outside the bar, that they have entertainment going on downstairs and they don't have police and the only security person is Brackett and they are otherwise not following their security plan by promising that the bouncer will not touch people. And we know that this is important because Oscar admitted that when the police came, he didn't tell them that Brackett picked him up and carried him out onto the street. He didn't tell them that Agent Thomas was a police officer. He didn't tell that to either the police or the ABRA investigator.[45]

Taking a breath, Mr. Hannon revisited Mr. Brackett's appearance in court, describing how he was dressed in a T-shirt, shorts, and flip-flops. He said, "so what does that say about the victim – that victim? He is not a victim. He didn't see himself as a victim. He didn't see anything that occurred that evening that he found at least in any way out of the ordinary. Quite frankly, he was pretty blasé about the fact that he saw the gun, and nobody is going to shoot me tonight."[46]

---

[43] Ibid, 348 - 349
[44] Ibid, 349 - 350
[45] Ibid, 350 - 351
[46] Ibid, 351

Mr. Hannon: *Now, I understand that the subjective and objective circumstances have limited relevance in this process. But was he a victim? Corporal Holubar had no idea that this trial was even going to happen. He thought once he gave the statement—*

Ms. Sawyer: *Objection, Your Honor.*

Judge Dixon: *I am not sure what your objection is.*

Ms. Sawyer: *My objection is to Marshall Brackett and Corporal Holubar's understanding about their status as victims. That objection was sustained at trial. Most of these arguments wouldn't be permitted in front of a jury. I am trying not to object, but it is getting a little far afield, Your Honor.*[47]

The objection was overruled.

Mr. Hannon moved on to Corporal Holubar and his failure to notify his command in Hawaii about the incident. He also questioned Corporal Holubar's clothing choice for his court appearance. He said, "I would think that his command would have trained in such a fashion that he would express a little more dignity and appreciation for the nature of what is going on here."[48]

Mr. Hannon: *With respect to Marshall Brackett … I think the Court should conclude that his approach to his obligation as a witness to limit his testimony to what he saw and what he heard and the like, perhaps escaped him. And he talked about credential issue. And got himself in a box and eventually had to say that when he had Agent Thomas in an arm bar – in a reverse arm bar, Agent Thomas, you know, whispers in his ear, I am a police officer and I am going to show you my credentials and somehow he gets them out with his left hand and gets them displayed and onto the hood of the car. … And we know from Jeffrey Cadle that didn't happen…*[49]

I suggest that all of that is important. Corporal Holubar is a remarkable Marine. He is smaller than I am. And has – apparently knows about Long Island ice tea by reputation and admits that in his circle, people drink it to get drunk fast. I guess anything else I have to say about that is outside the evidence. The only evidence is that it has five different types of alcohol …[50]

I want to elaborate on my factual argument and the motion to the judgment of acquittal that I was getting into regarding the alcohol. … Agent Thomas told you how much he drank. You saw what was on the bills. You heard what other people had to say. Lieutenant Charland has the great idea to do a breathalyzer, but not the fortitude to do it.[51]

---

[47] Ibid, 351 - 352
[48] Ibid, 352
[49] Ibid, 352 - 353
[50] Ibid, 353
[51] Ibid, 353 - 354

From there, Mr. Hannon talked at length about the decision Heath made to carry a gun that evening. He reminded the Court that Heath explained why he always carried a gun; he did not carry the gun to flaunt or intimidate others. Mr. Hannon said, "He chose to have it with him to be able to do his job so that when a family is slaughtered in the McDonalds and they learn that there is a law enforcement officer sitting in the McDonald's and they learn that he or she weren't carrying their weapon, they aren't outraged. That is a choice."[52]

He continued with police training in regard to signs of threats and verbal commands. Discussing different outcomes that could have occurred, he said, "I would suggest to Your Honor that intentionally drawing the weapon and turning the way that he did was permissible law enforcement conduct to protect the weapon and to act in self-defense. He did not shoot that gun."[53]

> Mr. Hannon: *I would rather that Your Honor credit the testimony of Agent Thomas. I would rather that the police at the scene credit Agent Thomas. I would rather that uniform officers who arrived at the scene who know nothing other than The Guards has called in a man with a gun in a dark shirt, go to the scene and handcuff both of them.*[54]
>
> *… Two men in armed combat with one another, but only Agent Thomas is handcuffed, because the lookout was for a man with a gun in a dark shirt. Brackett wasn't handcuffed because Officer Jeffery Cadle knew him.*
>
> Judge Dixon: *Mr. Hannon, can I interrupt you for a minute please? It was something you said just a moment ago. And I am paraphrasing, but I think what you said is even if I credit the Government's evidence, it was an act of self-defense if Mr. Thomas drew the weapon on his own accord to turn around to ward off what he thought were offenders, is that what you said?*
>
> Mr. Hannon: *Absolutely, Your Honor.*
>
> Judge Dixon: *Okay, I just want to make sure I had that clear.*[55]

Resuming, Mr. Hannon explained that his argument was supported by Mr. Bohrer's testimony, talking about a force continuum that would include presenting a weapon and pointing the weapon. The continuum would also include verbal commands.

Now, I don't believe that I made that specific argument. If I would have been asked, I would have said that Mr. Thomas was threatened when Mr. Brackett grabbed at his gun, and under those conditions, he could have used deadly force against Mr. Brackett.

---

[52] Ibid, 354 - 355
[53] Ibid, 356
[54] Ibid
[55] Ibid, 356 - 357

Judge Dixon responded to Mr. Hannon, explaining his understanding of my testimony. In part, he said, "his testimony did not seem to be that anyone happened to pass by the weapon and displaying no knowledge that the weapon was there somehow put the officer in a position to use that type of force to get the person away from him, that is, drawing the gun."[56]

Mr. Hannon responded, "That wouldn't make sense," and Judge Dixon said, "I agree."[57]

> Judge Dixon: *So the assault of the bouncer – using your argument – the assault of the bouncer grabbing Mr. Thomas from behind in a bear hug and then putting him down, justified Agent Thomas turning around with his gun to ward off that assault?*
>
> Mr. Hannon: *Yes, Your Honor. And to protect his weapon. And that is because if you take the continuum in terms of protecting your weapon, it doesn't matter whether the assailant in the beginning of the continuum knows you have it or not. If the assailant doesn't know you have a weapon and, obviously ... doesn't know you're a police officer, then there has got to be some more extensive cues to trigger some response, I have got to be concerned about this person, I have got to turn and face that person and the person is coming to me, I need to use verbal threats...*[58]
>
> *Now, the fact that Brackett didn't know he had a gun or claims he didn't know he had a gun is irrelevant to his conduct. Because he [Heath] knows not only does he have a gun, but it is coming loose. Or forget the fact that it is coming loose. Assume that it is not coming loose and he knows that he has a weapon, and it is securely settled in his holster and here is a man who assaulted him who is within arm's length of him.*[59]
>
> *Mr. Bohrer's testimony, his drawing the weapon and turning is part of that legitimate continuum. What Ms. Sawyer would have him do is run away ... He didn't. And if there is distance between him and Brackett, complete distance and Brackett has released him – suppose Your Honor has to ask himself, was this a gratuitous drawing of the gun for fear that this man would keep after him or not? We're playing the worst-case-scenario analysis here. And I think even under the worst-case scenario analysis where you ignore his character, you ignore his testimony, you ignore his demeanor and you ignore what I think Marshall Brackett admitted to, my position is that it is an exercise in self-defense and it is an exercise in protecting his weapon.*[60]

After further discussion of Heath's training, Mr. Hannon concluded, saying, "Unless the Court has any other questions, I would ask the Court to acquit Agent Thomas."[61]

---

[56] Ibid, 357
[57] Ibid, 358
[58] Ibid, 358 - 359
[59] Ibid, 359
[60] Ibid, 359 - 360
[61] Ibid, 361

The prosecution would have its chance for a rebuttal, but it was my perspective that Mr. Hannon made some good arguments. The questioning of Mr. Brackett's testimony on how Heath showed him his credentials and Cpl. Holubar's sobriety both seemed beneficial to the defense, but only if they were believed. Mr. Hannon's reexamination of the manager's testimony about the time the event occurred, the fact that a prosecution witness testified that the downstairs was open, the involvement of ABRA, and The Guards' security plan, were all good.

What I considered a gray area was Mr. Hannon's focus on the self-defense argument before Mr. Brackett grabbed at the weapon. Heath did have a right to self-defense because he was being assaulted. Did that right include drawing his weapon? Under the conditions Heath was in, it would not be unreasonable. However, Heath did not testify that he intentionally drew his gun.

Rebuttal Closing Statement

Ms. Sawyer used the next fifteen to twenty minutes to rebut the arguments Mr. Hannon had made in his closing. She began by stating, "it would be generous to say that he [Mr. Hannon] was mistaken at various points on both the facts and the law that govern the Court's decision in this case."[62] As an example, she questioned Mr. Hannon's interpretation of the security plan. However, the plan says if a guest is asked to leave and there is resistance, "... the next and final action is to call for police assistance."[63] The plan also says, "Never act aggressive or use physical force with guest."[64] She also stated, "He mischaracterized the testimony of the expert witness as it relates to weapon retention..."[65]

She then asserted that Mr. Viricochea was not trying to avoid the police or ABRA, noting that it was Mr. Viricochea who called the police. She compared this to Carole's actions, saying, "What did she do instead? ... Let's calm down ... We don't need to call the police."[66] Again, the prosecution seemed to want to attack or discredit Carole whenever it could.

Ms. Sawyer cut to the heart of the argument of self-defense, saying, "The defendant's own testimony has rendered that irrelevant. ... It was not until he was engaged in that struggle with Marshall Brackett that he became concerned for his safety ... Self-defense is irrelevant."[67] She added that the expert did not say anything about pointing a gun at someone as part of weapons retention.

---

[62] Ibid, 361 - 362
[63] The Guards Security Plan, Defense Exhibit 10, p 8
[64] Ibid, p 9
[65] Information from the trial transcript, Criminal Action Number 2010-CF3-16079, dated August 25, 2011, p, 362
[66] Ibid, 363
[67] Ibid

Ms. Sawyer: *He [Heath] was fairly explicit, in contrast, about the fact that that gun came out accidentally and he explained more than once exactly how that happened … Mr. Bohrer's testimony about the use of force continuum which Mr. Hannon wants to conflate with the idea of weapons retention, it is a use of force continuum, not a weapons retention continuum. And Mr. Bohrer talked about all of these steps that can be taken up to deadly force, none of which were taken because Mr. Thomas was never in any harm. He never felt a threat, by his own admission, until that gun became the subject of the struggle.*[68]

Judge Dixon: *Now, Ms. Sawyer, I think that in my ruling, depending on what the ruling is, that I may have to address both contentions; that is, whether the gun came out accidentally or not. A defendant is allowed to argue alternative theories. And so the alternative theory that I – that you were remarking on from Mr. Hannon was even if I discount Mr. Thomas's testimony that the gun came out accidentally, Mr. Hannon is arguing to me the alternative theory that I believe that Mr. Thomas drew the gun, his argument on behalf of Mr. Thomas is that he was acting in self-defense. And depending on what my ruling is, I may be called upon to have to consider both theories. Do you disagree?*

Ms. Sawyer: *I don't disagree. And I am happy to address the alternative theory.*

Judge Dixon: *… The way you were making the argument, it was as if under no circumstances would I ever have to address the alternative theory, because Mr. Thomas' testimony was that it came out by accident and, therefore, all I needed to do was rule on that issue.*

Ms. Sawyer: *… I think that the Court would come to the same conclusion under either analysis by Agent Thomas's testimony that it came out by accident, therefore there is no self-defense, by Agent Thomas', I suppose, alternate theory, he was – didn't see himself in any peril until the struggle. So, again, there is no – I suppose – well I will just address the law on that point.*[69]

So, Your Honor, unless the Court has any specific questions – I think I have addressed most of the arguments that Mr. Hannon has made that I would like to address – I just would leave the Court with one final thought. I think that one piece of the defendant's testimony that was most telling about what happened that night and it encapsulates for the Court precisely what was going on was what he said with the Court in fact asked him why it was that he didn't say anything on the way out of the bar as he was being carried out. And the defendant's response to this Court's question was extremely telling and that response was, I figured if I shouted and made a scene I would look even more ridiculous than I already did. And I think that was telling because it explains exactly what happened moments later outside. That as soon as he was released and had the opportunity, he wasn't going to look ridiculous anymore. And that's what happened that night, Your Honor.[70]

---

[68] Ibid, 364 - 365
[69] Ibid, 365 -366
[70] Ibid, 367

It is hard to ignore the spin that Ms. Sawyer put on the facts of the case in her final statements. Regarding Heath's silence while being carried out, Heath testified that he was thinking about defensive strategies and how best to defuse the situation. If, while being carried out, he had shouted, "Police, Stop," I believe the prosecution would have said a sober person would have been quiet; after all, drunks are boisterous and noisy. What is the normal reaction to an abnormal event? From a training perspective, Heath's actions were normal and expected. He was in an unexpected situation, and he was not panicked. Instead, he was thinking.

With the closing arguments over, Judge Dixon advised both sides that he was not going to make a ruling at this time; he would take a few days and make his decision. After everyone checked their schedules, the judge set August 30, 2011, to give his ruling.

The quote at the start of this chapter is ""If the facts don't fit the theory, change the theory."[71] In this case I believe the prosecution changed or interpreted the facts to fit their theory.

---

[71] An age-old adage, attributed to Albert Einstein, printed in the journal *Product Engineering, 1958*.

18A

Michael Morton: Concealing Exculpatory Evidence

In 1986, Mr. Michael Morton was employed as a supermarket manager, happily married with one child, and residing in Williamson County, Texas. On Michael's birthday the family celebrated by going out to dinner. Before going to work the following morning, Michael left a note for his wife, thanking her for the celebrations. The message included the fact that they did not make love on his birthday but ended with him expressing his love for her. While Michael was at work, an assailant entered his home, and his wife was raped and murdered. His three-year-old son witnessed the crime.

Michael was later arrested and charged with the crime, and in 1987 he was convicted and sentenced to life. At his trial, the prosecution theorized that he killed his wife because she refused to have sex with him on his birthday.

During the trial, the chief investigator, Sergeant Woods, did not testify, and the defense believed the prosecution was withholding evidence. This issue was brought to the judge's attention. The judge "ordered the prosecution to turn over all reports by Sergeant Woods so that he could conduct a thorough review."[1] Evidence that existed, but was not presented at the trial, included a report of a green van that was parked in the back of the home with a suspicious person inside, another report that the victim's credit cards had been used after the crime, and the eyewitness account of Michael's three-year-old son, who told his grandmother a "monster"[2] killed his mother. This evidence was not only not presented at trial, but it was also not given to the court - after the judge requested it.

Evidence that was presented during the trial included the sheets from the bed, where the crime occurred, which had semen stains, and a bloody bandanna found close to Morton's home. In 2005, a motion was filed requesting additional DNA testing in the Morton case. The motion was granted, but the bloody bandanna was excluded from the examination. Mr. Morton's DNA could not be eliminated from evidence found in the bed. It was his bed.

In 2011, five years later, the court allowed DNA testing of the bandanna and hair from the bandanna. The testing found DNA from the victim, Christine Morton, and

---

[1] CBS News, July 3, 2014, the innocence project and Michael-Morton.com
[2] Ibid

DNA from an unknown male. When the unknown male DNA was entered into a DNA database, it was matched to a Mark Norwood, a convicted felon. Mr. Morton was released and later exonerated. He had been wrongfully convicted and incarcerated for over 24 years.

After Michael Morton was released, "The Innocence Project filed a brief on Mr. Morton's behalf and the Texas Supreme Court ordered an unprecedented Court of Inquiry to determine whether Ken Anderson, the former prosecutor who went on to become a judge, had committed misconduct."[3] The Court of Inquiry found there was probable cause to charge Mr. Anderson with concealing exculpatory evidence and criminal contempt. Anderson was also investigated by the state bar association. Judge Anderson entered a guilty plea for his actions. He resigned from the bench, served ten days in jail, and surrendered his law license.

Should the other cases that Sgt. Woods investigated, and Mr. Anderson prosecuted, or presided over as a judge, be reexamined? Mark Norwood, the convicted felon who committed this crime, killed another woman two years after this crime.

References
Morton, Michael, *Getting Life: An Innocent Man's 25-Year Journey from Prison to Peace: A Memoir*, Published by Simon & Schuster, 2015.

---

[3] Ibid

PART III
The Verdict & Appeal

19

Guilty: The Decision, an Appeal, and Sentencing

TUESDAY, AUGUST 30, 2011

"The last of human freedoms—the ability to choose one's attitude in a given set of circumstances."

—Viktor E. Frankl

The mood in the courtroom on the morning of August 30 was somber, as most in attendance believed Heath would be found guilty. During the trial the court had heard false and misleading information from the prosecution, while the defense had been prohibited from entering information that would support a verdict of not guilty. Should the judge find Heath guilty, as was now expected, Mr. Hannon planned to appeal the verdict on Heath's behalf. Sentencing would be addressed later, if needed.

Speaking from the bench, Judge Dixon explained, "The defendant was before the Court on an indictment that charged two offenses. The first offense being assault with a dangerous weapon. The complaining witness or victim being alleged as Marshall Brackett. And the second count alleged assault with a dangerous weapon. The complaining witness or the victim being alleged, Brandon Holubar."[1]

The judge said he considered the testimony, the evidence, and the arguments by counsel in making his decision. The one count of assault had been dismissed during "the defendant's motion for judgement of acquittal,"[2] so the Court's concern was with the remaining count. Before delivering the verdict, the judge spent considerable time reviewing and summarizing the testimony.

The Decision

Judge Dixon: *I am not persuaded that the bouncer knocked Mr. Thomas' arm up while Mr. Thomas was trying to reseat the weapon in the holster and that the reason Mr. Thomas' arm came up with the gun in his hands. I am convinced – I am*

---

[1] Information from the trial transcript, Criminal Action Number 2010-CF3-16079, dated August 30, 2011, p 374
[2] Ibid, 375

convinced beyond a reasonable doubt that Mr. Thomas pulled the weapon from his holster, he turned to face the bouncer with the gun pointed in the bouncer's direction and it was either to intimidate the bouncer or show a superior show of force with respect to that struggle or to retaliate against the bouncer for what must have been an embarrassment event for him. I can't read Mr. Thomas' mind to determine why he would take such action, but I am convinced beyond a reasonable doubt that is what he did.

He certainly acted out of character that evening. Aggressiveness in his arguments with the wait staff about the poor service was not in accordance with the character testimony that the Court had received. But that conduct – testimony described by that conduct by the employees of the Guards was credible. The conduct – the testimony was also credible that the defendant smelled of alcohol, as one witness said "glassy eyed" and was a candidate for a field sobriety test.

With respect to the argument that Mr. Thomas had at the bar with the employees, once again here the descriptions — Corporal Holubar said the bartender said, "Calm down or we'll call the police," and the defendant responded, "I am the fucking police." Marina Yudina said that the defendant was cursing aggressively, yelling and screaming. Ms. Graciela Perez indicated that the defendant was complaining to the bartender [I think he meant the manager] asking if he wanted to explain in English or Spanish and that, at least from her perspective, people started applauding when the bouncer picked up Mr. Thomas to take him out.

Mr. Viricochea indicated that the man was very rude, using bad words. According to the defendant, all he was trying to do was give the names, O'Connor and Smith. For some reason, the individuals did not understand. And when he asked Mr. Viricochea if he was the Manager, Mr. Viricochea said, 'Yes' He proceeded to speak to him in Spanish after he acknowledged he spoke Spanish. And according to Mr. Thomas, it was the only comment by Mr. Viricochea, If you don't like the police that he responded – 'If you don't like it, call the police' that he responded, 'I am the fucking police.'

According to at least the testimony from Mr. Thomas, the description of events given by Cpl. Holubar, Marina Yudina, Graciela Perez and Oscar Viricochea, it just doesn't hold up with the way he described the testimony and I find those witnesses credible.

With respect to the marshal's [Marshall Brackett's] arrival at the scene where the argument was occurring, once again, comparing the testimony, Mr. Brackett said, sir, it's time to go, no response; tapped him on the shoulder, no response; touched him on the arm, pulled away twice. According to Mr. Holubar – Corporal Holubar the bouncer came over and said, sir, can you come with me? And then the bouncer attempted to escort the man, he pulled away. According to the defendant,

Mr. Thomas, he was not asked to leave. He did not hear the Manager say anything about calling security. No one asked him out. No one pushed him out. He had no idea who or why he was being picked up from behind. The Court finds that testimony is not credible.

A Law enforcement officer authorized to carry a firearm, for some reason, a stranger is picking him up and walking him out the door and he has no idea what is going on is not credible testimony to this member of the Court. Mr. Thomas knew what occurred and what was happening or, perhaps, inebriation has taken some effect.

Outside, while the struggle was going on according to Marshall Brackett, when he carried Mr. Thomas outside, he placed him on the sidewalk and he backed away. According to Corporal Holubar when the bouncer carried Mr. Thomas out to the street, he placed him down and he stepped back. According to both of them, Mr. Brackett and Corporal Holubar, it is at that point that Mr. Thomas began to turn with the gun in his hand. The only real difference in their testimony is, according to Mr. Brackett, Mr. Thomas turned to his right and according to Corporal Holubar, Mr. Thomas turned to his left. But according to both of them, a gun which has not been seen previously after the bouncer had stepped away, Mr. Thomas began to turn around and the gun was in hand. According to Mr. Thomas, while he was being carried out, he was trying to figure out who and why. According to Mr. Thomas, when he reached into his holster once he was put down, he still felt pressure and the presence of the person who carried him out. According to Mr. Thomas, the person grabbed him again and with his right hand, knocked Mr. Thomas's arm up and that is what caused the gun to come out of the holster. According to Mr. Thomas, when he turned slightly to his left, keeping his body between the gun and the person, it was at that point that the person – the bouncer reached around to his left, grabbed the gun, and the struggle continued.

The un-holstering of the weapon and the brandishment of the weapon, pointing it in the direction of the bouncer was not justified. There was no immediate threat. The bouncer had backed away. And it was an excessive response for the perceived assault of having been bear hugged, confined and carried out to the street.

Mr. Thomas' occupation as a law enforcement officer – a law enforcement officer who was authorized to carry a firearm, his occupation did not grant him privilege to draw his weapon under these circumstances and point it in the direction of Mr. Brackett. The Government has proven to my satisfaction, beyond a reasonable doubt, that Mr. Thomas did not act in self-defense or with any privilege grant him as a law enforcement officer.

The Government has proven to my satisfaction that there was an attempt or effort by Mr. Thomas to frighten the bartender [bouncer] with the service revolver, that the acts were done knowingly, intentionally and voluntarily. They were done with a firearm. And I find Mr. Thomas guilty of assault with a dangerous weapon.[3]

---

[3] Ibid, 399 - 403

Judge Dixon inquired if there were any questions, and there were none. The sentencing was set for November 4, 2011. The judge then opened the discussion regarding bond. Judge Dixon to Mr. Rickard: "What is the Government's position on bond pending sentencing?" Mr. Rickard responded, "The Government is requesting a step back, Your Honor," meaning Heath would go back to jail. Judge Dixon asked Mr. Rickard to explain his reasoning.

> Mr. Rickard: *The charge is serious, ADW [Assault with Deadly Weapon], gun. The defendant is not probation eligible and under the guidelines and would, but for the charging decision, potentially face a mandatory minimum. The defendant has testified in Court. And the Government takes very seriously Your Honor's finding that he testified incredibly, which I think should affect how Your Honor would weigh the promise to return to Court. And finally, all of the – the Government recognizes the defendant's distinguished career and all of the honors that he related and that Your Honor recounted, but I think at this point, now there is a conviction, now there is a presumption of detention, in some ways those credits kind of emphasize the dramatic change in position. And given that dramatic change in position, the Government does believe that he can't rebut the presumption that he is a danger and a flight risk at this time.*[4]
>
> Judge Dixon: *Mr. Hannon.*
>
> Mr. Hannon: *Your Honor knows the condition that Agent Thomas has been acting under during the pendency of this case for now over a year. And they include not drinking alcohol, to have a curfew, to not have a weapon which was released. And he is not carrying a weapon at the direction of his agency. This is the— this is, obviously, the first misstep in a remarkable career. And I don't believe that Your Honor can find that the conditions of release that are currently imposed upon Agent Thomas won't ensure his appearance for sentencing. And there has been no argument that he is a danger to the community under the circumstances that have been posed upon him heretofore. And I would ask the Court to continue him on those conditions until the time of sentencing. I simply don't believe there is anything about Agent Thomas or what the Court has heard to suggest that he is a person or character that would not appear or act out during that time period.*[5]
>
> Judge Dixon: *Thank you. I have considered the request of the Government counsel; I have considered the request of the opposition of the defense. Under DC Code, 1325(B), upon a conviction, an individual shall be detained unless the defendant demonstrates by clear and convincing evidence that he doesn't pose a danger to the community and is not likely to flee. Based on what I have learned throughout this trial and my – what I have learned throughout this trial, I am satisfied by clear and convincing evidence that there are conditions that can be set and therefore Mr. Thomas may maintain his*

---

[4] Ibid, 404 - 405
[5] Ibid, 405

current bond pending sentencing. I am going to reinstate, even though it may be superfluous I am going to reinstate the condition that Mr. Thomas shall not possess a firearm pending sentencing. The other conditions shall remain the same.

Mr. Rickard: *Your Honor, in an alternative the Government would ask for a condition of home confinement with high-intensity supervision.*[6]

The judge disagreed and then restated the date of November 4, 2011, for sentencing.

Judge Dixon obviously spent considerable time reviewing the testimony, given his lengthy summary. In his deliberations he seems to have given great weight to two areas of the evidence—the first being his belief that Heath's version of how the gun came out was improbable, and the second being the testimony of two witnesses whom he considered creditable and who testified that Heath turned with a firearm in hand while three feet from the bouncer.

Heath was upset, as one would expect, after hearing the verdict. He seemed more upset, however, that the judge thought he had lied in court. It would be two months before he learned his sentence.

A Motion for a New Trial

On September 19, 2011, the Hannon Law Group filed a motion in the Superior Court of the District of Columbia, Criminal Division, for a new trial and for a verdict of not guilty. The motion read in part:

> Rule 33 provides, in pertinent part, as follows:
>
> *On a defendant's motion, the Court may grant a new trial to the defendant if the interests of justice so require. If the trial was by the Court without a jury, the Court may – on defendant's motion for new trial – vacate the judgement, take additional testimony, and direct the entry of a new judgment.*
>
> *The Court found Agent Thomas guilty for three reasons. First, the Court believed that Agent Thomas lied under oath. Second, the Court believed that Agent Thomas apparent un-holstering and "brandishing" of his service weapon was an excessive response to the assault by Marshall Brackett. Third, the Court believed that the evidence presented in the Government's case alone was sufficient to permit the Court to find beyond a reasonable doubt that Agent Thomas intentionally un-holstered his service weapon to threaten Brackett and in doing so, did not act in self-defense.*
>
> *No spectator to the Court's verdict could misperceive the Court's vehement and wholehearted belief that Agent Thomas has lied to the Court under oath. So demonstrative was the Court in its verdict that even counsel felt accused of having knowingly sponsored perjured testimony.*[7]

---

[6] Ibid, 406

[7] Motion for a New Trial and to Enter a Judgement of Not Guilty, Superior Court of the District of Columbia, Criminal Division, Case No.: 2010 CF3 016079, Trial; Sentencing November 4, 2011, Heath P. Thomas' dated September 19, 2011, p 1 - 2

In his argument for a new trial, Mr. Hannon started with the fact that the Court believed Heath lied under oath and that Heath should have known who was picking him up. He questioned Mr. Viricochea's testimony in relation to the bar's security plan, which requires calling the police for a disruptive guest and prohibits the use of force by employees. Yet Mr. Brackett said that he frequently removed patrons by picking them up. Mr. Hannon also cited Mr. Brackett's testimony that he never heard profanity or a disturbance, further impugning the accuracy of Mr. Viricochea's testimony. He repeated Mr. Brackett's testimony about Heath showing his credentials, something that no one else witnessed.

Moving on to the so-called independent witness, Mr. Hannon noted that Corporal Holubar admitted to drinking a Long Island Iced Tea and a beer that evening just before the incident. Anyone with any knowledge of alcohol would conclude that someone consuming that much alcohol in a short amount of time would be intoxicated, which in turn would affect their perception of events.

Mr. Hannon then turned to the evidence that was not heard, emphasizing the defense's inability to enter evidence that supported Heath's version of events. Statements Heath made when arrested and a video demonstrating how the incident occurred, were excluded. Additionally, the Court limited the testimony of his expert, Shannon Bohrer. Mr. Hannon stated, "The Court did not articulate a reason for limiting the testimony of Mr. Bohrer, although the Government made several arguments for its exclusion."[8] He argued these omissions would have changed the course of the trial. The final two points in the motion dealt with Heath's argument of self-defense and for the judgment of acquittal.

Despite Mr. Hannon's efforts, the motion was not granted. This did not come as a surprise. Repeating ideas that were not believed the first time does not mean they will be believed the second time. One's confirmation bias can be stronger when one has ownership of the belief. Judge Dixon had made his decision based on his perception of the evidence and testimony presented in Court. For the judge to believe the arguments made in the motion, he would need a reason to disbelieve or, at a minimum, question his own positions. He would have to admit he made a mistake.

Sentencing Day
Early on November 4, 2011, the day of sentencing, I met Heath in the coffee bar in the courthouse basement. Heath told me that Mr. Hannon helped him prepare a written statement, but he decided not to use it. The statement included some standard remarks you hear in Court in sentencing hearings in which the defendant offers remorse for his actions. From Heath's perspective, if one appears to be apologizing for something he did not do, it becomes an ethical issue.

---

[8] Ibid, 12

Heath shared with what he intended to say:

Your Honor, I thank you for the opportunity to speak. For my entire adult life, I have served this country in positions of incredible importance and responsibility where the lives of people were at risk. For 25 years, the government has relied on [me] as indisputable. Major decision[s] about the implementation of important government assets and the potential of violence were made based on the intelligence I provided and assessments I provided. Ironically now the government states that my word is not credible, saying maybe I was drunk, maybe I was embarrassed, and that I am hiding behind my job. But this is a ridiculous supposition. I have been in much worse situations and acted according to my training. Embarrassment and ego are simply not traits I have.

Your Honor, I thank you for the opportunity to speak. It goes without saying that I am very distraught over how this has turned out, and you know that I will be pursuing an appeal. I understand that the Court must weigh the conflicting statements about what occurred inside the restaurant that night; in reflection, I can see how the Court would weigh the number of statements that are in conflict to my testimony, even though not all of the statements corroborate one another or each other for that matter. I never have disputed that I went up to the management to complain. I do however, maintain that certain actions…, the placing of hands on me by the bouncer was the catalyst to this situation.

As Mr. Hannon stated for me, I have worked hard to train myself to excel at what is required of me. I learned in the Navy that mistakes would cost me and others our lives. I worked hard not to make mistakes in my work. I take very seriously my obligation to protect and defend. I did not lightly make the personal decision never to go unarmed. I carried my weapon so no one could ever accuse me of not being in a position to prevent harm to another. Ironically, had my off-duty weapon not been in the shop for repair, it is unlikely that weapon would have fallen out of its holster.

I read the Prosecutor's sentencing memorandum. [The] Office has seen to be much more interested in how to "make an example" of me than actually looking for the truth. They take my use of the word "uncharacteristic" out of context and twisted it. I was only using this word to explain my use of profanity in stating I am a police officer. However, I can see that from the Court's perspective, these inconsistencies weigh against me, and I understand that. I only wish to reiterate; I never intentionally drew my weapon, nor did I ever intend to harm or scare anyone.

I am not sure I can say that I do regret any part of this entire episode, except for the profanity that I admit to. There is no doubt in my mind that I acted according to my training, fighting the biggest man I have ever fought in order to protect myself and those around us. But this event does not define me as a person. Nor does Your Honor's particular interpretation of the events of that night define me as a person. I know that Your

Honor is an experienced and highly regarded judge. I do not agree with your understanding of what occurred. I will continue to challenge your decision, as is my right.

But at the same time, Your Honor, should I fail in my effort to return to my life's dream of law enforcement, I will while it has and will affect my life, I plan to continue my life in a positive manner and will work to overcome this obstacle and move forward.[9]

After I read the statement, our conversation focused on what could happen if he read the words in Court. Normally, on a sentencing day, the person found guilty of an offense offers their apologies for the actions about which they have been convicted, and they appear contrite in front of the Court. Defense attorneys and judges often comment about the remorse before sentencing takes place. In cases where the defendants declare their innocence, they are often not viewed as remorseful, and in some instances, the sentencing appears to reflect the lack of remorse. In essence, Heath could be putting himself in a poor situation. His courtroom experiences were not unlike mine, and he understood the possibility and highly probable consequences. But he also expressed that he could not be contrite and apologize for something he did not do—it was not in him. Being found guilty of the alleged crime was not going to change him. He could not lie or even mislead the Court, and he had to be honest even if it caused him to be incarcerated. I wondered how the judge would respond to his statement.

At the specified time, we arrived in the court for sentencing. I was surprised that the courtroom was crowded. After the sentencing I realized that many of Heath's friends and co-workers were there for support, even after the guilty verdict.

Mr. Rickard, speaking for the government, focused on three items in the submitted sentencing memorandum.

> Mr. Rickard: *First of all, this was a violent act – a deliberate violent act with both uncertain and very dangerous consequences, not just for Mr. Brackett but for all others involved and anyone else out on the street that evening. The Government maintains that the act is all the more troubling in that it was also done by someone with a position, the authority to carry a weapon, a concealed weapon in the District of Columbia. And that by using that weapon in the way that it was used in this case, it represents a breach of that trust brandishing it in a personal dispute as it was here.*
>
> *Finally, the government in its allocution places importance on the conclusion that the defendant testified falsely under oath at trial. Which in and of itself is a bad thing, but it is made even worse again by the fact that the defendant is a law enforcement officer who's relied on to do just the opposite of what he did.*

---

[9] Mr. Heath Thomas written remarks he prepared for his statement to the Court on his sentencing date; November 4, 2011)

> *The government does recognize the defendant's character. His history and his government service was testified to – attested to in the letter submitted by the defense. But maintains that when all that is balanced against the nature of the offense, the need for the terms and the factors that I've just listed, that a short-split sentence of 18 months – ESS all but six months.*[10]

ESS is "execution of sentence suspended," meaning the Government wanted Heath incarcerated for six months. After serving six months he would be released and would be on probation.

The Defense
Mr. Hannon appeared greatly displeased with the sentencing recommendation. In his statement he described some missteps he felt he made, but also implied the recommendation for six months was or could be related to his professional relationship—or lack of relationship—with Mr. John Cummings, the chief of the felony major crime section in the U.S. Attorney's Office. He also implied that there was a possibility that the case was pursued and prosecuted because of his position in the case as the defense attorney, again relating to his experiences with Mr. Cummings.

> Mr. Hannon: ... *My comments are going to need to be a little lengthier than I anticipated as a consequence of the position that The United States Attorney for the District of Columbia has taken in his sentencing memorandum. And I note that with some significance that it was signed also by John Cummings, the chief of the felony major crime section who is here in the courtroom. And I'm going to need to address, if the Court permits me to, what I think are the credibility problems with that recommendation. And I want to begin by saying that any comments I make about the credibility of that recommendation are not directed at Mr. Rickard and Ms. Sawyer who were given this case to try.*[11]
> *I made two terrible mistakes in representing Heath Thomas. And the first mistake probably was a mistake of ego. Whether it would make any difference or not, I don't know. But imagine after the events on the street that night when a lieutenant had Agent Thomas locked up. That all the letters that you've received and the presentence report were provided to Ron Machen, the United States Attorney. I believe and Your Honor knows that's just my opinion that Your Honor never should have had to make the call that we asked you to make in this case.*[12]
> *For those who are here in the audience who don't know what the sentencing memorandum of the government says, they've asked the Court to incarcerate Heath*

---

[10] Ibid, 4 - 5
[11] Ibid, 5
[12] Ibid, 5 - 6

Thomas. And there are people in the courtroom who know him in a part of his life and there are people in the courtroom who haven't read the presentence report. And I'd like to just read a part of it, summarize a part of it.[13]

Mr. Hannon went through Heath's background, his family and their problems, and his striving to improve himself.[14] He presented Heath's Navy service, his efforts in becoming a demolition driver, his time with the Border Patrol and ending with Immigration Customs Enforcement.[15] His description was very complimentary.

After describing Heath's background, Mr. Hannon went back to what he termed his own mistakes.

Mr. Hannon: ... I made a mistake because I didn't believe that the young man who asked the Court to lock him up pending trial and who had assistant US attorneys going through the audience at the date of the first presentment giving people subpoenas to go to the grand jury would listen to me. And that lawyer filed a motion to disqualify me. And it was based upon conduct that he and I engaged in at the initiation of this case, that should never have been the subject of that motion and I renew my oral motion to you to unseal those papers so that the full record of this case is available to anybody who wishes to see it.[16]

And I was wrong not to try to have a dialogue with this person. Who during the course of the grand jury investigation, which took all of nine months tried to intimidate federal law enforcement officers and inevitably indicted a second count that was approved by his supervisor. And if I hadn't begged him to consider who this person was, maybe we never would have been here. I did try. I met with Richard Tischner who's now the — I'm told, running superior court operations. And our meeting was cut short by him repeatedly responding to text messages on his Blackberry. And I became personally offended and I shouldn't have and I walked out. And this was on the verge of the grand jury returning an indictment.[17]

I see Mr. Cummings here and I have to ask the Court for pardon because I tried cases against Key Mundy and Leroy Nesbit and Michelle Roberts when I was in the US Attorney's Office and Stephanie Duncan Peters and the best of the best. We always talked, except with Leroy because he never pled out a client to cooperate with the government. And we just killed each other in front of Eugene Hamilton and Carl Moultrie and Bob Scott and Don Smith, just went after each other hammer and tongue. And we were the best of the friends.[18]

---

[13] Ibid, 6
[14] Ibid, 6 - 7
[15] Ibid, 7 - 8
[16] Ibid, 8
[17] Ibid, 8 - 9
[18] Ibid, 10 - 11

Ken Monday once delivered personally some tapes to my house because they were Jencks. He said Mike, there's a tape recording of interviews with four witnesses on there and there's also a tape recording of my interview with my client. I'd appreciate it if you wouldn't listen to that one. I've never had a lawyer fail to shake my hand after a trial and that includes Mr. Rickard and Ms. Sawyer, except for one person. The person that signed this memorandum asking Your Honor to send Heath Thomas to prison for six years – six months, John Cummings.[19]

And he didn't emerge in this case until the verdict was coming in and now he's here at sentencing having signed this memo. I met Mr. Cummings when he was representing the government prosecuting a law enforcement officer for an offense far more heinous than this. It started out as a civil rights case, it ended up as an indicted misdemeanor. I met him, he seemed like a great guy. We went after each other hammer and tongue. It was a bench trial before Natalia Combs-Greene. And he ended up on the losing end of the stick. And in that case I had spent about three years telling everybody who would listen to me about the case. Except for Mr. Cummings because he really didn't want to listen to it. He was at the end of the trail. I had succeeded in having the government not indict it as a felony.[20]

The outcome of the case was that a woman ended up going down onto the sidewalk and breaking about 12 of her teeth as my client was defending people from marines who were attacking them at 2:00 in the morning in Columbia Heights. So we get all the way down to the misdemeanor and the government goes forward with the case without the victim. The victim is gone back to Namibia. And the star eyewitness identified herself as a lawyer in the State of New York. You can check it out on her website. Turns out she had failed the New York Bar.[21]

The judge interjected, "Mr. Hannon, I do have a time limit, which is 5:00 as requested by the chief Judge to end today's proceedings. I need to allow time to have Mr. Thomas to speak and for me to rule. So I will point that out to you."[22] On this day the proceedings had started at 4:08 PM. Mr. Hannon continued.

Mr. Hannon: *So I took my experiences with the people who were representing the government in this case, personally. I didn't try to drive through what I perceived to be their unwillingness to listen and naiveté. But I can't – and this is not – you know, this is not about me. Maybe it is, maybe some people would think it is about me. But I don't think it would be right for me not to – in representing Heath Thomas not to tell you that when*

---

[19] Ibid, 11
[20] Ibid, 11 - 12
[21] Ibid, 12
[22] Ibid, 12

> *Judge Combs-Green threw that case out, John Cummings refused to shake my hand and then promptly went up to put my client's name on the Louis list [sic; LEWIS, a database of police officers terminated for misconduct]. Even though he was not only acquitted but the case was thrown out on a – as it would be if there had been a jury sitting.*[23]
>
> *I apologize, Your Honor. I don't want this to be about me, but I am shocked at the recommendation of the United States Attorney in this case. And Your Honor may very well have a completely different view of the world than I do. I'm shocked that it was filed after the government already had read the sentencing memorandum. I can tell you, Your Honor, that Heath Thomas is everything that everybody says he is.*[24]
>
> *Notwithstanding Your Honor's verdict, another person without the training there would have been – there would have been bodily injury there. But again, that's my opinion, Judge.*[25]

At the close of Mr. Hannon's remarks, Judge Dixon offered, "Mr. Thomas, you have the right to be heard before sentencing, is there anything you'd like to say?"[26] Heath replied, "If I could, Your Honor."[27]

> His statement was slightly different and briefer than his written copy:
> Heath Thomas: *Your Honor, I thank you for the opportunity to speak. For my entire adult life I've served this country in positions of incredible importance in a responsibility where lives of people were at risk. During this time the government has relied on me as indispensable. Major decisions about implementation of important assets and the potential for violence were based on intelligence and assessments that I've provided.*
>
> *I find it difficult to see how my credibility is now shifted so much in lieu – in light of these – this incident. As Mr. Hannon stated for me, I've worked hard to train myself to excel at what is required of me. I learned in the Navy and in law enforcement that mistakes would cost me and others our lives. I worked hard not to make mistakes in my work and personal life, as often the line between work and personal life is blurred depending on the situation, especially in the vocation that I've chose.*
>
> *I take very seriously my obligation to protect and defend. I'm very disturbed at the disruption this has caused Mr. Brackett and all those involved. However, I can see from the Court's perspective how the inconsistencies raised during trial weigh against me and I understand that. I wish to reiterate, however, I never intentionally drew my weapon, nor did I ever intend to harm anyone. I do regret the outcome of this entire*

---

[23] Ibid, 12 - 13
[24] Ibid, 13
[25] Ibid, 14
[26] Ibid, 14
[27] Ibid

episode but this event does not define me as a person nor does the Court's particular interpretation of the events that night.

While this event has affected me and will continue to affect my life as it is pretty much ended my 25 years career and I now have to reinvent myself and go forward. I want to state to the Court that I do plan to move forward in a positive manner and will work to overcome this obstacle and continue to be a successful part of society.[28]

I was not the only person in the courtroom to understand and appreciate Heath's honesty.

The judge thanked Heath and continued with the sentencing.

The Sentence

Judge Dixon: *For me, the most difficult part of this case were the deliberations. The most difficult part was not the conduct of the trial, the most difficult part was not a determination of what the sentence should be. The difficult part was the deliberations. Because I made a reference during what I recall was an hour and 15 minute of findings of fact and conclusions of law. I made reference to the fact that a part of Mr. Thomas' actions on that evening were uncharacteristic.*

I heard the evidence. I understood that Mr. Thomas had lived an exemplary life. And this particular event, at least as far as everyone testifying was concerned, was something out of the ordinary. I considered and I believe the testimony of the bar patrons that Mr. Thomas had become upset. Mr. Thomas was arguing. And that here was a threat by the Manager to have him removed which he ignored. I believe that. I believe the fact that the bouncer attempted a couple of times to remove Mr. Thomas from the bar and that he more or less pushed him back. And that's why I also believed the bouncer's testimony about carrying Mr. Thomas out of the bar, which part is undisputed by anyone.

Mr. Thomas testified during his time on the stand that he wasn't quite sure what was happening at that point when he was being carried out of the bar. I believe he was bewildered but I also believe that he knew he was not being criminally attacked. I believe that he knew that he'd just been in an argument. And I believe that he'd been asked to leave. And I did not believe his implied testimony that that's not what he thought had occurred.

The bouncer testified that he walked or carried Mr. Thomas out the door, placed him on the sidewalk and started to back up to go back into the facility. That's when as Mr. Thomas turned around he saw this gun in Mr. Thomas' hand pointing at him.

Now, Mr. Thomas gives a different version. He says that as a result of being carried out, the gun was becoming loose and he was attempting to reseat the gun after he was

---
[28] Ibid, 14 - 15

put down by the bouncer and because the bouncer hit his hand while he was trying to reseat the gun, that lifted the gun up and when he turned around the gun happened to be in his hand. I did not believe that.

I was convinced beyond a reasonable doubt that number one, Mr. Thomas had a little too much to drink that night. That he was either aggravated or frustrated or perhaps angry that he had been tossed out of the bar. And in that instance uncharacteristically of anything anyone knew about him in the past, he pulled that gun and turned around at a minimum to show that he had the superior physical position at that point.

If Mr. Thomas had merely lifted up his shirt to show that he had a gun and was a law enforcement and hadn't pulled the gun the results would have been totally different. But that's not what happened. He did grab the gun, he pulled it out, he turned around and he pointed it in the direction of the bouncer. I am absolutely convinced beyond a reasonable doubt that's what occurred. And that's why the most difficult part of this case has been the deliberations. Because understanding what Mr. Thomas' reputation was, understanding what affect this case would have on his career, I needed to be convinced beyond a reasonable doubt with respect to the appropriate outcome.[29]

The presentence report writer when they completed their investigation in this case submitted a report to me that recommended a probationary sentence for Mr. Thomas.[30]

So for the offense that's before the Court Mr. Thomas is sentenced to 18 months in jail, the execution of all that sentence with the exception of four days is suspended and that amounts to time and thereafter he's placed on one year supervised probation with no conditions. I suspend a term of supervised release of three years. I impose court cost in the amount of $2500 to be paid within 6 months of today's date.[31]

The judge then advised Heath that he had a right to appeal within 30 days, and that concluded the proceedings.

After leaving the courtroom a small group gathered outside. There were brief conversations about the verdict and possible directions to pursue. Heath was upset, as one would expect, but he portrayed a calmness in the discussions. Everyone seemed to know that he was going to appeal, but little was said about the process.

Walking away from the group, my thoughts were mixed, knowing that appeals are rarely successful and simultaneously, at least in this case, believing there was more than sufficient grounds for an appeal. In my head I reviewed the incident, the trial, the players and witnesses and the outcome. I asked myself, what could have been done differently? I also felt that something was missing, and there was more to this story.

---

[29] Ibid, 16 - 18
[30] Ibid, 21
[31] Ibid, 21 - 22

19A

Cathy Woods: False Confession and More

In 1976, Michelle Mitchell called her mother for a ride because her vehicle had broken down on the highway. The 19-year-old was stranded but close to the University of Nevada–Reno, where she was a nursing student. When the mother arrived, she found her daughter's vehicle, but Michelle was missing. Several hours later, Michelle's body was found nearby in a private household garage. She was bound and her throat cut. The only evidence found at the crime scene was a discarded cigarette butt. A possible witness reported seeing a man fleeing the area.

The case went cold for three years until a patient in a mental hospital in Louisiana said she murdered a woman named Michelle in Reno, Nevada. The woman, Cathy Woods, was twenty-six years old when the crime occurred, was involuntarily committed when she was twenty-nine, and had been diagnosed with schizophrenia. Because Cathy was working in Reno when the crime occurred and because of her confession, she was considered a suspect. When interviewed, the details she gave "did not match anything reported about the crime."[1] Cathy also said she worked for the FBI and her mother was trying to poison her, neither of which was true. When questioned, she could not provide any evidence other than her confession. With just her confession, the authorities charged her with murder.

The case was tried in 1980; she was found guilty and sentenced to life without parole. A detective testifying at the trial said, "Woods told him she was a lesbian and she spotted Mitchell stranded by the roadside, whereupon she offered the student a lift. The detective said Woods claimed she made a sexual advance on Mitchell, got rebuffed, and, in anger, slashed the victim's throat."[2] A witness identified Woods as being near the crime scene on the date of the crime.

In 2013, the Rocky Mountain Innocence Project successfully petitioned for a DNA test in Cathy's case. The testing eliminated Woods from the evidence, connecting instead to an unknown male profile. In July 2014, the police were notified that the DNA matched Rodney Halbower, whose DNA had recently been added to the national database.

---

[1] "Woman Spent 35 years in Prison for Crime She didn't Commit; Exonerated Through DNA", Investigation Discovery.com, January 31, 2019.

[2] Ibid

Cathy's conviction was vacated in September 2014, and she was granted a new trial. The prosecution refused to re-prosecute, and in 2015 her conviction was again vacated (meaning the verdict was set aside). She had been incarcerated for 35 years. While incarcerated, she attempted suicide several times, including one instance of setting herself on fire.

Cathy's education was limited to an elementary school level, and she had "tremendous difficulty reading and writing."[3] The confession she reportedly made was not written, not recorded, and she was never asked to sign anything.

The witness at her trial in 1980, who testified that Cathy was in the area of the crime, was later "arrested for accosting a woman in a shopping center parking lot, and he was sent to prison."[4]

The killer, Rodney Halbower, identified with DNA, had been arrested for rape and attempted murder in Reno in late 1975 and was free on bond when he murdered Ms. Mitchell. In the Reno case, he was convicted of rape and attempted murder and sentenced to life. In 1986 he escaped and went to Oregon, where he assaulted and stabbed a woman, who survived. He was charged and convicted of that crime but was returned to Nevada to finish his sentence. In Nevada, he was paroled in 2014 and was returned to Oregon to serve a life sentence. Once back in Oregon, his DNA was collected and added to the national database, which resulted in the hit in this case. Halbower's DNA also matched two other homicides from 1976, the same year Mitchell was murdered. Those murders occurred in San Mateo, California. He was tried for both crimes and again sentenced to life.

References:
Mike Mcpadden, "Woman Spent 35 Years In Prison For Crime She Didn't Commit; Exonerated Through DNA", "How DNA from a cigarette butt proved Cathy Woods' innocence and led to a possible serial killer." *https://www.investigationdiscovery.com/crimefeed/...,* January 31, 2019

Kriti Mehrotra, "Michelle Mitchell's Murder: How Did She Die? Who Killed Her?"

The Cinemaholic, https://thecinemaholic.com/michelle-mitchell-murder/ November 29, 2020

Dennis Myers, "The case goes on Cathy Woods cleared in Mitchell murder" Reno News & Review, 03-12-15 https://www.newsreview.com/reno/content/the-case-goes-on/16511718

---

[3] Ibid
[4] The case goes on Cathy Woods cleared in Mitchell murder" Reno News & Review, 03-12-15

20

The Appeal and the Aftermath
NOVEMBER 8, 2011–MAY 9, 2013

"The evidence of intent to injure or frighten was insufficient to support a conviction of assault with a dangerous weapon."[1]

Heath Patrick Thomas was convicted of assault with a dangerous weapon on August 30, 2011, just over one year from when he was arrested. He was sentenced on November 4, 2011, and on November 8 of that year a notice of appeal was filed with the Superior Court of the District of Columbia, Criminal Division. Heath's appeal was filed by the Hannon Law Group.

One month later, on December 5, Mr. Hannon sent a letter to the Honorable Kathryn A. Oberly, saying that Heath was indigent and qualified for a Criminal Justice Act (CJA) appointed attorney. The CJA ensures that indigent individuals charged with a crime can have an attorney appointed to represent them. The act also allows reimbursement for services to the appointed attorneys, as well as for expert witness and investigative fees. Mr. Hannon wrote, "While I am not currently on the CJA Panel, I am requesting permission to proceed as his CJA Attorney and take the CJA amount in order to provide continuity of representation in an efficient manner."[2] Members of the CJA panel are appointed as needed, and since Mr. Hannon was not on the CJA panel, he was requesting to be appointed so he could be paid while representing Heath.

In the time between the guilty verdict and the Hannon Law Group trying to represent Heath as a CJA attorney, Heath had actively sought new representation for his appeal. Heath notified Mr. Hannon of his decision to seek another attorney, but this was after Mr. Hannon had sent the letter.

Mr. Hannon sent another notice to the courts, and the CJA authority withdrew the Hannon Law Group's appearance as representation for Heath in his appeal. During this same period, Ms. Barbara K. Kittay was appointed to represent Heath as his CJA attorney.

---

[1] Brief for Appellant, District of Columbia, 11-CFG-14222, Heath P Thomas v. United States of America, p 5
[2] Letter from the Hannon Law Group, to the Honorable Kathryn A. Oberly.

Appellant Brief to the District of Columbia Court of Appeals
After Ms. Kittay was appointed to represent Heath for his appeal, she submitted the appellant brief to the District of Columbia Court of Appeals.[3] In the brief, she presented two main issues at the center of the appeal:

> I: *Whether the trial court gave undue weight to the presence of a weapon and the complainant's overreaction, where the defendant, an off-duty law enforcement officer who was being removed from a bar, endeavored to secure a weapon that had jiggled loose from its holster, and the complainant (bouncer), unaware that the defendant was a law enforcement officer, immediately commenced to struggle with him to gain control of the gun.*
>
> II: *Whether the trial court unfairly limited the presentation of expert testimony regarding the nature of a law enforcement officer's training and, therefore, the reasonable reaction to a physical assault and a civilian attempt to disarm him of his weapon.*[4]

The brief gave the facts that Heath had been charged with two offenses and that, during the non-jury trial, one of the charges was dropped. It noted that at the time of the altercation, Heath was employed with ICE, and he was off duty. He was with friends and others, having an evening out, including dinner. The brief included the dispute with the bar manager and the fact that Heath had been physically removed from the bar. Ms. Kittay also stated that Heath had been found guilty, there was a sentence imposed, he was given credit for time served (four days), was on probation for one year, and was imposed a fine of $2,500.

Following the statement of the case, Ms. Kittay described essential points from the trial—for example, that Heath had trouble paying his bill at the Guards and attempted to complain to the manager. The brief said further that the manager believed Heath was "so disruptive, that he called for security to remove him (8/16/11 Tr. 127-28)"[5] It noted that the security guard had arrived, picked up Heath in a bear hug, and carried him outside.

"Once outside," the brief continued, "Brackett deposited the appellant on the pavement just beyond the sidewalk and turned to walk away. A moment later, seeing a gun in appellant's hand, Brackett rushed appellant, grabbed the gun, and struggled with him for possession of the weapon (8/16/11 Tr. 220-22)."[6] The brief noted that the struggle for control of the weapon had continued for several minutes, until the police arrived.

The government's case, including the testimony of the bar employees and Corporal Holubar, composed the next section of the brief. Brackett and Holubar, Ms. Kittay wrote, had both testified that Heath drew a weapon and turned to face the bouncer.

---
[3] Brief for Appellant, District of Columbia, 11-CFG-14222, Heath P Thomas v. United States of America. The brief is dated and was received by the Court on May 9, 2012.
[4] Ibid, under issues presented, p IV
[5] Ibid, 3
[6] Ibid, 3

Brackett grabbed the gun, and a struggle ensued. During the struggle, the weapon was pointed in the direction of the bar and Corporal Holubar.[7]

The brief said that the defense had included witnesses who were with the defendant at the establishment, character witnesses, and a training expert. Additionally, the defendant testified for himself. According to the brief, Heath had said "that he was securing it [the weapon] when Brackett lunged at him (8/22/11 Tr. 118-19) The defendant testified that his actions, thereafter, were pursuant to his law enforcement training, that an officer must not surrender, under any circumstances, possession of his weapon (8/22/11 Tr. 122), a principle that was supported in the testimony of his expert witness. (8/25/11 Tr. 272)"[8]

The brief's final argument was simple: "The evidence of intent to injure or frighten was insufficient to support a conviction of assault with a dangerous weapon."[9]

Legal Analysis

As part of the brief, Ms. Kittay presented her legal analysis of the case, stating, "The elements of 'intent to frighten' assault with a dangerous weapon are: 1) an act that reasonably would create in another person a fear of immediate injury; 2) committed voluntarily and on purpose, not by mistake or accident; 3) with the apparent ability to injure; and 4) committed with a dangerous weapon … Here, the mere presence of a weapon, combined with the absence of the critical fact that the defendant was a law enforcement officer, created such a perception of danger in the complainant, that his perceptions and the actions that followed, overwhelmed the simple fact that the weapon was being secured, not to brandish in any way … Here, despite the bouncer's observation of the weapon and immediate (and understandable, albeit erroneous) conclusion that he was in danger, appellant's actions to secure his weapon, that resulted in its display to others, was not a voluntary use of the weapon that was threating."[10]

The brief continued, reviewing Heath's right to carry the weapon—even off-duty— and his right to keep the weapon and not allow it to be taken from him. Ms. Kittay then addressed the argument that the trial court unfairly limited the presentation of expert testimony, beginning with procedural background:

> *Defendant proffered the testimony of at least two experts (and ultimately only was permitted to present a portion of the testimony of one expert) and asked the court to remedy the refusal of DHS and the U.S. Attorney to make available a third potential expert, the defendant's supervisor at ICE, Special Agent John Eisert. This witness, who the government has presented to the grand jury and whose testimony would have been received as more credible than the testimony of the paid witnesses, described the train-*

---

[7] Ibid, 4
[8] Ibid, 4 - 5.
[9] Ibid, 5
[10] Ibid, 8-9.

ing received by appellant and other ICE agents, and apparently told the prosecutors that in the same situation, his training would have caused him to shoot the bouncer, to maintain his weapon (8/23/11 Tr. 170), a conversation that the prosecutors denied (8/23/11 Tr. 230-31). The court refused to order the testimony of Agent Eisert.[11]

Included in the brief were the trial transcript from the judge's ruling on August 23, 2011, and his reasoning for not allowing Agent Eisert to testify. The brief continued, "The trial court also limited the paid experts' testimony, including this, most prejudicial limitation: 'I will not permit any expert testimony to be offered with respect to what was done or what could have been done by Mr. Thomas from the point that the bear hug was put on him until the time the weapon was grabbed' (8/23/11 Tr. 217)."[12]

This was followed by Judge Dixon's instructions, using the trial transcripts from August 25, 2011.

Other Legal Issues
As Ms. Kittay noted in the brief, one of the defendant's expert witnesses was an ICE official who was not allowed to testify to what he had previously told the prosecutors. The brief argued that "the Department of Homeland Security severely limited the scope of permissible testimony from Agent Eisert, and otherwise refused to authorize testimony about the propriety of appellant's conduct, given his training as a law enforcement officer (8/23/11 Tr.233) … Surely, the trial court could have been presented with the same testimony that would have carried more credibility than that of the paid witnesses – without objection of the witness's employer."[13]

The brief explained that the trial court also limited the testimony of the paid expert:

Specifically, the trial court declined to hear testimony about the interaction prior to the struggle over the gun. Trial counsel proffered expert testimony analogous to "accident reconstruction," in which his expert would recreate the circumstances under which the defendant needed to re-set his weapon in its holster, in the context of his law enforcement training, and express a reasoned conclusion about how the misunderstanding occurred (8/25/11 Tr. 274-76) …. [For] experimental evidence to be admissible, the conditions of the experiment must be 'substantially similar to those of the alleged occurrence.'" Butts v. United States, 822 A 2d 407, 414 (D.C. 2003), quoting Taylor v. United States, 661 A. 2d 636, 643 (D.C. 1995) "Differences in the conditions of the experiment may constitute "'fertile field for cross-examination' rather that grounds for exclusion of evidence." Id.[14]

---

[11] Ibid, 12
[12] Ibid, 14
[13] Ibid, 16 - 17
[14] Ibid, 17 - 18

> ... Where, as here, the critical question was the defendant's intentions in removal of his gun from its holster, the trial court undoubtedly would have been aided by a re-enactment of the "bear hug" and manner of carry used by the bouncer that the defendant claimed caused his gun to become dislodged, and the demonstration of what movements were necessary to re-secure the gun in the specific holster used by the defendant in the specific clothing he wore.[15]

The defense counsel questioned whether the court had believed Heath's struggle for his gun was reasonable:

> It is revealing that the issue of the struggle over the weapon, which was highlighted in the government's case, did not figure prominently in the court's ultimate findings of fact. Appellant suggests that, in part, this is because the expert testimony had established to the court's satisfaction that the appellant's actions were reasonable and indeed, consistent with his professional training. Appellant was seeking, through the entire defense he had proffered, to bring the same assistance to the court's evaluation of his conduct just prior to the struggle. The limitation of the expert testimony that precluded this additional assistance was quite prejudicial."[16]

Ms. Kittay further explained that the testimony from Agent Eisert and Mr. Bohrer should have been allowed because Heath's frame of mind, formed by his training, was central to his defense strategy:

> *The entire theory of defense, in this case, was "lack of intent to frighten." It depends on a reliable evaluation of the operation of the appellant's mind, that is, the motivation for his actions. And the motive for his actions was training. Therefore, an understanding of his training – the essence of the defense – should not have been limited. The court has the discretion to limit expert testimony, but the trial court unfairly limited the defense evidence here, when it denied the defense the impartial testimony of an official of its agency, denied testimony about the motivation and training for the re-holstering of his weapon, and denied discussion by experts about the imperative of weapon protection by law enforcement personnel."*[17]

District of Columbia Court of Appeals

The appellant brief was received at the Court of Appeals on May 9, 2012. The case was argued at the Court of Appeals on January 10, 2013, and the decision was rendered on February 27, 2013. The hearing was brief and started with one of the judges giving an

---

[15] Ibid, 18
[16] Ibid, 19
[17] Ibid, 20 - 21

oral review of the case. The review mentioned that Heath was intoxicated when the event occurred. Later, another judge on the court mentioned what Ms. Kittay had written in the brief that having an expert is like using an accident reconstructionist to "recreate the circumstances under which the defendant needed to re-set his weapon in its holster, in the context of his law enforcement training, and express a reasoned conclusion about how the misunderstanding occurred."[18] The judge seemed to agree with this argument.

The time allowed for arguments was short, and after the proceedings concluded, I met with Ms. Kittay, Heath, and several others outside the court. A central theme of our conversations was the court's openness to Ms. Kittay's position. While some thought the court was receptive, others were not optimistic. It was my thought that if the judges believed the trial court's decision and reasoning for the same, it could be easy to dismiss anything that an expert might offer. After all, from the appellate court's perspective, the lower court believed beyond a reasonable doubt that Heath was guilty. Conversely, it was my belief that if Ms. Kittay's argument that the expert could "express a reasoned conclusion about how the misunderstanding occurred," coupled with the analogy of the accident reconstructionist, the appeal could be granted.[19]

The Court of Appeals' Decision

The decision by the court was issued on February 27, 2013. Heath notified me by email of the decision on March 3, 2013, and in the email, he said he had been notified that day. The appeal was denied.

The court's written decision included a background for the case, the trial, and evidence, as well as its reasoning for the decisions. The reasoning excerpted portions of the transcript presenting the trial court's justification of the verdict. Reading the same words from the trial judge's opinion, it was easy to see why the Court of Appeals did not grant the appeal. In order to grant the appeal, the appellate court would have had to question the trial court's conclusions. It did not; the appellate court accepted the beliefs of the trial court as factual.

Another way of telling this story would be to start with "Once upon a time." I understand why Judge Dixon believed what he did, since there was not any substantive testimony that gave a different picture of the event, except for the defendants. I do not know whether expert testimony would have made a difference. For the court to believe another version of the event, the trial judge would have to have some doubts as to the veracity of the prosecution's witnesses, and he said in his decision that he found them believable. So, would the judge have found the experts' testimony not credible?

The justification that the Court of Appeals gave for its decision noted several precedents related to expert testimony:

---

[18] Ibid, 17
[19] Ibid, 17

Appellant now contends that the trial court unfairly limited his presentation of expert testimony. Our review generally is for abuse of discretion. See Girardot v. United States, 996 A 2d 341, 346 (D.C. 2010). 'Although the admission of expert testimony falls within the discretion of the trial judge, we have cautioned that because the right to confront witnesses and to present a defense are constitutionally protected, in exercising its discretion, the trial court must be guided by the principles that the defense should be free to introduce appropriate expert testimony.' Benn v. United States, 978 A2d 1257, 1269 (D.C. 2009) (internal quotation marks omitted). Expert testimony should be admitted 'if the opinion offered will be likely to aid the jury or the trial court in the search for truth.' Burgess v. United States, 953 A 2d 1055, 1062 (D.C. 2008) (internal quotation marks omitted).[20]

The justification argued was that any impact from denying the testimony wasn't sufficient to require that the decision be reversed:

On the record before us, even if we assume arguendo that the trial court erred in declining to disturb the DHS limits on Eisert's testimony and in restricting Bohrer's expert testimony as described above, we cannot find that the court abused its discretion, because, we conclude, any error was harmless – i.e., the impact of the (assumed) errors does not require reversal. See Abulquasim v. Mahmoud, 49 A. 3d 828, 837 (D.C. 2012) ("In evaluating a claim of abuse of discretion by the trial court, we must determine, first, whether the exercise of discretion was in error, and, if so, whether the impact of the error requires reversal" or, instead, was harmless) (internal quotation marks omitted).[21]

The justification noted the defense's arguments regarding the potential effect of the additional testimony:

Appellant argues that the trial court "undoubtedly would have been aided by a re-enactment of the [bouncer's] 'bear hug' and manner of carry used by the bouncer that [appellant] claimed caused his gun to become dislodged, and the demonstration of what movements were necessary to re-secure the gun in the specific holster used by [appellant] in the specific clothing he wore." He asserts that the demonstration would have included "expert explanation of [appellant's] turn ... which is part of the training to turn away from the perceived assailant[.]" The expert testimony, appellant claims, would have assisted "the court's evaluation of [appellant's] conduct just prior to the struggle.[22]

---

[20] Court of Appeals, No. 11-CF-1422, Heath Patrick Thomas (CF3-16079-10) Memorandum Opinion and Judgment, date, February 27, 2013, p 8
[21] Ibid, 8
[22] Ibid

The court was not convinced of the defense's argument:

We are not persuaded that the exclusion of such testimony prejudiced appellant. To begin with, appellant testified that the bouncer's bear hug only partially dislodged the gun, requiring appellant merely to push it back down into the holster once he was set down on the ground. According to appellant's testimony, it was not until the bouncer subsequently fell into him, grabbed at him again, hit his right arm, and "bladed" him, that the gun was forced out on the holster and his arm was forced upward as he grabbed onto the gun. Accordingly, there is no reason to think that expert testimony about the earlier, physically inconsequential "bear hug" and the response it might have necessitated would have assisted in appellant's defense.[23]

Further, as already described, in finding appellant guilty of ADW, the trial court expressly rejected appellant's account that "the bouncer knocked [appellant's] arm up" and that this was why appellant's "arm came up with the gun in his hands." The court found Brackett and Holubar credible, specifically citing their testimony that Brackett "backed away" and "stepped back" after placing appellant on the ground. In other words, the court discredited appellant's account about a perceived assailant hitting or "blad[ing]" him. The court's finding of guilt rested entirely on the court's credibility-based finding that the appellant took deliberate action (i.e., "un-holstering of the weapon and brandish[ing]" it toward the bouncer) before the bouncer saw the gun and grabbed the muzzle, and was not at all based on appellant's response afterwards, when he held onto the gun and struggled with the bouncer. And, of course, the appellant's experts were not on the scene, so that, as the trial court put it, they had no basis for opining about what transpired and what appellant "did, didn't do, could have done, [or] should have done, prior to the time the weapon was grabbed." For all these reasons, we see no likelihood that the proffered expert testimony – about why it was necessary for appellant to turn away from "the perceived assailant," or about what type of force appellant's training indicated might be warranted against an assailant who was trying to take his weapon – would have made a difference in the outcome of appellant's trial.[24]

One of the appellate court's reasons for denying the appeal was simple. Since the "bear hug only partially dislodged the gun," the appellant should have just pushed the gun back in the holster, so anything the expert would say would not help the defense. The Court of Appeals was sitting at an intersection—they did not see the accident, but they determined how the accident occurred by what others told them. Then they said that if an accident reconstructionist was hired, his or her opinion would not be valid because the expert did

---

[23] Ibid, 8 - 9
[24] Ibid, 9

not witness the accident. The Court of Appeals agreed that the defense was entitled to have the experts testify, but ultimately decided any error by the trial court was inconsequential, or as they said, it was "harmless," as it did not affect the outcome.

Life After the Appeal
Ms. Kittay sent Heath a letter dated March 3, 2013. A segment of her letter read, "I am required to advise you of the next steps you may take, because I do not see any non-frivolous reason to file a petition for rehearing or rehearing en banc on your behalf. An en banc petition must include a showing with particularity of how the panel of judges misstated the law or misapplied the facts. Unfortunately, although I am not pleased with the decision, I do not feel it meets the criteria for a petition of rehearing."[25]

She continued, "Arguably, your only avenue of further appeal is to seek a petition for certiori to the U.S. Supreme Court, but there, too, the likelihood that you can make any showing adequate to persuade the Court to entertain your case is very remote, because the D.C. Court of Appeals decided your case based on the review of mostly factual (rather than legal) findings. If you nevertheless believe that proceeding to the Supreme Court is appropriate, you can proceed pro se (representing yourself) with a petition for certiori, which must be filed within 90 days from the date of the decision."[26]

As Ms. Kittay noted, the appeal had been denied, not because the experts were limited, but because of the supposition that the believed or known facts would not have changed, even if the experts' testimony had not been limited. For that reason, the Supreme Court would not be interested in the case. For the rest of us, it raises the question, how does one know that their beliefs would not change with additional information? Examining this in reverse, if the expert testimony had not had the power to change the court's position on the facts or what the judges believed to be factual, there would have been no value in the expert testimony. If that were the expectation, then why limit the expert's testimony?

When I received the information from the Appeals Court decision, my first thought was, for the court to believe a different version of this event, the court would have to question the findings of the lower court. I wondered how many other appeals were denied, because of not questioning the lower court's decision.

In June of 2013, just five months after the appeal was denied, and almost three years after his arrest, Heath packed up an old truck and moved to Texas. He planned to stay with his mother. She lived in a nice home—a home Heath had purchased for her. When Heath was in Bosnia-Herzegovina, he earned additional wages (being in a combat area and not being taxed). Since his mom lived in an older home, Heath purchased a newer home, telling his mother that this was his

---

[25] Letter from Ms. Kittay to Heath Thomas, dated March 3, 2013, p 1, also Appendix O.
[26] Ibid, 1 - 2

retirement home. He asked her if she would live there so the home would not remain vacant. She moved in.

Heath had been in contact with his mother during his working career, and he was aware that she had some health and medical issues. But, when he arrived home, he realized her medical problems were more severe than she had revealed. Heath also knew that his brother had moved out, supposedly to be in the care of someone else. His mother said she had not been in contact with him for quite some time.

Shortly after Heath's arrival, his mother's health started declining, and he became her principal caretaker. We had numerous telephone conversations during this time, and it seemed that the medical professionals were unsure of everything that was going on with his mother. Heath, on the other hand, listened to each doctor and kept good notes. He had become her ombudsman. Even though his mother had other family members, from Heath's perspective, they seemed distant and reluctant to offer help.

During the time when her health was declining, Heath told me that they had some minor disagreements and some very deep conversations. As an example, if Heath purchased wine, his mother disapproved, possibly because of the circumstances when he had been arrested. Of course, her objection may have been related to the behavior of her husbands. It was not a critical issue for Heath, so he chose to simply not purchase any wine. They did not reconcile all their differences, but they came to some understanding that brought them much closer together. From my point of view, it seemed that Heath very much appreciated this time and developed a greater understanding of his mother, which resulted in a better understanding for both.

In August 2014, Heath wrote in an email:
I am writing to let you know that my Mom has begun the transition. She entered Hospice on Monday and it has been a steady move towards her new journey. All of you have known me for a long time and many have met my mother or at least heard me gripe about something she has done.

For what it's worth I believe that had I not had the life altering experience I had, I would not have come home when I did, and I would not have had the gift of caring for her this last 13/14 months. It pained her to see me go through what I did, but we talked a lot, and we were happy with where we got. I can't say we became friends, but that was not the nature of our relationship. She is not in pain and that is all I can ask for.

We will have a simple Mass per her wishes.[27]

---

[27] Email from Heath on August 14, 2014

A short while after the first email, Heath sent, "As an update, my mother gently and painlessly passed at 0112. She is being taken care of in the best way possible."[28]

I knew from our previous conversations that he wanted to take care of his mother—that he thought of it as a gift in some way, something that he could do. Even knowing this, it had never occurred to me that, because of his conviction, he was able to be there when she needed help. There are people who can take a horrible situation and find a lesson or at least something positive about their situation. Heath is one of those people.

We had a few conversations after his mother passed. I knew it was a difficult time for him since he was by himself. Although Heath had other family members, he was not particularly close to them. If you spend your life working with and around other people, and then that stops, it can require a significant adjustment. And from my perspective, Heath did well with that change. So, when Heath took on the responsibility of caring for his mother, I did not just view it as an obligation, but in some ways, I saw it as a different direction with purpose. But what I learned was that being home with his mother and being able to take care of her was more important to him than his conviction.

Of course, after someone passes, there are always certificates, notifications, and volumes of paperwork to be completed. Since most of Heath's extended family lived in the San Antonio area, notifying them was not an issue.

Heath did have his brother, Nathan, but he'd had no contact with him since returning to Texas. In attempting to locate Nathan, he found out that he had passed away. He does not know if his mother knew this. His mother never said anything if she had known.

Heath's early life is not an example of an upbringing that most people would reflect on and then predict that he would turn out to be the person he became. Saying that could reflect my own judgmental bias. However, there are many examples of individuals who, through adversity and challenges, have become persons whom we admire. I think Heath is one of them. I believe he learned early, matured, and became a responsible individual.

Heath is not a unique individual, and that is not a disparaging comment. There are many Heaths in the criminal justice system, and I have been truly fortunate to have known and worked with many of them. They are dedicated, hardworking, intelligent, and honest people—coworkers with whom I felt privileged to work and individuals who do not work just for a paycheck. They work hard to make the world safer because it is just the right thing to do. Honesty and integrity are in their DNA. These are individuals who do not seek recognition or awards, and when they receive them, they say they were just doing their job. In doing their job, they know that life is not fair, and they believe that is part of the job—to help make it fair. Heath was one of those hardworking and honest persons who made life a little safer for others.

---

[28] Email from Heath on August 15, 2014

20A

Lukis Anderson: When DNA Points in the Wrong Direction

In California, in 2012, the police investigated the homicide of Mr. Raveesh Kumra, a multimillionaire who lived in Silicon Valley.

Police collected DNA from the crime scene, which later implicated Mr. Lukis Anderson as a suspect. However, Mr. Anderson, who was homeless at the time of the crime, had a good alibi. Earlier on the day of the homicide, he was on the street in a semi-unconscious state. Emergency services were called, and he was attended to by paramedics and then transported to a hospital. While in the hospital he was under almost constant supervision; he was highly intoxicated and nearly comatose. Because of this, he was no longer considered a suspect.

How did this happen? The paramedics who responded to the murder of Mr. Kumra had treated Mr. Anderson earlier on the same day. When they responded to the homicide of Mr. Kumra, they unknowingly and unintentionally contaminated the crime scene with Mr. Anderson's DNA, "more than three hours later."[1] The DNA was picked up by the medics when they treated Mr. Anderson, and then later they left some of the DNA at the scene of the homicide. This is called transfer DNA.

Think of someone with chalk on their clothing, their shirt sleeves, and their person. Everywhere the person walks and on everything they touch, they can leave trace amounts of the chalk. DNA is like chalk, only it is invisible to our normal vision.

DNA has been widely used in convicting and exonerating persons. But unintentional, or possibly intentional transfer of DNA could be used to charge an innocent person.

DNA has been a valuable tool when determining innocence and guilt in thousands of criminal cases. However, this case demonstrates that if not collected correctly or if unintentionally transferred, DNA can implicate innocent persons. The importance of a thorough and complete investigation of all crimes should not be understated.

---

[1] "*When DNA Implicates the Innocent*," Reported in *Scientific American*, June 2016

Are there innocent persons who have been convicted because of DNA transfer? It is hard to believe that this was the only case of medics or other first responders transferring DNA. What would have happened in this case if Mr. Anderson had not been hospitalized at the time of the murder? Should more need to be done to ensure DNA transfer does not occur?

Reference

Peter Andrey Smith, "When DNA Implicates the Innocent," Scientific American June 2016. https://www.scientificamerican.com/article/when-dna-implicates-the-innocent/

21

Final Thoughts

JULY, 2021

"In matters of truth and justice, there is no difference between large and small problems, for issues concerning the treatment of people are all the same."

—Albert Einstein

In the case of *United States of America v. Heath Patrick Thomas*, the investigation conducted by the authorities was used to affirm what they had already concluded had happened. The prosecutor's office relied on the grand jury investigation, which was not unlike the nonexistent police investigation. As we have seen, there was never an investigation to determine what really occurred. From the moment the police arrived on the scene, Heath's guilt was assumed. This was not a complicated chain of events. A complete investigation would have involved interviewing all parties and then creating a timeline. Instead, a handful of witnesses, mostly employees of the bar, were interviewed, and their statements were never questioned. The statements of the witnesses who were with Heath were disregarded, as they were not believed.

The lack of earnest scrutiny was further exacerbated when the prosecutor's office failed to negotiate with the defense attorney.1 Heath was indicted after the grand jury, and the trial date was set.

Throughout the trial, many different versions of events were put forth, not just between the defense and the prosecution, but among the prosecution's own witnesses. How the prosecution and the judge failed to acknowledge these incongruities and contradictions is difficult to understand. The case the prosecution was making had no real substance, but they made it by creating a story. Not using the correct time should have been a clue—a big clue—that the narrative pushed by the prosecution was bogus. But, for a clue to be noticed, you must be looking for it.

---

[1] Mr. Hannon walked out of a meeting with Richard Tischner, while negotiating with the U.S. Attorney Office, about Heath's case, referenced in Chapter 18, Information from the trial transcript, Criminal Action Number 2010-CF3-16079, dated August 30, 2011, p 8 - 9

After the conviction, the court of appeals found that the lower court made no errors that resulted in harm. The court agreed that Heath should have had the opportunity to have his expert testimony heard, but it also said that it did not matter, as the outcome of the trial would not have changed. This, despite the fact that the appeals court did not know what the expert was going to say or the direction it would take the court. That is like someone driving down a road and being lost, so they decide to go faster – so they will not be late. The appeals court did not want to turn around even to see if the wrong road had been taken.

A case could be made that some individuals and organizations involved in this case had an agenda and, with that agenda, created their own reality to fit their positions. The person at the center of the entire incident—the manager, Mr. Viricochea—is responsible for starting and perpetuating the false story. Did he deliberately change the time of the incident to 10:30 instead of 11:58 p.m. to cover up the fact that the camera system was on (or not on), or did he turn it off after the incident occurred? Was the time changed to cover up that The Guards was not in compliance with its security plan by not employing off-duty officers? When the incident occurred, there had been entertainment in the basement, and there were two additional security persons, which Mr. Viricochea denied in his court testimony. Was the manager just frustrated that someone would complain to him about the poor service?

When the police were called and responded, did Mr. Viricochea have to justify his actions? If there had been no gun, would the police have been called? If these possibilities sound improbable, it could be argued they are more probable than Heath drawing his weapon because he was drunk and embarrassed.

More questions arise when we consider Mr. Hannon's comments about US Attorney John Cummings. Could the prosecution have pursued the case because someone in the U.S. Attorney's Office held a grudge against Mr. Hannon? Mr. Hannon brought up this possibility in the courtroom, and when he did so, I thought it was highly improbable. However, if The Guards were pushing for prosecution, could the office have taken the opportunity to pursue this case more forcefully than it might otherwise have done?

After Heath was arrested, he filed a civil suit against The Guards. Heath was confident that the charges against him would be dropped. Is it possible that the owners of The Guards pressured the prosecution to pursue the case to avoid possible financial judgements or even sanctions by the Alcohol Beverage Regulation Association (ABRA)? In an interview with one employee of the Guards, the employee told me that she happened to see the attorney for The Guards after Heath was convicted. She related to me that the attorney had said to her that The Guards no longer had to worry about the civil suit filed against them by Heath since he had been found guilty.[2]

---

[2] Interview of Alexandra Calomiris, an employee at The Guards. She was working when the event occurred. She was a bartender and was on break when Heath was carried out. The interview was via Telephone on October 22, 2014.

Between the chapters of this book, I have included some cases of individuals who were found guilty and incarcerated but were later found to be innocent. Examining and researching the cases was a learning experience in and of itself. It was not hard; in fact, it was easy—too easy—to find cases of individuals who had been found guilty of crimes they did not commit and then spent years incarcerated. In conducting the research, I found hundreds of cases. If one were to write and publish a book on innocent persons found guilty, the volume of materials could easily resemble a small set of encyclopedias. These are just the cases that we know of. If one can easily find hundreds of serious felony and death penalty cases where individuals were wrongfully convicted and sentenced, how many minor cases like Heath's exist?

While authoring this book, I had numerous conversations with various people about the premise of what I wanted to convey—the purpose and goal of the project. One individual was an attorney and judge from Houston, Texas, Mrs. Georgia H. Akers. She told me that if she would ever find herself being charged with a crime, there were two defense attorneys in Houston whom she would consider hiring.[3] Obviously, she has great faith in the two defense attorneys of whom she spoke, but what does that say about the rest of the legal field? Does our criminal justice system require an accused to have the best criminal justice attorney to prove that something did not occur?

Another individual with whom I spoke was a defense attorney in Washington, D.C., Mr. William Cowden. He was a former prosecutor with the U.S. Attorney's Office in Washington. When discussing the book with him, I mentioned that I had found some cases of wrongful convictions, and I intended to include a few summaries in the book. He asked me, "Would you like some more cases?"[4] He was offering me more examples to be included. What does that say about the system?

With so many cases being reversed in our judicial system, it is easy to see why innocence programs have proliferated around the country. While I applaud the investigators, the reporters, the attorneys, and the volunteers who give their time and energy to these cases, we also need to look at the other end. We need to examine the problem from the front end of the system—to prevent the back end from continually filling. Releasing innocent incarcerated people is a symptom of the real problem. The real problem is that innocent people are being incarcerated.

Where Do We Start?

I have been asked many times what changes to our justice system would I like to occur. We could start with research. Because of the significant volume of wrongful convictions and incarcerations, the data that could be helpful already exist. Studying the cases and extracting the data should provide useful information about how these

---

[3] Interview of Judge Georgia H. Akers Esq. Probate Judge, Houston Texas, now retired.
[4] Interview of William R Cowden Esq., a private attorney and former federal prosecutor.

wrongful convictions come about. Having a better understanding of how the problems were created should offer directions for correcting the issues.

For example, how many wrongful convictions exist because of a poor police investigation, coerced witnesses, withholding evidence, or corrupt officers, prosecutors, or judges? Using the research and the data to answer these questions should offer a direction and solutions. The sad part is that we already have a large volume of research materials because the problem of wrongful conviction is so significant, and these are only the ones we know of.

Beyond researching the data to understand the problem better, I would like to see some commitment from law enforcement administrators and trainers, lawyers, bar associations, the judicial system, and legislators to examine our criminal justice system. I understand that is a large expectation, but the system is so interconnected that a broad approach is needed. Honest and effective police reform should occur and could be a good start. However, if the prosecutors, defense attorneys, judges, and the entire system are not reformed, the benefits from police reform will be limited.

"Not everything that is faced can be changed, but nothing c
an be changed until it is faced."
—James Baldwin

Should There Be Consequences?

If there are individuals in our criminal justice systems who have contributed to some of the problems, should they suffer the consequences? In some of the cases, officers or attorneys have withheld information or evidence in a trial, leading to the wrongful conviction of the defendant. Later, when the information was revealed, the conviction was reversed. But you rarely hear of any consequences for the behavior.

Individuals in the criminal justice system have varying levels of authority. If one has the authority, should they not also be accountable?

As an example of consequences, if an officer or prosecutor has information that is not shared with the defense and the information is later used to exonerate the person, then the officer or prosecutor, at a minimum, should be fired, disbarred, or pay some restitution. I am not talking about a simple error; I am talking about the deliberate withholding of information that is critical for the defense. Would that deter the behavior?

In the case of Michael Morton, an innocent person was incarcerated for almost 25 years. The prosecutor, who later became a judge, was given ten days in jail for deliberately withholding evidence that sent an innocent person to jail—for life. That does not seem balanced. In the same case, the actual offender who killed Ms. Morton was later convicted in a separate case of the killing of another woman, two years after the Morton case. Not looking for the actual killer can and does have additional ramifications.

In the criminal justice community, we hear complaints about people who have knowledge of crimes, but they will not come forward. That mentality often infects the law enforcement community. In one case, an officer witnessed a fellow officer choking a handcuffed suspect. The officer intervened and stopped the choking. That was in 2006. An internal investigation by the agency ruled against the intervening officer, and she was fired in 2008. The officer took legal action, and in 2021, she was awarded back pay for the 15 years since the choking incident and a full pension.[5] In this case, other officers saw the negative consequences of doing the right thing and surely got the message. The culture needs to change.

Does that same code of silence among police affect lawyers and judges as well? If we—members of the criminal justice community—want to improve the system, we need to be responsible for our actions. We need to have rules and regulations that encourage whistle-blowers to step up. Of course, that is easy to say but more complicated to enact.

We know of cases where defense attorneys have requested DNA examination of evidence, and the prosecution refuses. In some cases, the defense attorneys take their case to the courts to redress their cause. Should prosecutors be required to justify the denial? Remember, while the state has the burden of proof, in many instances it is the DNA that refutes what the state has already proved. In the case of Ronnie Long (behind chapter 3), Mr. Long was incarcerated for 30 years before the evidence was known. Then, it took another 14 years for testing and exoneration.

> *"Most ailing organizations have developed a functional blindness to their own defects. They are not suffering because they cannot resolve their problems, but because they cannot see their problems."*
> —John Gardner

Early in my law enforcement career, I was told that life is not fair, and that was part of my job—to try to make it fair. We know that life is not just unfair; it is more unfair in some communities and especially within minority groups. To that end, society has been examining the unfairness and is proposing new laws for the purpose of moving in the direction of equality. Under our criminal justice system, our view of utopia is that we are all treated equally. This book does not profess to have all the answers, but it does shine a light in the right direction.

---

[5] Joseph Wilkinson, "Buffalo cop gets pension back 15 years" Reported in the New York Daily News, April 2021.

EPILOGUE

I have been asked to write what has happened to me since the end of my legal proceedings. As you can imagine, it was devastating. My life, as I knew it, came to an abrupt ending. I was terminated from my job at Homeland Security, about a month short of 20 years of service. I felt disgraced and wronged. I had always known our system had flaws, but in my experience, those flaws were mitigated by the individuals working in the system, but that is another topic.

I stayed in the region and completed my sentence of one year probation in Virginia. I must express my gratitude and thanks to Carole for her support during this extremely trying time. The probation office was interesting. There was an open opinion that I should not be there. They gave me one of their newer officers to give her experience monitoring a male; they had me do one drug test and said it was a waste of money to test me anymore. The officer came to where I was living once, then made me report in person two or three times. That was followed by moving from in-person reporting and phone reporting on an automated system. It was surreal.

During those 12 months, I went to a Virginia program to help offenders get employment; I thought they were going to help me, but by the second appointment, they asked me to be on a working group to help them develop a set of policies and procedures. Again surreal. They did have a therapist with whom I met regularly; she helped me talk out what I was going through mentally. She was instrumental in helping me cope with what was effectively the death of all the things that I thought made me who I am. She helped me re-realize that I was still the same core person.

In January of 2013, when a very good friend of mine, who has a remodeling and restoration company, offered me an entry-level job, I gladly agreed to it. I was a gopher for the guys who knew how to do the more skilled work. I also did demolition and clean-up. It was good honest work. I was happy to have it and thankful to my friend. I felt useful again. In this time frame, I decided I was going home to Texas. I had never liked the DC area and had no reason to stay, and I needed to go. At the end of June, I bought a truck, loaded it up, and drove home.

My mother was happy to have me back home permanently. Things were quiet for a while as I settled into a new routine of housework and taking her to doctor's appointments. Then I noticed my mom was having more difficulty doing things, and it was slowly getting worse. The next 14 months would become the hardest of my life and the most rewarding. As her health deteriorated, we began to have long conversations. Things long buried were brought up, questions asked, arguments debated. I can't say we fixed everything, but we did come to an understanding. I could go on about those 14 months, but I'll just say things happen for a reason, and I think if my incident hadn't occurred, I would have continued to focus on my career and not noticed the signs of my mom's health and I would not have had the opportunity to care for her. She passed away on August 15, 2014, the Day of the Assumption of Mary. We are Catholic, and this is a Holy Day of Obligation.

While taking care of her, I had some ideas of what to do next. Texas has some very good benefits for veterans, and as I had served honorably, I am eligible for them. I took the LSAT and scored well enough to be considered for law school. However, my research told me I was not automatically barred from the profession of being a lawyer, but I did have to wait five years to apply to attend law school. I would have to wait.

I had made some very frugal financial decisions, so I didn't need to work right away, but it would be good to get some funds coming in. I decided to go to the local unemployment office, the Texas Workforce Commission (TWC). I am not eligible for unemployment or really any assistance of any kind that I know of. The TWC has a program for veterans involved with the justice system, much like the offender program in Virginia, with resume writing, some placement assistance, etc. I talked to two caseworkers and told them my story; both were stunned; they asked for my resume and set up a follow-up appointment. I left them a resume and a curriculum vitae (CV).

The next appointment, they gave me some leads and asked me to tailor a new resume, so I did. Nothing bore fruit. I went back and asked what they thought, and one caseworker told me frankly, "Your resume and CV scare people. You sound like something from Assassin's Creed." It made me laugh, but I understood what he was saying. Half the time, I look at my work history and think "No one is going to believe this."

I did manage to get seasonal work at Amazon right after my mother died, but it only lasted a month. I have managed to get only five interviews in my job hunt. One was with a legal assistance group, who needed someone bilingual and with immigration law experience. I am both, but I got the impression that the group thought they couldn't afford me even though the grant was from TWC and TWC had recommended me.

I interviewed at a private law firm, and the paralegals who were bilingual loved me, the lawyer not so much. I did disclose my record. Two days later, they called and said that I would not be able to get into the local detention centers because of my conviction. I have contacts with the local ICE office and in their HQ; this was a convenient mistruth.

The third interview was with a hotel resort chain for a management trainee position. I disclosed my record, and at least they were honest and told me that they would recommend me, but human resources would override them.

The next interview was with the Texas Department of Fish and Wildlife, where I would be monitoring the health of the deer species in the hill country. The panel seemed to like me but were concerned that I did not have training in wildlife management, although they admitted it was an entry-level job. I think I didn't get the position because someone else did have that kind of training, not because of my record. I have been told repeatedly by Texas officials that they do hire individuals with records. It just depends on the position.

I also applied to be a bus driver for the local bus service; again, I disclosed my record. The interviewer was very complimentary and told me I was the most professional person he has interviewed, but he would have to have the department heads decide. He would call if they said yes. No call was forthcoming.

I have tried to add skillsets to make myself more marketable. I took an entry-level welding course and paid for a course in networking operations in information technologies (computer programs). Nothing yet; I have been lucky and have gotten two consulting grants from people who know me. But long-term gainful employment has eluded me.

Financially I have been lucky in that I made frugal choices that worked out. I right sized from the house I bought my mother and have little outstanding debt. It hasn't been easy or stress-free, but it's no use worrying about things you can't control. I couldn't retire because I was short of the age requirement of 50 and 20 years of service. My retirement is vested and waiting for me when I get to the minimum retirement age of 57.

I am not sure if I can't get work because of my record or my work history and qualifications. I sometimes feel that they don't even get to my record, more like the interviewer is intimidated by my experience. Maybe I'm not looking for the right jobs. I have been told that at seven years, my record becomes less critical; it's seven years since the arrest and five since the end of probation.

I keep busy with the upkeep of where I live, and I work out a lot. I started training to do an ultramarathon in Utah. Friends tell me to start a business, but I have never had the entrepreneurial bug. I did join the Knights of Columbus at my church, a noble organization with interesting dynamics, and I was initially very active with them, but not sure I will continue there; they have been a disappointment. I also volunteered with the Red Cross, especially after hurricanes, and found that rewarding; it felt good to be of service.

I don't know, but sometimes I think I was so immersed in my career and in what the mission was that I did not really look at life around me and now I am kind of forced to, and while I still have my down moments where I feel wronged, and I'll drink too much and lament what happened to me, I usually come to my senses and realize I have more than most and need to try and give back. What's hard is finding someone or some way that will give me the opportunity.

The last several years there have been quite a few changes, some very positive. I competed in several ultramarathon distances of 50K and 100K and plan on competing in 100 miler this coming year. My friends who run some of these races now employee me to help run them.

My new house has been good for me, but I also lost my pug Gnarley. He plunged over the rainbow bridge, and it felt strange being companionless for a while. On a very good note, I met someone very special, she is very capable and complementary, and our relationship is very positive. She is a partner. Now, my house feels more like a home.

I started a new part-time job, doing early morning stocking for a large building supply company. They liked my work, and my position was elevated to full time. It is interesting to have a job that I leave at work and have no reason to contemplate after my shift ends.

I don't know what will come next. I still think about what happened to me and see a lot of changes to my old career field, some of which Shannon and I talk about. It hasn't been an easy time, some of that was caused by my processing of what happened to me. I sometimes wish I was still "tilting at windmills" of "having an impact" as I did in my prior life, but that is a conversation for a later date.

V/R
Heath Thomas

ACKNOWLEDGMENTS

I want to thank everyone who helped me with this project, specifically my best friend, confidant and partner, my wife Sue. She is always my first reader and gives me honest critiques. The next thanks go to Heath. We stay connected, and I very much enjoy our long conversations. With the continued reporting of police misconduct, we always have something to talk about, not unlike two curmudgeons having coffee. Carole, Heath's girlfriend when this occurred, was extremely helpful, thank you.

A longtime friend, Carole Branaman, who early in the writing process gave me excellent feedback, and my niece Morgan Barr, who was instrumental in the early editing, both deserve credit. Mike Hillman, the editor for our local paper was a sounding board with good suggestions and Brian Barth, who with his suggestions and expertise in developing draft copies, was extremely helpful. I also want to thank the many officers and agencies that I have worked with during my career. I had the privilege of learning from numerous officers I worked with and others that I encountered. Several individuals who deserve a special mention include Tom Ingram, Steve Jessee, Jeff Wells, Wade Jackson, and Bill King. A special thanks to close friends, Dr. Anthony Pinizzotto, Mr. Edward Davis, and Mr. Robert Chaney, all of whom helped me with this project. Without mentioning other names, because I am sure I would leave someone out, I want to thank everyone who agreed to be interviewed and others who assisted with the project. The interviews were, from my perspective, critical in the development and content of the book.

Related to the development of the book, I want to thank the Frederick County Maryland writers club. I joined the club at the suggestion of an acquaintance and found out that you do not write something and then have it printed. The club itself and the resources that have been opened to me have been invaluable. I met the editor of the book, Katherine Pickett, POP Editorial Services, LLC, through the club. Her work was influential in the structure and completion of the final projecter.

Authoring this book has been a journey. I had written a few things before, but never a book. It is incredible what you can learn while writing. When I started the project, Heath gave me written permission to have the files. I obtained the materials and documents needed from Michael Hannon, Heath's attorneys. Three cardboard file boxes full of records. For the first six months, I wrote nothing; I just read and organized the materials.

When I started writing, I had an outline that I generally followed, but I kept finding new materials and documents, sometimes stuck in the wrong folder. It became apparent to me that the project would take a while, if for no other reason than the volume of materials.

The grand jury and trial transcripts filled more than one file box. Writing and editing what was important took longer than I had anticipated. The book could be described as the Cliff's Notes version. My intent was for the book to be a fair and objective representation of the materials. With the help of all the people mentioned above, I achieved that.

Authoring the book has been challenging at times, but it has also been a learning experience. With over four decades in law enforcement, I would never have believed how many innocent people are convicted of crimes. Heath and I talk about this and other problems, and I hope the book can influence some positive changes.

"A man who views the world the same at fifty as he did at twenty has wasted thirty years of his life." –Muhammad Ali

APPENDIX A

U.S. Department of Justice

Ronald C. Machen Jr.
United States Attorney

District of Columbia

Judiciary Center
555 Fourth St., N.W.
Washington, D.C. 20530

September 1, 2010

VIA EMAIL

J. Michael Hannon, Esq.
1901 18th Street, N.W.
Washington, D.C. 20009

Re: <u>United States v. Heath Thomas</u>
Case No. 2010CF3016079

Dear Mr. Hannon:

This letter is to confirm the pre-indictment plea offer for your client, Heath Thomas. **This plea offer will remain open until September 15, 2010 and the defendant must waive the preliminary hearing in order to take advantage of this offer.** However, the Government reserves the right to revoke this plea offer at any time before your client enters a guilty plea in this case. If your client accepts the terms and conditions set forth below, please have your client execute this document in the spaces provided below. Upon receipt of the executed document, this letter will become the plea agreement between your client and the Office of the United States Attorney for the District of Columbia. The terms of the plea offer are as follows:

1. Your client agrees to admit guilt and enter a plea of guilty to the following offense: **Attempted Assault with a Dangerous Weapon**, in violation of 22 D.C. Code, Sections 402, 1803 (2001 ed.). Your client understands that the offense of Attempted Assault with a Dangerous Weapon carries a penalty of "a fine not exceeding $5,000 or [] imprisonment for not more than 5 years, or both."

2. Your client understands that the Government will **reserve stepback** pending sentencing, **waive enhancement papers**, and will **reserve allocution** at sentencing, subject to the terms set forth in paragraph 5 of this agreement.

3. Your client understands that the Government agrees that it will not indict your client on any remaining or greater charges arising from the circumstances of this case. These offenses include, but are not limited to, **Assault with a Dangerous Weapon and Possession of a Firearm During a Crime of Violence.**

-1-

4. The parties further agree that your client, after taking an oath to tell the truth, shall agree to a proposed factual proffer in open court on the date of the plea.

5. Your client understands that the Court may utilize the District of Columbia Sentencing Commission's Voluntary Sentencing Guidelines in imposing the sentence in this case. The Government and your client agree that neither party will seek an upward or downward departure outside of your client's applicable guideline range. Your client further understands that the applicable guideline range will not be determined by the Court until the time of sentencing.

6. Your client agrees that this letter is binding on the Government, but not binding on the Court, and that your client cannot withdraw this plea at a later date because fo the harshness of any sentence imposed by the Court. The Government understands that your client is not bound by the Government's allocution, and may request a lesser sentence, subject to the terms set forth in paragraph 5, above.

7. Your client acknowledges and has been made aware that pursuant to the Innocence Protection Act, that there may be physical evidence which was seized from the victim, crime scene or from your client or from some other source that can be tied to your client that could contain probative biological material. Your client understands and agrees that in order to plead guilty in this case, your client must waive and give up DNA testing in this case and must execute the attached written waiver of DNA testing. Your client further understands that should he/she waive and give up DNA testing now, it is unlikely that he/she will have another opportunity to have the DNA tested in this case.

8. Your client also agrees that if any firearms or illegal contraband were seized by any law enforcement agency from the possession of or the direct or indirect control of your client, then your client consents to the administrative forfeiture, official use and/or destruction of said firearms or contraband by any law enforcement agency involved in the seizure of these items.

9. In entering this plea of guilty, your client understands and agrees to waive certain rights afforded to your client by the Constitution of the United States and/or by statute. In particular, your client knowingly and voluntarily waives or gives up his right against self-incrimination with respect to the offense(s) to which your client is pleading guilty before the Court which accepts your client's plea. Your client also understands that by pleading guilty your client is waiving or giving up your client's right to be tried by a jury or by a judge sitting without a jury, the right to be assisted by an attorney at trial and the right to confront and cross-examine witnesses.

Appendix A | 341

10. This letter sets for the entire understanding between parties and constitutes the complete plea agreement between your client and the United States Attorney's Office for the District of Columbia. This agreement supersedes all prior understandings, promises, agreements, or conditions, if any, between this Office and your client

                                    Respectfully,

                                    RONALD C. MACHEN JR.
                                  UNITED STATES ATTORNEY

By: _____
            Sean Lewis
            Assistant U.S. Attorney
            555 Fourth Street NW, Room 3816
            Washington, DC 20530
            Telephone: (202) 353-8815
            Facsimile: (202) 514-0477
            E-mail: Sean.Lewis2@usdoj.gov

APPENDIX B

List of Employees working August 28, 2010

Tara Novotny

Monica Rabinowitz

Alexandra Calomaris

Anna Zurawick

Oscar Viricochea

Cesar Siles

Roberto Sardan

Marvin Ventura

Mark Flemming

Filiberto Sueldo

Marshall Bracket

Mani M.

Graciela

Marina Yudina

Freddy Biloatoomez

Chea Primas

APPENDIX C

RECEIVED AUG 1 8 2011

DEPARTMENT OF THE NAVY
OFFICE OF THE JUDGE ADVOCATE GENERAL
1322 PATTERSON AVENUE SE
SUITE 3000
WASHINGTON NAVY YARD DC 20374

IN REPLY REFER TO:

5820
Ser 14/0157/T11325
August 15, 2011

VIA ELECTRONIC AND U.S. MAIL

J MICHAEL HANNON ESQ
HANNON LAW GROUP
~~[redacted]~~
WASHINGTON DC 20009

Dear Mr. Hannon:

RE: <u>United States of America v. Heath P. Thomas</u>, 2010 CF3 16079

    This office received your letter dated August 4, 2011, and Subpoena regarding the above matter. We have contacted the appropriate USMC officials where any such "documents reflecting any report by Marine Brandon Holubar regarding an assault that occurred on Aug. 28, 2010 at The Guards restaurant" would be located. We were advised by the appropriate USMC officials that no such documents exist.

    Should you have any questions or need additional information, you may contact Ms. Shirley Garris at (202) 685-5449.

Sincerely,

Christopher Jeter
LT, JAGC, USN, By Direction
Office of the Judge Advocate General
General Litigation

APPENDIX D

U.S. Department of Justice

Ronald C. Machen Jr.
United States Attorney

District of Columbia

Judiciary Center
555 Fourth St., N.W.
Washington, D.C. 20530

July 5, 2011

J. Michael Hannon, Esq.
Hannon Law Group
~~[redacted]~~
Washington, DC 20009

Via Priority Mail and E-mail to: jhannon@hannonlawgroup.com

Attorney Hannon:

    I write in response to your three recent letters, one dated June 27, 2011, and two dated June 23, 2011.

    First, in response to your request to offer two character witnesses by video-conference, I have several questions about how the presentation would work. As the case you cite suggests, the parties must verify that "there are measures in place to safeguard the important interests at stake." Do you have information on how the video-conference will work, both visually and technically? How would the oaths be administered? Would we expect any delay in relaying conversation? How would the witness's appearance be displayed to the jury? How much of the witness would be shown, and in what video resolution? How are the answers to these questions affected by the facilities at the Superior Court, and the witnesses's sites in Sarajevo and Heidelberg? Would the defense prepare all such facilities?

    Second, in response to your letter requesting whether the government's theory of the case is Attempted Battery Assault or Intent to Frighten Assault, be advised that the government may ask for either or both instructions at the close of evidence.

    Third, as to your request for statements of the defendant pursuant to rule 16(a)(1)(A), I'll provide those statements specified in the rule:

- First, as to recorded statements of your client, please find attached his post-arrest interview.
- Second, as to the written record of oral statements made by your client in response to interrogation from a government agent, I will send a supplemental letter shortly.
- Third, as to the substance of any oral statement made to a government agent, the defendant made statements to Ofc. Cadle, Sgt. Benton, and Lt. Charland. I'll

disclose these statements without regard to whether they were spontaneous or in response to questions, and without regard to whether the government intends to elicit them at trial.

- Your client told Ofc. Cadle that he was a police officer and that he was not drunk. Your client stated that the bouncer grabbed him from behind and carried him out of the bar. Your client stated, in substance, that the bouncer must have felt the gun, and that your client was trying to keep the bouncer from getting it. Your client stated that he was out with a female witness, and further stated that he had 18 years on.
- Sgt. Benton asked your client if he was a cop, and your client responded affirmatively. Sgt. Benton asked if there was an official that your client wanted him to notify, and your client stated he did not have the number for the official.
- Lt. Charland later asked your client if there was an official he should notify, and your client provided contact information.

Finally, I want to verify that you have not requested discovery pursuant to the remaining provisions of Rule 16. If you do intend to request discovery pursuant to Rule 16(a)(1)(C), please notify me and I will provide you with documents and a viewing letter with respect to tangible items of evidence. Regardless of whether you make such a request, I want to confer with you regarding whether you will stipulate to the authenticity of certain documents that the government may seek to introduce at trial, including bar receipts and the ICE firearms policy. Please let me know if you are willing to stipulate to the admission of these documents.

As noted above, I expect to send you a supplemental discovery letter shortly. Please do not hesitate to contact me with any questions or concerns.

Sincerely,

RONALD C. MACHEN
United States Attorney

By: Stephen Rickard
Stephen Rickard
Assistant United States Attorney
Felony Major Crimes
Room 3622
555 Fourth Street, N.W.
Washington, D.C. 20530
Office:
Fax:
E-mail: stephen.rickard@usdoj.gov

APPENDIX E

RFC'D NOV 2 9 2010

Angela Parrott, Esquire
First Assistant Federal Defender
Federal Defenders of Western North Carolina, Inc.
129 West Trade Street, Suite 300
Charlotte, NC 28202

November 18, 2010

Ronald C. Machen, Jr., Esquire
United States Attorney for the District of Columbia
United States Attorney's Office for the District of Columbia
555 4th Street, NW
Washington, DC 20530

Re: Heath Thomas

Dear Mr. Machen:

    I am writing you on behalf of Special Agent Heath Thomas for your consideration in determining whether to prosecute him based on his arrest the evening of August 28, 2010 for assault with a deadly weapon. I am hopeful that my letter gives you further insight regarding Mr. Thomas in your careful consideration of determining whether to proceed against him.

    I have been an assistant federal public defender for the past 14 years, admitted to practice in California and in North Carolina. My practice involves constant interaction with law enforcement. During the past 14 years, I have worked with law enforcement at all stages of federal criminal proceedings, from pre-indictment to appeal. For the most part, I have had good experiences with law enforcement. However, a few agents stand out as true leaders who exemplify all that an agent should be, and Mr. Thomas is one of those agents.

    I have known Mr. Thomas for approximately 12 years. We first met professionally, in early 1998. Mr. Thomas was an INS special agent working in Los Angeles, California, and he was the case agent in one of my cases. The case was a particularly egregious alien smuggling case with 6 defendants and 5 material witnesses. Per office policy, I was appointed to represent the material witnesses, or the victims in the smuggling case. The evidence was gruesome - two of my clients had been gang raped over a two-day period by the six smugglers, and the smugglers, using pliers, tore off half the ear of another of my clients. The compassion, empathy, and dignity with which Mr. Thomas treated my clients was outstanding. Mr. Thomas was just as professional and respectful with the defense attorneys who represented the defendants. The government could have tried its case in its sleep and obtained convictions, as Mr. Thomas' investigation was thorough, detailed, and complete. I also watched Mr. Thomas testify during that trial, and he was one of the most articulate agents I have heard in my career. Mr. Thomas stood out to me because he treated both sides equally, which does not happen as much as it should.

After this smuggling case was over, and approximately one year later, in 1999, Mr. Thomas and I began a personal relationship which lasted over three years. During this personal relationship and while living together, I also saw Mr. Thomas without his "agent" hat. Mr. Thomas is a man who takes his career very seriously and executes his work with the utmost professionalism. He is zealous and tenacious in his work, but always maintains a respectful demeanor.

In September 2001, while we were personally involved, I visited Mr. Thomas in Bosnia where he was the ICE representative in the U.S. Embassy, working with ICITAP. Mr. Thomas worked with foreign law enforcement and government officials and was held in high esteem by those who worked with him. Unfortunately, the events of September 11 took place during my visit. Rather than take any time off to spend it with me, Mr. Thomas immediately reported to the Embassy and other government officials to investigate terrorist activities. Mr. Thomas did not do this because he was ordered to do so, he did it because he cared about his country.

During the 12 years I have known Mr. Thomas, I can confidently say that he never lied to me, and I never saw him lie to anyone else. He is honest to a fault, not even capable of telling a white lie to make me feel better about a haircut.

I have had many opportunities over the years to observe Mr. Thomas in social situations. We have gone to restaurants and bars as a couple, and I have seen him out when we were not dating. Mr. Thomas has self control. He drinks socially, but never to the point of being out of control, drunk, or belligerent. I also have been with Mr. Thomas when officers conducted a traffic stop one evening when we were returning home. Mr. Thomas and I were riding on his motorcycle when the stop took place. The first words out of Mr. Thomas' mouth were not "I am law enforcement" but advising the officer that he was armed and where the officer could locate his firearm. The officer then proceeded to shove Mr. Thomas up against a brick wall. Mr. Thomas did nothing in response to the improper treatment he received. The officer's superiors arrived at the scene a few minutes later, and let us go home, with no citations. The next day, the chief of the police station called and apologized to Mr. Thomas, and indicated that the officer was a rookie who would not be hired after his probation ended.

I have also been with Mr. Thomas when men have made racial and derogatory slurs directed to him, relating to the fact that I am Caucasian and he is Latino. Mr. Thomas never reacted to these comments with a response or body language. I am positive that I would not have been able to restrain myself had such language been directed at me.

I am fully aware of the allegations against Mr. Thomas, and frankly, I do not believe the guard's version of what transpired based on what I know about Mr. Thomas. Mr. Thomas has black belts in Aikido and Judo, and I have seen him at the dojo practicing his art. The emphasis on these martial arts is to diffuse, redirect, and de-escalate a physical encounter. What is more, given the fact that Mr. Thomas takes his job so seriously, I believe that if he took his firearm out of his holster and brandished it, he would have shot the person and not just shown it to him.

I hope that my thoughts about Mr. Thomas assist you in your decision making, and if you have any further questions please call me at ▓▓▓▓▓▓▓▓. Thank you for your consideration.

Sincerely,

Angela Parrott

cc: Heath Thomas
    J. Michael Hannon, Esquire

APPENDIX F

Fw: Holubar

From: **Carole O'Connor** (███████████████) This sender is in your safe list.
Sent: Sat 2/08/14 11:57 AM
To: Shannon Bohrer ███████████████

On Tuesday, January 15, 2013 10:11 PM, Carole O'Connor ███████████████
This is the email that Hannon sent me asking me to contact Holubar.

----- Forwarded Message -----
From: J. Michael Hannon <███████████████
To: Carole O'Connor ███████████████>
Cc: ███████████████
Sent: Friday, August 12, 2011 1:41 PM
Subject: RE: Holubar

Carole,

Send him the following message exactly: "Hi – I am the friend of Heath Thomas, the federal agent, who goes on trial Monday. You might remember seeing and talking to me outside The Guards that night. Would you please call Heath's attorney, ███████████████. Thank you."

Do not respond to any messages you receive from him, as he will report this to the prosecutor. You can just pass them on to us.

Mike

From: Carole O'Connor [███████████████]
Sent: Friday, August 12, 2011 1:03 PM
To: J. Michael Hannon
Subject: Re: Holubar

Mike-
Sure, is it okay if I send him a message directly? Or should someone else try to do it? Emily Brant may have a facebook account. I'm sure I could find someone else if that is better.

Just let me know-
Carole

From: J. Michael Hannon <███████████████
To: ███████████████

APPENDIX G

About Us | Contact Us | Search

Remembering All of Law Enforcement's Heroes

| HOME | MEMORIAL PAGES | RESOURCES | GET INVOLVED | BLOG |

ODMP Remembers...

United States > U.S. Government > United States Department of Justice - Border Patrol > Border Patrol Agent Lawrence B. Pierce

Border Patrol Agent
Lawrence B. Pierce

United States Department of Justice - Border Patrol, U.S. Government

End of Watch: Thursday, August 17, 1995

Share this Memorial

Biographical Info

Age: Not available

Tour of Duty: Not available

Badge Number: Not available

Agent Pierce was killed when he was stabbed in San Ysidro, California, while trying to break up a fight in which another person had just been stabbed. The suspect was apprehended and charged with Agent Pierce's murder.

Print This Memorial >

Update This Memorial >

Incident Details

Cause of Death: Stabbed

Location: California

Date of Incident: August 17, 1995

Weapon Used: Edged weapon; Knife

Suspect Info: Apprehended

APPENDIX H

HANNON LAW GROUP
COUNSELORS AND ATTORNEYS AT LAW
1901 18TH STREET, NW
WASHINGTON, DC 20009

EST. MARCH 17, 2006

www.hannonlawgroup.com

August 17, 2011

J. MICHAEL HANNON *

DANIEL S. CROWLEY*+
EMILY E. BRANT †
PATRICK A. CORBUS
LAW CLERK

* ALSO ADMITTED IN MARYLAND
~ ALSO ADMITTED IN VIRGINIA
• ALSO ADMITTED IN CALIFORNIA
† ADMITTED IN MARYLAND ONLY
SUPERVISION BY J. MICHAEL HANNON

27 WOOD LANE
ROCKVILLE, MARYLAND 20850

11130 FAIRFAX BOULEVARD
SUITE 310
FAIRFAX, VIRGINIA 22030

OF COUNSEL

CHARLES I. CATE•+
DONALD LEWIS WRIGHT
WILLIAM CLAYTON BATCHELOR•+

VIA ELETRONIC TRANSMISSION ONLY

Stephen Rickard
Katherine Sawyer
Assistant United States Attorneys
Felony Major Crimes Unit
555 Indiana Avenue, N.W.
Washington, D.C. 20530

Re: <u>United States of America v. Heath P. Thomas</u>, Case No.: 2010 CF3 16079

Dear Mr. Rickard and Ms. Sawyer:

    Heath P. Thomas intends to call as expert witnesses Shannon B. Bohrer and Kenneth H. Kelly. Their resumes were provided to you. Mr. Bohrer and Mr. Kelly will be available to you in the courtroom tomorrow morning at 10:00 a.m. to discuss their opinions in more detail with one or both of you. I intend to call them as witnesses after the luncheon recess tomorrow. In addition, Mr. Bohrer produced a videotape which I will show to you during the luncheon break tomorrow. I believe it is about 18 minutes long.

    Mr. Bohrer will be offered as an expert in law enforcement and, in particular, use of force, off-duty carry, and holsters. Mr. Bohrer is expected to render the following opinions: (1) Heath P. Thomas is a highly trained, qualified, and experienced law enforcement officer, particularly in the use of force; (2) during the incident of August 28, Heath P. Thomas exercised considerable restraint in the level of force he employed; (3) Heath P. Thomas would have been well within his training and standards in law enforcement to have used force against Marshall Brackett before the struggle outside The Guards; (4) during the struggle with Marshall Brackett, Agent Thomas was faced with the potential use of deadly force against him or others; (5) Agent Thomas was trained in numerous defensive and offensive tactics to retain his weapon at all costs; (6) the circumstances of the struggle would have justified Agent Thomas in "firing the assailant off the gun": i.e. firing the weapon to get Brackett to let go of the weapon; (7) Agent Thomas was wearing an authorized off-duty holster which is designed for concealment; (8) the holster contains only a single retention system, that of friction between the holster and the weapon; (9) in the circumstances in which Agent Thomas found himself, any trained officer would be concerned about the dislodgment of the weapon from the friction holster; (10) Agent Thomas

Letter to Stephen Rickard
July 19, 2011
Page 2 of 3

was acting pursuant to his training to secure his weapon and to prevent it from falling into the hands of Brackett or any other civilian in the area; (11) once the struggle with Brackett ensued, Agent Thomas had the training and the ability, and would have been justified, in using even more aggressive force against Brackett including deadly force; (12) it is highly improbable that Agent Thomas had his finger in the trigger guard of the weapon; (13) once Brackett grabbed the weapon, Agent Thomas no longer controlled the weapon as to its muzzle direction except to attempt to direct it away from himself and others; (14) Agent Thomas could have gained control of the weapon through the defensive measures in which he was trained, but withheld such extreme measures in order to bring Brackett into a stalemate; (15) it is unlikely that Agent Thomas was impaired by alcohol at the time; (16) at all times, Agent Thomas acted consistent with his training as a law enforcement officer; (17) the investigation by MPD of the use of force by a law enforcement officer was inadequate.

Mr. Bohrer will also testify to the training that Agent Thomas received relevant to this incident. He will also address the varying scenarios propounded by Marshall Brackett and Brandon Holubar as to the events outside The Guards. In either scenario propounded by these gentlemen, Mr. Bohrer believes the above opinions apply. He will also illustrate his testimony with a videotape of a demonstration performed by Agent Thomas and a colleague. In addition, Mr. Bohrer may opine about varying standards in law enforcement regarding carrying weapons while drinking alcohol and the individual decisions made by law enforcement officers regarding this practice.

Mr. Bohrer is basing his opinions on his experience, which is well outlined in his resume and on the internet. He has watched the trial, he has interviewed Agent Thomas, and he has conducted a view of The Guards. He has reviewed the exhibits and the Jencks material provided by the government.

Mr. Kelly will testify as an expert in the field of martial arts in the context of law enforcement and its complement to weapons training. Mr. Kelly is expected to render the following opinions: (1) Heath P. Thomas is a highly trained, qualified, and experienced martial arts expert; (2) during the incident of August 28, Heath P. Thomas exercised considerable restraint in the level of force he employed; (3) Heath P. Thomas would have been well within his training and standards in law enforcement to have used force against Marshall Brackett before the struggle outside The Guards; (4) in refraining from using force while inside The Guards, Agent Thomas showed restraint in order to prevent his weapon from being dislodged and becoming available to a civilian; (5) during the struggle with Marshall Brackett, it is unlikely that Agent Thomas had only one hand on the weapon; (6) Agent Thomas was trained in numerous defensive and offensive tactics to retain his weapon at all costs; (7) it is highly improbable that Agent Thomas had his finger in the trigger guard of the weapon; (8) Agent Thomas could have gained control of the weapon through the defensive measures in which he was trained, but withheld such extreme measures in order to bring Brackett into a stalemate; (9) it is unlikely that Agent Thomas was impaired by alcohol at the time; (10) at all times, Agent Thomas acted consistently with his training.

Letter to Stephen Rickard
July 19, 2011
Page 3 of 3

    Mr. Kelly has reviewed the same materials as Mr. Bohrer. He has also interviewed Thomas Snowden, Agent Thomas' longtime martial arts instructor. Mr. Kelly has viewed the videotape produced by Mr. Bohrer. Mr. Kelly has also interviewed Stan Huff, a colleague of Agent Thomas.

    I can assure you that had your colleagues and supervisors afforded appropriate attention to this case, this information could have been provided long ago.

    Thank you for your courtesies.

                          Sincerely,

                          s/J. Michael Hannon

                          J. Michael Hannon

APPENDIX I

Superior Court of the District of Columbia
CRIMINAL DIVISION
SUBPOENA

UNITED STATES
DISTRICT OF COLUMBIA

vs.   Case No. 2010 CF3 016079

Heath P. Thomas

To: Mark Flemming
2915 M Street, NW, Washington, D.C. 20007

YOU ARE HEREBY COMMANDED:

To appear before the Criminal Division room/courtroom __215__ of the Superior Court of the District of Columbia, 500 Indiana Avenue/Judiciary Center, 555 Fourth Street, N.W., Washington, D.C. on the __15th__ day of __August__, 20 __11__, at __9:30__ (a.m.)/p.m. as a witness for __Heath P. Thomas__

[X] and bring with you __Cell phone records for August 28, 2010.__

and do not depart from the Court without leave thereof.

WITNESS, the Honorable Chief Judge of the Superior Court, and the seal of said Court this ____ day of ____

To service Processor 7/22

Officer in Charge ____ District ____

Attorney for Government/Defendant

Phone No. (202) 232-1907

Authorization as required by D.C. Code § 14-307 and *Brown v. U.S.*, 567 A. 2d 426 (D.C. 1989), is hereby given for issuance of subpoena for medical records.

Date	Judge

RETURN ON THIS SUBPOENA IS REQUIRED ON OR BEFORE THIS DATE:

[ ] I hereby certify that I have personally served, or have executed as shown in "**REMARKS**," the above subpoena on the individual at the address below.

Name and Title of Individual Served	Address (If different than shown above)

[ ] I hereby certify that, after diligent investigation, I am unable to locate the individuals, company, corporation, etc., named in above subpoena for the reason(s) as shown in "**REMARKS**."

Date(s) of Endeavor	Date and Time of Service

REMARKS	Signature of Title of Server

APPENDIX J

Shannon B. Bohrer
15436 Sixes Road
Emmitsburg, Maryland 21727

Education:
A.A. Degree in Law Enforcement and Corrections from the Community College of Baltimore, Baltimore, Maryland. B.S. Degree in Criminal Justice Administration from the University of Baltimore, Baltimore, Maryland, and a Master in Business Administration from Frostburg State University, Frostburg, Maryland. Additional Graduate work in Adult Education, University of Virginia and Virginia Tech.

Employment and Work History:
Winterbilt L.L.C., Criminal justice training, program development, expert witness and consulting for criminal justice community.
Maryland Police and Correctional Training Commissions, Range Master and Use of Force Administrator, April 1999 – March 2010.
Federal Bureau of Investigation, Instructor, firearms training unit, Quantico, Virginia-May 1, 1995 to April 29, 1999
Maryland State Police, Undercover police officer, uniform road patrolman, criminal investigator, road supervisor, duty officer, assistant barrack commander, teacher, firearms instructor/armorer, program manager -1968 to 1995

Current employment is part-time/self-employed, Teaching and presentation work for the Institute for Intergovernmental Research through the Bureau of Justice Assistance. Additional part-time work includes presentations for officer safety, supervising for safety and research on critical incidents and expert witnesses.

My last full-time position involved writing entrance and instructor-level programs, teaching all levels, supervising range employees, and managing the range complex. The range complex was used by 35 local, State, and federal agencies. The position included conducting research, primary and secondary, and keeping current with training methods. The role also involved communicating and working with law enforcement departments from all over the State, developing special programs as requested, and certifying all firearms instructors and programs in the State. Additionally, I administered the Firearms Safety Program.

My position with the Federal Bureau of Investigation involved teaching firearms to entry-level students, researching and updating programs, and working on special projects. Programs included Deadly Force research and the National Academy. The National Academy program was a 15-hour non-credited course on management issues related to training and the use of deadly force in law enforcement.

Shannon Bohrer
Employment and Work History: Cont.

My last position with the Maryland State Police was as the Agency Firearms Instructor/Armorer in the Training Division. The position involved writing programs and courses for 97 field instructors to teach and writing and teaching recruit-level and in-service classes. Responsible for reviewing agency shootings and use of firearms equipment, research of firearms and firearms-related equipment and critical incidents, developing and teaching firearms instructor schools, and developing and teaching courses for requesting agencies. Additionally, I coordinated the scheduling, use, and maintenance of a training facility, the Liberty Firearms Range, with other State Police units and 25 local, State, and federal agencies.

Specialized Experience:
July 1996, wrote and taught the "Deadly Force Management" course for the F.B.I. National Academy.
November 1998, a panel member on an FBI SATCAST program on "Deadly Force Management."
January 1999, assisted in coordinating, developing, and teaching a one-day course/workshop program on deadly force issues for the United States Attorney's Office in Washington, DC.
From 1999 thru 2005, guest instructor for the "Perspectives on the Use of Force" presented for the United States Attorneys Office, Department of Justice, F.B.I. Academy Quantico, Virginia.
From 1999 thru 2006, assisted with a special project, *"Violent Encounters*, A Study of Felonious Assaults on Our Nation's Law Enforcement Officers ."This was a grant for a continuation of two previous research projects: *"Killed in the Line of Duty"* and *"In the Line of Fire".*
April 2004, 2005, 2006, 2007, 2008, and 2009 a presenter at the International Law Enforcement & Educators and Trainers Association Conference, Chicago, Ill.
June 2004, a panel member for "The Nature & Influence of Intuition in Law Enforcement", sponsored by The U.S. Department of Justice, F.B.I., Behavioral Science Unit, American Psychological Association and the National Institute of Justice, at Marymount University in Virginia.
January 2005, a presenter and member at "The Future of Law Enforcement, Safety Training in the Face of Terrorism," F.B.I. Academy, Quantico, Virginia.
September 2007, program developer and instructor for the "Perspectives on the Use of Force" presented for the United States Attorneys Office, Department of Justice, MPCTC Firearms Training Unit Sykesville, Maryland.
December 2008, panel member and presenter for CIAG, (Critical Incident Analysis Group) on "Suicide by Cop" conference at the University of Virginia.
January 2009, guest presenter "Deadly Mix" United State Secret Service, Beltsville, Maryland.
August 2009, panel member for NIJ grant project "More Precise Deadly Force Metrics: Developing New Tools for Research & Practice." with Bryan Vila, Ph.D., Washington State University, Spokane, Washington.
Presenter for Law Enforcement Safety classes; "The Deadly Mix" Bureau of Justice Assistance Grant project, sponsored by Fairfax County Police Department, Fairfax, Virginia, 2010.
Guest lectured at the National Academy in a "Violence in America" class taught by the Behavioral Science Unit.

Shannon Bohrer
Specialized Experience, Cont.

Guest lectured at the Maryland State Police Academy on communication skills, listening, and study habits.
Testified and given depositions in both state and federal courts as an expert witness on the use of force by police officers.

Articles published:
"Lesson Plans" *Police Marksman*, May/June 1996
"Foot Chases" *F.B.I. Law Enforcement Bulletin*, co-written, May 2000
"Technique Accuracy & Speed" *Police Marksman*, March/April 2004
"Off-duty Training" *Police Marksman*, co-written, March/April 2004
"The Power & Influence of an Instructor, *ILEETA Digest*, June 2004
"Finger off the Trigger" *Police Marksman,* July/August 2004
"How Presentation Affects Student Learning – 10-06 Rules", *ILLETA Digest* December 2004
"After Firing the Shots, What Happens?" *F.B.I. Law Enforcement Bulletin*, September 2005
"When the Hair on the Back of Your Neck Stands Up – Listen To It" *Police Marksman* September/October 2005
"The Deadly Mix" is a chapter in the book "W.I.N. Critical Issues in Training and Leading Warriors" by Brian Willis, 2008.
"The Deadly Dilemma, Soot or Don't Shoot?" co-written, *F.B.I. Law Enforcement Bulletin*, March 2008
"Law Enforcement Perspective on the Use of Force – Hands-On, Experiential Training for Prosecuting Attorneys", *F.B.I. Law Enforcement Bulletin*, co-written, April 2009.
"Police Investigations of the Use of Deadly Force Can Influence Perceptions and Outcomes." *F.B.I. Law Enforcement Bulletin*, co-written, January 2010.
"What I Learned With Experience, I Wish I Knew Before Experiencing," a chapter in a book titled If I Knew Then, Life Lessons From Cops on the Street", by Brian R Willis, April 2010

Continuing Education:
Maryland State Police Entrance Level Academy 1968
Maryland State Police Annual-In-Service 1968-1995
Maryland State Police Firearms Instructor School 1985
Maryland State Police Officer Survival Instructor School 1987
Monadnock PR-24 Baton Instructor School 1987
Maryland Police and Correctional Training Commissions Instructors School 1989
Beretta U.S.A. Armorer School 1992
U.S. Secret Service Firearms Instructors School 1992

Shannon Bohrer
Continuing Education, Cont.

Calibre Press Street Survival School 1993
U.S. Department of Justice, Officer Survival School/Seminar 1993
NRA Rifle Instructor Development School 1994
Smith & Wesson Pistol Armorer School 1994
Walther Armorer School 1995
Sturm, Ruger (pistol, revolver, Mini-14) Armorer School 1995
Smith & Wesson Revolver Armorer School 1995
Remington Shotgun Armorer School 1996
Glock Armorer School 1997
Jerry Barnhart's Tactical Pistol Training Course 1998
Jerry Barnhart's Tactical Pistol and Rifle Course 1998
Federal Bureau of Investigation, Counter-Sniper Course 1998
Range Development & Operations Conference, National Rifle Association 2000
Glock Armorer School 2003
Colt Defense L.L.C. Armorer Certification, 2007
Sturm, Ruger, Mini 14 Armorer School, 2007

Affiliations:

Personal:

References:
Upon request,

APPENDIX K

Law Enforcement Perspective on the Use of Force
Hands-On, Experiential Training for Prosecuting Attorneys

By ANTHONY J. PINIZZOTTO, Ph.D., EDWARD F. DAVIS, M.A., SHANNON BOHRER, M.B.A., and ROBERT CHENEY

In 1998, Washington, D.C., experienced a period of high crime and violence with a number of incidents involving officers who used deadly force. These cases generated media attention concerning alleged abuse of deadly force by members of the police department. Citizens began demanding a judicial review of these shootings. At the same time, the city selected a new police chief from an outside agency. The new chief requested assistance from the U.S. Attorney's Office of the District of Columbia to review these use-of-force cases, as well as any subsequent ones that might occur. To this end, the U.S. attorney requested assistance from the director of the FBI to create a training program for senior prosecutors of the newly established Civil Rights Unit responsible for investigating the use of deadly force by law enforcement officers. The goal of the training was to give these attorneys a realistic experience that would help them gain a better understanding of the use of force from a law enforcement perspective.[1]

The authors developed an initiative that included collaborative efforts by both firearms training and behavioral science personnel at the FBI Academy. The main intention of the project centered on placing prosecuting attorneys in the shoes of officers on the street who may become involved in deadly force incidents.

The authors based the program on a variety of factors, such as law enforcement experience and training, the interrelated aspects of research, and case consultation. Together, they had a combined amount of law enforcement service equaling more than 100 years that included actually employing deadly force, investigating such actions, and extensive training in the use of firearms. Their research focused not only on the use of deadly force against law enforcement but also by officers themselves. It involved numerous in-depth interviews with officers who had survived critical incidents where subjects had used force against them, as well as with offenders convicted of murdering law enforcement officers or feloniously assaulting them. The resulting publications detailed the varying perspectives of these officers and offenders.[2] The authors also consulted with members of local, state, and federal law enforcement on the aspects of perception, memory, and recall during a critical incident; wound ballistics; action-reaction models; sensory distortion; and facing edged and other weapons, including hands and feet.[3]

THE PROGRAM

To give attorneys the perspective of an officer, the authors employed an interactive video simulator that played scenarios requiring the participants to decide whether to engage the use of deadly force. Some of these allowed such

The main intention of the project centered on placing prosecuting attorneys in the shoes of officers...who may become involved in deadly force incidents.

action and others presented a no-shoot situation. The different scenarios enabled the attorneys to describe and justify their actions in a particular set of circumstances and generated discussion from other attorneys in the classroom who witnessed the events.

These discussions, held prior to replaying the particular scenario, had the attorneys who acted as officers describe in detail as much as they could recall concerning the circumstances of the incident, including descriptions and actions of the alleged offenders; activity of any partners present; number of shots fired, if any; who fired the shots; and justification for the use of force, if used. The attorneys who played the role of witnesses then had to describe what they saw at the scene. After these exchanges, the authors replayed the specific scenario. The results and highlights of the discussions that emanated from this hands-on training follow.

Justification of Action

After each scenario, the attorneys had to explain their actions as officers. In a large segment of the cases, most of the attorneys fired their weapons *only* after being shot at. They based their justification for shooting on the fact that their lives were in clear and present danger. They identified this threat not only as the presence of a weapon but because the suspect had fired at them first.

Ballistic Issues

While many attorneys did shoot and could justify their actions, most fired only one or two rounds and, in many cases, did not incapacitate their assailants. When questioned, the attorneys stated that they believed only one or two shots would disable someone. Additionally, they assumed that their shots actually hit the subjects. In some instances, however, this proved incorrect as some of their shots clearly missed their intended targets.

Subsequent instruction to the attorneys included dispelling the "one shot drop" myth. The authors explained that a person, upon being shot, generally does not become immediately powerless, unlike many portrayals in television shows and movies.[4] Experts agree that the only true instant incapacitation is caused either by the disruption of the central nervous system or from significant blood loss wherein individuals lose 20 percent of the volume of their blood, which can take 8 to 10 seconds to accomplish.[5] In situations where officers must fire their handguns, considered as defensive weapons, these rarely result in the instantaneous debilitation of their assailants. This is why officers are taught to continue to shoot until the threat ceases or is eliminated.

Perception, Memory, and Recall

During initial discussions of the scenarios, the attorneys acting as officers and those cast as witnesses disagreed on several important issues: what occurred on the scene, how many shots were fired, and who shot first. Only after the class reviewed each scenario did the participants reach an agreement as to what had happened and the number and origin of shots fired.

The attorneys also achieved a better understanding as to why witnesses often contradict each other. They came to realize that witnesses can differ slightly or even profoundly about what took place, and their recollections may change over time. Memory, in most situations, is

constructive; it does not operate as a videotape recorder. Under critical or traumatic circumstances, perception, memory, and retrieval have a greater likelihood of being affected by the intensity and duration of the event.[6]

Action Versus Reaction

The two-phase model of action versus reaction demonstrates why, in some instances, officers are killed or debilitated without returning fire with their service weapons. In the action phase of one scenario, the attorneys saw the offender draw a handgun and point it at the officer who is taken by surprise. Then, in the reaction phase, they witnessed the officer attempt to draw and fire *quicker* than the offender who can simply pull the trigger. Because this is not possible in most situations, officers are killed or wounded before they can react to the threat.

This model also explains why officers sometimes have shot someone in the back while both consciously and truthfully believing that they shot the person in the chest. In these cases, the individuals turned and ran as the officers drew their weapons. Because of the time lag between the officer's decision to draw and fire the weapon and the physical completion of the act, the person had the opportunity to change position. Action versus reaction is linear and compatibility dependant; that is, action does not always beat reaction.[7]

Myths and Misconceptions

As the attorneys participated in the interactive video scenarios, some made comments and statements that often appeared founded in myths from television shows and movies. As one attorney noted, "The major benefit is educating us about the realities of a shoot. I had no idea that things really went down as they did. I bought into the Hollywood mythology entirely."

Edged Weapons

Collectively, the attorneys reported that they did not view edged weapons to be as great a threat to their safety as firearms. However, edged weapons are the second leading cause of homicides in the United States behind handguns.[8] Assailants continue to kill more people with edged weapons than with rifles and shotguns combined. As such, law enforcement officers follow the safety rule of 21 feet: if a subject armed with an edged weapon comes within 21 feet before an officer can draw and fire a weapon, the officer could be seriously injured or even killed.[9]

Other Weapons

The attorneys thought that a person without any visible weapon was not a threat. But, in fact, if officers are incapacitated by a punch or a kick, their own service weapons can be taken and used against them.

Decision Making

Another myth held by the attorneys involved the decision-making process. When an officer in a movie decides to shoot someone, it often is portrayed in slow motion, appearing to give the officer more than enough time. In fact, officers have only a split second to decide whether to shoot. Moreover, they often must form this crucial decision based on limited information.

Subjects Killed

Many of the attorneys believed that law enforcement officers kill a much greater number of subjects than can be substantiated by facts. In reality, officers often refrain from

During initial discussions of the scenarios, the attorneys acting as officers and those cast as witnesses disagreed on several important issues....

the use of deadly force. Several studies have demonstrated that the majority of officers had many more opportunities to use justifiable deadly force than actually did. "After all, in more simplistic terms, it often is not the officer's *decision* to use deadly force but the suspect's *actions* that require it."[10]

THE FINDINGS

This first training effort was well received by the attorneys who attended. They offered positive feedback, expressed an appreciation of the insights and materials presented, and recommended expanding the training to other attorneys within the U.S. Department of Justice. Comments from the attorneys included—

- "Very helpful, informative, eye-opening, at times even moving."
- "Thanks for giving the course. It sure has made me rethink deadly force cases."
- "I have a newfound respect for law enforcement training and decision-making processes."
- "I learned a lot about action/reaction and how most deadly force scenarios happen much faster than one would think."

The authors eventually expanded the course in both time and content. Most important, they added a live-fire exercise so the attorneys could experience actually using a firearm. Attendees at these subsequent classes included attorneys for state and local governments, trial attorneys from the U.S. Department of Justice, Civil Rights Division, as well as general counsel for large police departments. Commanders of units within these law enforcement agencies charged with the responsibility of investigating deadly force incidents also attended these additional classes.

The training proved a learning experience for both the attorneys and the instructors. The attorneys willingly participated and raised many issues. The authors instructed them to question everything they encountered in the training, and they did. From their inquiries and comments, several important issues arose. One student approached two of the authors and expressed the need for expanded training on perception, memory, and recall. She told them that prior to this training, she thought all officers involved in a deadly force incident should report exactly the same story. But, after attending the training, she realized that individuals can view similar circumstances in different ways, and those specific memories, in fact, may change over time.

As for the authors, they fully recognized that the attorneys never could experience certain realities firsthand. These obviously would include the actual consequences of using deadly force, such as post-traumatic stress disorder, media scrutiny, excessive legal review prior to the return to duty, stress placed on family members, and peer pressure. Losing a gunfight in a simulator never can compare with losing one on the street. But, giving prosecuting attorneys the experience of making a decision in the use of deadly force—with limited information and in a fraction of a second—can have far-reaching effects long after they complete the training.

THE RECOMMENDATIONS

The authors recommend that local and state law enforcement agencies consider developing training programs for attorneys charged with reviewing the use of deadly force by their officers. These departments should take into account several issues when developing this type

Losing a gunfight in a simulator never can compare with losing one on the street.

of training. Using scenarios that are simple, slow moving, and with obvious choices will cause participants to believe that the decision-making process is easy. They may not fully understand and appreciate the complexities and difficulties of the issues being taught. Conversely, fast-paced, high-speed, and complicated scenarios tend to overwhelm attendees. They may believe that the instructors are trying to make them fail. After all, this training should be difficult and challenging but obtainable.

Law enforcement agencies also may want to offer a similar course for those outside the criminal justice system, such as members of the media, civic organizations, seated grand juries, and human-interest groups. Many departments conduct citizen academies and could include this training in the existing curriculum.[11]

CONCLUSION

The goal of this hands-on, experiential training was to place U.S. attorneys in the shoes of objective, reasonable law enforcement officers who must use deadly force. The attorneys experienced anxiety in reporting the decisions they made during these high-stress but nonthreatening scenarios. It gave them some insight into what officers may experience when their lives and those of the citizens they have sworn to protect are in jeopardy. While remaining objective and emotionally distant in each investigation, these attorneys now have additional information to make clear, equitable reviews. They also have gained a significant understanding of the effects of these agonizing events on those law enforcement officers compelled to use deadly force. ✦

Endnotes

[1] For additional information on legal issues surrounding the use of force by

APPENDIX L

Contact Us
- Your Local FBI Office
- Overseas Offices
- Submit a Crime Tip
- Report Internet Crime
- More Contacts

Learn About Us
- Quick Facts
- What We Investigate
- Natl. Security Branch
- Information Technology
- Fingerprints & Training
- Laboratory Services
- Reports & Publications
- History
- More About Us

Get Our News
- Press Room
- E-mail Updates
- News Feeds

Be Crime Smart
- Wanted by the FBI
- More Protections

Use Our Resources
- For Law Enforcement
- For Communities
- For Researchers
- More Services

Visit Our Kids' Page

Apply for a Job

Feature

Police Investigations of the Use of Deadly Force Can Influence Perceptions and Outcomes

By Shannon Bohrer, M.B.A., and Robert Chaney

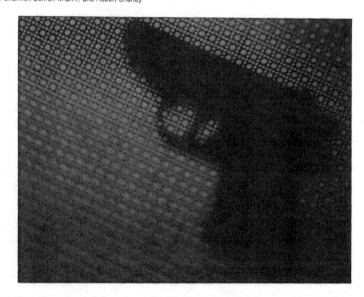

Basic law enforcement training covers using force, including deadly force, and investigating even those involving assaults and shootings by police. The relationship between these two e the use of force and the police investigation of this use of force—can have far-reaching consequences, both good and bad, for the public, the department, and the officers involved.

The law enforcement profession spends considerable time and resources training officers to firearms and other weapons and to understand the constitutional standards and agency polic concerning when they can employ such force. Society expects this effort because of the pos consequences of officers not having the skills they need if and when they become involved ir critical incident.

In addition to receiving instruction about the use of force, officers are taught investigative tec They must reconstruct the incident, find the facts, and gather evidence to prosecute the offer And, historically, they have done this extremely well. But, is the same amount of attention pa examining the investigative process of the use of deadly force and how this can affect what c after such an event? Are there any reasons why the police should approach the investigation officer-involved shooting differently? To help answer these questions, the authors present an overview of perceptions about these events and some elements that law enforcement agenc incorporate into investigations of officer-involved shootings that can help ensure fair and judi outcomes.

PERCEPTIONS OF DEADLY FORCE

All law enforcement training is based on the two elements of criticality and frequency. Skills t
officers need and are required to have to perform their duties fall into both:
1) how often they use them and 2) how crucial it is to have them. Training officers to handle
potentially lethal incidents, by nature, is vitally important. Investigating officer-involved shooti
constitutes a critical function, but, for most departments, it does not occur that frequently. On
examining training needs from the perspective of preparation for the event does not necessa
into account what can occur afterward. Just because the officer had the right to shoot and th
evidence supports the officer's actions may not guarantee a positive, or even a neutral, rece
from the public.

In addition, *who* the police shoot seems to mold some perceptions. For example, a bank rob
armed with a shotgun presents a different connotation than a 14-year-old thief wielding a kni
Sometimes, it is who the police shoot that also can set the tone for the direction of the invest
surrounding the incident.

The Officer's Perception

Mr. Bohrer, a retired Maryland State Police sergeant, is the range master for the Maryland Police and Correctional Training Commissions in Sykesville.

Mr. Chaney, a retired homicide detective, currently serves as the deputy director of the Office of Intergovernmental and Public Liaison, U.S. Department of Justice.

Interviews conducted with offic
have been involved in shootin
revealed that while many were
trained for the event, they ofte
not prepared for the investigat
afterward.[4] Some believed tha
investigations centered on finc
something that officers did wrc
they could be charged with a
a violation of departmental pol
Others felt that the investigatic
for the protection of the agenc
not necessarily the officers inv

Officers can have broad perce
that often depend upon their
experiences of being involved
critical incident or knowledge
has happened to other officers
A trooper with the Arizona De
of Public Safety commented, "
choose to take that man's life.
chose to die when he drew a
an officer. It was not
my choice; it was his."[7]

The Public's Perception

Perceptions by the public of officer-involved shootings usually are as wide and diverse as the
population, often driven by media coverage, and sometimes influenced by a long-standing b
mistrust of government.[8] Documented cases of riots, property damage, and loss of life have
in communities where residents have perceived a police shooting as unjustified. Some memt
the public seem to automatically assume that the officer did something wrong before any
investigation into the incident begins. Conversely, others believe that if the police shot somet
individual must not have given the officer any choice.

The Department's Perception

Departmental perceptions can prove diverse and difficult to express. For example, when inte one chief of police advised that "it is sometimes easier to go through an officer being killed in of duty than a questionable police shooting."[9] The chief was referring to the public's response including civil unrest, to what was perceived as an unjustified police shooting. At various leve however, administrators may feel that a full and fair investigation will clear up any negative perceptions by the public. While not all-inclusive, departmental perceptions include many ins when an officer-involved shooting was viewed with clear and objective clarity before, during, the investigation.[10]

ELEMENTS OF THE INVESTIGATION

Few events in law enforcement attract the attention of the media, the political establishment, police administration more than an officer-involved shooting. In some instances, such intense can affect the investigation. Is this scrutiny related to the incident, the investigation, or both? affect the focus and outcome of the investigation? And, conversely, can the investigative proc influence this close observation of the incident?[11]

With these issues in mind, the authors offer six elements for investigating officer-involved sh While they are not meant to be all-inclusive or broad enough to cover every conceivable situa they can be useful as a guide.

The Investigators

The first element involves investigators who have correct and neutral attitudes. Not all officer suited to conducting police-shooting investigations. Examining such incidents requires open-experienced investigators who have empathy toward the involved officers and members of th general public. Starting with the right investigators will ensure that the process has a solid fou

If possible, at least two primary investigators should oversee the case from the beginning unt end. They should be responsible for such activities as supervising the crime scene investigat reviewing witness statements and evidence and laboratory reports, and coordinating with the justice system. They should not be heavily involved in the initial routine investigation except f handling the interaction with the involved officers, including taking statements.

The Crime Scene

The second element entails the appropriate response to and protection of the crime scene. F or criminal investigators should protect the site. They need to take their time and broaden the protected area, possibly adding a safety zone beyond the immediate vicinity. They should es press area with a public information officer available to respond to media inquiries.

Before inspecting the crime scene, the investigators should videotape it and the surrounding then periodically videotape the area, along with any crowds and parked vehicles, during the the examination. Such information may prove valuable later in locating additional witnesses. should use up-to-date technology and evidence-gathering methods, calling on experts as ne

Before releasing the crime scene, the investigators should consult with the criminal justice of who will be responsible for the case. It can be easier to explain the circumstances of the incid while still in control of the location where it occurred.[12]

The Involved Officers

Removing the involved officers from the scene as soon as possible and taking them to a sec location away from other witnesses and media personnel constitute the third element. The investigators need to explain to the officers that these actions will help maintain the integrity case. They also should invite the officers to stay within a protected area to participate in the f investigation. When possible, they should only take statements from the involved officers onc clearly understand all of the facts and crime scene information. Moreover, in the initial and ea stages of the investigation, authorities never should release the names or any personal inforr the involved officers.[13]

Sometimes, it is beneficial for involved officers to revisit the crime scene later to help them re events. If at all possible, the investigators should accompany them.

It is important to keep the involved officers informed. Someone should contact them on a reg basis. In many agencies, the officers have advocates, including peer support, union represer and legal aid. Keeping the officers advised may require the investigators to go through the advocate.[14]

The Civilian Witnesses

The fourth element highlights the importance of investigators gaining the confidence and res civilian witnesses. After all, they need their assistance. In most cases, investigators should h them the same way as involved officers.

Before interviewing the witnesses, investigators should have a full understanding of the crim and the facts of the shooting. If any statements conflict with the crime scene examination or information from other people who observed the incident, investigators should have the witne view a crime scene videotape or take them back to the site to help them recall events. They wish to consult with the criminal justice investigating authority beforehand to ensure that the does not invade the privacy or cause harm to the witnesses. And, of course, investigating au never should release any information concerning the witnesses.

The Criminal Justice Authorities

The fifth element, the need to have these cases vetted through the criminal justice process a as possible, proves critical to the involved officers, their families, and their employing agencie Sometimes, backlogs may delay report completion but should not hinder clearance procedur Close consultation with the appropriate criminal justice authority may alleviate the need for a completed formal report if a written statement for the proper authority confirms the facts. For example, medical examiners and ballistic experts can provide their findings to investigators v formal reports to follow.

Presentations of the investigation should include all videotapes, photographs, and copies of statements, investigative reports, and other necessary documents. Throughout the criminal ju proceedings, investigators should update the involved officers and their departments about t progress of the case.

The Media

As the final element, the department's public information officer should contact the media be representatives approach the agency.[16] In the early stages of the investigation, the departme should demonstrate that it wants to cooperate with the media. By informing the public throug releases and interviews, the agency shows that it is investigating the incident and that as infc can be released, it *will* be. Departments should remember that the proverbial "no comment" gives the impression that the police are hiding something.

Without a positive relationship with the media, poor communication between the public and the police can d creating a lack of faith in the management and operatio department and mistrust from all parties. The time to pre press releases for officer-involved shootings is *before* o occurs.

In addition, agencies should encourage the media to pri air stories on the responsibilities of officers and the train conducted to enhance their abilities. General informatio shootings, simulator experiences, and the perspective of the reasonable objective officer can develop a cooperative association.[17] Such a collaborative effort between the police and the [media is] not a magic pill and will not alleviate all of the public misperceptions and problems. However, [it may] reduce or prevent false perceptions, especially with officer-involved shootings.[18]

Finally, investigators should review all of the related printed materials and media interviews t[o identify] further witnesses and, if needed, interview them as soon as possible. Sometimes, these indiv[iduals] may not understand why the police would want to interview them after they have talked to the [media,] so a diplomatic approach can prove helpful. This highlights the importance of a positive work[ing] relationship that often can result in shared information between the media and the police.

CONCLUSION

Often, it is not a law enforcement shooting that generates negative consequences, but, rathe[r,] how the involved agency handles the incident that can foster and feed misperceptions. As a [Santa] Monica, California, police officer pointed out, "No one knows about the hundreds of instance[s a] police officer decides not to shoot. Perhaps, no one cares. After all, people say we're trained [to] handle such things, as if training somehow removes or dilutes our humanity."[19]

While the six elements presented in this article may not be all-inclusive, they offer an outline [to] reduce the negative events that sometimes occur in these situations. Having the appropriate investigators and a positive working relationship with the media constitute the bookends of a[n] effective process. After all, the right investigators are the foundation for a thorough investigat[ion, and] a cooperative connection with the media forms the basis of public understanding. Joining tog[ether] and sharing information can help both the police and the media deal with officer-involved sho[otings in] a fair and judicious manner.

Endnotes

[1] Darrel W. Stephens, foreword to *Deadly Force: What We Know*, by William A. Geller and M[ichael] S. Scott (Washington, DC: Police Executive Research Forum, 1992).

[2] For an overview of legal concerns, see Thomas D. Petrowski, "Use-of-Force Policies and T[raining: A Reasoned Approach," *FBI Law Enforcement Bulletin*, October 2002, 25-32 and Part Two, November 2002, 24-32.

[3] Shannon Bohrer, Harry Kern, and Edward Davis, "The Deadly Dilemma: Shoot or Don't Sh[oot," *FBI] Law Enforcement Bulletin*, March 2008, 7-12; Larry
C. Brubaker, "Deadly Force: A 20-Year Study of Fatal Encounters," *FBI Law Enforcement Bu[lletin*,] April 2002, 6-13; and George T. Williams, "Reluctance to Use Deadly Force: Causes, Conse[quences,] and Cures," FBI Law Enforcement Bulletin, October 1999, 1-5.

[4] Anthony J. Pinizzotto, Edward F. Davis, and Charles E. Miller III, U.S. Department of Justic[e,] Federal Bureau of Investigation, *In the Line of Fire: Violence Against Law Enforcement* (Was[hington,] DC, 1997); and *Violent Encounters: A Study of Felonious Assaults on Our Nation's Law Enfc[rcement] Officers* (Washington, DC, 2006).

[5] Interviews with students attending the Management Issues: Law Enforcement's Use of Dea[dly] Force course taught at the FBI's National Academy from 1995 through 1999. The FBI hosts f[our 10-] week National Academy sessions each year during which law enforcement executives from a[round] the world come together to attend classes in various criminal justice subjects.

[6] Feedback from students attending the Instructor Training Liability Issues course taught at t[he FBI] Firearms Instructor Schools, Sykesville, Maryland, from 2001 through 2009.

[7] American Association of State Troopers, *AAST Trooper Connection*, September 2008.

[8] U.S. Department of Justice, Community Relations Service, *Police Use of Excessive Force: Conciliation Handbook for the Police and the Community* (Washington, DC, June 1999). This publication provides options for addressing controversy surrounding the use of excessive or [deadly] force and offers guidelines for resolving community disputes. Readers can access http://www.usdoj.gov/crs/pubs/pdexcess.htm for the June 2002 updated version.

[9] In 1993, Edward F. Davis was an instructor in the FBI Academy's Behavioral Science Unit [who] interviewed the chief about police and the use of force. The chief's comment could be miscor[strued] because it was part of a larger dialogue about police use of force and community relations, a[nd]

it demonstrates perceived and sometimes real concerns. Specifically, the chief was referring fact that the department seemed to pull together when an officer
is killed and the opposite often occurs when the shooting is questioned in the media.

[10] Because of Robert Chaney's (one of this article's authors) extensive experience in investig police shootings while serving with the Washington, D.C., Metropolitan Police Department ar reviewing such incidents for final disposition when later employed by the U.S. Attorney's Offic the District of Columbia, he understands the value of the process and how this can affect pub perceptions and investigative outcomes.

[11] William A. Geller and Michael S. Scott, *Deadly Force: What We Know* (Washington, DC: F Executive Research Forum, 1992).

[12] Robert Chaney's (one of this article's authors) experience includes a close working relatio with the criminal justice authority (in his case, the criminal justice authority was the U.S. Attor Office). The close working relationship can be critical with shootings that have
the potential for negative publicity.

[13] U.S. Department of Justice, Community Relations Service, Police Use of Excessive Force Conciliation Handbook for the Police and the Community.

[14] Laurence Miller, "Officer-Involved Shooting: Reaction Patterns, Response Protocols, and Psychological Intervention Strategies," *International Journal of Emergency Mental Health* 8, ((2006): 239-254.

[15] Henry Pierson Curtis, "Deadly Force Investigations Can Take Years in Some Florida Cour *Orlando Sentinel*, November 11, 2007; Todd Coleman, "Documenting the Use of Force," *FBI Enforcement Bulletin*, November 2007, 18-23; and Geller and Scott.

[16] For additional information, see Brian Parsi Boetig and Penny A. Parrish, "Proactive Media Relations: The Visual Library Initiative," FBI Law Enforcement Bulletin, November 2008, 7-9; D. Sewell, "Working with the Media in Times of Crisis: Key Principles for Law Enforcement," Enforcement Bulletin, March 2007, 1-6; and Dennis Staszak, "Media Trends and the Public Information Officer," FBI Law Enforcement Bulletin, March 2001, 10-13.

[17] Brook A. Masters, "Under the Gun: I Died, I Killed, and I Saw the Nature of Deadly Force,' *Washington Post*, February 13, 2000.

[18] Anthony J. Pinizzotto, Edward Davis, Shannon Bohrer, and Robert Chaney, "Law Enforce Perspective on the Use of Force: Hands-On, Experiential Training for Prosecuting Attorneys, *Law Enforcement Bulletin*, April 2009, 16-21.

[19] Geller and Scott, 1.

Accessibility | eRulemaking | Freedom of Information Act/Privacy | Legal Notices | Legal Policies and Disclaimers
Privacy Policy | USA.gov | White House
FBI.gov is an official site of the U.S. Federal Government, U.S. Department of Justice.

APPENDIX M

Reprinted from "Police Marksman" July/August 2004

Unintentional Discharges, Finger off the Trigger?

By Shannon Bohrer, MBA

Officer Smith (not his real name) is in a foot chase with subject in a residential area that borders a business district. The subject Officer Smith is chasing was reported to be armed, but has not displayed a weapon. Officer Smith had his issued handgun in his right hand with his trigger finger indexed along the frame, and his radio in his left hand. Officer Smith's thoughts were; I am so close to catching him that I should holster my handgun. Almost at the same moment, the subject turned a corner of a private residence, ran into a large bush, which was against a tall fence and bounced back. Officer Smith turned the same corner and literally ran into the back of the subject.

Officer Smith and the subject ended up on the ground and Officer Smith then secured and handcuffed the subject. The subject then asked, "Why did you shoot me?". Officer Smith responded, "Why did you run?" When the collision of the subject and Officer Smith occurred, Officer Smith's 9mm pistol discharged and a round struck the subject in the lower back and then exited approximately 10 inches higher. The subject knew immediately he had been shot, whereas Officer Smith did not immediately realize that he had fired his pistol. Another officer, less than 50 feet away, heard the shot and his initial thoughts were that the subject has shot Officer Smith.

Question #1, How does an officer's pistol discharge without the intent of the officer?

In almost every academy, police are taught to keep their trigger finger off the trigger and indexed along the frame. Until they are ready to fire, that is, if you are going to shoot, then put your finger on the trigger. When officers are taught this technique, many are just told it is done for safety – period. It should be taught that the safety of keeping your finger off the trigger is because of Dr. Enoka's study on Involuntary Muscular Contractions, 1991.

According to the study, there are three factors that can cause an officer to experience an unintentional discharge with a handgun. The three conditions include: *startle response, balance disturbance and a fair amount of force with the non-shooting hand.* If the officer has his/her handgun out of the holster and the trigger finger is on the trigger when one of these three conditions occurs, the officer's trigger finger can move the trigger to the point the weapon fires, without an intent by the officer to discharge the weapon.

Startle Response

If an officer has his/her handgun out with the finger on the trigger, searching a building, covering a suspect, etc., and an external event startles the officer, the officer's trigger finger can move the trigger and cause the gun to fire – unintentionally. An officer is searching a building, using light and noise discipline, the officer reaches for a door knob and just as s/he turns the knob, a cat jumps and screams from under the officer's feet – and bang. The result – bullet door – it may be embarrassing, but in most cases it could have been prevented if the officer had his/her finger off the trigger.

Balance Disturbance

If an officer has his/her handgun out with the finger on the trigger, running after a suspect and trips, losing their balance, the officer's trigger finger can move the trigger and cause the gun to fire – unintentionally. Just before a dynamic entry an officer is in line with other officers, with his/her weapon out and finger on the trigger, moving forward next to a wall. The officer with his/her finger on the triggers stumbles and loses balance – and bang. The result – bullet leg for the officer in front of the officer that strumbled. In most cases the unintentional discharge could have been prevented if the officer had his/her finger off the trigger, and the weapon was pointed in a safe direction.

Fair Amount of Force with the Non-Shooting Hand

If an officer has his/her handgun out with their finger on the trigger and uses the free hand in an attempt to control a subject, the officer's trigger finger can move the trigger and cause the gun to fire – unintentionally. The cause is an "interlimb interaction," meaning that what one hand does, influences the other hand. An officer is arresting an individual and has his/her handgun in their shooting hand, finger on the trigger. With the free hand, the officer attempts to control the individual – and bang. As the non-gun hand uses more force to control the subject, the shooting hand contracts with an "interlimb interaction" and the officer's trigger finger moves the trigger to the rear. The shot was unintentional, and in most cases could have been prevented if the officer had his/her finger off the trigger.

After the Study

After the study, officers everywhere were trained and told to keep their fingers off the trigger, until they are going to shoot. Unfortunately, not all departments follow these simple guidelines. Some agencies train officers to keep their fingers off the trigger, unless they are getting ready to shoot, or might be getting ready to shoot. The trouble with the training is that the trigger finger ends up on the trigger when the officer is not shooting and can be subjected to; startle, balance, or interlimb effects.

Many departments/agencies adopted training and policies that were intended to keep the officers trigger finger off the trigger until they were going to shoot, believing the training and policy would keep the firearms from discharging. While teaching officers to keep their trigger fingers off the triggers until they were shooting greatly reduced the unintentional discharges, it did not eliminate them.

Officer Smith was positive his trigger finger was indexed on the frame and off the trigger

Although Officer Smith *was positive he had his finger off the trigger*, being startled, losing his balance and using both hands to avoid a collision, Officer Smith's gun went off – meaning his finger *was on the trigger*. At the civil trial, Officer Smith's expert witness testified that the combination of all three conditions; balance, startle and interlimb interactions, could cause the officer's finger to leave the touch point and end up on the trigger. The expert had witnessed this in simulated training events.

In Officer Smith's case, a combination of all three conditions caused Officer Smith's Trigger finger to leave the indexed position – to the trigger – and then pull the trigger, without Officer Smith's intent.

Some of you reading this article may be saying something like "Male Bovine Fecal Material." You may think that teaching students to keep their trigger finger off the trigger will prevent all unintentional discharges, it does not. There are those rare instances where an officer's trigger finger is indexed along the frame, and because of a combination of events, like Officer Smith' case, the finger goes to the trigger and bang – and its unintentional.

Question #2, If keeping your trigger finger off the trigger does not prevent all unintentional discharges, what does?

Keeping the officer's trigger finger off the trigger does not prevent all unintentional discharges, but it would probably eliminate, or has the ability to eliminate many of them. Therefore, *teaching officers to keep their finger off the trigger until they are going to shoot, not that they might shoot, but are going to shoot, should be the standard.*

Some Thoughts on Training

There is some evidence that the officer, while keeping his/her finger off the trigger, should keep a curvature in the trigger finger using the tip of the finger as the touch part. The idea or thought is that if the trigger finger contracts, due to balance, startle or "interlimb effects" the trigger finger will fall behind the trigger, inside the trigger guard. The anecdotal evidence for this strategy does exist, but conversely the space behind the trigger on many of the common firearms used by law enforcement, is not sufficient for a trigger finger. Another idea is for officers to have a curvature in the trigger finger with the touch point behind the trigger, and yet another theory is that if the officer's indexed trigger finger is "straight," it is less likely to fall to the trigger?

The small amount of research on the above practices is not sufficient to make generalized statements of fact. Additionally, the facts are that officers have different sized hands and fingers and there are different sized firearms and operating systems. Add these generalities to the fact that officers are human and can make mistakes, then maybe the prevention of all accidental discharges does not appear to be possible?

Suggested Training

In "Involuntary Muscle Contractions and the Unintentional Discharge of a Firearm," by Roger M. Enoka, Ph.D., 2003, (see references), Dr. Enoka offers suggested training to reduce unintentional discharges. The training should be scenario based that is likely to cause involuntary contractions that could induce unintentional discharges of a weapon, the training should include stress, simulating field experiences with high arousal levels, and the training should be offered more than once a year. Static training and/or closed motor skills, firing a standard qualification course, is thought to accomplish little in the reduction of unintentional discharges by involuntary muscle contractions.

Standard Rules

To help reduce unintentional discharges, officers should be taught to follow the simple safety rules. While these rules are quit common, many times they become espoused theory rather than theory in use. Rules don't prevent accidents, only the actual practice of the rules can prevent accidents.

1. *Keep your finger off the trigger until you are going to shoot.* This will not always prevent the trigger from being pulled, (Officer Smith's case) but it should greatly reduce the number of times that it can occur.
2. *Keep the muzzle of the weapon pointed in a safe direction.* If – the officer has an unintentional discharge and the weapon is pointed in a safe direction, the probability of injury is greatly reduced. *The laser rule*, keep it pointed in a safe direction.
3. *Teach officers why they need to keep their finger off the trigger.* If you could talk to ninety-nine percent of all officers, just before they have an unintentional discharge, they would tell you that would not happen to them. This could be related to the fact that they do not know that it could happen (Enoka studies).

Conclusion

How many Officer Smiths have had unintentional discharges? In this case, Officer Smith, as a defendant in federal court, was found not guilty/liable. However, how many other officers have had similar experiences that resulted in departmental charges, both civil and or criminal charges? How many officers have departments given up because they did not believe that the officer did not intent to fire his/her weapon? We have no idea how often the unintentional discharge of a firearm occurs? While significant research and examination of the issue has been done, a lot more is needed.

If we use the above suggested training and teach every officer to keep his/her finger off the trigger and never point the weapon in an unsafe direction, I do not know if we would eliminate the problem, but I do believe it would be significantly reduced.

References:

Williams, George T., "Teaching Finger Indexing", The Police Marksman, January/February 2004 edition.

Enoka, Roger M., Ph.D., "Involuntary Muscle Contractions and the Unintentional Discharge of a Firearm", Law Enforcement Executive Forum, Volume 3, N2, 2003. **A must read for every firearms instructor**

Artwhol, Alexis, Ph.D., "No Recall of Weapon Discharge", Law Enforcement Executive Forum, Volume 3, Number 2, 2003, Illinois Law Enforcement Training and Standards Board.

Grossi, David M., "Unintentional Discharges: A Training Concern", The Police Marksman, March/April 2004 edition.

Arizona Department of Public Safety Staff Report on Interlimb Interactions, "Sympathetic Squeeze", November 2991, December 9, 1991 and February 11, 1993.

Enoka, Roger, M., Ph.D., University of Arizona, Tuscon; a review of a presentation on Involuntary Muscular Contraction and Accidental Discharge of a Firearm, IALEFI Conference, September 25, 1991.

Author

Shannon Bohrer was a Maryland State Police Officer for 27 years. He retired in 1995 as the agency range master. He then taught at the FBI Academy in the FTU and National Academy until 1999. He is currently the Range Master for the Maryland Police and Correctional Training Commissions. He can be reached at sbohrer@dpscs.state.md.us or 410 552-6300.

asb.djk.dmwsbdjk

APPENDIX N

Off-Duty Training - What Constitutes a Threat?
by Shannon Bohrer, MBA, and Holly L. Knepper, Esq.

Law enforcement training is continually improving. In recent years technology alone has catapulted training faster than anyone would have thought possible. Officers are better trained and better able to deal with the diversity of problems they face than at any other time in history. Officers have instant communications, a variety of tools to resist physical threats, better driving skills, body armor, the latest in handgun technology and less lethal forms of force. While this improved training has had a positive impact on law enforcement, there is one area that seems to have been neglected.

The Problem

Generally, officer training relates to the knowledge, skills and attitudes the officer needs while on-duty. But sometimes the officer needs to use job-related skills *while the officer is off duty*. According to Law Enforcement Officers Killed and Assaulted (LEOKA) law enforcement lost 643 officers in the line of duty from 1992 to 2001. Ninety-two of these deaths occurred while the officers were *off-duty*. In other words, **14.3% of officers killed in the line of duty in the last ten years were killed while off duty.**

These numbers are alarming, particularly because they have been in front of law enforcement for a long time. A review of the "Summaries of Felonious Incidents" reported in LEOKA for the last ten years teaches us that the problem is evident and continuous. Even with improvements in training, off-duty deaths have not been reduced. While we train officers with the skills they need for on-duty performance, how much training do we give them for what happens off-duty?

"On June 4, at approximately 3:40 a.m. a 5-year veteran of the ____Police Department was shot and killed while working off duty as a security guard." LEOKA 2000.

Any category of officer deaths totaling more than 14% should be specifically addressed in training. Training police to survive includes training officers about what constitutes a threat and then dealing with the threat. The training process begins with basic training in an academy and field training, and continues with annual training. Since one out of seven officers killed are killed while off-duty, it is clear that off-duty performance can be a threat. Therefore off-duty training is a critical issue that should be addressed by every department, in entry-level and annual training.

"An officer with the ____ Police Department was killed during an altercation at a gas station at approximately 7:45 p.m. on July 14. The 21-year old police officer, who had nearly 2 years' law enforcement experience and was off duty at the time of the incident, had stopped with two of her friends to get gas." LEOKA 2000.

Training Questions

What training does your department give relating to off-duty responsibilities? Does your department have rules governing off-duty behavior? Are you required to take police action while off duty? Are you required to be armed while off duty? If so, are you required to carry handcuffs? Are there regulations about consuming alcohol? If you are required or permitted to be armed while off duty, are you expected to intervene if you see a crime, or just be a good witness? If you make an off-duty arrest, how do you communicate with other officers? Do you have access to a radio to call for backup? If you have a radio, are you in range to call, or could you be in an unfamiliar 'dead zone'? Is your firearm accessible? If you are in your own car, do you have all the equipment you usually carry in your cruiser? These questions, and many more, must be examined and considered as training topics to protect off-duty officer safety. Does your officer survival training cover off-duty situations?

Two off-duty officers are in a business establishment when the business is robbed. The officers had their departmental identifications and badges on their persons, but left their firearms in their vehicle. When the robbers discovered the badges and identification, one officer was shot in the back of the head. "The victim officer was transported to a local hospital where he died two days later." LEOKA, 1997.

Self Protection

Should an officer be armed while off-duty? Some departments require officers to be armed at all times if they are in the jurisdiction; some simply permit it. Departments may regulate off-duty weapon selection, or even prohibit officers from being armed off-duty.

Off-duty police officer, exiting a business establishment, was ambushed, shot, and killed in an execution-style shooting. "Evidence shows that victim detective's death was directly related and in response to arrest and prosecution in which the victim participated in 2001." LEOKA Updates, January 2003.

Individuals who officers arrest often live or work in the same geographic area as the officer, so it is predictable that officers will meet some of their arrestees while off-duty. A large segment of off-duty officers assaulted and killed each year are victims of revenge type assaults, some for nothing more than giving out a traffic ticket. Police officers should be effectively trained in how to protect themselves - and the public - when they are off-duty.

"The 36-year-old detective answered a knock at his back door and was shot once in the front upper torso with a .38 caliber semiautomatic handgun." " The trio had come to the victim's residence with the intention of preventing the detective from testifying against the 32-year-old in a Theft by Deception case." " The 14-year veteran detective was transported to the hospital, where he underwent surgery but died of his wound in early morning hours." LEOKA 1995.

Legal Issues

"If we don't regulate it/know about it/train on it, we are not responsible" is not the appropriate response to the problem of keeping off-duty officers safe and reducing your department's exposure to liability. It should come as no surprise that departments may be held liable for their officers' off-duty conduct. Departments should not assume they are liability-proof for events that occur while officers are off-duty and out of uniform.

Lawsuits are commonly brought against officers and departments under 42 U.S.C. §1983. This federal law provides that a municipality may be liable under §1983 if the execution of one of its customs or policies - including inadequate training - deprives someone of their constitutional rights.[1] To impose liability on either the actor or its municipality employer, the harmful action must be taken by someone acting "under color of law" (e.g., a police officer). No single fact, such as being off-duty or out of uniform, answers the question of whether an officer was acting "under color of law." *See, Layne v. Sampley*, 627 F.2d 12 (6th Cir.1980); *Stengel v. Belcher*, 522 F.2d 438, 441 (6th Cir. 1975); *and Simmons v. City of Evanston*, 1992 WL 25712 (N.D.Ill. 1992). Liability may be imposed in cases where the department had nothing to do with the off-duty conduct, but a court finds the officer would not have gotten into the situation if he or she were not a police officer. *See, Revene v. Charles County Commissioners, et al.*, 882 F.2d 870, 872-873 (4th Cir.1989); *Ott v. City of Mobile*, 169 F.Supp.2d 1301, 1307 (S.D.Alabama 2001).

Departments that allow officers to perform functions for which they are not trained - on-duty *or* off-duty - are taking enormous risks. Departments may be liable for officers' off-duty conduct if they fail to train officers how to handle off-duty encounters. *Brown v. Gray*, 227 F.3d 1278 (10th Cir. 2000) (off-duty officer shot and killed civilian after traffic altercation; verdict against city upheld, where department had 'always armed/always on duty' policy, but did not train officers on handling foreseeable off-duty encounters). There is no fixed rule about when off-duty conduct will lead to departmental §1983 liability, because it depends on the specific facts of each case. Courts look at all the facts of each case to make that decision. It is impossible to predict exactly which situations will present themselves to your off-duty officers. But if you fail to train your officers on how to handle predictable off-duty encounters, you are taking unacceptable risks with your officers' safety and your department's exposure to liability.

---

[1] In *City of Canton v. Harris*, 489 U.S. 378, 109 S.Ct. 1197 (1989), the Supreme Court set the standard for failure to train cases under 42 U.S.C. §1983 by saying that circumstances, a municipality may be liable for inadequate police training when the failure to train demonstrates "deliberate indifference" to the constitutional rights of persons with whom officers are likely to come into contact, provided the failure to train was the result of the municipality's policy or custom.

Training is Required

If an *on-duty officer* is assigned to stake out a bank because of a tip the bank will be robbed, what are the officer's rules for engaging and arresting? What communication would you expect from an officer if the robbery occurs, and when would you expect it? You should expect any officers inside the bank not to engage the suspects, and to lock the doors after the suspects leave. You should expect officers outside the bank to engage the suspects, and the officers inside and outside will probably communicate with each other as the robbery develops. Of course, you would expect this to be planned in advance, along with a *Plan B*.

But what happens when an *off-duty officer* enters the same bank while the robbery is in progress? If the off-duty officer pulls his/her weapon, would someone think they are one of the bad guys? If the off-duty officer makes an arrest, will the responding on-duty officer know the off-duty officer? The off-duty officer's judgment, decision skills, and training are critical for surviving off-duty incidents.

An off-duty police officer and his wife were leaving a hospital after visiting their newborn son. The officer and his wife were walking toward the parking lot when they saw a man walking toward the hospital, brandishing a gun in a threatening manner. The officer pushed his wife into some shrubs, and then jumped out of the man's way. The officer made eye contact with the man and asked if he was all right. The man responded, "No, man. everything is not alright," then raised the gun and shot the officer, who died two days later. LEOKA 2001.

An effective and popular training method involves scenarios and role-playing, where the trainee 'plays' a uniformed officer, with access to radio, baton, spray, backup and firearm, and makes decisions as the scenario unfolds. What would off-duty officers do in the same scenarios? Off-duty officers, without uniforms or equipment, would have fewer alternatives and would have to rely on themselves. Procedures should be worked out in training, where officer safety is not in jeopardy. There is no guaranteed training that will eliminate all off-duty deaths, but training should go a long way in reducing the numbers.

"The 19-year veteran sergeant was riding in his personal vehicle with his wife within a block of his house when three males in a passing truck shot the windshield of the sergeant's vehicle. The sergeant followed the individuals and identified himself as a police officer." The officer was shot with a handgun by one of the individuals and died the next day. LEOKA, 1998.

Conclusion

It is unsafe and unwise to operate on the belief that officers will only act in an on-duty capacity. Officers *must* be trained on how to handle off-duty encounters.

Implementation of effective policy and training for the off-duty component of the officer's job is critical for reducing risks to officer - and public - safety, and reducing exposure to liability. Departments may consider implementing scenario-based training for off-duty officers based on other officers' past off-duty encounters, along with other scenarios your department reasonably believes will face your own officers in their off-duty hours.

In the landmark study "Killed in the Line of Duty," two of the selected cases were officers that died while off-duty. Consider this excerpt from an article about that study:

"Unfortunately, the officers involved in these tragic incidents are not alive to tell their side of the story. One thing is certain, however. At the time of their deaths, their departments did not have established procedures for how officers should perform police functions while off duty - procedures that might have saved their lives." Above and Beyond the Call of Duty – Preventing Off-Duty Officer Deaths, FBI Law Enforcement Bulletin, April 1996.

Notes

LEOKA uses eight categories to describe the circumstances at the scene of the incident of the officers' deaths.

LEOKA 2001 numbers are: 70 officers killed in the line of duty, excluding the 72 officers that died on September 11, 2001. Of the 70, 11 were off-duty, or 15.7 % for the year.

If all of the 72 officers that died on September 11, 2001 were on duty, the ten-year total would be 715 officers that died in the line of duty and 92 off-duty, which equates to 12.8%.

How many officers are assaulted while off-duty? The number of officers shot and killed while off-duty is readily found in annual the LEOKA reports, but the *numbers of officers assaulted while off-duty is not known or published*. It would be beneficial for training purposes, to know how many off-duty officers are assaulted each year, what weapons were used, the circumstances, etc.

The liability section of this article does not address departmental liability for incidents involving officers' secondary employment. See, *e.g.*, *Gutierrez v. City of Mesquite*, 2001 WL 1343624 (N.D.Tex. 2001) (mem. op.) (denying officers' and city's motion to dismiss §1983 action, where off-duty officers working secondary as department store security received no training or supervision for their off-duty actions, although department approved its officers employment there, and allowed them to use city services (uniforms, badges, city dispatch and databases)).

References

"Law Enforcement Officers Killed and Assaulted," U.S. Department of Justice, Federal Bureau of Investigation, 100 Custer Hollow Road, Clarksburg, WV 26306. (annual report issues from 1992 to 2001, plus monthly updates).

"Attack Me – I'm Off Duty," John W. Kurzeja, published in *The Police Marksman* July/August 1990. The Police Marksman, 6000 E. Shirley Lane, Montgomery, AL 36117.

"Above and Beyond the Call of Duty – Preventing Officer Deaths," Edward F. Davis, M.A., and Anthony J. Pinizzotto, Ph.D., published in the *FBI Law Enforcement Bulletin*, April 1996, U.S. Department of Justice, Federal Bureau of Investigation, 10th and Pennsylvania Avenue, N.W., Washington, D.C. 20535.

"Killed in the Line of Duty," Anthony J. Pinizzotto, Ph.D., and Edward F. Davis, M.A., Uniform Crime Report Section, Federal Bureau of Investigation, U.S. Department of Justice (1992).

Summaries of Referenced Cases

Layne v. Sampley, 627 F.2d 12 (6th Cir.1980). Appeals court upheld $16,000 jury verdict in §1983 case against officer, holding that jury had enough evidence to conclude the officer acted under color of law. Officer had earlier responded to a domestic disturbance call; Layne took it badly and later left word with dispatch he would "fix" the officer. A few days later, Layne encountered the officer, who was off-duty, with his wife, in his own car, and had his service weapon (which he was authorized but not required to carry off-duty). The ensuing argument ended with the officer shooting Layne with the service revolver.

Stengel v. Belcher, 522 F.2d 438, 441 (6th Cir. 1975). Court upheld jury finding that officer acted under color of law for purposes of §1983, and upheld $831,000 jury verdict against officer for his off-duty intervention in bar fight, which ended when he shot and kill 2 men, and paralyzed a 3rd. The court noted departmental regulation required the officer to take police action "in any type of police or criminal activity 24 hours a day," and to carry his firearm and mace at all times while off-duty.

Simmons v. City of Evanston, 1992 WL 25712 (N.D.Ill. 1992). After an altercation with his estranged wife, an off-duty officer went to the station, typed up a criminal complaint against his wife for misdemeanor battery, took it to a judge, and got an arrest warrant. The wife was arrested, processed, released, and ultimately found not guilty, but in the meantime could not file charges or get a protective order against her husband because *she* was the subject of criminal charges. Department's officers routinely initiated misdemeanor complaints without supervisory approval, and there was no rule governing the investigation of cases involving off-duty officers. In the wife's §1983 lawsuit against the city and police chief, she alleged the failed to make rules or provide training or supervision to prevent officers from taking official action in cases where they have a personal interest. Denying the chief's and city's motion for summary judgment, the court held that by not promulgating preventative rules, policies or training, chief and city acquiesced in the officer's use of his office to cause his wife's arrest, and noted that even if motivation is personal, action could be taken 'under color of law' if officer invoked authority of his office to accomplish it.

Revene v. Charles County Commissioners, et al., 882 F.2d 870, 872-873 (4th Cir.1989). Off-duty deputy sheriff driving his own car followed Revene and pulled in behind him when Revene reached his destination. An altercation ensued, and ended when the deputy fatally shot Revene. In the §1983 action against county officials, defendants got the case dismissed by arguing the deputy was not acting under color of law when he shot Revene. Plaintiff appealed; the appeals court reversed and held the deputy being off-duty, out of uniform, and driving his own car was not dispositive, because outward indicators are not alone determinative of whether an officer is acting under color of law. "Rather, the nature of the act performed is controlling." By local law, deputies are on duty 24 hours per day, and expected to take police action on any matter coming to their attention at any time. The court noted that "any action purportedly taken pursuant to this authority would be under color of state law whether the deputies 'hew to the line of their authority or overstep it.'"

Ott v. City of Mobile, 169 F.Supp.2d 1301, 1307 (S.D.Alabama 2001). Non-uniformed, off-duty officer driving his personal car became involved in an altercation with Mardi Gras revelers. At some point, he flashed his badge, identified himself as a police officer, and got his departmental firearm from his car. The altercation ended when he struck one reveler in the head with the butt of his pistol, and fatally shot another man. In the §1983 lawsuit against the city, the city tried to win summary judgment by arguing the officer was not acting under color of law during the incident. While the court did not rule that the officer *was* acting under color of law, there was enough evidence to send that issue to trial. A number of factors go into assessing whether an off-duty, plainclothes officer acts under state law: flashing a badge; display or use of department-issued weapon; identifying himself as a police officer; arrest or attempted arrest of an individual. *A person acts under color of state law when he acts with authority possessed by virtue of his employment with the state, "including misuse of power made possible only because the employee is clothed with the authority of state law."* (emphasis added).

Brown v. Gray, 227 F.3d 1278 (10th Cir. 2000). The City and County of Denver Police Department ("Denver") had a departmental policy that officers were always on duty and required to take police action in any matter coming to their attention. Officer Gray, who was off-duty, out of uniform, and driving his own car, got into a traffic dispute with Clinton Brown, which ended with Gray shooting Brown several times with his service revolver and Brown permanently injured. Brown sued Gray and Denver, and settled with Gray before trial for $150,000. Brown's §1983 claim against Denver went to trial; the jury verdict against Denver was $400,000.

On appeal, Denver argued Brown did not produce enough evidence to establish Denver's liability for Gray's off-duty actions. The appeals court affirmed the verdict, and held there was enough evidence for the jury to hold Denver responsible because it inadequately implemented its always armed/always on duty policy. Officer training made no distinction between on- and off-duty scenarios. Gray testified he felt ill-equipped to handle the encounter because he lacked his uniform, patrol car, and radio, and never received training on how to handle this type of situation off-duty. Gray testified he was instructed that simply identifying himself verbally as a police officer while off-shift should be sufficient to control the situation. There was also testimony that this kind of situation was foreseeable, because officers are often alerted to suspected criminal activity when they are off-shift; the always armed/always on duty policy made this kind of encounter anticipated. The jury properly concluded Denver's failure to train on off-duty encounters showed deliberate indifference to constitutional rights of people officers would encounter while off-duty. The police academy commander testified a conscious decision was made not to distinguish between on-shift and off-shift scenarios in the training program, despite that off-shift officers would be without their radios, uniforms, and marked cruisers. The commander acknowledged the always armed/always on duty policy was risky for officers, but insisted no further training was necessary. The jury properly concluded Gray's shooting of Brown was directly attributable to his position as a Denver police officer, and to the lack of instruction he received on how to be 'always armed/always on duty' while off-shift.

Authors
Shannon Bohrer was a Maryland State Police Officer, retiring in 1995. He then taught at for the Department of Justice at the FBI Academy in Quantico, Virginia, from 1995 until 1999, and he is currently the Range Master for the Maryland Police Training Commission in Sykesville, Maryland. Mr. Bohrer received his B.S. degree from the University of Baltimore and his M.B.A. degree from Frostburg State University. Mr. Bohrer can be reached at sbohrer@mpctc.net.

Holly L. Knepper, Esq., is an Assistant Attorney General and counsel to the Maryland Police and Correctional Training Commissions. Ms. Knepper received her B.A. *cum laude* from Millersville University, and J.D. from Widener University School of Law. She can be reached at hknepper@mpctc.net.

APPENDIX O

Appendix

Barbara E. Kittay, Esquire
11140 Rockville Pike, Suite 100-284
Rockville, Maryland 20852

March 3, 2013

Mr. Heath P. Thomas
3453 Martha Custis Drive
Alexandria, Virginia 22302

Dear Mr. Thomas:

As we discussed, this morning, I am very sorry to advise you that the Court of Appeals has affirmed your conviction. Enclosed please find a copy of the Memorandum Opinion and Judgment, dated February 27, 2013.

Pursuant to the Court of Appeals decision in *Qualls v. United States*, 718 A.2d 1039 (1988), I am required to advise you of the next steps you may take, because I do not see any non-frivolous reason to file a petition for rehearing or rehearing *en banc* on your behalf. An *en banc* petition must include a showing with particularity of how the panel of judges misstated the law or misapplied the facts. Unfortunately, although I am not pleased with the decision, I do not feel it meets the criteria for a petition for rehearing.

Arguably, your only avenue of further appeal is to seek a petition for *certiori* to the U.S. Supreme Court, but there, too, the likelihood that you can make an showing adequate to persuade the Court to entertain your case is very remote, because the D.C. Court of Appeals decided your case based on the review of mostly factual (rather than legal) findings. If you nevertheless believe that proceeding to the Supreme Court is appropriate, you can proceed *pro se* (representing yourself) with a petition for *certiori,* which must be filed within 90 days from the date on the decision of the D.C. Court of Appeals (February 27, 2013).

If you want further to discuss matters pertaining to your appeal and the decision, you should feel free, as always to call me. I hope that in all other ways, this letter finds you well, and I'm so sorry that we could not be more successful in this appeal.

Sincerely,

Barbara E. Kittay, Esq.

/Enclosure
Memorandum Opinion
Dated Feb. 27, 2013

REFERENCES

Prior to the development of this book, I obtained written permission from Mr. Heath Thomas, allowing me to review the materials in sections A through L listed below. The majority of materials were given to me by Heath's attorney, J. Michael Hannon, Esquire. The materials were contained in three cardboard file boxes. The location of any materials not obtained from Mr. Hannon is noted.

Section A
Grand Jury Transcripts
Superior Court for the District of Columbia, Criminal Case No. 2010-CF3-16079.
Grand Jury No. August 5, Superior Court for the District of Columbia
555 Fourth Street N.W., Washington, D.C. 20530.
Wednesday, September 1, 2010, Testimony of MARSHALL BRACKETT, commencing at 11:15 a.m.
Sean Lewis, Assistant United States Attorney.
U.S. v. Heath Thomas EXHIBIT 5 (defense exhibit), CASE NO 2010 CF3 016079.

Superior Court for the District of Columbia, Criminal Case No. 2010-CF3-16079.
Grand Jury No. September 2, Superior Court for the District of Columbia
555 Fourth Street, N.W. Washington D.C. 20530.
Thursday, September 23, 2010, Testimony of BRANDON HOLUBAR, commencing at 10:38 a.m.
Sean Lewis, Assistant United States Attorney.
U.S. v. Heath Thomas EXHIBIT 6, (defense exhibit) CASE NO 2010 CF3 016079.

Superior Court for the District of Columbia, Criminal Case No. 2010-CF3-16079.
Grand Jury No. September 2, Superior Court for the District of Columbia
555 Fourth Street, N.W. Washington D.C. 20530.
Monday, September 27, 2010, Testimony of OSCAR VIRICOCHEA, commencing at 12:43 p.m.
Sean Lewis, Assistant United States Attorney.
U.S. v. Heath Thomas EXHIBIT 8 (defense exhibit) CASE NO 2010 CF3 016079.

Superior Court for the District of Columbia, Criminal Case No. 2010-CF3-16079.
Grand Jury No. September 2, Superior Court for the District of Columbia
555 Fourth Street, N.W. Washington D.C. 20530.
Friday, October 1, 2010, Testimony of CAROLE O'CONNOR, commencing at 9:30 a.m.
Sean Lewis, Assistant United States Attorney.
U.S. v. Heath Thomas EXHIBIT 33, (government exhibit) CASE NO 2010 CF3 016079.

Superior Court for the District of Columbia, Criminal Case No. 2010-CF3-16079.
Grand Jury No. September2, Superior Court for the District of Columbia
555 Fourth Street, N.W. Washington D.C. 20530.
Friday, October 8, 2010, Testimony of MARIA YUDINA, commencing at 12:19 p.m.

Sean Lewis, Assistant United States Attorney.
U.S. v. Heath Thomas EXHIBIT 7, (defense exhibit) CASE NO 2010 CF3 016079.

Superior Court for the District of Columbia, Criminal Case No. 2010-CF3-16079.
Grand Jury No. September 5, Superior Court for the District of Columbia
555 Fourth Street, N.W. Washington D.C. 20530.
Thursday, October 21, 2010, Testimony of TERRY SPRADLIN, commencing at 1:11 p.m.
Sean Lewis, Assistant United States Attorney.
U.S. v. Heath Thomas EXHIBIT 24, (government exhibit) CASE NO 2010 CF3 016079.

Superior Court for the District of Columbia, Criminal Case No. 2010-CF3-16079.
Grand Jury No. September 6, Superior Court for the District of Columbia
555 Fourth Street, N.W. Washington D.C. 20530.
Friday, October 22, 2010, Testimony of JANE SMITH, commencing at 3:57 p.m.
Sean Lewis, Assistant United States Attorney.
U.S. v. Heath Thomas EXHIBIT 27, (government exhibit) CASE NO 2010 CF3 016079.

Superior Court for the District of Columbia, Criminal Case No. 2010-CF3-16079.
Grand Jury No. October 2, Superior Court for the District of Columbia
555 Fourth Street, N.W. Washington D.C. 20001.
Friday, October 22, 2010, Testimony of KAUSHIK RATHI, commencing at 12:00 p.m.
Sean Lewis, Assistant United States Attorney.
U.S. v. Heath Thomas EXHIBIT 10, (defense exhibit) CASE NO 2010 CF3 016079.

Superior Court for the District of Columbia, Criminal Case No. 2010-CF3-16079.
Grand Jury No. October 1, Superior Court for the District of Columbia
555 Fourth Street, N.W. Washington D.C. 20530.
Monday, October 25, 2010, Testimony of GRACIELA PEREZ, commencing at 3:00 p.m.
Sean Lewis, Assistant United States Attorney.
U.S. v. Heath Thomas EXHIBIT 9, (defense exhibit) CASE NO 2010 CF3 016079.

Superior Court for the District of Columbia, Criminal Case No. 2010-CF3-16079.
Grand Jury No. February 5, Superior Court for the District of Columbia
555 Fourth Street, N.W. Washington D.C. 20530.
Friday, March 11, 2011, Testimony of JOHN EISERT, commencing at 10:57 p.m.
Sean Lewis, Assistant United States Attorney.
U.S. v. Heath Thomas EXHIBIT 23, (government exhibit) CASE NO 2010 CF3 016079.

Section B
Trial Transcripts
Day 1 Trial Transcript, Monday August 15, 2011. Transcript, including certification, 111 pages.
SUPERIOR COURT OF THE DISTRICT OF COLUMBIA, CRIMINAL DIVISION UNITED STATES OF AMERICA VERSUS HEATH PATRIC THOMAS, DEFENDANT. Criminal Action Number 2010 -CF3 – 16079, Volume I of III, Washington, D.C.
Bench trial, before Honorable HERBERT DIXON, Associate Judge, in courtroom 215.
On behalf of the of the Government: STEPHEN RICKARD, Esquire and KATHERINE SAWYER, Esquire, Assistant United States Attorneys.

On behalf of the Defendant: MICHAEL HANNON, Esquire, Washington D.C. ALSO PRESENT: EMILY BRANDT. Jurtiana Jeon, CSR Official Court Reporter. Transcript certified on March 27, 2012. The trial commenced at 11:57 a.m. and the proceedings concluded at 3:34 p.m.

Day 2 Trial Transcript, Tuesday, August 16, 2011. Transcript, including certification, 196 pages.
SUPERIOR COURT OF THE DISTRICT OF COLUMBIA, CRIMINAL DIVISION UNITED STATES OF AMERICA VERSUS HEATH PATRIC THOMAS, DEFENDANT. Criminal Action Number 2010 -CF3 - 16079, Washington, D.C.
Bench trial, before Honorable HERBERT DIXON, Associate Judge, in courtroom 215.
On behalf of the of the Government: STEPHEN RICKARD, Esquire and KATHERINE SAWYER, Esquire, Assistant United States Attorneys.
On Behalf of the Defendant: MICHAEL HANNON, Esquire, Washington D.C., ALSO PRESENT: EMILY BRANDT.
Jurtiana Jeon, CSR Official Court Reporter. Transcript certified on March 28, 2012. The trial commenced at 11:34 a.m. and the proceedings concluded at 4:49 p.m.

Day 3 Trial Transcript, Wednesday, August 17, 2011. Transcript, including certification, 180 pages.
SUPERIOR COURT OF THE DISTRICT OF COLUMBIA, CRIMINAL DIVISION UNITED STATES OF AMERICA VERSUS HEATH PATRIC THOMAS, DEFENDANT. Criminal Action Number 2010 -CF3 - 16079, Washington, D.C.
Bench trial, before Honorable HERBERT DIXON, Associate Judge, in courtroom 215.
On behalf of the of the Government: STEPHEN RICKARD, Esquire and KATHERINE SAWYER, Attorney at law, Assistant United States Attorneys
On Behalf of the Defendant: MICHAEL HANNON, Attorney at Law, Washington D.C., ALSO PRESENT: EMILY BRANDT.
Janice R. Hunt, RMR Official Court Reporter. Transcript certified on March 5, 2012. The trial commenced at 11:34 a.m. and the proceedings concluded at 4:49 p.m.

Day 4 Trial Transcript, Wednesday, August 18, 2011. Transcript, including certification, 160 pages.
SUPERIOR COURT OF THE DISTRICT OF COLUMBIA, CRIMINAL DIVISION UNITED STATES OF AMERICA VERSUS HEATH PATRIC THOMAS, DEFENDANT. Criminal Action Number 2010 -CF3 - 16079, Washington, D.C.
Bench trial, before Honorable HERBERT DIXON, Associate Judge, in courtroom 215.
On behalf of the of the Government: STEPHEN RICKARD, Esquire and KATHERINE SAWYER, Esquire, Assistant United States Attorneys.
On Behalf of the Defendant: MICHAEL HANNON, Esquire, Washington D.C., ALSO PRESENT: EMILY BRANDT.
Jurtiana Jeon, CSR Official Court Reporter. Transcript certified on March 28, 2012.
The trial commenced at 11:27 a.m. and the proceedings concluded at 4:50 p.m.

Day 5 Trial Transcript, Monday, August 22, 2011. Transcript, including certification, 169 pages.
SUPERIOR COURT OF THE DISTRICT OF COLUMBIA, CRIMINAL DIVISION UNITED STATES OF AMERICA VERSUS HEATH PATRIC THOMAS, DEFENDANT. Criminal Action Number 2010 -CF3 - 16079, Washington, D.C.
Bench trial, before Honorable HERBERT DIXON, Associate Judge, in courtroom 215.
On behalf of the of the Government: STEPHEN RICKARD, Esquire and KATHERINE SAWYER, Esquire, Assistant United States Attorneys.
On Behalf of the Defendant: MICHAEL HANNON, Esquire, Washington D.C., and EMILY BRANDT, Esquire, Washington D.C.

Sherry T. Lindsay, RPR Official Court Reporter. Transcript certified on February 14, 2012.
The trial commenced at 11:44 a.m., the ending time is not documented in the transcript.

Day 6 Trial Transcript, Tuesday, August 23, 2011. Transcript, including certification, 69 pages.
SUPERIOR COURT OF THE DISTRICT OF COLUMBIA, CRIMINAL DIVISION UNITED STATES OF AMERICA VERSUS HEATH PATRIC THOMAS, DEFENDANT. Criminal Action Number 2010 -CF3 – 16079, Washington, D.C.
Bench trial, before Honorable HERBERT DIXON, Associate Judge, in courtroom 215.
On behalf of the of the Government: STEPHEN RICKARD, Esquire and KATHERINE SAWYER, Esquire, Assistant United States Attorneys.
On Behalf of the Defendant: MICHAEL HANNON, Esquire, Washington D.C., and EMILY BRANDT, Esquire, Washington D.C.
Sherry T. Lindsay, RPR Official Court Reporter. Transcript certified on February 14, 2012.
The trial commenced at 10:39 a.m., the ending time is not documented in the transcript.

Day 7 Trial Transcript, Thursday, August 25, 2011. Transcript, including certification, 131 pages.
SUPERIOR COURT OF THE DISTRICT OF COLUMBIA, CRIMINAL DIVISION UNITED STATES OF AMERICA VERSUS HEATH PATRIC THOMAS, DEFENDANT. Criminal Action Number 2010 -CF3 – 16079, Washington, D.C.
Bench trial, before Honorable HERBERT DIXON, Associate Judge, in courtroom 215.
On behalf of the of the Government: STEPHEN RICKARD, Esquire and KATHERINE SAWYER, Esquire, Assistant United States Attorneys.
On Behalf of the Defendant: MICHAEL HANNON, Esquire, Washington D.C., and EMILY BRANDT, Esquire, Washington D.C.
Sherry T. Lindsay, RPR Official Court Reporter. Transcript certified on February 23, 2012.
The trial commenced at 11:08 a.m., the ending time is not documented in the transcript.

Day 8 Trial Transcript, Tuesday, August 30, 2011. Transcript, including certification, 36 pages.
SUPERIOR COURT OF THE DISTRICT OF COLUMBIA, CRIMINAL DIVISION UNITED STATES OF AMERICA VERSUS HEATH PATRIC THOMAS, DEFENDANT. Criminal Action Number 2010 -CF3 – 16079, Washington, D.C.
Bench trial, before Honorable HERBERT DIXON, Associate Judge, in courtroom 215.
On behalf of the of the Government: STEPHEN RICKARD, Esquire and KATHERINE SAWYER, Esquire, Assistant United States Attorneys.
On Behalf of the Defendant: MICHAEL HANNON, Esquire, Washington D.C., and EMILY BRANDT, Esquire, Washington D.C.
Sherry T. Lindsay, RPR Official Court Reporter. Transcript certified on February 23, 2012.
The trial commenced at 11:08 a.m., the ending time is not documented in the transcript.

Day 8 Sentencing Transcript, Friday November 4, 2011. Transcript, including certification, 23 pages.
SUPERIOR COURT OF THE DISTRICT OF COLUMBIA, CRIMINAL DIVISION UNITED STATES OF AMERICA VERSUS HEATH PATRIC THOMAS, DEFENDANT. Criminal Action Number 2010 -CF3 – 16079, Washington, D.C.
Sentencing before Honorable HERBERT DIXON, Associate Judge, in courtroom 215.
On behalf of the of the Government: STEPHEN RICKARD, Esquire and KATHERINE SAWYER, Esquire, Assistant United States Attorneys. On Behalf of the Defendant: MICHAEL HANNON, Esquire, and EMILY BRANDT, Esquire, The Hannon Law Group, 1099 18th St., N.W., Washington D.C. 20009.

Mahalia M. Davis, RPR Official Court Reporter. Transcript certified on February 27, 2012. The Sentencing commenced at 4:08 p.m., and concluded at 4:49 p.m.

CD's
CDS-R disk, copies of court transcripts, dated 8-15-11, 8-16-11, 8-17-11, 8-18-11, 8-22-11. 8-23-11,8-25-11 and 8-30-11.

Section C
Court of Appeals Transcript
DISTRICT OF COLUMBIA COURT OF APPEALS, No. 11-CF-1422.HEATH PATRICT THOMAS, APPELLANT, V. UNITED STATES, APPELLEE, Appeal from the Superior Court of the District of Columbia (CF3-1609-10) Argued January 10, 2013, Decided February 27, 2013. MEMORANDUM OPINION AND JUDGEMENT
Stamped February 17, 2013

Section D
Alcoholic Beverage Regulations Documents and Transcripts
ALCOHOLIC BEVERAGE REGULATION ADMINISTRATION (ABRA) and related DOCUMENTS
A-4 ALCOHOLIC BEVERAGE CONTROL BOARD MEETING TRANSCRIPT
DISTRICT OF COLUMBIA ALCOHOLIC BEVERAGE CONTROL BOARD MEETING, FACT FINDING HEARING. IN THE MATTER OF: The Guards, Inc. t/a The Guards, 2915 M Street, N.W., Retailer CR, License No. 916, Case No. 10-251-00188, Felony Assault Outside of Establishment. Dated January 19, 2011.
U.S. v. Heath Thomas EXHIBIT 14, CASE NO. 2010 CF3 016079.
THE DISTRICT OF COLUMBIA ALCOHOLIC BEVERAGE CONTROL BOARD, In the matter of: Guards Inc., t/a The Guards, Fact Finding Hearing at premises, 2915 M Street, N.W., Washington D.C. 20007, REQUEST TO TERMINATE MPD REIMBURSABLE DETAIL. ORDER, Request denied. Dated, February 16, 2011.
U.S. v. Heath Thomas EXHIBIT 31 Case NO. 2010 CF3 016079.

ALCOHOLIC BEVERAGE REGULATION ADMINISTRTION CASE REPORT. Case number 10-251-0018, Date of Occurrence August 28, 2010, License Number BRA 916, Trade Name, The Guards, 2915 M Street, N.W., Washington D.C. The Security plan is attached.
The Guards Security Plan, 2008.
U.S. v. Heath Thomas EXHIBIT 11, CASE NO. 2010 CF3 016079.

D.C. OFFICE OF DOCUMENTS AND ADMINISTRATIVE ISSUANCES, CHAPTER 11, SPECIAL POLICE, MAY 2010. U.S. v. Heath Thomas EXHIBIT 29, CASE NO. 2010 CF3 016079.

The Guards Security Plan. Stamped Exhibit 3, and Def. 11. Plan was written by the Guards, submitted to the District of Columbia, Alcoholic Beverage Control Board, (ABC), dated 2008.

Alcoholic Beverage Control Board's official response to The Guard's request to eliminate the reimbursable detail, p 1 dated February 16, 2011.

A one-page document titled, The Guards License #ABRA-000916: 1/20/11. The document lists the Investitive History of The Guards, from 12/10/05 through 8/31/10. Eleven incidents are listed.

Written statement of Mark (bartender) of the incident.
U.S. v. Heath Thomas, EXHIBIT 17, CASE NO. 2010 CF3 016079
Not dated.
Written statement of Cesar Siles (waiter) of the incident.
U.S. v. Heath Thomas, EXHIBIT 16, CASE NO. 2010 CF3 016079
Not dated.

Section E
US Immigration and Customs Enforcement Documents
Letter from U.S. Immigration and Customs Enforcement, to Emily Brant, Hannon Law Group, authorizing agent Eisert to testify, with restrictions.
Dated August 16, 2011

Interim ICE Use of Force Policy, July 7, 2004.
U.S. v. Heath Thomas, EXHIBIT 33, CASE NO. 2010 CF3 016079.

Interim ICE Firearms Policy, July 7, 2004.
U.S. v. Heath Thomas, EXHIBIT 36, CASE NO. 2010 CF3 016079.

US Immigration and Customs Enforcement Guidance for Primary Firearms Holsters, December 2004.
U.S. v. Heath Thomas, EXHIBIT 37, CASE NO. 2010 CF3 016079.

Section F
Filings and Correspondence between Superior Court for The District of Columbia Criminal Division – Felony Branch, Us. Department of Justice and the Superior Court of the District of Columbia, Criminal Division, United State of America, and Hannon Law Group

U.S. Department of Justice, Ronald C. Machen Jr. to Carole O'Connor, informing her of a subpoena for her to testify in front of the grand jury on August 31, 2010.
Dated August 30, 2010, Appendix Document.

Letter to Hannon Law, from U.S. Department of Justice, District of Columbia, signed by Ronald V. Machen Jr. United States Attorney, offering a pre-indictment plea offer for Heath Thomas.
Dated September 1, 2010, Appendix Document.

Letter to Hannon Law, from U.S. Department of Justice, District of Columbia, signed by Stephen Rickard, responding to request from Hannon Law to 1. offer character witnesses by video conference, 2. inquiry of governments theory of case (Attempted Battery Assault or Intent to Frighten Assault, and 3. Request of statements of the defendant when arrested. Letters of request dated June 27, 2011, and June 23, 2011.
Dated July 5, 2011. Appendix Document.

Letter to Hannon Law, from U.S. Department of Justice, District of Columbia, signed by Stephen Rickard, a follow up responds to the letter of July 5, 2011, with additional statements from witnesses. Original requests from Hannon Law Group, dated June 27, 2011, and June 23, 2011.
Dated July 19, 2011. Appendix Document

Superior Court of the District of Columbia, Criminal Division, United State of America, v. Heath Thomas, Criminal Case No. 2010-CF3-016079, Heath P. Thomas' reply in support of his motion to compel discovery, responding to the Governments Opposition to his Motion to Compel Discovery.

Submitted by Hannon Law Group. Dated July 29, 2011.
Dated August 2, 2011.

U.S. Department of Justice, Ronald C. Machen Jr. to Hannon Law, response for discovery of names and contact information for witnesses in letter of July 19, 2011, that were not subpoenaed for trial.
Dated August 5, 2011.

Superior Court for the District of Columbia Criminal Division – Felony Branch. United State of America, v. Heath Thomas, Criminal Case No. 2010-CF3-016079, notice of filing, Letter to J. Michael Hannon, Esq, from Steven Rickard, Assistant United States Attorney. A letter responding to Mr. Hannon's request for information on Ms. Vetlugina, and Mr. Holubar.
Dated August 15, 2011.

Superior Court for the District of Columbia Criminal Division – Felony Branch. United State of America, v. Heath Thomas, Criminal Case No. 2010-CF3-016079, notice of filing, Letter to J. Michael Hannon, Esq, from Steven Rickard, Assistant United States Attorney. A Governments Opposition to Defendants second motion to compel discovery.
Related to statements made by Ms. Vetlugina.
Dated August 15, 2011.

U.S. Department of Justice, Ronald C. Machen Jr. to Hannon Law, from Stephen Rickard, informing the defense of conflicting information, on the color of the bouncer's shirt.
Dated August 15, 2011, Appendix Document.

Superior Court of the District of Columbia, Criminal Division – Felony Branch. United State of America, v. Heath Thomas, Criminal Case No. 2010-CF3-016079, notice of filing, from Stephen Rickard to Michael Hannon. David Evans, Deputy Assistant Director of the Department of Security's National Firearms and Tactical Unit, states his belief that in and of itself, drawing a firearm is not a use of force.
Dated August 15, 2011.

Letter from Hannon Law Group to Assistant United States Attorneys, Stephen and Katherine Sawyer Re: United States of American v. Heath P Thomas, Case No. 2010-CF3-016079. Felony Major Crimes Unit, advising of defense expert witnesses.
Dated August 17, 2011.

Superior Court of the District of Columbia, Criminal Division, United State of America, v. Heath Thomas, Criminal Case No. 2010-CF3-016079, Hannon's Law Group's Support of Heath P Thomas' memorandum in His Motion for Judgment of Acquittal.
Dated August 18, 2011.

Superior Court of the District of Columbia, Criminal Division, United State of America, v. Heath Thomas, Criminal Case No. 2010-CF3-016079, Hannon's Law Group's Support of Heath P Thomas' Motion for a New Trial and to Enter a Judgement of Not Guilty.
Dated September 19, 2011.

Superior Court of the District of Columbia, Criminal Division, United State of America, v. Heath Thomas, Criminal Case No. 2010-CF3-016079, Judgement in a Criminal Case, Sentence of the Court.
Dated November 4, 2011.

Superior Court of the District of Columbia, Criminal Division, United State of America, v. Heath Thomas, Criminal Case No. 2010-CF3-016079, notice of filing an attached video, referenced in Defendants Motion for a New Trial, from Hannon Law Group.
Dated November 8, 2011.

Superior Court of the District of Columbia, Criminal Division, United State of America, v. Heath Thomas, Criminal Case No. 2010-CF3-016079.
Notice of Appeal by Hannon Law Group. Dated November 8, 2011.
District of Columbia Court of Appeals. No 11-CF-1422, Heath P. Thomas v. United States, CF3-1607910. On consideration of the motion of counsel for appellant to withdraw appearance as counsel of record, J, Michael Hannon, Esquire, withdrawing counsel, and Barbara Kittay, Esquire, appointed to represent appellant.
Dated December 29, 2011.

Section G
Subpoenas

Superior Court of the District of Columbia, Criminal Division, Subpoenas, for the United States District of Columbia vs. Heath P Thomas, Case 2010 CF3 016079. To Vincent Wells, ordered to appear on the 15th of August, as a witness for Heath P. Thomas. There is no indication that the summons was served.

Superior Court of the District of Columbia, Criminal Division, Subpoenas, for the United States District of Columbia vs. Heath P Thomas, Case 2010 CF3 016079. To Donnell Butler, ordered to appear on the 15th of August, as a witness for Heath P. Thomas. With a yellow sticky note attached to the summons, written the note: served by EEB on 7/25.

Superior Court of the District of Columbia, Criminal Division, Subpoenas, for the United States District of Columbia vs. Heath P Thomas, Case 2010 CF3 016079. To Alcoholic Beverage Administration Regulation (ABRA) Human Resources Coordinator, Camille Robinson. With a yellow sticky note attached to the summons, written the note: emailed 7/26.

Superior Court of the District of Columbia, Criminal Division, Subpoenas, for the United States District of Columbia vs. Heath P Thomas, Case 2010 CF3 016079. To The Guards Restaurant c/o Hossein Shirvani. With a yellow sticky note attached to the summons, written the note: Given to the Server Process on 7/22.

Superior Court of the District of Columbia, Criminal Division, Subpoenas, for the United States District of Columbia vs. Heath P Thomas, Case 2010 CF3 016079. To Cesar Siles. With a yellow sticky note attached to the summons, written the note: served 8/9, The Guards.

Superior Court of the District of Columbia, Criminal Division, Subpoenas, for the United States District of Columbia vs. Heath P Thomas, Case 2010 CF3 016079. To Mark Flemming. Unknown if served.

Superior Court of the District of Columbia, Criminal Division, Subpoenas, for the United States District of Columbia vs. Heath P Thomas, Case 2010 CF3 016079. To Ciro Salcedo. With a yellow sticky note attached to the summons, written the note: served 8/9, The Guards.

Superior Court of the District of Columbia, Criminal Division, Subpoenas, for the United States District of Columbia vs. Heath P Thomas, Case 2010 CF3 016079. To Julie the Waitress. With a yellow sticky note attached to the summons, written the note: Not Served.

Section H
Other Correspondence

Character Letter from Angela Parrott, Esquire, addressed to Ronald C Machen Jr., Esquire, U.S. Attorney. Dated November 20, 2010.

Character Letter from Eric N. Larson, an international prosecutor in Bosnia Herzegovina, addressed to, To Whom It May Concern, supporting Heath Thomas.
Not dated.

Character Letter from Stephen Kontos, US Army, Europe, to Mr. Ronald Machen U.S. Attorney, supporting Special Agent Heath Thomas.
Dated 10 November 2010

Character Letter from J. S. Martin, Lorton Virginia, addressed to Ronald C Machen Jr., U.S. Attorney for the District of Columbia. Supporting Heath Thomas.
Not dated.

Character Letter from Letter from Francisco Burroia, addressed to Ronald C Machen Jr., Esquire, U.S. Attorney. Supporting Heath Thomas.
Not dated.

Character Letter from David Mitchell, addressed to Ronald C Machen Jr., U.S. Attorney for the District of Columbia. Supporting Heath Thomas.
Not dated.

Character Letter from Thomas E. Snowden, Chula Vista, Ca., addressed to Ronald C Machen Jr., U.S. Attorney for the District of Columbia. Supporting Heath Thomas.
Dated 11/3/10.

Email Character Letter from Paul D'Agostino, addressed to Ronald C Machen Jr., U.S. Attorney for the District of Columbia. Supporting Heath Thomas.
Dated November 18, 2010.

Letter from Hannon Law, to General Counsel of the Navy, requesting all documents reflecting any documentation of incident reports submitted by Marine Corporal Brandon Holubar regarding an alleged assault that occurred against him on August 28, 2010.

Attached to the letter is a Subpoena from the Superior Court of the District of Columbia, August 2, 2010.
Dated August 4, 2011

Letter from the Department of the Navy, to J. Michael Hannon, replying to inquiry of documents, dated August 4, 2011. No documents found.
Dated August 15, 2011.

Letter from the Law Offices Marteli, Donnelly Grimaldi and Gallagher P.A., to the Hannon Law Group, executing a tolling agreement in the Matter of Heath Thomas, dismissing a lawsuit.
Dated October 4, 2011.

Letter from Barbara E. Kittay, Esquire, advising Mr. Heath Thomas of options if his conviction is upheld by the court of appeals. Dated January 10, 2013. This is the same day the case was argued.

Section I Metropolitan Police Department Documents
Metropolitan Police Department, complaint /Suspect Statement, of Brackett, Marshall C.
Dated 8-29-10, 1220 hours.

Metropolitan Police Department, complaint /Suspect Statement, Mark (Bartender).
Dated 8-29-10, 1220 hours.

Metropolitan Police Department, complaint / Statement of Holubar, Brandon Scott. Dated 8-29-10, 0025 hours.

Metropolitan Police Department, complaint / Statement of Viricochea Oscar. Not dated.

Transcript of Agent Thomas Interrogation, August 29, 2010, 0242 hours, 2nd district DC Metro Police Station.
U. S Government Exhibit 99 Case No, 2010, CF1 018988, U. S. v. Heath Thomas.
Metropolitan Police Department, Incident Based Event Report, Internal Document, marked, Not for Public Distribution. (Found in the ABRA documents)
Dated August 29, 2010.

Superior Court for the District of Columbia, United States V. Thomas, Heath Patrick. The document appears as a statement of Charges.
Dated August 29, 2010.
6A Police Personnel. D. C. Office of Documents and Administrative Issuances. Regulations for Special Police and Campus and University Special Police.
United States V. Thomas, Heath Patrick, EXHIBIT 29, CASE NO. 2010 CF3 016079.
Dated May 2010.
Ofc. J. Cadle W C, copy of handwritten notes, in upper left corner, dated 3-4-2011 and in upper right-hand corner (AUSA note)
S Andelman, (officer) copy of handwritten notes, dated on top 8-29-2010.
DVD-R, marked Thomas, Heath 10-124552, Det. Tabron D2-1386, copy of integration, copy made 8-23-10.
Exhibit 100 Case, no. 2010 CFI018988, U.S. v. Heath Thomas.
CD-R, United States v. Heath Thomas, 2010 – CF3-16079, copy of radio call, TAC Radio Run and 911 call.

Section J
Interviews of Witnesses
A one-page document titled List of Employees (The Guards) working August 28, 2010. The list includes 16 names.

Interview materials listed below were created during the book development.
List of witnesses that were contacted, to be interviewed.

Interview documents and notes, including copies of letters mailed to witnesses, along with an interview format used for Guard employees.
Notes and emails and contacts with Heath Thomas
Notes and emails and contacts with Carole O'Connor
Notes of interview of Michael Hannon, in his office, September 25, 2014. Mr. Hannon was also contacted by telephone and email, on several other occurrences.

Notes of Interviews of The Guards employees
Notes of Interview of Shay Primas, September 30, 2014
Notes of Interview of Tara Novonty, October 21. 2014
Notes of Interview of Alexandria Calomaris, October 22. 2014
Notes of Interview of Freddy Biloatoomez, September 30, 2014
Notes of Interview of Brandon Holubar, November 16, 2014
Notes of Interview of Marshall Brackett, September 26, 2015

Other Interviews
Notes of Interview of Charles Cate, October 28. 2014
Notes of Interview with Angela Parrott, March 20, 2015
Notes of Interview with Terry Spradlin, October 21. 2014
Notes of Interview with Trevor Hewick, June 8, 2013
Georgia Akers, Esquire and Barry Coburn, Esquire

Section K
Other Materials
Bowling Green State University. A study funded by the National Institute of Justice found that police officers are arrested about 1,000 times each year. The study found that 5,545 officers were arrested between 2005 and 2011., www.bgsu.edu/news/2012/01/.
Schmidt, Richard A. Motor Learning & Performance, From Principles to Practice, Human Kinetics Books, Champaign IL., published 1991, Chapter 2, Processing Information and Making Decisions, p 15 to 25.
Pinizzotto, Anthony J. Ph.D. Use of Deadly Force Seminar, Outline on Perception and Memory, FBI Academy, Quantico Virginia, Presented January 19, 1999.
Heath Patrick Thomas, written statement to the Judge, for his remarks on the date of sentencing, November 4, 2011. The document is not dated.
Joseph Wilkinson, "Buffalo cop gets pension back 15 years" Reported in the New York Daily News, April 2021. https://www.nydailynews.com/news

Section L
Sub-Chapter Materials
Omar Abdel-Baqui, "Michigan man imprisoned for nearly 4 decades exonerated after witness admits lying," *USA Today*, December 14, 2020. https://www.usatoday.com/story/news/nation/2020/12/14/jackson-michigan-walter-forbes-exonerated-4-decades-prison/6537810002/.
Omar Abdel-Baqui, "Michigan man imprisoned for nearly 4 decades exonerated after witness admits lying", Detroit Free Press, USA Today December 14, 2020.
Mary Wisniewski, "Illinois man freed after 20 years in prison gets $20 million", Chicago Tribune (Reuters) dated March 20, 2015. *Rob Warden,* Juan Rivera, National Registry of Exonerations, Posting Date: Before June 2012. Last Updated: 11/21/2019 https://www.law.umich.edu/special/exoneration/.
Harmeet Kaur and Amanda Watts, "A Black man is freed from prison 44 years after he was wrongly convicted of rape", CNN, August 28, 2020. (https://www.cnn.com)
Ken Otterbourg, Ronnie Long, National Registry of Exonerations (umich.edu), www.innoceneporject.org. Posting Date: 9/14/2020, Last Updated: 5/4/2021.
Richard Schlesinger, "Walking Free - 48 Hours - investigates the David Camm case", on ET/PT on CBS, Associated Press aired August 3, 2014 (This story first **aired** on November 30, 2013)
Linsey Davis, "Former Indiana Trooper David Camm Found Not Guilty After 3rd Trial in Family's Slaying. *David Camm found not guilty after two convictions for killing wife, two kids."* ABC News, October 25, 2013. https://abcnews.go.com/US/indiana-trooper-david.
David Camm - National Registry of Exonerations, no reporter listed. https://www.law.umich.edu/special/exoneration/.
Posting Date: 10/25/2013, Last Updated: 5/26/2021.
The National Registry of Exonerations, associated with the University of Michigan Law School and https://www.law.umich.edu/special/exoneration/Kenvin Lee Green, no reporter listed.
Posting Date: Before June 2012, Last Updated: 6/20/2020.
Steve Broader, "The case of Thomas Haynesworth," The Washington Post, February 14, 2011.
John Schwartz, "Virginia Man Jailed for 27 Years is Exonerated.", The New York Times, December 6, 2011.

Christopher Zoukis, "$9 Million Settlement in Baltimore Wrongful Conviction Case", The Criminal Legal News, October 2018, Filed under Settlements, wrongful Conviction, Maryland location, online at https//www.criminallegalnews.org.

Maurice Possley, Mr. James L Owens, The National Registry of Exonerations, before June 2012, last updated: 5/6/2019, https://www.law.umich.edu/special/exoneration/.

Jennifer Dhanaraj, "After serving 17 years, New York man freed from prison," *New York Daily News*, June 3, 2014.

Josh Soul, "Wrongful, 17-year conviction ends for 'framed' Brooklyn man," *New York Post*, June 3, 2014.

Rob Warden, Mr. Kirk Bloodsworth, The National Registry of Exonerations, before June 2012, last updated: 10/6/2021 https://www.law.umich.edu/special/exoneration/.

Raju Chebium, "Kirk Bloodsworth, twice convicted of rape and murder, exonerated by DNA evidence," subtitled, "After spending two years on death row, Kirk Bloodsworth was cleared by DNA evidence that was nearly destroyed," CNN, June 20, 2000.

Full title: KIRK NOBLE BLOODSWORTH v. STATE OF MARYLAND, Court: Court of Appeals of Maryland, Date published: Sep 3, 1986, Citations Copy Citations, 307 Md. 164 (Md. 1986) 512 A.2d 1056 Bloodsworth v. State, 307 Md. 164 Case text Search + Citator*https://casetext.com/case/bloodsworth-v-state-1*.

Johnny Magdaleno, "She was wrongfully convicted and imprisoned," The Indianapolis Star, October 15, 2020.

Bluhm Legal Clinic Center on Wrongful Conviction, "Kristine Bunch," Northwestern Pritzker School of Law, www.law.northwestern.edu/legalclinic/wrongfulconvictions/exonerations/in/kristine-bunch.html.

Jason Hanna and Ed Payne, "Alabama inmate freed after nearly 30 years on death row", Associated Press, April 3, 2015.

The Equal Justice Initiative https://eji.org/cases/anthony-ray-hinton, April 3, 2015, no author given.

Bryan Stevenson, The Milbank Tweed Forum, https://www.law.nyu.edu/news/bryan-stevenson, April 3, 2015.

Deborah Fleck, "Joyce Ann Brown, a longtime advocate for the wrongly convicted, has died," The Dallas Moring News, June 13, 2015. www.innocenceporject.org, posting date before June 2012, updated: 6/13/2015.

Bluhm Legal Clinic Center on Wrongful Convictions, "Joyce Ann Brown," Northwestern Pritzker School of Law, www.law.northwestern.edu/legalclinic/wrongfulconvictions/exonerations/tx/joyce-ann-brown.html, no date or author given.

The Wilton Dredge case, National Registry of Exonerations (umich.edu), no author listed, posting date: Before June 2012. No author listed, and no date posted.

Kelly V. Landers, P.A. Criminal Law, "A Tale of Exoneration, Does Innocence Matter in Florida?" a blog post, November 9, 2015, kvlcriminallaw.com.

William Dillon, www.innocenceporject.org, no author listed, posting date: before June 2012, last updated: 2/21/2019.

William Dillon, "Unlock the Truth", Innocence Project of Florida, https://www.floridainnocence.org/william-dillon.

Terri Sundquist, "Justice 27 Years Too Late, The William Dillon Story," Promega, January 17, 2011, www.promega-connections.com/justice-27-years-too-late-the-william-dillon-story/.

Henry McCollum and Leon Brown, North Carolina Coalition for Alternatives to the Death Penalty, nccadp.org/henry-McCollum-Leon-brown, published 2018.

Thomson Reuters," Henry McCollum, Leon Brown freed after 30 years in prison,"

CBC News website, September 03, 2014, www.cbc.ca/news/world/henry-McCollum-Leon-brown-freed-after-30-years-in-prison-1.2753737

Bryan Pietsch, "Cleared of Murder," New York Times, May 17, 2021.

The Equal Justice Initiative, https://eji.org/news/glenn-ford-exonerated-released-after-30-years-louisiana-death-row, posted 03-18-14. The Death Penalty Information Center www.deathpenaltyinfo.org) posted July 30, 2015.

Alexandria Burris, "Glen Ford, Exonerated Death Row Inmate, Dies," *USA Today*, June 29, 2015. https://www.usatoday.com/story/news/nation/2015/06/29/glenn-ford-exonerated-death-row-inmate-dies/29489433/.

CBS News, July 3, 2014, the innocence project and Michael-Morton.com

Morton, Michael, *Getting Life: An Innocent Man's 25-Year Journey from Prison to Peace: A Memoir*, Published by Simon & Schuster, 2015.

Mike Mcpadden, "Woman Spent 35 Years In Prison For Crime She Didn't Commit; Exonerated Through DNA", "How DNA from a cigarette butt proved Cathy Woods' innocence and led to a possible serial killer." https://www.investigationdiscovery.com/crimefeed/..., January 31, 2019.

Kriti Mehrotra, "Michelle Mitchell's Murder: How Did She Die? Who Killed Her?"

The Cinemaholic, https://thecinemaholic.com/michelle-mitchell-murder/ November 29, 2020.

Dennis Myers, "The case goes on Cathy Woods cleared in Mitchell murder" Reno News & Review, 03-12-15 https://www.newsreview.com/reno/content/the-case-goes-on/16511718.

Peter Andrey Smith, "When DNA Implicates the Innocent," Scientific American June 2016. https://www.scientificamerican.com/article/when-dna-implicates-the-innocent/.

PHOTOGRAPH/MATERIALS INDEX

There are 29 items listed in the photograph/material index. They feature 18 courtroom exhibits used during the trial, with 2 of the exhibits being repeated in three chapters. Heath supplied 7 photographs of his professional life. Mr. Adam Enatsky, a professional photographer, contracted by the author, took 2 photographs simulating the exterior of The Guards Restaurant under low lighting conditions. The author supplied 3 photographs, the holster, the inert plastic gun by itself, and the inert plastic gun in the holster.

Chapter 2
Inside of bar with view of pillar. The table Heath's party sat at was behind the pillar.
Inside of bar looking at the first set of exit doors to the atrium area.
View of the front entrance door from the street.
View from the atrium with the front door closed.

Chapter 6
Heath in Navy uniform
Heath in diving gear
Heath at Graduation with his mother.
Heath with his mother at a sporting event.
Heath in front of his patrol vehicle
Heath in Bosnia
Heath receiving an award.

Chapter 7
Bar tab from the Guards, Government Exhibit 15.

Bar tab from the Guards, merchant copy, Government Exhibit 16.

Chapter 8
View of the street from the atrium with the front doors open.

Chapter 9
View of the street from the front door.
 Photograph simulating the lighting conditions and distances of what could be observed on the night of the incident. Gun in right hand, viewed from right side.
 Photograph simulating the lighting conditions and distances of what could be observed on the night of the incident. Gun in both hands viewed from left side.

Chapter 10
Restaurant tab from Old Glory, Government Exhibit 13.
Three restaurant tabs from Old Glory (merchant copies), Government Exhibit 14.
Bar tab from the Guards, Government Exhibit 15.
Bar tab from the Guards, merchant copy, Government Exhibit 16.

Chapter 11
View of pillar, blocking the view of the front table.

Chapter 13
Bar tab from the Guards, Government Exhibit 15.
Bar tab from the Guards, merchant copy, Government Exhibit 16.
View of the steps to the entrance from the street.
Ms. Carole O'Connor looking to the street from the front doorway.

Chapter 14
Photo of holster
Photo of plastic inert gun and holster
Photo of holster on belt with the plastic inert gun in a holster
The author will provide complete source information for the content in the book.

Apprentice House is the country's only campus-based, student-staffed book publishing company. Directed by professors and industry professionals, it is a nonprofit activity of the Communication Department at Loyola University Maryland.

Using the latest publishing technology and an experiential learning model of education, Apprentice House publishes books in untraditional ways. This dual responsibility as publishers and educators creates an unprecedented collaborative environment among faculty and students, while teaching tomorrow's editors, designers, and marketers.

Eclectic and provocative, Apprentice House titles intend to entertain as well as spark dialogue on a variety of topics. Financial contributions to sustain the press's work are welcomed. Contributions are tax deductible to the fullest extent allowed by the IRS.

To learn more about Apprentice House books or to obtain submission guidelines, please visit www.apprenticehouse.com.

Apprentice House Press
Communication Department
Loyola University Maryland
4501 N. Charles Street
Baltimore, MD 21210
Ph: 410-617-5265
info@apprenticehouse.com • www.apprenticehouse.com

Printed in the USA
CPSIA information can be obtained
at www.ICGtesting.com
CBHW060913070624
9642CB00002BA/3